CHINESE STORIES FROM TAIWAN
1960-1970

The Pale Moonlight. Ink painting by Ho Hwai-shouh (1969)

Chinese Stories from Taiwan: 1960–1970

JOSEPH S. M. LAU, *Editor*

TIMOTHY A. ROSS, *Assistant Editor*

Foreword by C. T. Hsia

COLUMBIA UNIVERSITY PRESS   NEW YORK

1976

LIBRARY OF CONGRESS CATALOGING IN PUBLICATION DATA
Main entry under title:
Chinese stories from Taiwan, 1960–1970.
  Translated from Chinese.
  Five of the stories were published in the compiler's
T'ai-wan pen-ti tso-chia tuan-p'ien hsiao-shuo hsüan,
published 1972.
  CONTENTS: Ch'en, J.-H. The last performance.—
Wang, W.-H. Flaw.—Ch'en, Y.-C. My first case. [etc.]
  1. Short stories, English—Translations from Chinese.
  2. Short stories, Chinese—Translations into English.
  3. Short stories, Chinese—Taiwan.   I. Lau, Joseph S.M.,
1934–   II. Ross, Timothy A.
PZ1.C44   [PL2658.E8]   895.1'3'01   75-43971
ISBN 0-231-04007-5
ISBN 0-231-04008-3 pbk.
Columbia University Press
New York   Guildford, Surrey
COPYRIGHT © 1976 COLUMBIA UNIVERSITY PRESS
PRINTED IN THE UNITED STATES OF AMERICA

895.13

L366c

1976

The editors acknowledge with gratitude the permission granted by the publishers
listed below for use of copyrighted lyrics in the story "Cicada."
The Aberbach Group of Music Publishing Companies, for "Five Hundred Miles,"
by Hedy West, copyright © 1961 and © 1962 by Atzal Music, Inc. Used by
permission.
Al Gallico Music Corporation, for lyrics from "The House of the Rising Sun,"
copyright Al Gallico Music Corporation.
Warner Bros. Music, for lyrics from "The Times They Are a-Changin'," copy-
right © 1963 M. Witmark & Sons. All rights reserved. Used by permission of
Warner Bros. Music.
Comet Music Corporation, for "Blue Jay Way," by George Harrison, © 1967
Northern Songs Ltd. All rights for the USA, Canada, Mexico, & The Philippines
controlled by Comet Music Corp. c/o ATV Music Group. Used by permission.
All rights reserved. International copyright secured.
Maclen Music, Inc., for "A Day in the Life," by Lennon/McCartney, © 1967
Northern Songs Ltd., and "Revolution I," by Lennon/McCartney, © 1968
Northern Songs Ltd. All rights for the USA, Canada, Mexico & The Philippines
controlled by Maclen Music, Inc. c/o ATV Music Group. Used by permission.
All rights reserved. International copyright secured.

To my uncle W. S. LAU
and
To my brother S. K. LAU

CONTENTS

FOREWORD

Because only three writers from Taiwan (Nieh Hua-ling, Shui Ching, Pai Hsien-yung) are included in my *Twentieth-Century Chinese Stories* (1971), I expressed my hope in the Preface that "it will be possible for me or some other scholar to prepare in the near future an anthology exclusively devoted to Taiwan fiction." I am very pleased to report that in less than five years my hope has come true with the publication of Joseph S. M. Lau's *Chinese Stories from Taiwan: 1960–1970*, which includes, in addition to Pai Hsien-yung, ten important authors brought up and educated in Taiwan. A few months earlier, the National Institute of Compilation and Translation of the Republic of China brought forth an even more comprehensive *Anthology of Contemporary Chinese Literature: 1949–1974*, representing years of work by a team of translators headed by Professor Chi Pang-yuan. Over a thousand pages in length, it includes representative pieces by twenty-two poets and seventeen essayists (Vol. I), and twenty-three stories by seventeen writers (Vol. II). Since the University of Washington Press will soon serve as its distributor in North America, the reader of the present volume can easily turn to that anthology for an even larger variety of Taiwan literature. In 1971 I did not anticipate that the Western reader's curiosity about this literature could be so amply met in a matter of a few years.

So rich is Taiwan fiction that only five authors (Huang Ch'unming, Lin Huai-min, Pai Hsien-yung, Wang Wen-hsing, and Yü Li-hua) appear in both the *Anthology* and *Chinese Stories from Taiwan*, and of these five, only Pai Hsien-yung is represented in both places by the same selection—"Winter Nights" (or "One Winter Evening"). The three anthologies, if I include mine, yield a total of thirty-seven stories by twenty-five writers; the number of stories is significantly enlarged if we include several earlier anthologies published in Taipei and individual translations appearing in such journals as *Renditions* and *The Chinese PEN*.[1]

Of the older story writers included only in Professor Chi's *Anthology*, mention must be made of the novelist and journalist P'eng Ko; the women writers Lin Hai-yin, Meng Yao, and P'an Jen-mu; and the three retired officers who began their literary career even while serving in the army—Chu Hsi-ning, Ssu-ma Chung-yuan, and Tuan Ts'ai-hua. But since the sixties represent a far more exciting literary decade for Taiwan than the fifties, the very fact that Joseph Lau has concentrated on the so-called second-generation writers of that decade has made his volume a richer anthology of fiction than Professor Chi's, though I am not saying that the writers appearing only in the latter are any less worthy of serious attention by the Western public. While Professor Lau could have added stories by Shui Ching, Shih Shu-ch'ing, and possibly Ou-yang Tzu (all represented in the other two anthologies), the eleven chosen are undoubtedly among the most important writers of the decade, and most of them have continued to make vital contributions in the seventies. Five or six of the stories chosen were critical sensations at the time of their first appearance in magazines, while the rest certainly represent their authors at their best.

In Taiwan as in the United States, increasing numbers of serious writers are being identified with the university where they have received advanced training and where they are often subsequently employed as teachers. But despite this irreversible trend, our eleven writers still maintain a healthy balance between those who stay in academe and those who do not. Six have been identified as members of the academic school (*hsüeh-yuan p'ai*) because they have all received some graduate training in America: Chang Hsi-kuo has a Ph.D. in Electrical Engineering and the other five (Ch'en Jo-hsi, Lin Huai-min, Pai Hsien-yung, Wang Wen-hsing, Yü Li-hua) have Master's degrees in literature, journalism, or creative writing. Yet of the six, only Pai Hsien-yung

[1] For a listing of four such anthologies, see Preface, n. 4. Among other stories by authors represented in this volume, we may note Howard Goldblatt's translation of Huang Ch'un-ming's "Sayonara, Tsai Chien" (*The Chinese PEN*, Taipei, Autumn 1975), and Pai Hsien-yung's "The Eternal Yin Hsueh-yen" (tr. by Katherine Carlitz and Anthony C. Yu) and "New Year's Eve" (tr. by Diana Granat) in *Renditions*, No. 5 (Hong Kong, Autumn 1975).

and Wang Wen-hsing have been fully identified with an academic career. Conversant with the "two cultures" because of his technological training, Chang Hsi-kuo has so far alternated between university teaching and industrial research; in his spare time he writes not only novels but a newspaper column. A college teacher of English, Lin Huai-min has in recent years won new fame as a dancer and choreographer, though he still writes occasionally. Of the two women writers, Yü Li-hua teaches part-time while Ch'en Jo-hsi has recently found employment in a bank. Both make their homes in North America and have growing children to care for.

Wang Chen-ho, a student of Western literature who visited America for a year, could be listed among the academic group. But judging by his life-style and the style of his fiction, he clearly belongs with the remaining four of our authors: Ch'en Ying-chen, Ch'i-teng Sheng, Huang Ch'un-ming, and Yang Ch'ing-ch'u. These five are all natives of Taiwan (as are Ch'en Jo-hsi and Lin Huai-min of the first group) whose parents and grandparents lived under Japanese rule, and they themselves can draw upon memories of a more backward Taiwan before the National Government took steps to improve its living conditions. Other than their passion for writing, these writers seem not to have tied themselves down to a specific profession or line of business that would facilitate their social advancement. While biographical information on some of them remains extremely scanty, the stories these five have written would certainly indicate their familiarity with villages, small towns, and the humbler walks of life in a big city like Taipei or Kaohsiung. In comparison with the second-generation mainlanders, therefore, these writers (and Ch'en Jo-hsi in the early phase of her career) would certainly seem to be more provincial (in the geographical sense of the term) in their imaginative sympathy and choice of subject matter.

To turn from the authors to the stories themselves, we may begin by comparing the fiction of the sixties with the fiction produced on the mainland during the thirties, with which the reader is more familiar. Since the thirties stand out as a golden decade for writers of the leftist persuasion, one difference we detect right away is that no comparable dominant ideology governs the stories of our collection even though we catch in several a pervasive tone which may be loosely defined as Existentialist. Another obvious difference is that, while the fiction of the thirties is highly patriotic in its expression of anti-Japanese sentiments, the fiction of the sixties has actually shied away from the strident patriotism of the fifties to assert a provincial or regional character. Many anti-Communist novels were produced in that decade, but by the late fifties we saw the rise of a new generation of writers and readers who, while retaining their full identity as Chinese and nostalgic about the mainland in their own fashion, are much more interested in what is going on in Taiwan and America (since they may go there someday) than in what happened on the war-torn mainland of the thirties and forties. The emergence of a Taiwan-oriented regional fiction, then, would seem to be symptomatic of a general disenchantment with patriotic cant among the young, whereas in the thirties a patriotic fiction of regional emphasis was produced in direct response to the steady expansion of Japanese aggression. In particular, Manchurian regionalists like Hsiao Chün, Hsiao Hung, and Tuan-mu Hung-liang received wide acclaim in the middle thirties because student readers then were keenly concerned about the fate of Manchuria, which had already fallen into Japanese hands. Today, Taiwanese regionalists have found comparable favor among the young because Taiwan is the only Chinese province left which they can proudly claim as their own.

Yet, though differing in ideology, mood, and geographical awareness, the writers of this volume certainly share with their predecessors in the thirties an emotional identification with the young and the poor. Then as now, writers empathize with their young intellectual heroes for their discontentment with society, their yearning for a better world, or their despair over their sense of futility, even though the more flippant youths who ape foreign ways are as a rule satirized. While the more academic writers of today do not go out of their way to search for proletarian experience of social significance, they are no less drawn than the regional writers to the peasants, factory workers, soldiers, and prostitutes for their social maltreatment and economic deprivation. Though of all the writers in the present collection only Ch'en Ying-chen has been suspected of leftist leanings, it is a sure sign of the continuity of modern Chinese fiction that they should have inherited this dual allegiance to the young and the poor.

But, compared with the mainlanders in the thirties, the Taiwan population today is surely enjoying better times. Mainly thanks to the successful implementation of a governmental program of agri-cultural reform which has enabled the farmer to till his own land, the evil landlord—a ubiquitous villain in the fiction of the thir-ties—has disappeared from the scene and is not to be found in any of our stories. Leaders of business and industry in Taiwan have certainly become more benevolent or at least disguised their greed by handling their public relations more competently so that the sensual pot-bellied merchant (*ta-fu ku*) and the harsh manufac-turer bent on oppressing his factory hands—both stock figures in the earlier mainland fiction—are scarcely visible in the present collection. Though a prosperous businessman of the American type, Hu Hsin-pao, the suicidal hero of Ch'en Ying-chen's "My First Case," is actually depicted as a tormented intellectual. The sons and daughters of the well-to-do in Lin Huai-min's "Cicada," pleasure-seeking but easily bored, certainly remind us of the equally frivolous youths in the Shanghai world of Mao Tun's *The Twi-light* (*Tzu-yeh*), but the former have acquired a knack for Exis-tentialist talk, which makes them somewhat more serious and sympathetic.

The feudalist tradition, with its rigid code of morality, which has been the main target of attack among such novelists of the thirties as Pa Chin, has also dwindled in influence despite the Government's active promotion of Confucian teaching. Ch'en Ying-chen, who appears bothered by this type of promotion, en-hances our pity for Hu Hsin-pao by portraying the inspector of the suicidal case as one who, in his new state of wedded bliss, fully identifies himself with Confucian morality so that he may the more smugly condemn Hu for his moral turpitude. This attempt at topical satire, however, remains half-hearted to the extent that we retain a rather nice impression of the inspector for the objec-tive, if not altogether sympathetic, way he examines the case. The other writers, insofar as they appear bothered by feudalist morality, are mainly concerned with the sway it has enjoyed in the past.

Yü Li-hua, a novelist best known for her depiction of Chinese intellectuals in America, has chosen for "In Liu Village" her childhood milieu in rural Chekiang. This gives her a chance to explore the psychology of a country woman bound to the traditional ways, rather than the frustrations and infidelities of her typical heroine—a more or less emancipated Chinese wife in America. Ts'ui-o, a victim of sexual assault by the puppet village head, faces the implacable enmity of her mother-in-law and subsequently the mistrust and estrangement of her husband, but it is characteristic of the author that the arch-villain of the story is not the village head but the feudalist mother-in-law who breaks Ts'ui-o's spirit and almost ruins her life.

"Enemies," Yang Ch'ing-ch'u's grimmer story with a comparable village setting, tells of a Taiwanese girl who, having abandoned her newborn son in a public toilet, faces persecution by the Japanese police. More sadistic than any landlord in the work of Chang T'ien-i (the most powerful short-story writer of the thirties), they line up all the unmarried girls of the village and squeeze their exposed breasts in order to identify the guilty one. Yet the Japanese police are conducting this search in the name of Confucian morality, and insofar as the heroine would not have disposed of her son in this callous manner but for her uncle's adamant opposition to her lover, he is surely the principal cause of her tragedy. The uncle is not without nobility in defending his family name and enduring torture by the Japanese; yet if he had not been such a rigid adherent to a feudal code of honor, the lovers could have been happily married and the child born in wedlock.

It is surely a sign of improved social conditions in Taiwan that both stories explicitly concerned with the inhumanity of the feudalist tradition—"In Liu Village" and "Enemies"—should take place in villages under Japanese occupation: contemporary reality in the province offers the writers few opportunities to observe the blind moralist who would trample upon the young in the name of Confucian morality. Indeed, middle-class parents in Taiwan have long ceased to coerce their children to marry against their wishes. They send their daughters to America in the expectation that they may marry a Chinese Ph.D. and live happily ever after, but often to their disappointment (in stories not represented in this volume) they may marry a Caucasian instead or else remain spinsters, too proud in their unhappiness to admit defeat and return home. Left to their own devices to cope with life's problems, the liberated young have really nothing to hold against the tradition except the feeling that it has somehow inhibited them from enjoying their freedom with as much abandon as their American friends. Thus even T'ao Chih-ch'ing, the emancipated but still unhappy heroine of "Cicada," feels justified in complaining, "We Chinese have never learned to really let ourselves go. Five thousand years of culture weighs down on our backs like a great big stone. We're so inhibited we can't even breathe."

It may be of further interest to observe that this caustic critic of Chinese culture and potential rebel doesn't have much of a choice except to attend Sarah Lawrence College once her sister in America has got her admitted there. T'ao Chih-ch'ing marries in time, has two children, and joins a Peking opera club for relaxation. One cannot say her taste has changed for the worse by shedding her earlier passion for rock music, but in her eyes her new life-style in America must be a shame, since Peking opera represents cultural bondage and rock music represents youth and liberation. Despite her brief fling among her friends in Taipei, then, she has turned out to be as considerate of her parents' feelings as an obedient daughter of an earlier era. Whatever her own state of happiness, they should be very proud of her for having taken all the right steps toward bourgeois respectability.

Even during the May Fourth period, of course, tradition was never something entirely to be repudiated. With such leading iconoclasts as Lu Hsün and Chou Tso-jen, the traditional way of life is inevitably identified in their minds with the innocent delights and sorrows of their childhood and recalled with affection whenever they are not consciously attacking the social evils of their day. Now that the traditional way of life is fast disappearing under the impact of Taiwan's accelerated pace of industrialization, many essayists are writing in the nostalgic vein to capitalize on the public's insatiable appetite for information about the old China. One of the unobtrusive but important themes of this volume is surely its nostalgia for a simpler and more tranquil mode of existence within the context of the island's rapid economic growth. Ch'en Jo-hsi's "The Last Performance" underscores the rapid decline of the traditional Taiwanese opera, showing that even small-town audiences are bored by this form of old-fashioned entertainment. The heroine is admittedly a singer of waning popularity, and yet her addiction to heroin suggests the prevalence of an underground culture destructive of rural values. Similarly, though Wang Wen-hsing's "Flaw" is the timeless story of a boy's awakening to his sexual needs and the perfidies of the adult world, still the mysterious and unprincipled woman whose beauty enthralls him is also the owner of the new building that portends ruinous change for Tung-an Street, one of many such streets in Taipei during the author's childhood, where "cats could be seen strolling lazily along the tops of the low walls, from one house to the next. The whole landscape was filled with glistening green foliage and delicately fragrant odors from the profusion of flowers and plants in the front yards." Since this female swindler rudely awakens the boy from his sweet dream of first love by absconding with the savings of many residents of that street, she certainly appears to be the ominous symbol of a meretricious commercial culture which will in time overtake the whole city of Taipei.

In Chang Hsi-kuo's "Earth," however, the nostalgia of some recent college graduates over their lost youth does not imply an awareness that society has in the meantime changed for the worse. It stems rather from their sense of entrapment in a society which offers them few opportunities for self-advancement or meaningful service. So during a brief reunion they play chess and have some boisterous fun in a futile attempt to regain the sense of happiness they had as high school classmates. It is certainly poignant that these youths in their early twenties should behave so childishly and at the same time sound so very cynical and resigned about their future prospects. Yet there does seem to be no road open except to pursue graduate studies in America, as one of them, Hsiao-yü, eventually does.

The young intellectual in modern Chinese fiction has always appeared at his noblest as a fighter against traditionalist and imperialist forces. That none of our stories features such a hero invites, of course, the obvious explanation that the second-generation writers of Taiwan have been cut off from the leftist tradition of heroic defiance that flourished in the thirties. Yet the National

Government on Taiwan has always actively encouraged a literature of national heroism, and even today such writers of military background as Chu Hsi-ning and Tuan Ts'ai-hua are happily cooperating, but not necessarily writing at the level of propaganda. The younger writers' reluctance to depict Japanese aggression or Communist tyranny indicates, finally, their refusal to compromise their talent by writing about things of which they have no first-hand knowledge. While they may be far less sanguine than the older patriotic novelists in their expectations of a triumphant return to the mainland, they are certainly aware of the traumatic effects of violent dislocation experienced by mainlanders lucky enough to have escaped Communist tyranny. For both the suicidal hero of "My First Case" and the veterans of the civil war in "Earth," the forced retreat from their homeland provides key psychological clues to their present state of unhappiness or resignation. But neither Ch'en Ying-chen, a Taiwanese, nor Chang Hsi-kuo, who was only five when he left with his family for Taiwan in 1949, could have referred to the civil war in other than oblique terms. Of all the second-generation writers Wang Wen-hsing alone has written about the war in the absence of personal knowledge. But his long story "Dragon Sky Restaurant" (*Lung-t'ien lou*), which recounts the Communist siege of Taiyuan, the capital of Shansi (one of the goriest episodes of that war), turns out to be a philosophic fable about life, death, and fate with probably little correspondence with reality. Only the opening and closing sections of the story describing the survivors' reunion at the restaurant are done in impressive realistic colors.

Nor could the second-generation writer, as has been indicated earlier, depict the intellectual as a fighter against tradition. Tradition is no longer of sufficient social and moral authority to affect his life-style; he can adopt whatever style pleases him so long as he does not voice antigovernment sentiments or engage in subversive activities. And once he goes to America, he can turn Communist if he wants to. But wherever he goes, the uncertainty of his personal future and the national future weighs heavily on his own mind. Thus, in recent Taiwan fiction, the intellectual has turned inward, finding no concrete ideal to serve and no identifiable enemy to fight against, and we find in our stories several little

Hamlets pondering the meaning of life, including the two suicides in "My First Case" and "Cicada" (though Lin Huai-min does not say for sure whether Fan Ch'o-hsiung, a delicate youth susceptible to every kind of allergy, drowns himself deliberately).

In my conclusion to *A History of Modern Chinese Fiction* I pondered "whether the study of Western literature has in any significant manner enriched the spiritual life of the Chinese," since it seemed to me that modern Chinese novelists have by and large failed to emulate their Western masters in writing stories that leave the reader deep in thought over their philosophic meaning and psychological revelations. Recent Taiwan fiction, however, would certainly seem to mark a new departure, at least in its fondness for philosophic rumination. By the late fifties a significant number of writers, both of fiction and poetry, have discovered Existentialism as a mode of thought attuned to their own sense of dilemma in not knowing what to do next. Though failing to display in their own lives the Existentialist courage to stand by any absurd cause, these writers are certainly bothered by the horror of unreflective existence on the one hand and the no less horrible conviction, on the other, that it is thinking that makes life miserable. Thus the suicidal hero of "My First Case" repeatedly muses, "That man should go on living is really strange" and "Why is man able to drag on day by day, knowing all the time that he doesn't know what he's living for?" Li Lung-ti, the hero of Ch'i-teng Sheng's "I Love Black Eyes," finds the desire to hold on to life in the absence of thought even more appalling. When people in the street, alarmed by the rising flood, scramble to get to the roofs by means of ladders, he thinks indignantly, "How shameless people who fight for survival like this are. I'd rather stand here and cling to this pillar, and just die with it." T'ao Chih-ch'ing in "Cicada," on the other hand, equates thought with pain, "In fact, we shouldn't think of anything; we can go on living. And after we've lived, we won't have to think of anything, we won't have to think."

Such thoughts, baldly presented without the poetry of *Hamlet* or the erudition of *Herzog*, may strike the Western reader as rather tame. But I believe that the new philosophic fiction, while claiming no originality in the realm of thought, should nonetheless command his respect for the way the second-generation writers

construct their fables to illuminate certain kinds of human predic-
ament. Joseph Lau has observed with justice that nearly all such
writers "have attempted at one time or the other the parabolic
form during their formative years," [2] and of the stories in this
collection, "I Love Black Eyes" certainly stands out as an arresting
parable despite, or rather because of, its intentional moral ambigu-
ity. An uncommunicative sort of person, Li Lung-ti is seen by his
neighbors only because he takes strolls. Apparently in love with his
wife and depending on her for support, he nevertheless shows a
Dostoevskian strain of cruelty when refusing to acknowledge her
identity in front of all the victims of the flood staying on the roofs.
He does so because he is caught in the compromising situation of
befriending a young and frail prostitute and believes that it will be
impossible to talk reason with his wife under the circumstances.
He does drive her insane with jealousy by his refusal to communicate, but would she be in this pass if his entirely commend-
able action is duly explained? Why talk about "this huge and
treacherous gulf" separating him from his wife when it is entirely
of his own making?

The only plausible explanation for Li Lung-ti's odd behavior is
that, in rescuing the prostitute, he has finally done something
which makes him proud of himself. In thus equating his manhood
with this duty, he apparently feels that, so long as they are
stranded together, he should make her completely happy as her
friend and protector and proffer her the illusion of total devotion.
In the end, after seeing her off by train to start a new life at her native place, he decides to take a few days' rest and then look for his
missing wife and make up with her. But can she be reconciled
after the gross insult and humiliation she has received?

The intellectual hero has no place in Wang Chen-ho's "An Oxcart for Dowry" and Huang Ch'un-ming's "A Flower in the Rainy
Night," which are deservedly two of the most celebrated stories in
the style of Taiwanese regionalism. Yet precisely because they do
not deal with the quandaries of intellectuals, Wang and Huang
have succeeded eminently (as has not been the case with the
overtly philosophic Ch'en Ying-chen and the intentionally baffling

[2] Joseph S. M. Lau, "The Concepts of Time and Reality in Modern Chinese
Fiction," *Tamkang Review* 4, No. 1 (Taipei, April 1973), p. 32.

Ch'i-teng Sheng) in singing the praises of man for his arduous struggle toward decency and dignity no matter whether his attempt ends in failure or success. Despite their tribulations, the oxcart-carrier of Wang's story and the prostitute-heroine of Huang's embrace life with a wry stoicism or exuberant optimism that would put to shame the many easily despondent youths we meet elsewhere in this volume. It would seem that, compared to these two, they haven't suffered at all. [3]

"An Oxcart for Dowry" begins with a restaurant scene where five young villagers show Wan-fa, a deaf man in his middle forties, open contempt for his acquiescence in cuckoldry for the sake of his economic betterment. The author shares their mockery of his hero (since his is a comic tale), in much the same fashion that Lu Hsün exposes Ah Q, a shiftless village youth of comparable destitution, to repeated ridicule. But far from being made a symbol of national shame, Wan-fa is an honorable man despite his manifest inability to maintain his family at a subsistence level. He wants to own an oxcart badly, but somehow can never raise enough cash to buy one. In this respect, he invites comparison also with Camel Hsiang-tzu, the title hero of Lao She's famous novel, who is forever frustrated in his desire to own a ricksha. It is only with the generous assistance of the clothes peddler Chien that Wan-fa finally owns an oxcart, but he has to pay the humiliating price of condoning that man's open adultery with his wife Ah-hao.

On one level, the story is surely a tall tale since there is no reason in the world for the peddler to be friends with Wan-fa and his wife by moving into an abandoned hovel by the graveyard when he could have better and more convenient lodgings elsewhere in the village, and there is no reason whatever for him to persist in a liaison with Ah-hao, who is "at least ten years older"

---

[3] Chang Hsi-kuo, among others, is aware of the vast contrast between intellectuals and men of the soil. While sympathetic to the college graduates and mainlanders in exile for their frustrations, he titles his story "Earth" in honor of an old man known by the nickname Shih-t'ou-tzu ("Rock Man," or "Kid Stone," as in John Kwan-Terry's translation) who untiringly works over a tract of rocky land without giving up hope. "All these thirty years," someone comments in admiration, "he has lived in that thatched hut there, every day digging up the rocks and carrying them away." He is a modern version of the legendary Foolish Man Who Removed Mountains.

and hideous to boot, when he could, with his money and attractive wares, buy the favors of younger women. Realistically, too, there is little reason for Wan-fa to wax indignant over his wife's adultery to the point of refusing the peddler's help since, as an impotent husband, he cannot be jealous for reasons of sexual rivalry. But since Wang Chen-ho is a serious student of Western literature, all these improbabilities would indicate that he has designed his immensely funny tale as an allegory. Chien, who comes out of nowhere to meddle in the affairs of Wan-fa's family, can surely be seen as something of the Devil himself who has made a wager with God to test this man of infinite patience, a Chinese Job almost, who has already sold three daughters out of economic necessity. Chien comes to the destitute family, therefore, as a tempter, and though deaf, Wan-fa dislikes him right away because of his offensive body odor (a palpable sign of his evil). Ah-hao becomes increasingly friendly with the peddler after he hires her son, and Wan-fa, though financially relieved by having one less mouth to feed, becomes increasingly suspicious. He guards Ah-hao day and night, and the lovers can only outwit him by putting him in a state of drunken sleep. Twice Wan-fa sends the Devil packing, and twice Chien promptly leaves the neighborhood without a protest. But each time during his absence Wan-fa meets some unforeseen misfortune, and it is only following his own imprisonment that he submits to the reality of his wife's open adultery. Thus the Devil wins, and Wan-fa is bribed into a state of contentment with the gift of an oxcart.

The five villagers at the restaurant, in mocking Wan-fa, would seem to be traditional moralists on the side of God venting their anger over His apparent defeat, but they don't realize, of course, to what lengths he has gone to maintain his honor. He is far less corruptible than Camel Hsiang-tzu, who is too easily discouraged after each calamity and in the end courts his own ruin. We retain to the end our great liking for Wan-fa and cannot feel superior to him for his eventual reconcilement with the Devil, who has won his cunning battle through bribery. Starvation is no joking matter, even if cuckoldry for a man of dire poverty and sexual impotence remains laughable.

If Wan-fa is a Chinese Job eventually rewarded with good fortune through his defeat, then Pai-mei, the heroine of "A Flower in the Rainy Night," can be seen as a saintly woman possessed by a beatific vision of her own destiny, who rises triumphant above her tribulations as a lowly prostitute. Thoroughly believable on the realistic plane, her story, nevertheless, calls for a religious or allegorical interpretation if only to bring into clearer definition our wonderment over her inexhaustible humanity. No other heroine of modern Chinese fiction radiates her kind of glory as a visible embodiment of faith and hope in a largely God-forsaken world. The title heroine of Hsü Ti-shan's *Yü-kuan* is a woman of comparable saintliness, but she is a Christian missionary conditioned to the habit of moral introspection and unexposed to the dehumanizing forces at work in a third-class brothel. Her struggle to eradicate selfishness from her bosom, therefore, partakes less of divine rapture than of Pai-mei's determination to emerge from the lower depths of degradation to find self-fulfillment.

Traditional Chinese poetry loves to depict the imaginary sorrows of languid courtesans without touching upon their actual degradation as human beings. Even the courtesans in the colloquial *San-yen* tales, whose sufferings are more real, are nevertheless seen as genteel young ladies endowed with wit and beauty. It is a measure of modern Chinese literature's enhanced respect for human dignity that, at the beginning of this century, we at last come across a pair of lower-class prostitutes utterly believable and sympathetic in their helplessness in Liu Ê's *The Travels of Lao Ts'an* (*Lao-ts'an yu-chi*, 1903–4). Pai-mei and her younger companion Ying-ying can be seen as the direct descendants of Ts'ui-hua and Ts'ui-huan, and the story of their friendship at the brothels and their accidental, happy reunion on a train is told with a realism by turns heart-rending and heart-warming that Liu Ê would have loved.

In accordance with a vicious Taiwanese custom, both girls are sold by their poverty-stricken parents when very young to their foster mothers (or foster parents), who in turn rear them for the brothels. Sold to a brothel at fourteen, Pai-mei has been a peripatetic prostitute for fourteen years when the story opens. The single most moving passage occurs, I believe, when on a visit to her foster mother she gives a bitter retort upon being called "rotten baggage":

"Yes, I'm rotten baggage—rotten baggage that you sold off fourteen years ago. Think about it—what kind of life were the eight of you living then? And how are you living now? Now you have a house to live in. Yü-ch'eng's graduated from college and has gotten married. Yü-fu's going to senior high school. Ah-hui's married. Do you eat any worse, or wear any worse clothes than anybody else? Where would you be today without this 'rotten baggage?' "

Yet despite Pai-mei's stinging denunciation of her ingratitude, her foster mother at least cares enough to urge that she quit her trade and marry. Huang Ch'un-ming, though verbose and careless at times, cannot be accused of the kind of sentimentality that is partial to prostitutes by painting all their exploiters in a bad light. He neither condemns Pai-mei's mother for selling her daughter nor censures the fishermen in quest of pleasure after their rough days on the sea. He actually describes with relish young fishermen gobbling down supposedly aphrodisiac parts of raw male fish in preparation for their brief holiday among the prostitutes: it is surely not their fault that they have no girl friends to turn to for sexual relief.

Both Ts'ui-hua and Ts'ui-huan become concubines, thanks to the kindness of Lao Ts'an and his friend Huang Jen-jui. Ying-ying, too, is lucky enough to meet an army officer who offers marriage. At twenty-eight, however, Pai-mei is too much of a veteran at her trade to expect salvation in this fashion, but the sight of Ying-ying glowingly happy on the train with her three-month-old son so arouses her maternal instinct that she is determined to achieve motherhood without benefit of a husband. She eventually chooses a nice young fisherman to be the instrument of her impregnation and returns to her real mother's home to wait out her term.

In time she does have a son even though she almost risks her own life in delivering him. The scene of childbirth may appear overlong for some tastes; yet the author is surely intimating that it is a life-and-death struggle for a veteran prostitute to regain the full measure of her humanity by bringing forth a male child with all its promise of a bright future.[4] In a sense, the good luck she brings

---

[4] Chin Hsi-tzu, the heroine of Ch'en Jo-hsi's story, is equally maternal. But as a heroin addict, she has to entrust her infant son to the care of some other woman in order to assure for him a better future.

to her village after an absence of twenty-three years is as much a miracle as her successful impregnation by the man she chooses to be her unborn child's father. At a time when abortion has become legalized in so many parts of the world, it is surely heart-warming, if I may use that word once again, to read a story where copulation strictly for the purpose of procreation and the agony of childbirth are described in all their sanctity as indispensable means for a woman's redemption. Of all the stories in this collection, "A Flower in the Rainy Night" speaks most eloquently of man's endurance and triumph, and of his vision for a bright future. Huang Ch'un-ming is surely one with Faulkner in believing that it is the writer's duty "to help man endure by lifting his heart, by reminding him of the courage and honor and hope and pride and compassion and pity and sacrifice which have been the glory of his past." [5] Among earlier modern Chinese writers, Shen Ts'ung-wen alone has proudly fulfilled the Faulkerian injunction to lift man's heart with a large corpus of distinguished fiction. Huang Ch'un-ming can already be seen as a worthy successor to Shen Ts'ung-wen; if he continues to be productive and does not dissipate his imagination by writing carelessly, he may even turn out to be China's Faulkner.

In reviewing the contents of this anthology, I have stressed the second-generation writers' tendency toward despair when they contemplate the fate of intellectuals like themselves facing an uncertain future, and these same writers' humanitarian bond with the poor whose very ignorance of local and world politics renders them immune to despair and whose very struggle for survival and decency reminds us that hope and love are still with us after all. The Western reader at all knowledgeable about modern Chinese literature perhaps should not be surprised by the presence of both of these two worlds—one of intellectual despair and the other of humanitarian hope and optimism—in recent Taiwan fiction. But because he is used to more violent forms of nihilism and despair in the recent literature of his own culture, I believe he is likely to be

[5] Quoted from Faulkner's "Speech of Acceptance upon the Award of the Nobel Prize for Literature," *The Faulkner Reader* (New York, Random House, 1959), p. 4.

more deeply impressed by the stories about the sorrows and joys of the simple folk and their amazing capability to survive and stay human despite the odds against them. Though Western in form and technique, this fiction of Taiwanese regionalism claims a linear descent from the folk tradition of Chinese literature which began with the songs of ordinary lovers, farmers, and soldiers in the ancient *Book of Poetry (Shih ching)*.

I have so far failed to discuss Pai Hsien-yung's "Winter Nights" because, while it is poignantly expressive of Taiwanese experience, it stands apart from the other stories for its conscious attempt to encompass the whole range of modern Chinese experience through the conversation of two old friends who had been active student leaders at the May Fourth (1919) demonstrations in Peking. One is an eminent professor of Chinese history at Berkeley on a brief visit to Taipei and the other an obscure professor of English poetry at a local university whose youthful ambition for patriotic and revolutionary endeavor is symbolized by his great love for Byron but whose only present resemblance to that poet is his lameness. But the disparity in the worldly fortunes of these two friends pales to insignificance when, through their reminiscences, we see a more glaring contrast between their youthful patriotic ardor and the placid determination of the English professor's son to study physics in America, preferably at Berkeley, upon his graduation from college. While T'ao Chih-ch'ing shows obvious discontent with her life in America and while, in the epilogue of "Earth," Hsiao-yü, lately transferred from a mid-Western college to the California Institute of Technology, is at least aware of something missing from his life despite his growing smugness, we can be sure that the young physicist will be single-minded in his pursuit of academic success in America. He represents the "happy" Chinese of his generation eagerly looking forward to permanent exile in this country and repudiating the patriotic tradition of his father's generation without a trace of regret.

There is little need to dwell on "Winter Nights," since I have already discussed it at some length in a recent article of mine and

Joseph Lau has devoted a whole article to the collection *Residents of Taipei* (*Taipei jen*), of which the story forms a part.[6] Suffice it to say that Pai Hsien-yung is the most nostalgic of the writers represented in this volume, since in the present story, as in nearly all his mature stories, he contrasts the diminished lives led by the Chinese in Taiwan and America with their more glorious or heroic past on the mainland and unequivocally declares his emotional allegiance to the past. And it is because even young readers little disposed to applaud patriotic rhetoric are capable of responding to this kind of nostalgia that the stories of Pai Hsien-yung, with their unmatched artistic finish, have in recent years exerted such a strong appeal.

But one cannot indefinitely refer to the mainland in the past tense and ignore its Communist present. The massive transformation of the land and people under the most totalitarian of governments in China's history, of course, has received intensive journalistic attention in Taiwan and Hong Kong as well as in America. But ever since Eileen Chang's escape in 1952, for some twenty years no creative writer approaching her stature has been able to leave the mainland and write about the Communist experiment there from first-hand experience. In November 1973, however, Ch'en Jo-hsi managed to arrive in Hong Kong with her husband and two young sons, and they have subsequently settled in Vancouver, Canada. An idealist imbued with the desire to serve her unseen fatherland, Ch'en Jo-hsi had gone there with her husband in the autumn of 1966, during the unleashing of the Cultural Revolution, and suffered through seven years of hell. The price she pays in personal suffering, however, has meant a maturing of her art and a deepening of her understanding of the Chinese people. The series of stories she has been writing since her return to freedom, not represented in this volume because they appeared too late for inclusion, uncovers a new, tragic range of Chinese experi-

[6] See C. T. Hsia, "The Continuing Obsession with China: Three Contemporary Writers," *Review of National Literatures* 6 (Special Number: "China's Literary Image"), No. 1 (Spring 1975), and Joseph S. M. Lau, " 'Crowded Hours' Revisited: The Evocation of the Past in *Taipei jen*," *Journal of Asian Studies* 35, No. 1 (November 1975).

ence hitherto inaccessible to the second-generation writers of Taiwan.[7]

Ho Hwai-shouh (1941–), whose ink painting, "The Pale Moonlight," perfectly complements the anthology as an example of contemporary Chinese art at its best, is himself a noted writer from Taiwan with two volumes of critical essays to his credit. But his primary vocation is painting, and I believe he is exceptional among painters of his generation for his stubborn refusal to imitate current Western fashions and his subtle transformation of the traditional Chinese style for the projection of a somber individual vision. All his best paintings haunt us with their desolate or spectral grandeur, as does his present rendering of a nocturnal Taipei suffused with the pale light of a large moon.

C. T. HSIA

Columbia University
February 1976

---

[7] *Mayor Yin* (*Yin hsien-chang*), her new collection of stories, has just been published by Taipei's Yuan-ching ch'u-pan-she. My promised introduction will appear in a subsequent printing of the book.

PREFACE

In 1972, I edited the Chinese collection, *Selected Short Stories by Six Taiwanese Writers.*[1] Two of the criteria used in my selection process were: that the writers represented be of Taiwanese origin and that their stories be a genuine reflection of the native sentiments about Taiwan.

In a way the present anthology can be considered an extension of my earlier efforts, not only because it has included five of the six stories in that collection,[2] but also, more importantly, because it is guided by the same editorial concern that the stories reflect the Taiwanese experience. The only difference is that in this anthology the emphasis is on the authors' background and education. I have de-emphasized their geographical associations for two reasons. Firstly, I want to give a larger variety of the Taiwanese experience as felt and recorded by a larger variety of writers regardless of their ancestral origins. Secondly, as can be seen in the biographical notes preceding each story, all the authors in this anthology, Taiwanese and Mainlanders alike, have one thing in common: they were raised and educated in Taiwan in a homogeneous system, and they are all Mandarin-speaking. Under these circumstances, it is little wonder that the work of a native Taiwanese sometimes reads more like that of a Mainlander writer and vice versa. In view of this successful integration among second-generation Taiwanese and Mainlanders who were either born or raised in Taiwan after the establishment of the Nationalist Government

---

[1] *T'ai-wan pen-ti tso-chia tuan-p'ien hsiao-shuo hsüan* (Hong Kong: Hsiao-ts'ao ch'u-pan-she, 1972). The six writers included are Ch'en Jo-hsi, Wang Chen-ho, Ch'i-teng Sheng, Shih Shu-ch'ing, Huang Ch'un-ming and Yang Ch'ing-ch'u.

[2] Regrettably, my several letters to Ms. Shih Shu-ch'ing requesting permission to translate her story "The Last Descendant of Job" ("Jo-po-ti mo-i") were either delayed or misplaced. When I finally heard from Ms. Shih, it was only one month before the deadline for manuscript submission to the publisher.

on the island in 1949, the usual distinction between a "Taiwanese" writer and a "Mainlander" writer is no longer viable. For, whatever they write, these second-generation authors cannot but reflect upon their adolescent experience in Taiwan. In this respect the young Mainlander writers are sharply different from their predecessors, whose imagination has largely been centered on their experience in mainland China.[3]

The eleven stories included here can by no means be regarded as exclusively representative of the best efforts of the second-generation writers. There must be others equally worthy of inclusion that have escaped my attention. But since this is the first English anthology of Taiwan fiction published outside the Republic of China,[4] I sincerely hope that other anthologists will make up for this unfairness in the near future.

A note of explanation is in order for readers unfamiliar with the exchange rate between the New Taiwan Dollar and the U.S. dollar. At the time these stories were written, the rate was forty to one. All the prices quoted in this anthology are in the New Taiwan Dollar.

In preparing this anthology for publication, I have received generous support from a number of individuals. First of all, I would like to thank all the translators who have graciously given of their time and labor. Dennis T. Hu, Project Assistant and doctoral candidate in the Department of East Asian Languages and Literature at the University of Wisconsin at Madison, deserves special mention for painstakingly rechecking every manuscript. His efforts are equivalent to those of an assistant editor.

Grateful acknowledgments are due to the following publishers

[3] I have dealt with this aspect of the Mainlanders' psychology in my essay "How Much Truth Can a Blade of Grass Carry?" in the *Journal of Asian Studies*, XXXII, No. 4 (1973).

[4] In the Republic of China, at least five anthologies have appeared. The first four are published by Taipei's Heritage Press, the fifth by the National Institute for Compilation and Translation, Taipei. (1) Nancy Chang Ing, tr., *New Voices: Stories and Poems by Young Chinese Writers* (1961); (2) Nieh Hualing, ed., *Eight Stories by Chinese Women* (1962); (3) Lucian Wu, ed., *New Chinese Stories: Twelve Short Stories by Contemporary Chinese Writers* (1961); (4) Lucian Wu, ed., *New Chinese Writing* (1962), and (5) Chi Pang-yuan et al., eds., *An Anthology of Contemporary Chinese Literature, Taiwan: 1949–1974*, 2 vols. (1975).

and editors for permission to use the stories which first appeared in their magazines: Lin Hai-yin, Publisher-Editor of *Ch'un wen-hsüeh*; Pai Hsien-yung, Publisher-Editor of *Hsien-tai wen-hsüeh*; Wei T'ien-ts'ung, Editor of *Wen-hsüeh chi-k'an*; Nancy Chang Ing, Editor of *The Chinese Pen*; Roy E. Teele, Editor of *Literature East and West*; and Chu Hsi-ning, Editor of *Hsin-wen-i yüeh-k'an*.

I would also like to thank Anthony C. Yu of the University of Chicago for his translation of Wang Ching-wei's poem appearing in the story "Earth"; David Diefendorf of Columbia University Press for his expert editing; Martha Fisk for typing some of the manuscripts; Anita Brown for reading the proofs; the Asian Literature Program of the Asia Society for helping defray part of the editorial expenses; and the Graduate School of the University of Wisconsin at Madison for providing me with a summer grant and the award of a project assistantship.

J. S. M. L.

Madison, Wisconsin
October 10, 1975

CHINESE STORIES FROM TAIWAN:
1960–1970

Ch'en Jo-hsi (pen-name for Ch'en Hsiu-mei) was born in Taipei, Taiwan, in 1938. From 1957 to 1961, she was an English major at National Taiwan University. Upon graduation, she came to the United States to further her studies at Mount Holyoke College and Johns Hopkins University. She received an M.A. degree from Johns Hopkins' Writing Seminars in 1965.

In 1966, she left the U.S. for Nanking with her husband Tuan Shih-ao and from 1966 to 1973 was Lecturer in English at Nanking's Huatung Institute of Hydraulic Engineering. Mrs. Tuan is presently residing in Vancouver with her husband and two children.

Under her maiden name and pseudonym, she had published a number of stories in *Wen-hsüeh tsa-chih* when she was an undergraduate student. Five of these were translated into English and published as an anthology by the Heritage Press (Lucy H. Ch'en, *Spirit Calling: Tales About Taiwan*, 1962).

"The Last Performance" ("tsui-hou yeh hsi") first appeared in *Hsien-tai wen-hsüeh* (No. 10, 1961). It is a story about narcotism in which the author, as I commented in my essay "How Much Truth Can a Blade of Grass Carry?," "has managed to register in the space of six pages an unforgettable note of anguish in the 'lower depths' of Taiwan."

The Last Performance -

H'EN JO-HSI

Translated by TIMOTHY A. ROSS *and* JOSEPH S. M. LAU

After a quick drum roll came a solitary stroke of the brass gong. Chin Hsi-tzu strode onto the stage, raised both hands gracefully, pressed them to her cheeks, then lowered them to her chin. Next, with hands in her sleeves, she moved to the varying rhythm of the gong, one step at each beat, advancing to the center of the stage. She mumbled a couplet, and then turned about, lowered her head, and went through a door. Two paces brought her to a table; she pulled out a chair and sat down. "Ah . . ." As the gong sounded, Chin Hsi-tzu's hoarse throat dryly forced out: "I . . . Hsüeh-mei . . ."

She sang the lines woodenly, meanwhile absent-mindedly glancing at the large red playbills stuck up on the theater's bulletin board. The last performance, "Heroes of the Great Sung Dynasty," was finally finished, but to attract more of an audience they had added "Hsüeh-mei Thinks of Her Lord." Those four distinct brush-written characters flew and danced before her eyes, making her a little dizzy. She felt that her lips were dry and cracked, her tongue sticky, and each phrase came out broken and disjointed, as though pressed out from beneath a grindstone. If only, her heart began to groan, she could drink a little cider. Looking to the front, she vaguely saw a glass of cider among a pile of yellow and black heads; the glass was transparent, and was filled with shiny yellow cider. She stared at it greedily. The glass began to expand. It extended up and down, left and right, and the cider gradually began to stir, and then, like a wave, it billowed up and flooded the room, finally rising to the top of the theater, so that the walls and the heads below were all submerged. . . .

Suddenly the wood-slats sounded, and the three-stringed guitar began to weep. She was startled, and unconsciously she rose, moved to the front of the stage, and began to sing:

3

"Hsüeh-mei laments her sad fate.
Thinking of her lord
Her tears fall—"

As she sang listlessly on the stage, her eyes sized up the house: only half of the thirty rows of wooden benches were occupied, and most of the audience were old people and small children. The old women, paper fans in hand, glanced obliquely at her as they listened. The men were smoking cigarettes and taking great gulps of soft drinks. The children ran about in the rear and fought each other. The boy who sold ice hawked his wares in a low voice, looking for customers with one eye while watching her on stage with the other. From backstage came the sounds of heavy things being dismantled and of wardrobes being moved about; a heavy and impatient sound.

She felt exhausted and disappointed. This was the third time she had been to Lu-chou District, and although business was never good, it had never been as bad as this. She remembered her first visit, at eighteen—it was already ten years ago—when the tickets had been sold out early, and a hundred "standing room" tickets in addition. Red paper strips carrying pledges of cash gratuities had been stuck up all the way to the front entrance by admirers. Men and women, captivated by her, had waited every night by the stage door to see her. Four years ago, when she was here, a nearby movie house was showing an American film. But even with the actress kissing her man in public, her legs and bosom almost bare, Chin Hsi-tzu's show was still enjoying a packed house. After the show, the patrons, as they walked home, would still be discussing her singing and acting.

The local opera was declining rapidly, and everyone knew that, on stage and off.

She could faintly see a plump woman who looked like Lotus sitting alone in the corner. The lamplight was too dim, and the distance too great, so she couldn't see very clearly. She was puzzled, for Lotus was supposed to come tomorrow. A few days before, someone had come with a message that she was ready to take Ah-pao. Should she just let her come in vain? Like the last time? She really could not part with Ah-pao. That wasn't Lotus, was it? She stole another glance. *Ai,* she thought, my eyesight's getting blurred for sure.

Now she felt weak in all her limbs, her whole body began to sway, and she thought only of kneeling, or lying down on the floor, holding onto something, grasping it tightly, and giving it a bite. She felt her stomach beginning to contract and churn. Her eyes were blurring more and more, and her feet trembled slightly. Even by exerting all her strength, she could only temporarily restrain them from leaving their places. She wanted to kneel down, to lie down, or simply to clutch something.

The wood-slats sounded faster, the guitar's strumming became more rapid and the tone went higher. Straining, she drew a deep breath, prepared her throat, and opened her lips. There was no sound. Her throat was dry, and not a single note would pour forth. She could not sing. The guitar played on alone, and the wood-slats beat on by themselves. The audience grew restive, and a humming sound arose as they whispered to one another. Amidst catcalls and malicious guffaws, a cigarette butt landed at Chin Hsi-tzu's feet.

She stood on the stage, concealing with her long sleeves her hands, which clutched tightly as her long fingernails dug deeply into the flesh. The pores on her face suddenly opened, and warm sweat forced its way out. The guitarist and the wood-slat player were both staring at her, and playing all the louder, all the faster.

At that very moment, she threw out her chest and ground her teeth, while all the blood in her body seemed to swell up and her feet trembled like branches in a storm. She opened her mouth, summoned all her strength, and a single word pressed its way out of her throat: "Ah—." The humming of voices abruptly fell off, as everyone craned their necks toward the stage and watched her with considerable surprise.

She felt as though her throat were a stretch of drought-stricken land beginning to crack, and it seemed to be oozing drops of blood, dripping as she sang. Her stomach walls were like bellows, expanding and contracting dreadfully, and her limbs trembled like willow twigs in the winter wind.

Her whole body shivered. She couldn't even stand, and soon she was going to fall down. With all her might, she struggled and forced herself to sing on. A child came out from backstage carrying a glass of cider for her. She raised her left hand to hide her face, and took the glass with her right hand. She brought it to her lips, drank it down in one gulp, and then greedily scoured the rim with the tip of her tongue. The corners of her lips were wet, but she had no time to wipe them dry. She had to hurry on and sing along with the guitar.

The cider enabled her to temporarily regain a little of her strength and consciousness. She saw another performer come on stage. And she heard a child crying backstage. That headstrong cry was Ah-pao's, and he was waiting to be nursed. She suddenly remembered the fortune-teller. A few months before, at Yang-mei, the fortune-teller had told her: "This child's fate is for adoption; unless you give him to someone else, I'm afraid he won't last too long. . . ."

"I don't believe it!" She shook her head. Suddenly she realized that she was still singing opera. While doing the lines smoothly, she swept the audience with her eyes. That woman in the corner was dozing off, and she did look like Lotus, the Lotus who would not be the least perturbed even if the heavens fell. Ah-pao's crying was growing louder, and she felt that she couldn't bear up any longer. Her eyes watered, her nose ran as if everything was going to flow out; without a shot she absolutely couldn't bear up.

The forty-watt bulb hung in the middle of the backstage area, and its dim light fell on the disorderly pile of trunks, costumes, masks, tables, and chairs, making a ragged and uneven shadow. Chin Hsi-tzu pushed aside the curtain and stumbled in. The lamplight and the shadows interwove and danced before her eyes, and the made-up faces of the other actors flashed, became distorted, and expanded. In an instant, Chin Hsi-tzu's world turned unreal. She groped for the small table against the wall, took hold of a chair, and sat down. She opened the drawer, and tried her hardest to keep her eyes open in order to look for the hypodermic syringe.

"Wa-ya . . . wa . . ." Ah-pao's unrestrained crying pierced her heart. Nearby, men were dismantling the sets, and hammer blows struck intermittently. She couldn't see anyone. She couldn't see anything around her. In her world there was only the needle. Putting everything aside, she hastily uncovered the needle point and stuck it into a small vial. As she briskly raised her left hand, her long sleeve fell back, and with head lifted and eyes fixed on the back of her left hand, she quickly jabbed the needle into the flesh with her right hand.

She closed her eyes, then opened them again. Before her, everything seemed to grow brighter. She saw the untidy, opened trunks, and the row of costumes hanging on the wall like corpses. She smelled the familiar, rotten and unhealthy odor of mildew and sweat, combined with the pungency of Paradise cigarettes. Together with the smell of talcum powder and cold cream, it formed a sticky, damp atmosphere which hung in the air everywhere. Gradually the backstage area began to grow brighter, and all the props were gilded with a layer of golden light. The table and chair around her had completely changed shape, instantly turning as splendid as a palace. A cluster of false beards hanging beside the table began to waggle, and smiled at her. She felt herself growing light, as gently as a lump of sugar quickly melting and dissolving in hot water. A feeling of warmth ran through her entire body, as though she were in a man's embrace, and she felt an incomparable satisfaction, a satisfaction that left her no room for other thoughts.

Suddenly, a dreadful, harsh cry exploded in the void. The shattering sound penetrated her eardrums and struck directly at her brain. Shaken, she blinked, and saw Ah-pao and old Aunt Ho.

Ah-pao was crying in Aunt Ho's arms, while his two small hands tore at her blouse and the legs, thin as match-sticks, kicked in weak fits. Mucus and tears flooded his ashen face, forming a swamp in which his little eyes and nose drowned. His dark lips were distorted to a funnel shape, and his mouth writhed. He cried at the top of his lungs, and his face turned the color of a shelled duck egg gone rotten. Old Aunt Ho, eyes shut, was trying very hard to rock him, and was muttering some indistinct words to soothe him. Suddenly she could no longer hold onto him, and the child rolled out of her arms and fell onto the floor. His whole body convulsed, trembled, and then seemed to be paralyzed, like a hedgehog.

Chin Hsi-tzu hurried over. As the child's limbs convulsed her heart began to sink. Let Lotus take him! She began to feel wearied. Old Aunt Ho picked the child up and he curled up in her arms, crying weakly. The make-up man came to help Chin Hsi-tzu take off her costume. Chin Hsi-tzu took the child from Aunt Ho, who limped off to prepare the powdered milk. The child wriggled in Chin Hsi-tzu's arms, searching for the nipple, his mucus and tears leaving a moist trail across his chest. She unfastened her brassiere, baring the left breast, which was dry and flat. The child gnawed at the nipple, sucking hard, and his crying gradually grew weaker. Chin Hsi-tzu frowned; the child's baby teeth were chewing her nipple, biting into her lungs and her heart.

"Aunt Ho!" She closed her eyes and groaned. "Come on, hurry up!"

Aunt Ho poured the powdered milk into the baby bottle.

"Shall I add the white powder, or not?" the old woman asked.

The child, sucking and getting no milk, pulled at the nipple violently. Chin Hsi-tzu's fingers started to cramp.

"Yes, do!"

Aunt Ho grumbled, shook her head helplessly, and tottered over to the place where Chin Hsi-tzu had just been resting. She opened the drawer and took out a small package of morphine concentrate. After pouring some into the baby bottle, she replaced the nipple, shook it twice, and gave it to Chin Hsi-tzu.

As she watched the child greedily sucking at the bottle, Chin Hsi-tzu's heart was yet more distressed and chilled, and the hatred she had felt toward the child was all changed momentarily to guilt. My darling baby . . . Mother's sin has passed down to you through her milk! Her nipple was sore, but she frowned and endured it.

"The powdered milk is running out, Chin Hsi-tzu," Aunt Ho reminded her, going over to help a worker with the packing. Chin Hsi-tzu did not answer. She did not feel like thinking. The gong sounded again.

Chin Hsi-tzu hastily gave the child to Aunt Ho to hold, and stood up, fastening her brassiere. The make-up man came quickly over to help her put on her costume, and as the wood-slats sounded her cue for the second time, she made a dash for the stage, with the make-up man trailing her, tying up her belt from behind.

(*The wicked minister Wen-hsi tried to seduce Hsüeh-mei on a terrace overlooking the rear garden; Hsüeh-mei is doing embroidery in her boudoir.*)

Chin Hsi-tzu sat at one corner downstage, going through the motions of threading a needle, guiding the thread, and tying it off. The stage was dead silent; there was only the scratchy, lonely weeping of the guitar. She was so preoccupied with her own troubles that she had lost all interest even in this role, her best; it was merely a matter of mechanically reproducing what she had memorized. She glanced down from the stage; the woman who had been sitting in the corner was gone, and suddenly she felt a little disappointed.

Ah-pao's convulsed face appeared in that woman's place. Over the yellow and black heads of the audience, she saw Ah-pao's convulsed face, a shattered duck's-egg of a face. Oh, let Lotus raise him. Her resolve was beginning to waver. The difficulties of bringing up Ah-pao appeared, all at once, in her mind's eye. She had been willing to sacrifice everything for the child, if only she could keep him, and for this resolve she had let pass an opportunity to be married as a second wife, and had lost the love of the crowd, . . . but it seemed that she had exchanged all that for an even sadder result. She simply didn't dare think of it. She had only to close her eyes and the image of a tramp addicted to both drugs and gambling appeared in sharp relief. Is this my child's future? The thought made her tremble. She had tried to give up the drug, for Ah-pao's sake, and during the months of her postpartum confinement she had suffered quite a few times, but she had never been able to do it. In order to live, she had to keep on performing. However, the local opera at this time was in decline, and the acting life now was a far cry from the good old days. Ten years before, lead roles had been hers to choose, and she had been able to live for a month on her pay from a single show. Now, if the manager were dissatisfied, he could dismiss her at any time. She had foreseen this vicious, interlocking chain long ago: survival, drugs, survival . . . it bound her tightly, and there was no way she could set herself free. She loved to sing opera, and except for singing opera, she did not even know what she could do. She understood clearly the way young lead actresses usually ended up: as they grew older, they either married a businessman, as Lotus had, or they bought a few girls for service in a teahouse or a brothel which they would eventually own. But she was only twenty-eight! If she could pull herself together, she could very well go on singing for several years more, and save a little money. . . . But, in that case, she would have to spend half a year breaking the drug habit, and moreover she would have to give up the child. Ah, she would have to think it over carefully. All this mess was tangled as hemp. . . .

As the show ended, an actor in the robes of a court attendant came out and bowed to the audience. He had daubed three spots of white powder on his nose, and wore his red, melon-shaped cap askew.

"Ladies and gentlemen, our opera troupe has performed here for ten days, and we're most grateful for your patronage. Starting tomorrow, we will be performing in the Ta-hua Theater in T'ao-yüan, and we hope that you ladies and gentlemen will frequently honor us with your presence. Any of you who would like to obtain pictures as souvenirs are welcome to remain. . . ."

The audience all got up, some whispering in groups, others fluttering their paper fans, and began to leave. A few hung around in their seats undecidedly, but when they saw that the others were leaving, they left too. In a little while, the whole theater was deserted, and there remained only a janitor girl, lazily closing the windows.

Everyone was disappointed, and Chin Hsi-tzu even more so. The drummer, the wood-slat player, and the guitarist threw down their instruments and yawned to their hearts' content. The bustle started backstage with the sound of water being gulped, of trunks being dragged across the floor, of mocking laughter, and of insults and scolding, all blended together.

She was removing her head ornaments. Ah-pao crawled over to her legs, stood up by holding onto her leg, and looked up at her out of his sharp eyes. Aunt Ho had wiped away the tears and mucus, and his small face was clean and tidy. She forgot the thick make-up and powder on her face, and swept him up, kissing his face and little hands. The child beamed at her, showing three tiny teeth, and his whole body wriggled with pleasure. His little hand patted his mother's nose, and he kept saying "*Mo, mo.*" Suddenly her mind cleared. She hugged Ah-pao tightly, and kissed his little face again and again.

"Chin Hsi-tzu, you're coming along with the others tomorrow, right? You want your trunk tidied up and packed?" asked a workman standing in front of her trunk. "Eh, . . . oh, . . . yes, yes." She clasped Ah-pao's face and kept rubbing her lipstick on it.

Aunt Ho, in the corner, shook her head. Chin Hsi-tzu glanced at her, but pretended she had not seen. My child. Oh, such a lovable little face, she reminded herself.

"Chin Hsi-tzu."

She looked up and found the manager of the troupe standing before her, glaring brutally and directly at Ah-pao. She felt a little uneasy, like a conscience-stricken wrongdoer, and despite herself her heartbeat speeded up.

"What was wrong with your throat tonight? Your voice got lower and lower, and Ah-pao's crying got fiercer and fiercer!"

"I'm sorry. Aunt Ho was too busy to feed him . . ."

"I've told you before, an opera troupe is not a nursery. If you wanted a kid so bad, then why didn't you leave with that tea merchant? Huh? Tonight, for the first time, nobody asked for a picture! Chin Hsi-tzu, I'm not the kind to turn my back on a person, but we just can't go on like this; we've all got to eat. Our contract is up next month, so you'd better give it some thought. I'm serving you notice ahead of time." His plump body went striding off without looking back, leaving her standing there stunned.

The backstage noise reverberated in Chin Hsi-tzu's ears, intensified, and at last exploded; she closed her eyes.

"*Ma-ma-ma!*" Ah-pao was jumping around in her arms. She opened her eyes, and the child showed his teeth in a smile. His eyes danced with laughter, and his thin lips formed a curve. It was a lovable look, tempting her to play with him. She gazed intently at that smile. It was gradually broadening, broadening. She saw the bloom of that earlier smile, so beguiling and wild. Suddenly she was frustrated and tense; she felt so oppressed by it that she could not breathe.

She had buried that smile more than a year ago, and now it came back to life in Ah-pao. All at once, they returned, those decadent, undisciplined days, those days which Chin Hsi-tzu with all her might wanted to forget; they all came back. That smile had had a frightening attraction for her, she had gone mad for it, had taken to drugs for it, had even had a baby. Those had been dreadful days! As Chin Hsi-tzu recalled them in pain, she felt that those days had stopped up her throat and pinched her neck, so that she couldn't turn her head or breathe; the memories made her tremble all over, uncontrollably.

The child smiled at her with his fixed eyes, and his thin lips formed a captivating curve, showing three teeth as he chuckled at her. Chin Hsi-tzu stared at him, stared and stared, and her face twisted. Suddenly she stood up, and put the child on the floor.

"Oh, you needn't get my trunk ready. Lotus is coming tomorrow, and I'll have to leave a day late."

Hearing that, Aunt Ho, still in the corner, sat up straight, rubbing her eyes. Chin Hsi-tzu stood up, straightened herself, and went on removing her head ornaments. The child crawled on the floor alone.

Wang Wen-hsing was born in Fu-chou, Fukien, in 1939. A classmate of Ch'en Jo-hsi and Pai Hsien-yung, he received his B. A. degree from National Taiwan University and an M.F.A. from the University of Iowa. Before *Hsien-tai wen-hsüeh* was established in 1960, he was, like his classmates, a frequent contributor to *Wen-hsüeh tsa-chih*, where some of his best stories had been published.

An ardent advocate for the Westernization of modern Chinese literature (see his Preface to *The Newly Carved Statue [Hsin-k'e-ti shih-hsiang]*, 1968), Wang Wen-hsing had received little attention until the first installment of his controversial *Change in the Family (Chia-pien)* appeared in *Chung-wai wen-hsüeh* (I, No. 4, 1972). It became an instantaneous sensation. Special groups at various universities met to study its meaning, particularly its highly idiosyncratic style. Newspapers and magazines devoted generous space specifically for the discussion of this story. Though the public's views on this work range from admiration to aversion, there is no doubt that Wang Wen-hsing has written a piece of fiction that will be a subject of debate for years to come.

In April 1973, Taipei's Huan-yü ch'u-pan-she put together the six magazine installments into a book of 294 pages. Its length is about two-thirds of *Madame Bovary*, yet it has taken Wang seven years to finish, roughly two years longer than Flaubert had presumably spent on his classic. If sales volume can in any way be used as an indicator of success, Wang Wen-hsing has not labored all these years in vain, for the second edition of *Change in the Family* followed the first by two months.

"Flaw" ("Ch'ien-ch'üeh") first saw print in *Hsien-tai wen-hsüeh* (No. 19, 1964); the English translation appeared in *The Chinese Pen* (Autumn 1973). Wang Wen-hsing is currently Associate Professor of English at National Taiwan University.

Flaw-

WANG WEN-HSING

Translated by CH'EN CHU-YÜN

I must have been eleven that year, because I had just enrolled in junior high. At that time we were still living on Tung-an Street, our earliest home in Taipei, and had not yet moved to Tung-hua Street, after which we moved again to Lien-yün Street. But it has always been my impression that the earlier the home, the better it seemed; every time we moved, it was to a less attractive place. Perhaps it was the nostalgia for early childhood, strongest for the earliest years, that gave rise to such an illusion.

Tung-an Street was a quiet little alley, with less than a hundred families along its entire length. Slightly curved around its middle, the street stretched all the way to the great gray river at the end. Actually, viewed from the vantage point of the river bank, there were very few pedestrians on the street, which, with its palish body and meandering path, was virtually a small river itself. Such was the tranquil picture when I was eleven; later, as small cars were allowed to pass through the street, the atmosphere of quiet seclusion was lost altogether. My present reminiscences hark back to the era before the arrival of the cars.

In any event, on Tung-an Street at that time cats could be seen strolling lazily along the tops of the low walls, from one house to the next. The whole landscape was filled with glistening green foliage and delicately fragrant odors from the profusion of flowers and plants growing in the front yards. Flowers especially took to Tung-an Street; they bloomed in the spring and in the fall. Most unforgettable, however, were the evenings of that tiny street, when silent street lamps illuminated the darkness of the road. Night seemed even quieter than day. The little grocery stores, unlike their counterparts in the crowded city, closed at half-past nine. Midnight began at half-past nine. Night enjoyed its deepest and longest sleep on this street. Light breezes rustled among the leaves

15

while remote stars twinkled in the skies, and after a few hours, night passed and day broke. In the early morning mist, the owners of the small grocery stores, still unlike their counterparts in the city, began taking down the wooden panels of the shops.

In spring that year, a young seamstress opened a shop at the end of the street near the river. It was at a time when Taipei, still untouched by affluence, was just beginning to prosper, and a number of three-storied buildings could be seen cropping up here and there. Ever since the previous winter, we children had been watching with interest the construction of such a building on the vacant lot in front of our houses. Our feelings were excitement mingled with sadness; we were excited because, as children, we felt an immense satisfaction with all novel experiences—new sights, new sounds, new objects, new undertakings—and sad because we were losing our favorite playground for after-school ball games. The building was completed in spring, and the young woman moved in. The house consisted of three compartments, and was three stories tall. The young woman and her family occupied the entire compartment on the right, while the second and third floors served as family rooms. It was said that she owned the entire building and we children had naturally assumed that she would occupy all the space herself, but it turned out she reserved only one compartment for her own use and offered the others for rent. A week after they had been taken she changed her mind and sold them off. And we felt a slight tinge of regret for her that she had been able to occupy only a part of the building.

I was a precocious child then, although I looked at least two years younger than my eleven years. Like all underdeveloped children however, my mental growth compensated for my physical weakness by being two years beyond my age. One day, I discovered that I was in love with the young woman. The realization dawned upon me during the spring vacation, right after the soft spring showers, in the blossom-filled month of April.

Being a sensitive and inward child, I had an instinctive fear of glamorous and sophisticated women, and took only to those with kind faces (I still do even now). The woman at the dressmaking shop was exactly the type I like.

She was about thirty-five or so, and did not wear much make-up (this was very important). She wore neither rouge nor powder on her face and only a tiny trace of lipstick on her lips, which were often parted in a white warm smile. Her eyes were not only beautiful, but, even more important, glowed with gentle kindness. My love for her stemmed not only from approval of her looks, but was rooted in sincere admiration for the goodness of her character as well.

Love in a precocious child, like a heavy blossom atop a frail stem, was a burden too heavy to bear. Only then did I realize the consuming nature of love; if the blazing flames were the joys of love it was the burning of the fuel itself which made these flames possible. I found it impossible that true happiness could consist in achieving joy from the masochistic burning of one's own self. Although I had been in the world for a mere eleven short years then, I had undergone enough minor suffering to be able to devise a means of avoiding pain. That was: if you happened to form an emotional attachment to a certain thing or a certain person, the best thing to do was to immediately look for a fault therein, upon which you would then be able to withhold your affection and thus lighten the burden. During the next few days, I often concealed myself directly opposite her shop and scrutinized her with cold detachment, in an effort to discover some ugliness in her. But the longer I watched, the more beautiful she seemed. I realized then that love had so deeply embedded itself that there was no way of uprooting it. I would have to live with it.

It was already the last day of the spring vacation. I made up my mind to enjoy it to the full by playing outdoors for the whole day. Early in the morning, I went over to our new playground (which had been relocated at the vacant lot in front of the garbage heap beside the grocery store) to wait for the other children to gather. We started our ball game much earlier that morning than usual— it must have been before eight o'clock, for our shrill cries woke an office worker living in one of the wooden buildings. Still clad in his pajamas, he opened the window and leaned out to scold loudly. Our ball often hit the ragged old woman who kept a cigarette stand next to the garbage heap and she tried to chase us away with a broom, but as she lacked the strength and energy, could only stand brandishing her broom like a sentinel in front of her

stand, hitting out at whoever ran near her, but we were all careful
to stay away. On top of it all, Ah-chiu's pet mongrel kept dashing
among us madly. For some reason or other he seemed to have
picked me for his target, jumping on me repeatedly and causing
me to fall several times. It was only when Ah-chiu's mother appeared and summoned him and his four brothers back to breakfast
that we finally broke up the game and dispersed. The sun had
splashed the entire street golden by then. Thick greenery clustered
over the tops of the plaster walls. Market-bound housewives were
already holding summer parasols to ward off the sunlight, whose
beams had become so strong lately that some buds were bursting
into flower before their time. I felt thirsty and wormed my way
into Liu Hsiao-tung's yard in order to drink from their faucet.
Water flowed over my face and neck, where I left it for the sun to
dry. As I passed the dressmaking shop, I saw the young woman
standing in the doorway talking with another lady, teasing now
and then the baby the latter held in her arms. I climbed up the
incline at the end of Tung-an Street, walked down the steps on the
other side and headed for the river.

The river under the sunlight was alive with undulating glitter,
like a million thumb-tacks rising and falling in rhythm. On the
opposite bank, two ox-carts were crawling along the sandy beach.
Standing under a newly budding tree, I could smell the fragrance
of the baked earth along the river bank and feel the coolness of the
river breeze on my skin. As I walked away from the tree, I raised
my voice and started singing "Crossing the Sea in Summer."
Keeping time with my hands, I went singing all the way up the
river. I walked into a bamboo grove, found a relatively flat patch of
land and lay down.

In front of me stretched the river, glimmering through the bamboo leaves; at my back was a piece of farmland colorful as a Per-
sian rug. The huge patches of green were rice paddies; big blocks
of rich dark brown were earth freshly plowed but yet unsowed;
slender strips of light green, like the thin glass squares used under
microscopes, were bean tendrils, while the golden patches were
vegetable blossoms, swaying in the spring breeze. The short dark
figures of the farmers could be glimpsed working in the distance,

and occasionally the faint odor of manure drifted in from the fields.

I lay quietly, thinking of all kinds of whimsical things, but they were all happy thoughts; I allowed my fancies to roam like the breeze-driven clouds in the sky. I turned over, and, resting my chin upon my arms, gazed at the river through the bamboo leaves. I thought of the young seamstress. I had no one in whom I could confide my love, only the river. Later this river also became the witness to my pains in learning to swim. I would often steal away from home, make my way alone to the river under the summer sun, and, bracing myself against fears of drowning, would try to teach myself the art of floating above water. But I never did succeed. I gave up my efforts finally, because I no longer had the courage to struggle.

The river could not respond to my confidences. I returned to my former position on my back and covered my face with a handkerchief.

I lay until the sun had traveled directly overhead, then removed the handkerchief and sat up. Thinking that my mother would be waiting for me to go home for lunch, I stood up and headed for home. The farmers had all disappeared from the fields. Probably they too had gone home to eat.

At home I saw our Taiwanese amah. She had not gone home yet and was still doing the ironing. As soon as she saw me, she asked:

"Young Master, have you seen my Ch'un-hsiung?"

I replied that I had not.

"Weren't you playing with him outdoors?"

I said I was not.

"I can't think where he could've gone. I told him to come and help me mop the floors, but there hasn't been a trace of him all morning. My Ch'un-hsiung just can't compare with Young Master, Ma'am. Young Master is smart, and works hard; so young and already in junior high; he'll be in senior high next, and after that, a top official," she said, shaking out one of my father's shirts.

Our amah often praised me thus, remarking that I would proceed to senior high school after finishing junior high. She could not imagine a college education beyond that of senior high, so after that, I was to become a high official.

Mother answered her in broken Taiwanese, "It'll be the same with you. Ch'un-hsiung will also go to school, also earn money and support you."

"Thank you, Ma'am, thank you. But I was born to suffer, Ma'am. Ch'un-hsiung's father died early, leaving me alone to raise him. I have no other hopes, only that Ch'un-hsiung will be like Young Master, work hard in school, study in junior high and afterwards in senior high. No matter how hard I have to work, wash clothes all my life even, I want him to be educated."

"He won't disappoint you," my mother replied.

Amah only sighed.

That kind old woman. I still remember her broad tan face, like a piece of dark bread, warm and glowing, the perfect blending of simple goodness and unpretentious love. Where she had gone, no one knew. As I grew older, gentle people like her were harder and harder to come by. They are not the kind to adapt easily within an increasingly complex society, I suppose. I also recall another minor detail about her, the result of the peculiar powers of childhood observation: I often noticed her bare feet, with ten stout toes fanning out, pattering along on the shining floors of our house. The reason I found this extraordinary perhaps was that we all wore slippers in the house and there were many pairs of spare slippers in the hallway reserved for guests. Amah probably had never become used to this alien custom and thus never wore any. I often mused to myself then that even if she consented to wear slippers like the rest of us, where would we find such a large pair to fit her?

That was the last day of the spring vacation. Another detail I remember was that I went out and bought a diary that afternoon. A certain fascination for the surrounding phenomena, interest for the musings within my mind (for my newly-sprung love), and for spring itself urged me to imitate Liu Hsiao-tung's elder brother and keep a diary. All my thoughts for the day were faithfully recorded that evening in the first entry of my diary.

After the spring vacation, love continued to plague me, as if urging me to some action, to do something which would bring me closer to her, albeit only in my feeling. I thought of taking something to her shop and asking her to mend it for me (a sorry means of courtship, I admit). But that shop of hers took only women's clothing. I could not think of anything else, so one day I finally brought along a Boy Scout jacket with a missing button to her shop.

Her shop was tastefully furnished. Pictures cut from Japanese fashion magazines adorned the walls, and a vase of bright red roses stood on a small table in one corner. Four girls were sitting in the room, talking and laughing among themselves as they pedaled on machines spread with pieces of brightly colored material.

"What do you want, little one?" A rounded-faced girl wearing a string of imitation pearls lifted her head and asked.

"I want a button sewn," I said, turning to the seamstress, who stood at the table measuring a dress, "Can you do it?"

The woman took my jacket and said: "Ah-hsiu, sew the button on for him." She handed the jacket over to the round-faced girl, then turned and went on with her measuring.

I felt the sorrow of rejection.

"Which button is it?" the girl asked me.

I told her, with my eyes on the woman.

"How much?" I asked the woman.

"A dollar," replied the girl.

The woman seemed not to have heard my question, for she did not even lift her head. My grief sank its roots into the depths of my heart. But after a while I saw the woman put on a pair of glasses, and curiosity took the place of sorrow. I found it strange that she should wear glasses, as if it were the least probable thing in the world. I did not like the way she looked with glasses; she no longer looked like herself. Moreover, she was wearing them too low. They made her look old and gave her an owl-like expression.

Suddenly aware that I had stood gazing in the shop much longer than necessary, I asked the round-faced girl:

"Can I come back and get it later?"

"No, stay. It'll be ready in a minute."

I waited nervously in the shop for her to finish. I glanced again at the pictures of the Japanese women on the walls. They were all very pretty, with dazzling smiles, but strangely, their eyelids all had only single pleats. I looked again at the roses in the corner.

They were still flaming red. Feeling that they seemed to be redder than roses usually were, I took a more careful look and discovered that they were plastic flowers.

After a while, a boy came down the stairs, munching a piece of fruit. He was taller than I, also in a Boy Scout uniform, and was wearing a pair of glasses. With sudden intuition, I realized this was her son. I had seen two smaller children with her, but had never seen this one; like all newcomers to the neighborhood, he never came out to join our games. Amidst surprised confusion I, who was secretly in love with his mother, watched him as he went upstairs again with a water bottle.

After the button had been replaced, I hurried out the door with the jacket. In the doorway I met our amah coming in. Afraid that she would report me to my mother, for I had come to the shop without her knowledge, I slipped away as unobtrusively as I could.

Despite the fact that I had been received with cold indifference at her shop, that I had seen a son of hers who was much older than I, my love did not change; the love of a child does not change easily. I still gave her all the passion of my eleven years.

Thus I loyally allowed my love to continue, without hope, without fulfillment, and without anyone's awareness. This hopelessness, however, colored my love with a nuance of melancholy beauty. Actually, I could not tell whether this sense of futility gave me sorrow or happiness. But I was sure of one thing, that with such love I was happier than adults in one respect. I was spared any unnecessary anxiety; I did not have to worry over the fact that one day my love would suddenly come to an end. As long as my admiration existed, my love existed. Looking back now, I should say I was quite happy then.

The trip I made to her shop, I recall, was the only time I undertook such a venture. I never found another opportunity; besides, for some reason I suddenly lost all courage, and found myself deeply ashamed over the incident. Whenever I thought of myself going into her shop on the mere pretext of replacing a button, my shame would grow until the experience became a positive terror, causing me to sweat in anguish. For three days afterward I did not have the heart to pass in front of her shop. Courage is a strange thing: the first plunge should never be merited as true courage until tested by subsequent tries.

Although I was never in her shop again, I was often in front of it. Opposite her shop was a dry-goods store which sold all kinds of tidbits for children and at which I frequently stood vigil. Munching on a cracker, I watched as she moved around in her shop. Sometimes I would see her husband, a man of thirty-some, riding a motorcycle and said to be working in a commercial bank. Strangely enough, I never felt a trace of jealousy for this man. This showed, I suppose, that I was still a long way from maturity. I did not seem to realize the full significance of the word "husband." I thought of him as merely another member of her household, like her brother, her uncle, or her brother-in-law. But should she be talking with another man, for instance if she chatted momentarily with the barber next door, my jealous rage would lead me to visualize the barber lying on the ground with a dagger in his heart.

Thus the days slipped by, one after another, like the turning pages of my diary. Soon it was summer and the end of the school term approached. I began to worry about my grades; I was very weak in algebra, and was afraid I would not be able to pass the finals. My algebra teacher had already warned half-jokingly that he expected to see me again next semester. I shook with fear; I had never in my life had to repeat a grade, and now the threat loomed large. Yet mingled with the anxiety was a sense of unbound expectation, expectation for the freedom, the happiness, and the unlimited possibilities of the summer vacation. Under the dark shadow of the finals, I sat for hours on end with the algebra text in front of me, but, instead of studying, I often simply gazed at it anxiously. I grew thin and pale.

Finally, the heavy, burdensome finals were over. All the students hurled themselves into the free skies of the summer vacation like birds escaping from captivity. I was merely one ecstatic soul among thousands. Countless youngsters, burdened by the exams, had eagerly awaited the arrival of the summer vacation, and, in waiting had imagined that it would never become a reality, otherwise their joys of expectation would have been cancelled by the pains of suffering.

That first morning of the vacation, I opened my eleven-year-old eyes to the riotous singing of birds and a world brilliant with sunshine. Exams were a thing of the past. No matter how badly I did on them, they were no longer on my mind. All children, perhaps, are unable to worry over the past. Sitting up in bed, a shiver of excitement told me beyond a shadow of doubt that the summer vacation had finally arrived. That certainty did not come from any indication on the calendar, but from a certain sound, a certain odor, a patch of sunlight, all distinctively characteristic. I heard the shrill buzz of the cicadas, saw the reflection of a basin of water shimmering on the ceiling, smelled the cool fragrance of mothballs as my mother took out our winter clothing from the trunks and laid them out in the sun—and I knew that this was it. Happiness was that child as he jumped out of bed.

Each year with the awareness of summer came the reminder to sort out our fishing gear. We would rummage among the coal bins in the kitchen and come out with a slender bamboo pole which our mothers had put aside (and which we had painstakingly whittled ourselves), take it to the bathroom and, with great effort, try to clean it, thinking of the great catches in store this year, although for the most part we were only able to catch frogs.

I found my fishing pole that day as usual, and cleaned it up as before. But holding it in my hands I all of a sudden felt that it was much too homely. It was my own handiwork, of which I had once been so proud, but now I saw its crudeness. I felt that I needed a brand new fishing pole, a *bona fide* one, not a plain home-made one like this. I wanted one with a reel, a tinkler, and one that was gracefully pliant like a whip. I made up my mind to ask my father to buy me one. I had high hopes of getting it, because I had an indisputable reason: I was *eleven*.

I threw my fishing pole back into the coal bin.

I headed for the garbage heap to look for my friends. It had been two whole weeks since we played our last ball game, all because of the final exams. Our mothers would not let us play.

I passed by the dressmaking shop, hoping to catch a glimpse of the young woman, but today her shop was closed. She must be out with her family. I felt a little disheartened. I saw her every day, but one day in which I did not was enough to give me that feeling of voidness.

My friends were already in the middle of a game. I hurriedly joined in and immediately became involved in the ferocious battle. We played happily until noon. The side I was on lost and they blamed me, while I blamed myself for joining the wrong side. But we all determined valiantly to fight again tomorrow and win. As I walked home, the dressmaking shop was still closed. Again I experienced a loss.

At home my mother was complaining over the fact that Amah had failed to show up that morning to do the laundry, and that if she was too busy to come she should have sent Ch'un-hsiung over with a message. Then she turned upon me and said that I had disappeared all morning like a pigeon let out of the cage; she wanted me to go and look for Amah, but she could not even find me. I was surely headed for trouble if I played like that every day, and I should not spend all my time in ball games even though it *was* the summer vacation. Naturally, these words were ones I liked least to hear.

After lunch I felt drowsy. The white-hot sunshine outside made it hard to keep my eyes open; in the room a few flies were buzzing intermittently upon the dining-room table. Unconsciously I dozed off for about ten minutes. Awaking, I gazed at the bright sunlight outside the window and the flies on the table in the room and a familiar sensation dawned upon me. How could I have forgotten? Summer vacations were always boring after all.

Just then Mrs. Liu, who lived next door, came over for her daily chat with my mother. With hair curlers bobbing she stepped in the doorway and asked:

"Is your mother at home, little one?"

"I'm in the kitchen, Mrs. Liu," my mother called, "Find a seat and I'll be out in a minute." But Mrs. Liu had already traced the voice into the kitchen.

Then they both emerged. My mother's hands were covered with soap suds. She found a piece of cloth and started wiping them.

"How come you're doing the wash yourself?" Mrs. Liu asked as she sat down.

"Amah didn't show up today, I thought I might as well."

"That's what I came to tell you," Mrs. Liu said, setting her curlers bobbing again, "You know what's happened to Amah? She's lost all her money. Twenty thousand dollars of savings, and she lost it all last night. No wonder she's sick."

"Oh? Is that so? I didn't know she had so much saved up." My mother remarked in surprise.

"All the money she earned by working day and night as a washerwoman, saved up bit by bit. She says she was saving for her son's education. Bad luck that she should lose it all. But this time lots of other people on our street were hard hit too. Mrs. Yeh lost ten thousand—seems like she just put the money in a couple of days ago, and it being the money for the fuel coupons of her husband's office at that. Mrs. Wu lost three thousand. It's all that witch's fault, and now the whole family's skipped."

"Who're you talking about?"

"That woman in the dressmaking shop. You can't imagine how unscrupulous she is. One hundred fifty thousand, gone just like that. Who'd believe she was capable of doing such a thing? Everyone saw that her business was good and trusted her, saw that she offered higher interest, of course, and never dreamed she would suddenly skip out like that. Sheer betrayal, that's what it is."

"Unbelievable," my mother mused, "she seemed to be such an honest person. Oh, poor Amah, what is she going to do . . ."

I did not stay to hear my mother finish. I ran out of the house and headed straight for the dressmaking shop.

The shop was still closed. A few women were standing near the doorway chatting. I stood gazing at the shop as pieces of the conversation nearby drifted into my ears.

"They left in the middle of the night. No one knows where they are now."

"They could report her to the police, have her arrested."

"No use. All she'll have to do is declare herself bankrupt, and she wouldn't have a care in the world. Besides, now that she's got the money, the law can't touch her."

"It was all planned," another said, "You notice she was in a hurry to sell most of this building as soon as she moved in."

"They say she sold this shop of hers last week too."

A few maids were peering in from the windows on the right. I went over and looked in through a small pane of glass: the room was empty, all the sewing machines and the furniture were gone.

"Just imagine, she didn't even pay the girls their wages. How mean can one get?"

Hearing this I suddenly felt my ears burn with anger.

Mrs. Liu had already left when I got home. Seeing me, my mother murmured:

"Unbelievable, just unbelievable. People are getting worse and worse. More people get rich and more cheating goes on. People are getting prosperous, but if morals go bad, what's the use of all this prosperity? Luckily we aren't rich; otherwise, who knows? We might also have been duped."

Our family was not rich. My father was teaching in a high school then, and, in Taiwan, a teacher was by no means well off. But was Amah well off? Why cheat her out of all her money? And those girls who had worked for nothing, why deprive them of their wages?

I went with a book up to the rooftop that evening; I had decided to heed my mother and do a little studying. The sky above was a soft quiet blue. I sat on the reddish tiles and leaned my head against the railing.

I could see the dressmaking shop down across the street. The door was still closed; the chatting women had gone.

Thinking of the young woman, of her comely yet gentle face, I found it hard to believe that she was a fraud. But she *was a fraud.* Every time I told myself the truth, my heart contracted in pain.

I still cherished my love for her. I wanted to keep that love. I closed my eyes and thought of her lily-like face—yet I was always reminded of her flaw. I saw the ugliness of that face; and the flower hung down and withered.

Dusk slowly enveloped Tung-an Street; wisps of pale smoke began to curl from the chimneys nearby. The scene in front of me got misty, and I discovered that my eyes were filled with tears.

Oh, youth, perhaps my sadness then was due not only to a woman's having disappointed me, but to the discovery that some element in life had been deluding me, and had been deluding me for a long time. The sorrow and the anguish of the discovery disturbed me deeply.

From that day on, I understood a bit more; I learned that disillusions were an integral part of life, and that more disillusions were to come. From that day on, I forgot the beauty of that woman, although I never could forget the details of this incident. No wonder; that was my first love.

Ch'en Ying-chen (pen name for Ch'en Yung-shan) was born into a
missionary family in Taiwan in 1936. He studied English at Tamkang
College and was graduated in 1960. A frequent and enthusiastic contributor to *P'i-hui, Hsien-tai wen-hsüeh,* and *Wen-hsüeh chi-k'an,* he
had been a leading figure among the native Taiwanese writers until he
was arrested by the Taiwan Garrison Command and sentenced to ten
years' imprisonment in 1968 for his alleged anti-government activities.
(He and other political prisoners were granted amnesty in August 1975
after President Chiang Kai-shek's death on April 5 of the same year.) In
"How Much Truth Can a Blade of Grass Carry?" I have assessed the
significance of his writings thus:

> Ch'en Ying-chen may not be a great writer; his output is relatively small
> and his style is at times embarrassing, yet he is a very important writer. He
> is important because he is unique. Almost alone among his contemporaries,
> he addresses himself to some of the most sensitive problems of his time. "The
> Country Teacher" ("Hsiang-ts'un chiao-shih," 1960), a semiautobiograph-
> ical account of the consequences of disillusionment among Taiwanese in-
> tellectuals after Taiwan's restoration to China during the initial stage, is
> one such example.

"My First Case" ("Ti-i-chien ch'a-shih") first appeared in *Wen-hsüeh
chi-k'an,* No. 3, 1967. A collection of his essays, movie reviews, and
stories can be found in Joseph S. M. Lau, ed., *Selected Stories of
Ch'en Ying-chen (Ch'en Ying-chen hsüan-chi,* 1972).

My First Case–

CH'EN YING-CHEN

Translated by CHEUNG CHI-YIU and DENNIS T. HU

On graduation I was sent to this small town. It's been almost a year now. This morning, the manager of the hotel burst into our bedroom without knocking. My newly-wed wife screamed and hurriedly covered herself with a blanket. I was really angry. The manager looked frightened, and backed out into the sitting room in a fluster. I put on my trousers, walked out from the bedroom and closed the door behind me.

"Blundering fool!" My wife had already started yelling in the other room.

As I was really angry, I suppose I did not look too amiable either.

"Sorry, sorry." One hand on his chest, the manager had a piteous look on his small face. "Sorry, sorry."

"What do you think you're doing, huh?"

"Actually it's that . . ."

"Ass! Blundering fool! What an ass!" My wife said in the bedroom.

The manager looked at me with extreme helplessness in his eyes. "Sorry, Mr. Tu. I'm so frightened," he said. "A guest died at our hotel."

"A guest died?"

"My God, yes. A guest died," said the manager. "You must come over and take a look."

I told him to leave everything as it was, and he went away. I began to feel somewhat excited though I knew that it was not right, and I just could not suppress the feeling. I went back into the bedroom and took off from the hanger my flannel uniform, which was distributed not long ago.

"That stupid fool! You've got to arrest him!" My wife was thumping the bed. Her slightly reddish hair lay randomly on the

29

pillow. I went over and kissed her. "That fool!" she was still grumbling.

"A man died at the hotel," I told her.

She suddenly screamed again, pushing me far away. She stared at me; her eyes were not big, but they were bright after a good night's sleep.

"You're the wife of a policeman," I smiled. "This is my first case."

"Oh, yes," she said.

I bent down to look in the mirror to see whether I needed a shave. I saw her lower her head, scratching her disarrayed hair.

"Oh! How frightening!" she said.

I always remembered what Instructor Wei once said when I was still in school: investigation of a case is an art, is philosophy, psychology, and methodology . . . I was determined to be a good policeman. All this my wife did not understand.

"This is my first case," I said.

My uniform was new. It was a pity that the cap was old. Now my wife, still lying in bed, had put on her glasses, and began reading a novel.

"Come home early," she said. "How frightening!"

"Ah, investigation of a case is philosophy, is . . ." I said. But my wife naturally did not understand all this.

It was about 6:00 P.M. when the senior officer from the county department arrived. I had all the information put in order, and gave it to him.

"Very good," the senior officer said, "very good."

"This is my first case," I humbly told him.

He repeated, "Very good," and began to read the preliminary materials I supplied. "Hu Hsin-pao, thirty-four." As he read he took a breath, looking so very professional.

"Yes, sir."

"He had a good job . . . he came such a long way to kill himself."

"Yes, I think there must be a reason behind it," I said.

"Very good, there must be a reason behind it."

He put the materials on the table and stood up. Although the lights were on, it seemed a little dark in the room. The dead man

Hu Hsin-pao lay on the bed; saliva dripped from the left corner of his mouth, wetting the pillow and the collar of his pajamas. Li, the medical officer, uncovered him, touching this place and that on the dead body. The senior officer put a cigarette between his lips, and I hurried to light it for him.

At last the dead man was totally undressed. He was well-built. Perhaps because he had led an easy life, a thick layer of fat had accumulated around his waist though he was only about thirty. But you could still see that he once had a strong body. With the heavy eyelids closed, there was almost a sort of shyness on his face; this made me lose the nerve to look straight at his virile-looking sexual organ. The senior officer, smoking, coughed lightly.

"How long has he been staying here?" he asked.

"Three days," I replied. I was afraid that the senior officer would detect my uneasiness caused by the somewhat shy expression of the dead man. This would in turn betray my inexperience. Luckily he was only looking at the pallid corpse.

"Very good," he said in a low voice.

Medical Officer Li covered the body with a blanket, without dressing it. In an instant it looked as though the dead man were just asleep. I did not get into the habit of sleeping naked until after I was married, and the scene suddenly gave me a strange feeling. Li took off his gloves, picked up a small, greenish bottle from beside the bed, and examined it under the light.

"Suicide?" asked the senior officer.

"There's no evidence of murder," replied the medical officer.

"Very well," the senior officer turned to me, "there must be a reason."

"Yes, sir," I responded instantly, "there must be a reason."

"This is your first case, you said?"

"Yes, sir."

"Then," he said, "then, it will be very important to you."

"I'll do my best," I said respectfully.

I offered him a cigarette; he said he did not care for any. I offered it to the medical officer; he thanked me, and I lit it for him. The senior officer picked up my materials and went through them quickly.

"These people are your leads?" asked the senior officer.

"Yes, sir. During the last three days they talked to him, and there are various types of relationships here," I said. "The manager of the hotel, a physical education teacher, and in addition, a woman by the name of Lin Pi-chen."

"I'm handing it over to you," he said.

"I'll certainly do my best."

The senior officer stretched out his hand to shake mine. I felt the tenderness of the handshake and was deeply moved. He got into his red jeep and drove away in the dusky twilight. He waved at me from the car, and I saluted at the door of the hotel. There was quite a crowd in the streets.

"What's happened, Mr. Tu?" a farmer was bold enough to ask.

"What's happened? A man was killed."

"A man killed?" he asked. "Who was killed?"

"Don't blab. Aren't you afraid that the dead man would follow you home?"

The farmer spat on the ground at once. "Follow me home? Damn it! Damn it!" he said.

The crowd laughed, and parted to let me pass. Quite imperceptibly, the sky had been strewn with a few early stars. Suddenly I missed my wife at home a little. Yet this was my first case. It was really important.

"Go home now," I said to the crowd. "There's nothing to see here. Go home now."

1.

The next morning I set up for Hu Hsin-pao's case a special file.

"Lin, the head of the Community Bureau, and I—we didn't finish work until eleven last night," my assistant Patrolman Chou said. "His wife's really pretty."

"Whose wife's pretty?" I asked.

"The dead man's. It was almost nine-thirty when they arrived, and they shipped the body back the same night." Putting a cigarette between his thick lips, he continued, "I just wonder what made him do it."

I put the file in order, carried it under my arm, and said, "I'm going to the hotel."

Chou stood up mechanically and put on his cap.

"It's all right," I added quickly, "I can go by myself."

Chou sat down as mechanically as he had stood, took off his cap, and put it in the upper right corner of the table with great care.

"What made him do that?" he said casually. "Such a pretty wife!"

Outside it was a really fine day, not a cloud in the sky.

The manager, Liu Jui-ch'ang, still wore his sad countenance, yet he was quick to greet me: "Oh, it's you, Mr. Tu. Please take a seat, take a seat."

"Thank you," I said, "sorry to bother you again, but I need your help."

The rooms here were divided only by fiberboards, but they had been repainted recently. There was an old pin-up of a nude, foreign woman on the wall near the bed. Liu offered me a cigarette and busily lit it for me. His thin hands were shaking so much that I could not help laughing, and the match was blown out. He lit another one, hands still trembling.

"There's nothing serious, Mr. Liu," I said, "relax."

"How am I supposed to relax?" he asked, forcing a smile. Yet the smile did not disperse the gloominess on his face. "A man picked our place for killing himself. See what tough luck it is?" He stammered along, "Now my business will be ruined."

Liu Jui-ch'ang seemed to have lost a lot of weight in one night. His face looked somewhat twisted, like a cookie drenched overnight by dew. I opened my file, and crushed the cigarette butt in the ashtray. "Don't you ever read newspapers?" I asked. "In some hotels, grenades are thrown, barrages are fired, and people cut into pieces, but it's business as usual."

"Oh my! Oh my!" He looked at me thoughtfully with his small, greyish eyes.

"Now tell me again," I said, "how he came here, how he rented . . ."

Liu Jui-ch'ang straightened his body, one hand grasping the other. He looked at me, making an effort to smile, "I told you all yesterday: he came to my place that afternoon, . . ." He was anxious to please me. "Where am I to start?"

I began to feel a little irritated. I looked into the file and said, "He came on the sixteenth, at about four in the afternoon."

"Yes, yes," he said seriously.

"You said that he came and asked for a room. He looked at several, but wasn't satisfied."

"Yes, yes. After that he said, 'Your rooms here are bad.' "

"Uh-huh."

"Then I showed him that one. The bed there's new. But he didn't think it good enough. He walked to the window and opened it. He looked at the little cement bridge over the ditch and said the bridge was pretty."

"Good."

Liu Jui-ch'ang leaned forward, stretched his neck and said, "Pardon?"

"Nothing. Go on."

"He said the bridge was pretty, and he wanted that room. As soon as he began to take off his coat and undo his necktie, I wanted to leave, and I asked him for his identity card for registration. He asked me the name of our place. I told him. I looked at the identity card and said, 'You've come a long way.' He said, 'Yes.' I said, 'You're on a business trip?' He answered, 'No.' He said he just came for a change of pace."

"Uh-huh."

"I thought the man was simply on a leisure trip," he continued. A thin veil of sadness enclosed his curved body. "Going places, leisure trip, that's what I say. He opened the closet and hung up his clothes. Then he stared into the mirror in the closet, rubbing his face with his right hand. 'Never mind,' he said, 'I want to sleep for a while now.' And he closed the door and went to bed."

We became silent. Liu Jui-ch'ang stared at his bony ankles in the plastic slippers. I suddenly thought of the big, arched feet of the dead man, whose soles, with their fungus infection, had a whitish-green color to them.

"Originally this was a grocery store," Liu Jui-ch'ang suddenly said. "Life wasn't too bad either. If only the place weren't turned into a hotel, there wouldn't have been all this tough luck."

The foreign woman on the wall was smiling mischievously, but rather wickedly too. I suddenly discovered that on the fiberboard wall there were several small holes secretly pierced for peeping, and each hole was filled up with little pieces of paper. I had never known the existence of such tricks before, and could not help laughing slyly.

"Really," Liu Jui-ch'ang said, "in such a small town, there's not much point running a hotel. Sometimes for days the hotel stays empty and I don't get a cent. Really."

"Oh, why don't you take it easy," I said.

"We've been law-abiding people for generations," he said abjectly. "We have no desire to make it big, but we don't want this kind of messy business either, you know."

His dim, greyish eyes turned even dimmer because of the trouble. I felt a little disgusted. "There was a woman who visited him," I said.

"That was during the last night," he said in a low voice. "Mr. Tu, she asked for Mr. Hu by name. She's from some other place, that's for sure. I didn't call the woman in for him, I swear."

"Enough, enough."

"Yes, sir, yes sir."

"So he said to you, 'What is life for?' . . . No, he said to you, 'Why does man . . .' How did he say it?"

"It's like this." He again made an effort to sit up straight. I could see that he was really a timid, law-abiding citizen. "But the woman really came to visit him on her own."

"Okay. Enough of that. You understand?" I said. "I know you're a good man. Of course I know. Your older brother is a farmer, your younger brother has a job in the city—all upright and law-abiding. Very good. Of course I know."

"Yes sir, yes sir," he murmured.

"Just don't call in women for your guests next time. I came for the dead man's case; when I ask a question, just tell me all you know. Now tell me, how did he say it?"

Liu Jui-ch'ang leaned forward and listened, nodding continuously. "It's like this," he humbly answered. "At that time, he said, 'You're doing good business, eh?' I turned my head and saw him lying on the bed, with his back to me. I said, 'In such a small country town, how could business be good?' 'Ah,' he said, 'then how do you manage?' I answered, 'How do I manage—how else? Just drag on day by day.' 'Day by day, day by day,' he said, 'I'm tired of it.' I felt funny, and I laughed. He turned around and looked at me. There was nothing peculiar about the way he looked, except that his eyebrows were so dark and thick. Am I right?"

"Yes."

"I said to him, 'You're young and able; you earn good money; and you travel around on vacation trips. What a life you have!' He smiled, smiling faintly like this. Then he sighed and said, 'Ah, young and able, yet suddenly to find no way to go.' He smiled again."

"What did he say he couldn't find?"

"He said he couldn't find a way to go, smiling when he said it. You don't know how his smile could put you so much at ease. Then he suddenly sat up, crossing his long, lean legs. 'There must be bugs here in this bed,' he said. 'No joking,' I said, 'your bed's a new one.' He again smiled faintly, moving his left hand on the bed. 'Actually it doesn't matter whether there're bugs,' he said. He began to scratch his back with his right hand, letting out his broad chest like a dove." As Liu Jui-ch'ang was thus speaking, he imitated the action with his narrow chest, and took out a pack of Golden Horse cigarettes from his breast pocket. He looked small and thin, and repulsively comical.

"That line, how did he say it? 'Man lives . . .' What is it?"

"He said," Liu Jui-ch'ang replied, "he said it didn't matter whether there're bugs—let me tell you from the beginning and you'll know. Who could have guessed that he came here to kill himself?"

I began to feel bored. He talked like a scatterbrain. Besides, I really wanted to smoke, but unfortunately I had forgotten to bring my cigarettes.

"Yeah, yeah," I muttered impatiently.

Now he crouched again, sinking deep into his seat. The sunlight came through the window and shone on the right side of his body, making him look gloomy and scared.

" 'It doesn't matter whether there're bugs,' he said. He scratched his back sometimes with his right hand, sometimes with his left, like this. 'What does matter,' he said, 'is that yesterday I was still busy on my way to some place, and today suddenly you can't see what's before you, as though someone's wiped it off with an eraser.' He still smiled faintly, in a way that wouldn't worry you a bit. Not a bit, Mr. Tu. This is true. I may not be good at a whole lot of things, but at least I know how to read a person's mind by observing his facial expression."

I really wanted to smoke now, and this blockhead was bragging about how well he could read minds! I laughed.

Liu Jui-ch'ang continued the narration in his thin and sorrowful voice. "He laughed quietly. Like this: 'Ha, ha.' Then he stopped scratching. He walked over to the window and stood there silently. I knew he was looking at the cement bridge. 'There're lights at both ends of the bridge,' he said. 'The light at this end's been broken long ago,' I told him, 'but the one at the other end shines brightly when night comes.' "

I began to pretend that I was looking for my cigarettes in my pocket, but Liu Jui-ch'ang took no notice.

"He stretched out his hands and held the window-sill. He was a big fellow, wasn't he?"

"Yes," I replied weakly.

He finally saw that I was searching for a cigarette and offered me one, lighting it for me too.

"He was so big that you could tell at a glance that he was a Northerner. It stated on the identity card that he was the manager of a big company. And so young, too. You see, no one could have known that he came here to kill himself."

"There must be a reason." The cigarette cheered me up in no time. "Business, love, money . . . there must be a reason. Tell me how he said that line."

"You see," he said, "he stood beside that window, holding his hands up high grasping the window frame . . ."

"You told me yesterday that he said something to you." My anger rose. "Tell me first how he said it. We've got to find some motive for his suicide, right?"

"Yes sir, yes sir," he said. "He stood beside the window. 'That man should go on living is really strange,' he said."

" 'That man should go on living is really strange'?" I asked.

" 'That man should go on living is really strange.' That's what he said."

"You told me something different yesterday."

"What else could I have said?" This gloomy, timid man was angry. "What else could I have told you?" he asked unhappily. "Talking about it makes me feel that he's still alive. He shouldn't—why should he come to my place to kill himself?" Liu

Jui-ch'ang was obviously agitated. He must be scared to death by the whole thing.

"Well," I said tiredly, " 'That man should go on living is really strange'—how is it so strange?"

"Yes. 'How is it so strange?' I asked him. He said, 'There're lights burning at both ends of the bridge.' I told him that only the light at the other end still worked; the one at this end was broken. 'This bridge, it looks so similar to the one I remember, except that there're no lights; it also arches its back this way, like a cat,' he said. He picked up a pack of cigarettes from the coffee-table and gave me one. Such a pretty pack. They were American cigarettes. I was so gratified. He smoked for a while silently. 'I was only eighteen,' he began, again smiling faintly. 'The whole group of us walked day and night and passed three provinces without any rest. One night, there was no moon, but stars were all over the sky, like yellow beans scattered on the ground. People up front said, "To-night we can have some sleep." And all of us lay down, one by one. I saw in the starlight a bridge, arching its back like this. There was a fourteen-year-old following me all the way. I said to him, "Let's go to sleep under the bridge. It'll be less dewy there in the night." He said, "Okay," but at that same moment his legs gave way and he dropped to the ground. I tried to pull him up, and found out that he was dead.' Then he smiled again, like this. He said, 'Everyone was asleep; I was the only one who was awake the whole night. I stared at the shadow of the bridge; it simply arched itself quietly.' "

I began to feel that I was only wasting time with this fool.

"This is my first case," I stated seriously, "I must have it properly investigated. This is very important . . ."

"Yes, yes," he replied, "that's why I'm freely reporting to you, and in such detail. He said he'd go to see that bridge the next day. I left his room, and he turned off the light and went to sleep."

"Never mind, that's it then." But I was still rather frustrated. "I remember you told me about a line he said."

"He went out very early the next morning. I saw him walking to the small bridge on the ditch. That day he didn't come back until night," he continued.

He stood up and opened the window. It was becoming warm. He looked haggard in the sunlight by the window. He lit himself a cigarette, his fingers piteously trembling all the time.

"Mr. Tu," he said, "the next day he came back to the hotel, and told me that he had played basketball in the primary school court for half the day, still laughing that expressionless laugh. You just wouldn't have worried about him, Mr. Tu."

Liu Jui-ch'ang looked out the window. Tainted clouds evenly filled the whole sky. I suddenly remembered that my wife had bought a fish two palms broad this morning. She would put two pieces of red pepper on the fish and serve the dish on the dinner table.

"Mr. Tu," he was still looking out of the window, "he then asked me to bring him water for a bath: he'd played basketball for half a day. I said to him, 'You like exercise so much, no wonder you've got such a strong body.' He smiled faintly, like this. Then he said, 'Why's man able to drag on day by day, knowing all the time that he doesn't know what he's living for?' "

"That's the line!" I shouted. " 'Why's man . . .' Say it again: 'Why's man . . .' "

Liu Jui-ch'ang was startled. He repeated carefully, " 'Why is man able to drag on day by day, not knowing what he is living for?' That's about what it was," he said.

" 'Why is man able to drag on day by day . . .' " I muttered to myself.

"Probably that's what he said," he murmured.

I began to feel weary. In this handsome dead man Hu Hsin-pao, there might, after all, not be any great mystery. I thought of the somewhat shy expression on his face, of his thick and tightly closed eyelids: his was a strong and healthy body, showing no sign of hunger, of being weak or emaciated. Yet this was my first case.

"Now," I said, "now tell me about the third day. You said that he went to have a haircut. Right?"

"Right," he replied gloomily, "it rained early the third day, you remember."

"Yes."

"It rained early. When he woke up and came to the front desk for the newspaper, it was almost 11:00 A.M. 'Did it rain in the morning?' he asked. He seemed to be in a good mood. Then he stood next to my desk and read the paper. I offered him a chair but he smiled and said he was doing fine. He leafed through the paper—there's nothing in the papers, you know, always about the American air raids somewhere, day after day—and he returned it to me. 'I haven't slept so well for a long time,' he said, touching his unshaven chin. 'I'll go outside and take a look at your streets in the afternoon.' 'Your streets.' That's what he said. I asked him about his trip to the cement bridge the day before. 'I was only eighteen,' he said with some sadness. 'Ah, only eighteen.' 'You're still young,' I said, 'and you look fine and strong.' He faintly smiled at me. 'Another eighteen years have passed,' he said. 'It makes one so happy thinking about things in the past.' "

" 'It makes one so happy,' " I repeated.

"Yes, that's what he said: 'It makes one so happy.' " Liu Jui-ch'ang shook his small and gloomy head slowly. "Mr. Tu, he was like that. You wouldn't have worried a bit about him. You ought to put in a good word for me. No one could have stopped him; he had it all planned to come here and kill himself, and there was nothing you could have done, Mr. Tu."

"Fine," I said, "then he went to have a haircut."

"Yes, yes," he said, "he washed his face and brushed his teeth, ate his lunch, and went out. At about eight, a woman came. 'Is there a Mr. Hu Hsin-pao staying here?' she asked. I said, 'Yes.' 'I'm a friend of his,' the woman said. 'Ah, but he's not here right now. He's gone out,' I said. 'I'll wait for him in his room,' the woman said. Seeing that I was hesitant, she added, smiling, 'Wouldn't it be all right if you lock me in?' I smiled too, and let the woman in his room. When he came back, I noticed his hair and asked, 'You had a haircut?' He didn't answer, just scratched his head. I told him there was a lady waiting for him in his room, and he hurriedly went in."

So that's how it was, I thought. And afterwards, that night, he died.

"It was past three o'clock in the morning that the woman left. I got out of bed to open the door for her. He accompanied her to the door. I smiled at him. He smiled too, somewhat shyly. You see, Mr. Tu."

"Then he died," I said, standing up.

"Mr. Tu, please put in a good word for me," he said dejectedly. "Please put in a good word for me, Mr. Tu. I'm losing on the rent, plus the bedding he used too."

I picked up an envelope from the file and handed it to him. "He left this rent for you," I said.

He stared, motionless, at the envelope. It was not sealed, and "Hotel Chia-pin" was written on it. I began to long for my lunch—that fish, two palms broad.

"It doesn't hurt you," I said. "Didn't I tell you? Men are killed, bodies are cut into pieces, and grenades go off in hotels. . . . None of that affects business."

Liu Jui-ch'ang stood there looking absent-minded. I put on my cap. New caps for the summer season would be distributed in the second half of the month.

"It seems as though he's still staying in that room of his," he said in a low voice. "Man has always been like this, dragging on to live. Just keeps dragging on."

"Did he say that?" I asked.

He stared at me with his grayish dark eyes. "It's me who said that," he laughed in a silly way, crimping his face. "I've dragged on for half my life. Better to drag on in hardship than to die in peace."

"Better to drag on in hardship than to die in peace," I echoed. I had a joyous feeling, like the feeling of one whose office hours were just over. Liu Jui-ch'ang was counting the money, and repeating in his low voice incessantly, "Better to drag on in hardship than to die in peace. . . ."

Then I left. At my back, unenthusiastically, and in a monotone, Liu Jui-ch'ang asked me to stay for lunch. He also muttered a lot of other stuff. It was still so unbearably hot that I became all the more famished.

2.

The teacher of physical education in the primary school was Ch'ü I-lung, forty-two years of age, a Northerner. At three o'clock in the afternoon, I telephoned him at his school. "This is my first case," I said. "You're a veteran in security work. I hope I can learn something from you."

"Ha! Ha!" his laughter came through the distance. "Don't be modest. I'll be expecting you then."

Mr. Ch'ü I-lung waited for me in the gymnasium. He was not big, but well-built. I offered him cigarettes and he poured me tea. From the classrooms outside came the sound of students reading aloud.

"I was playing basketball that morning in the court," he said, looking out the window. Just outside was a worn-out basketball court. A shortish woman teacher was leading a group of students from the lower grades, languidly doing exercises. They threw their small hands to the left and to the right, as if they wanted to throw away the sticky sunshine on their bodies.

"I saw him walking out from the fields back there. And he stood there, right by that low fence. Then he came in through the gate, and stood under the tree next to the court."

There was a tree next to the court, standing there all by itself.

"We didn't speak to each other. I played basketball and he just looked on," he said. "I made a good shot, and he smiled. 'Ah,' I said in my mind, 'This man knows basketball.' 'You're looking for someone?' I asked him, still playing. 'Just taking a walk,' he said. 'I came from the other side of the bridge.' "

"There're lights on both ends of the bridge; one still works, the other's broken," I told him.

"Yes," he said, "I said to him, 'Come and play a game.' 'No,' he said, 'I haven't played for a long, long time.' But he'd already taken off his jacket, and walked onto the court. I passed him the ball; he turned around and shot. He missed, but, friend, such a beautiful move! Beautiful move!"

I always got poor grades in physical education. Yet I expressed my admiration.

"And we played one-on-one on the court." Then he lowered his voice, "Friend, let me tell you frankly: he played really well. We played until a class had to use the court. He was going to leave; I wouldn't let him. I bought him cold drinks in the canteen. Then we sat here, right here, like you and me now. Only I was sitting in your place, and he was sitting in mine."

He laughed. I could not tell whether it was oil or sweat that was glimmering on his dark face. Everyone in his profession looked alike. Over the low fence outside the window, the morning-glory flowers were blooming, everywhere red and purple.

"And we talked," he said. "I said to him, 'You play well.' He smiled, somewhat shyly. 'I haven't played for a long, long time,' he said. 'It's so nice to play again.' I went over there to switch on the electric fan and had it adjusted so that it turned back and forth between the two of us. 'That's the best thing to do when you're in a bad mood,' I said."

"Yes," I went along with him. "Really the best thing for cheering you up."

"Once you're on the court, you forget everything," he said with light-hearted ease. "I started to play a lot again two years ago, after my son's death."

"Oh," I responded respectfully.

"Let me tell you frankly, my friend," he said earnestly, "that son of mine, he was nice. Let me tell you frankly today, he was really a good boy."

"Yes, yes," I answered with some sadness.

"He made good grades in school, was polite, well-disciplined and had a sense of propriety," he said. But there was no trace of sorrow on his face. "Imagine when I was at his age—my God, what an easy life I had! Let me tell you frankly today: I was District Chief of the Community Bureau at twenty, riding on a white horse when I went out, surrounded by guards, a squad leading the way, and another squad following. This is no bull, either, my friend."

"Yes, sir," I said humbly.

"I got whatever I wanted," he laughed, "I got whatever I wanted. Then I went to school in Shanghai, and took up sports. I played soccer at first. The National Tournament. That really was something."

"Yes," I smiled.

"There's more—go check newspapers of the time," he said. "There was a city-wide dance contest in Shanghai—I won the first prize in tango." He laughed loudly and continued, "But as for my son, he was only three when I brought him here, and all through his short life he lived with me in hardship. Times changed. My happier days were gone a long time ago. Two years ago he was run over by a car. I was so depressed, and I started playing basketball again. Once you're on the court, you forget everything."

He poured me some more tea, and I offered him another cigarette.

"Come on now, take it easy."

"Oh, I'm all right," he said, his hands rubbing his coppery, tanned arms. "I didn't shed a tear for my son. You know what he said?" He was smiling.

I was puzzled for a while, and asked, "Who?"

"That man. I also talked to him about my son. Guess what he said. This: 'After all, living's not necessarily better than being dead, and being dead is not necessarily more blissful than being alive.' His words made me feel good. I didn't shed a tear for my son, I thought. Maybe I'd been in the same frame of mind all along."

"The past's past," I said. "Try not to think about it any more."

"He was not like you," he laughed again. "Know what he said? 'It makes one so happy thinking about the past.' "

"Ah."

"You won't understand, my friend." He sipped some tea, taking care not to drink in the floating tea leaves. "You won't understand. You're still young, much too young."

"Yes, I guess," I scratched my head.

"Let me tell you frankly today," he said seriously, "we're now nothing worth talking about. I don't mean to talk about myself; let's talk about him. He told me his family owned a bank. You entered the front door of his house in the morning, and by the time you found your way out the back door, it was evening. Do you believe that? I do." He glared at me, nodding his head slightly.

I said in a hurry, "I do too."

"Afterwards he and the other students—actually the whole school—moved to the south. He told me. And he was the only son of the family. They would put him on their knees and spoon-feed him even after he was ten years old. When he was about to leave for the south, his father fastened heavy pieces of gold on his belt, and there was also a fine Mongolian blanket. But they discarded things along the way. One night he undid his belt and flipped it into the river, and there went the string of shiny gold-pieces, sinking to the bottom. No lie.

"Oh, my." There was regret in his voice. "Then he told me how he began to play basketball," he continued. "They came to Taiwan, the whole group of them, and waited for registration. 'It was horrible then,' he said. 'Every day there were students falling sick or dead. While in Canton some relatives had given me a few silver dollars. I spent half of them on bananas and with the rest I bought a basketball. I played basketball day and night, and soon forgot my plans for college. But that was also the way I saved myself,' he laughed. 'It makes one so happy thinking about the past,' he said."

Mr. Ch'ü I-lung threw the cigarette butt out of the window. Outside, it was still a gloomy, cloudy sky. It looked like it was about to rain, but not quite yet. The lonely tree by the basketball court made a vain gesture, stretching in the empty space.

"He told me, 'That son of yours, although he did have a hard life, he had you, his papa, taking care of him, and he studied in school peacefully for several years.' This is right. I thought at the time: 'The Ch'ü family finally got a fine child. I've fooled around half my life. In this half that's remaining, even if I have to work myself to death, I'll let him study what he wants, and go wherever he wants.' There's no end to it if you want to talk about how I fooled around." He laughed loudly again. "It's partly the circumstances, and partly the times. He said that too. 'The wheel of fortune turns,' he said. 'So what you have doesn't pass down to your son—nor had I any share in what my father had had. I was just a kid of nineteen then, and I kept thinking: my family had sent me off with more loving care and attention than ever, and I had gone through so much and survived, so there had to be some meaning to it. And I worked myself to death studying. I worked myself to death taking all kinds of examinations. Yet, so what? Now I'm somebody in society, I'm married, and I have a daughter. Yet, so what?' he said. And he laughed rather maliciously."

"The fellow was a little stubborn, wasn't he?" I asked.

He glanced at me with a trace of disdain, then smiled to himself. I was a little scared.

"Maybe so," he said. "He said that suddenly he didn't know how he had lived until then, and how he was going to live afterwards. 'There's a good analogy,' he told me. 'It's as if you've been sailing for a long time, and suddenly the compass is broken, the charts defaced, the wireless damaged, and even the wind stops blowing.' Boy, what a way to put it!"

"Yes, oh yes." I was puzzled.

"I'd worked whole-heartedly for my son, I'm telling you the truth. In my younger and happier days, I never gave a thought to such things. I gave myself whole-heartedly to fighting the Communists. I'm telling you frankly today, I lived among them, face to face and shoulder to shoulder. I showed the Communists no mercy." As he spoke, his bright eyes flashed in his dark face. "Whenever I arrested Communists," he said, "I had them buried alive. I'm telling you frankly today, my friend. I fought them whole-heartedly. It was quite something, let me tell you. I was responsible for having no less than six or seven hundred of them buried alive." He became quite excited, and one could visualize his courageous style and professional competence.

"You served your country and your people well—you sure did." I was full of respect.

"But those days are long past." He was somewhat disconsolate. "When my son was buried, for no reason at all I suddenly thought of the Communist bandits. I said to myself, I won't care about anything for the rest of my life. But, my friend, bear in mind that I am not like that man, the one we've been talking about. The day my son was buried, I swore that I wouldn't be hard on myself any more. As long as I have enough to eat, and a place to sleep, I wouldn't ask for anything else. I simply wouldn't be hard on myself, not like him."

"He was too stubborn," I said critically.

He glared at me quickly. In his eyes there seemed to be an inexplicable contempt, which made me uneasy. But he laughed again, forgivingly. "Stubborn? Yes," he said, "but now that he has died, so what? I heard about his death yesterday morning and I was in a pensive mood for a long, long time. To tell you frankly, I fully understand what he felt. I told him about my child, 'I lived happily for that son of mine: saved money for him, hung on to old clothes for his sake.' He was bouncing the ball, listening. Then he aimed at the basket, and made a long shot. The ball went in the basket with a swish and fell down, bouncing on the ground. He looked at the basket and said, 'I have a wife, and two children too. When I get home from work, my older daughter always comes and embraces my right leg,' he looked at his right leg when he spoke. 'But, so what?' he said. 'Though the laughter and voices of my wife and children fill my ears, my heart's dead silent. I only hear people and things of the past flowing noisily by me,' he said."

"This is terrible," I said. "If a man keeps thinking about one thing day and night, he's bound to go crazy—at least that's what the psychologists say."

"But I'm not like that," he said. "After my son died—oh you don't know how obedient and diligent he was, not like me at all. After my son died, I thought of only one thing. 'Now,' I told myself, 'all right, now what am I going to do with the rest of my days?' For this son of mine, I forgot my pride; I forgot my women—one in Tsingtao, and one in Shanghai. I forgot them all. There was only my son. Then he died and I had nothing left, right? Nothing left."

"Nothing?"

"Nothing," he said, sipping some tea and swallowing it carefully. "Yet I'm not like that man. I wouldn't be hard on myself, not like him. 'I hope you won't be like me,' he said. I was shooting baskets, and the ball kept bouncing off the rim. He just stood there, his arms crossed on his chest. 'Supposing we're to count the days we have to suffer through from today on—I have more days,' he said with a friendly smile. 'I'm just kidding. Hope you don't mind.' Of course I didn't mind. Let me tell you frankly, my friend. When I was young, I did everything I wanted to. I drank, picked fights, enjoyed life, everything; so when my road came to an end, I was resigned. You said he was stubborn; maybe you're right. Why? Because his road came to an end, yet he wouldn't accept it. I won't be hard on myself, not like him."

"Man must not be stubborn, right?"

"Right," he said seriously. "But there are things you don't understand. For us, there had been so many changes. You don't understand. People were separated from their families, and their property deeds changed to wastepaper overnight. Yes, the wheel of fortune turns. I've said this before: it's like the firework displays at night—no matter how bright and beautiful they are for a while, in the end it's just pitch darkness. So, when you reach the end of your road, you've got to resign yourself to it. If you don't, if you're stubborn, you end up like him. Right, my friend?"

"Yes, yes," I said, though I did not quite understand him.

"But you," he said, staring at me. "How about you?"

"Me?" I was taken aback, and my face almost changed color.

"You're different," he said forgivingly, "entirely different. How old are you?"

"Twenty-five."

"Twenty-five?"

"Yes." I could not help feeling ashamed of myself.

"Twenty-five," he said. "In other words, you grew up here safely and peacefully for twenty-five years. Your relatives and friends are all around . . . you can take things for granted, like a tree: it grows naturally."

"Like a tree?"

"He's the one who said it. We finished playing basketball. He walked over there, took down the jacket he had hung on the tree, and said, 'It would be nice if man could be like a tree.' I asked, 'Why?' 'From the time it buds, a tree grows in the earth, stretching its roots downward into the ground, budding upward into the air. It grows naturally. Who can be happier than a tree?' "

"I think perhaps he was a philosopher?"

"Possibly," he said, hesitantly. " 'But as for us,' he said, 'we're like branches cut off, lying on the ground. Either because of the dew, or because there is still water in them, they can live for a while. Yet when the north wind blows on them, and the sun shines on them, they are bound to wither.' That's what he said."

I did not say anything. I was thinking about the philosophical question of whether I was a tree. Bells in the school rang again.

"When a road comes to its end, you've got to accept it. Then, maybe you still have another. Maybe there's never really been a road to begin with," he said. "But if you don't accept it, you'll end up like him. That's how it is."

"Yes," I started to pick up my file.

"So, my friend," he said, "for me, this is a very simple case. I've seen too many cases like this."

"Thank you very much, sir," I said, humbly shaking his lean and bony hand. "You've taught me a lot, really."

He shook my hand forcefully. You could sense what a brave and competent soldier he had once been.

"Oh no," he laughed, "the past's the past. You're young and promising. The future belongs to people like you."

I could not help feeling timorous under his gaze, which seemed somewhat derisive. He said when I was free I was welcome to come and talk to him again. I said I would. And I said good-bye to him.

It was dusk. The sky was heavy with clouds. But the green crop in the field was waving rhythmically in the warm, evening breeze. When I looked up, I saw the two small hills behind the airport, like a woman's breasts, forming tender curves in the smoke of twilight. When my wife lay down on her back in bed, her breasts were just like this, looking so rich and fertile. A tree mischievously grew on the very spot where the nipple should be; it made me laugh jovially—the joviality one feels when one hears a dirty joke. But in the next instant I suddenly began to think about futile questions such as whether man lived like a tree.

3.

For two days, the senior officer had been contacting various agencies, and I received from them background information concerning the mysterious Lin Pi-chen. On the fourth day, I received a telephone call from the senior officer telling me that he had arranged for me to have an interview with her. "You said that this was your first case," he said on the telephone from the distance.

"Yes, sir."

"This girl's damned liberal! Mother's!" He suddenly laughed, as if trying to laugh away the foul language he had slipped into before a subordinate.

"Yes, sir."

"Show your competence, your class, and style."

"Yes, sir."

I read the materials over and over on the northbound train: Lin

Pi-chen, twenty-five, college graduate, chemist with Dunlop Taiwan Chemical Company, single.

The train was running fast. The fields, bathed in the autumn
sun, seemed to revolve slowly outside the window around an invisible point. I was smoking, and suddenly, because I was going to
interview a college graduate, felt anew the long forgotten sadness
of not having been able to pass the college entrance examinations.
I worked so hard then. It was so hot and the sun shone so fiercely
in my home town. But under the mango tree behind my house,
you always got a balmy breeze. And there I spent days and days
reading aloud, trying to build up my English vocabulary.

The meeting place was a European-style cafe called the "Honolulu." From the second floor, one could see through the big picture window the unbelievably crowded streets. Here and there
were indoor plants in pots; together with the light brown curtains,
they created an atmosphere fit only for drinking tea and chatting.
Maybe because it was noon, I was the only customer in the whole
place. The cashier-girl was totally absorbed in reading a thick
novel. As a boy was serving me coffee, music started to flow
languidly in the room.

I never had any coffee until I was married. A friend of my wife's
had sent us two cans of instant coffee. Since they said coffee could
help to keep one alert, I drank one cup each morning (from a
small, pretty Japanese cup, a piece from my wife's dowry) so that
my colleagues would not tease me by saying that I was always tired
after marriage, as they did Li, who had married half a year earlier
than I did. But unexpectedly I quite liked it once I tried it, so in
less than a month I finished the two cans. But as it was not available in the small town, I did not drink it any more.

I was thinking about this when I heard someone coming upstairs. I turned around and saw Inspector Keng of the local police
force accompanying a young woman up the stairs. I stood up.

"You're early," Keng said with a smile.

I immediately felt sorry because Keng was in uniform. He almost looked like he was escorting a prisoner. But this young
woman, who was, of course, Lin Pi-chen, did not seem a bit embarrassed.

"This is Mr. Tu," Keng said, introducing me to her.

"How do you do? Sorry to have to trouble you," I said.

She smiled, and nodded almost unnoticeably.

"I must go now," Keng said, and he left.

We sat down almost at the same time. The music was still playing. She took a blue pack of cigarettes from her handbag and put a cigarette between her lips. I lit it for her.

"You smoke?" she asked.

"I just finished mine," I said, smiling.

We quietly listened to the music, which drifted slowly about the room like a paper airplane.

"I learned about his death the next day, when I went home from work," she said.

"Did you receive a letter from him?"

She shook her head. Her hair, slightly brown, rested smoothly on her shoulders. The small boy served her coffee. She was sitting with her back to the light, but I could still see that she had a fair complexion.

"I live next door to him—only a courtyard divides us. But we're in two different apartment buildings. They live on the fourth floor, I live on the third."

She dextrously put the sugar cubes into the coffee. Only then did I realize that the small cup of cream was for the coffee too.

"Before we met, I often watched him wash his face in the morning. He shaved very carefully, and he always filled his mouth with white foam when he brushed his teeth."

Stirring her coffee with the small silver spoon, she smiled alone in her memories, as if oblivious to my presence. Her eyes, which would have been very good-looking if they had had double eyelids, tenderly stared at the milky, brownish, small whirlpools in the cup.

"That morning, since it was my day off, I lay alone in bed," she said, "and I vaguely heard somebody weep on the other side of the courtyard. I immediately recognized it to be little Hua-hua. He always loved this older daughter of his best."

Her hand holding the cigarette was short and plump; it made me think of a carp caught out of the old pond in front of our house back in my hometown. The carp was black, but her hand was white as the stalk of the cabbage.

"I wrapped myself in my nightgown and rushed out. Little Hua-hua was crying at where he usually washed his face. People on the fifth floor were looking down, people on the second and third floors looking up; in the courtyard a fat milkwoman, holding her bicycle, turned her whole face upwards. Three policemen walked out. All were silent, only little Hua-hua was crying."

I quickly took out one of my cigarettes, and lit it, fearing that she might insist on my smoking her foreign cigarettes, but she did not seem to have that in mind. I gave her a small envelope Hu Hsin-pao left for her. She looked at the words written on it, taking care not to tear them up.

"I was wondering how you were able to find me so soon. So it was because my address was on this," she smiled. Between her lips one could see her small, fine, but slightly irregular teeth. Three keys with a key-chain slipped out from the opening of the envelope. Her smile slowly diminished. Caressing those keys, she looked saddened.

"He died after you had left him, on that very night," I said.

She looked into the envelope, but did not find anything else. Playing with the keys, she pushed them to the middle of the table, and they lay there peacefully, shining with dull, reflected light.

"So," I continued, "could you tell us why he . . . Let's say, were there any indications?"

"We were lovers," she lit another long, white cigarette, and inhaled deeply, so deeply that her pearl necklace—which looked a little muddy—moved slightly.

"Of course you knew he had a wife," I said in a low voice.

"Of course."

Suddenly she was silent. I did not know when it was that the music had stopped.

"Of course I knew," she whispered. She sipped a small mouthful of coffee, and before she put the cup down, lost in reflections, she took another sip. "His wife's really pretty. After we had gone together, I still frequently saw him come home with his family after picnics. They looked so happy, and yet somehow they didn't make you jealous. Anyway, I don't know anything about him at all." She seemed a little worked up. " 'Isn't this good enough?' he

said. I didn't even know his name. I gave him a name—Jason,* a
mariner in Greek mythology. He liked that name very much. He
liked the story of the mariner. We didn't want to know too much
about each other. 'Isn't this good enough?' he said." Her voice
choked with feeling. "You know, he was not the type that talked,"
she said, lowering her head. "That day, he made a long-distance call to me. I was working on a very important experiment.
Mr. Ebenstein * doesn't allow us to take calls when we're working.
I didn't know who was calling. Besides, we had just agreed that we
should leave each other."

"That's to say," I sharply asked, "you had a quarrel?"

Her face and her slightly brown hair slowly shook, expressing
the negative. "He just said he wanted to leave me. But I wasn't too
worried, because that wasn't the first time. He always came back
after a while, always quietly coming back to me. I'd learned not to
ask questions, and just let him have me. That way it seemed that
he'd never really left; he'd just gone for a short trip and come back
again. He looked so tired when he came back, and yet always so
affectionate."

"Miss Lin," I explained with some difficulty, "we feel that there
has to be a reason."

"Reason?" she said. "I loved him, Mr. Tu. I loved him madly.
But he didn't tell me anything. Yesterday I was thinking all day: I
fell in love with a mariner. One just didn't know where he came
from, and he only came when his ship was in port. He came
because he wanted me. Giving myself to him, I didn't have time
to think about anything else. He was a mariner."

I sighed. Suddenly I did not know how to continue the interview. Yet I still asked patiently, "What I mean is, he said he and
you should part. There must have been a reason."

She became silent. The music quietly started again. A bald
man, wearing sunglasses, was drinking a large glass of orange juice
at a table in the corner, at the same time intently reading the
newspaper.

"He said our relation was based on deception."

* English in the original.

"He loved his wife and his daughters—was that what he meant?"

She shook her head emphatically.

"Not in that sense. He loved his wife and his daughters, yes, I should say yes. He looked after his family as a good gardener looked after his garden. He often lifted little Hua-hua up high in the air, laughing so loudly that people in both buildings could hear him."

"Then I don't understand."

"He said he thought at first he could make me happy," she explained with difficulty. "Make me live, and hoped that he himself could also find happiness. That's his reason for living." She smiled helplessly, seeming dissatisfied with her own words. She continued, "But later he said that that wouldn't do, that it was deception."

I began to light another cigarette.

"Try this," she said, putting her deep-blue pack of cigarettes in front of me.

"I'll just stick to mine," I said.

She started once more to play with the cold keys peacefully lying in the middle of the table. "You still don't understand, do you?" she said with a friendly smile.

"No, I don't."

She suddenly stared straight at me. After a while, she said, "He's the first man that satisfied me."

We each silently smoked our cigarettes. She waved the match exaggeratedly, then threw it into the ashtray. Maybe it was to help her to speak; still, one had to admit that she smoked too much for a young woman.

"Perhaps you know whose daughter I am." Her lips, with the cigarette between them, curved into a smile. As for her family, just knowing that they owned the enterprises producing the most famous brands of tooth paste and underwear in popular use, you could guess how rich they were. Her father's name frequently appeared in the papers, and he was usually described by the press as "one of the province's most important magnates of industry," or some such.

"Yes, we all know," I said.

"My father always claimed how much he loved my late mother. He cried and cried every year on the anniversary of her death; he does that even now."

The music had become very lively, and she just kept on smoking. Her hand holding the cigarette really looked like the carp of my hometown, short and plump. When you lifted it out of the water, it simply lay still on the grass, not stirring a bit.

"In my junior year in high school, my father brought a woman back from Japan, together with two small children," she said in a melancholy voice. "I immediately moved out, and have lived by myself ever since. Because of this, I turned wild." She smiled in self-mockery.

I did not notice until now that the bald man with dark glasses had fallen asleep sitting. I had thought that he was listening to us, and was wondering how he could have such good hearing. In regular intervals, his head briskly nodded slightly towards the left, then was raised as briskly again.

"Yes, he's the first man that satisfied me," she said. " 'You make me live,' I told him." She was sitting with her back to the light, but I could still see her face turn red all at once.

"Then, he suddenly looked at me silently. 'I make you live? Really?' I said, 'My parents gave me life, but it's you who make me live.' And he laughed happily. I never saw a man laugh so happily before. 'Now,' he said, 'now I live in order to make you live. This is an excellent cause,' he said."

The music suddenly stopped. Only hollow sounds came out of the microphone. There was a beach near my hometown. I remembered when I was still a child, I once put a shell to my ear there on the beach, and heard a similar hollow sound. In the season when the sun shone most fiercely, the whole beach was just shiny, white sand. But the armed soldier, facing the sea, stood there indefatigably, all by himself.

"Telephone call for Mr. Pai" came from the loudspeaker repeatedly.

Nodding, the bald man with dark glasses finally woke up. He finished his half glass of orange juice. No one went to the cashier to answer the call, and the music began again.

"From then on, he concentrated on living the sort of life we had together. At that time, he concentrated so much that he almost forgot himself. 'To be able to make your life flutter,' he said, 'makes me so happy.' Then one day he suddenly said, 'Birdie' * (Mr. Ebenstein, my boss, called me 'Birdie'; he said I looked like a sort of bird in Australia), 'we're just deceiving ourselves. Let us leave each other.' 'Didn't you say you liked to see my life flutter?' I said, 'Jason, my parents gave me life, but it's you who make me live—don't forget that.' I cried, but he left me all the same. I still saw him shaving every morning on the fourth floor. When he saw me, he still smiled at me unpretentiously. 'Good morning,' he'd say, his mouth full of white foam. He still went out with his pretty wife and little Hua-hua on holidays. His wife's really pretty."

"He was really a hard man to understand," I said, "really hard to understand."

Lin Pi-chen began to smile. Now the bald man in dark glasses was leaving. It turned a little dark outside in the streets, but they became even more crowded.

"Then he came back. Sometimes it would be a phone call, sometimes a letter. 'Birdie, I'll be waiting for you at a certain time in a certain station. It's near the beach there. Wear the yellow pleated skirt,' he would say. And he would leave again. Mr. Tu, he was a very unhappy man. But he didn't look it at all. At the most, sometimes he looked a little tired, and that's all. He always smiled so kindly."

The small boy served us two more cups of coffee.

"I don't want any more," Lin Pi-chen said.

Now I was the first to pour the small cup of cream in the steaming hot coffee. It was nice to have a cup of coffee after smoking so much. We were silent for a while.

"You said that he called you long distance the previous day . . ." I began.

"Yes," she said thoughtfully, beginning to wind her fine, delicate watch. "Mr. Ebenstein doesn't allow us to take calls when we're working. So after lunch I asked the operator, and she told

* English in the original.

me no message had been left. About five o'clock he called again. 'Birdie, Birdie,' he said. He sounded high-spirited. He told me where he was. 'On a business trip?' I asked. I almost cried: I had missed him so much those several days. 'No,' he said, 'I just suddenly had the urge to take a trip.' I cried. My mariner had come back again. 'Jason, Jason,' I whispered. He seemed to be saying something, but I didn't hear him. 'I've got to attend a meeting right now,' I said loudly, 'I'll come to see you.' Then I hung up."

"Yes . . ." I said expectantly.

"After work I hurriedly caught the first train to that town. Luckily there was only one hotel, and I easily found him. He wasn't in then. The manager said he'd gone out. The windows were left open, through which you could see a whole stretch of paddy fields. Over the ditch arched a small, broken-down stone bridge. His room was very clean; he was always neat and tidy. There was a stack of letter paper on the desk. On one piece was written: 'Pao-yüeh, little Hua-hua.' Nothing else."

"Pao-yüeh?" I asked, "Who's Pao-yüeh?"

"His wife," she replied.

"No," I searched in my file. "It says here: Hsü-hsiang."

"It's his wife," she smiled with a taint of loneliness. "He told me. Before that I never knew his wife's name. Hsü-hsiang is correct, but Pao-yüeh's the name he called her by."

"Oh, I see."

" 'When I was a kid, I very much liked a little girl who was about my age. She was the daughter of our cook,' he said. 'That little girl was so pretty.' He was laughing, thinking of the past. 'They seemed to call her little Pao-yüeh; I didn't know what the characters for it were, but that's how they said it,' he said. He married his wife because she looked like her."

She picked up another of her long, white cigarettes. I lit it for her.

"Thank you," she said, exhaling a puff of greenish smoke. "He had never talked about his wife that way before. 'She's a very obedient woman,' he said. But this little Pao-yüeh of his hometown was a headstrong child. No matter what, she simply wouldn't play with him, and so always ended up beaten by her mother.

'Every time I wondered why little Pao-yüeh hated me so,' he said. 'Even now, I still feel so lonely,' " she repeated his words sadly. "His wife's so pretty."

"Everyone says so."

"I'd never seen him have that kind of passion to talk about his wife before. It so happened that her own family had a fruit garden in the hills, which reminded him of the apple orchard of his home town—he told me this. She had not had much education. 'Yet even though we're quite well-off,' he said, 'she does all of the housework every day, conscientiously and all by herself.' He asked, 'What makes her live so persistently?' Sometimes he even thought that she'd known long ago about our relationship. 'Yet she still lives happily and strongly,' he said. 'It's frightening.' "

"But we didn't find the piece of letter-paper you mentioned," I said. "All we saw was a pile of blank paper, with nothing on it."

"I tore it up," she lowered her head and smiled.

"Oh, I see."

"I was jealous," she said. "I'd never heard him talk about his wife with such nostalgic affection. 'Ignoring all contempt, disregard and deception, and living courageously, unremittingly,' he said. 'This is really frightening.' "

"You quarrelled?"

"I didn't go all the way there to hear him talk about that, did I?" She was a little shy. "But you could never quarrel with him. He smiled so tenderly. 'Fool,' he said. I told him, 'You shouldn't have phoned me—you're a liar. You always loved your wife. You have a dual personality. You're small, you're a coward.' And I cried."

Now they played only light, pleasant tunes. There were more customers. Two lovers talked endlessly, and even kissed in front of all the people. Only the potted plants stood still, like specimens.

" 'Birdie, Birdie,' " she began again, then paused, suppressing her emotion. " 'Birdie,' he said. 'You little fool, I really couldn't resist the impulse to call you.' He looked so lonely." She took out from her bag a small, square, green handkerchief, and wiped away the glimmering tears. She smiled apologetically. "And yet, at that time, I didn't know whether I was more angry or hurt. I insisted on going home. 'Now that you've come,' he said, 'why don't you stay till tomorrow?' He tried to take me, but simply couldn't. This distressed him. 'I'll let you go if you insist,' he said. 'Return the keys to me,' I said. 'Little fool,' he said, 'I will, but not now.' "

"And then?"

"And then I went home. I took a taxi back the same night."

"It's just that," I thought, "a pessimist tired of living. It's just that." I drank up the coffee. "Thank you very much," I said. "Sorry to have taken so much of your time."

She smiled. "I thought he would come back just like before. He was just an unhappy mariner." She picked up the keys on the table, threw them into her bag, and said, "He could open my door without making a sound." She whistled with admiration, and smiled helplessly.

We walked down the stairs of the "Honolulu," and she briskly jumped into a taxi.

"Good-bye, Mr. Tu," she said.

The cab soon vanished in the evening of the city. It had cooled off a bit. There was an evening breeze, bringing with it the noise and dust of the city. I was thinking: I should bring home some cream along with the two cans of coffee this time.

I spent a whole week writing the case report. Only in writing it did I begin to understand fully what Instructor Wei once said: what is most needed in the modern world is some kind of a philosophy of life. Throughout his life Instructor Wei regarded handing down the traditional eight virtues of our culture as his divine duty, and spent more than thirty years promoting them with unswerving perseverance. Frankly speaking, even I, who was always looked upon by Instructor Wei as among the best of his students, did not realize fully until now that the modern world was so evil, corrupt, and decadent. No wonder the wise and the humanitarian were so alarmed. How admirable was Instructor Wei's perspicacious foresight!

This was a case of a pessimist committing suicide. It was just that. But lying behind this was the fact that the country was in a moral crisis, and traditional values had been forsaken. Hence, I spent three-fifths of my report talking about how people's wrongful desires could be re-directed and kept on the right course, how the eight virtues could be put into practice, and how, consequently, the world would find itself in righteous peace. As for the true

meaning of peace, I could not remember where, but I had read
something like this:

How is harmony among things in the world achieved? Only when they
are attracted to each other by their very nature will their behavior be in
harmony. In physics, only subjects of opposite polarity exert mutual attraction; those with the same polarity repel each other. For the cases in
which substances of similar nature do display an affinity it is because
there are dissimilarities within the similarities, and what pulls them
together is the former, not the latter. Types of dissimilarities are varied
and numerous. To cite some major examples: the *yin* and the *yang* in the
living world, the leader and the follower in human relationships, the odd
and even numbers in mathematics, etc. It is out of dissimilarities that opposition arises. In the universe, and for something as colossal as the solar
system, the sun represents leadership, the *yang*, while the planets represent the followers, the *yin*. Because of a difference in nature they attract
each other, resulting in the activities of the system. At the other extreme
is the atom. There the respective counterparts are the protons and the
electrons. Dissimilarities again give rise to the functioning of the atom.
In the case of a nation, the roles are the leader on the one hand and government officials and the people on the other. Dissimilarities lead to the
exercise of polity. In the same way odd and even numbers make mathe-
matical operations possible. In short, attraction and harmony are indispu-
tably the result of dissimilarities in nature. The similarities and dissimilarities of one group interact with those of another in a complicated
manner. The universe is the thus-harmonized composite, taking the form
of an electro-magnetic field.

How could one help but feel sorry when confronted with the
muddled world that's ours? What Instructor Wei had once said
was absolutely right: to be a security officer in the modern world,
one must be versed in philosophy and ethics. Day in and day out a
security officer saw and heard nothing but violence, debauchery,
and indulgence. Without a firm and profound ethical footing, was
it not highly probable that he would fall all the faster into the dark
abyss of evil?

By the time I was done with the last page of the report, it was
deep into the night. My wife had fallen asleep a long time ago. In
the lamplight and in her underwear, she lay in a very tempting
way. I was thinking that conjugal love was different from the all-
embracing love for the world and the country. As sages and wise-
men of old had proclaimed, conjugal love was the ultimate expres-

sion of human nature. Humankind depended on it for propagation, and familial order and all manners of benevolence and goodwill depended on it for maintenance of their effectiveness. My heart was thus filled with a happiness so wild that I almost heard it beat.

And I turned off the light.

In real life, Ch'i-teng Sheng is Liu Wu-hsiung (1939–   ), a native Taiwanese writer whose language and imagination are as strange as his pen name. He is a graduate of Taipei Normal College. In my essay "The Concepts of Time and Reality in Modern Chinese Fiction" (*Tamkang Review*, IV, I, 1973) I have noted:

> Among the practising parable writers, Ch'i-teng Sheng is perhaps the most consistently parabolic. While his contemporaries have either given up writing (like Ts'ung Su) or given up the form (like Shih Shu-ch'ing), he has pursued his parabolic dreams as if he were capable of nothing else. On first reading, his stories may appear as offensive to traditional taste as they are outlandish in character. His "First Sight of Dawn" ("Ch'u-chien shu-kuang," 1965) opens like this: "Surprised at seeing each other; one Sunday afternoon express train was dashing along the coast toward the south, T'u Chi Se ran into one of his schoolmates Ma. . . ." If the translation appears syntactically un-English, it is because the syntax in the original is un-Chinese. But what is more un-Chinese about Ch'i-teng Sheng is his habit of nomenclature. Of course, the name T'u Chi Se (literally, "earth give color") in romanization means as much or as little as Tu Tzu-mei, but in Chinese it sounds as foreign as To-erh-ssu-t'ai (Tolstoy) or Sha-shih-pi-ya (Shakespeare) simply because of its unfamiliarity among Chinese personal names.

Compared with his other stories, "I Love Black Eyes" ("Wo ai hei-yen-chu," in *Wen-hsüeh chi-k'an*, No. 3, 1967) is perhaps the most intelligible of his writings, not only because its hero has an intelligible Chinese name but also because it has a story to tell, however strange it may seem. In addition to a slim collection of poems (*Wu-nien chi* [*Collected Poems: 1966–1971*], 1972), Ch'i-teng Sheng has to his credit three volumes of short stories: *Stalemate* (*Chiang-chü*, 1969), *Freeing the Rat* (*Fang sheng shu*, 1970), and *Leaving the City* (*Li ch'eng chi*, 1973).

I Love Black Eyes -

CH'I-TENG SHENG

Translated by TIMOTHY A. ROSS *and* DENNIS T. HU

With a woman's green raincoat hanging on one arm, and black umbrella in hand, Li Lung-ti left home quietly without telling his aunt. He stood in the bus-stop shelter by the side of the road, waiting for a bus to get into the city. It was evening, but on a rainy day, especially in winter, the magnificent colors of twilight were not to be seen. One only felt that all around, imperceptibly and gradually, dusk was falling. He was over thirty years of age. Nobody quite knew what his occupation was. But the impression which his constantly contemplative manner gave people was not exactly that of an optimistic man. The only times those who lived in the area saw him, he was strolling; they were all going to the city to work, so why was he alone so free and idle? He found no cause, on meeting people, for either greetings or small talk. Sometimes one would see in his company a small, pretty woman, but no one knew whether they were husband and wife, or brother and sister. The only known fact was that he stayed in this residential district with a woman by the name of Ch'iu, who had lost her husband five years before.

Li Lung-ti saw a bus charge along like a monstrous beast having just stormed through a solid jungle of dazzling steel barricades. The wheels rumbled. Inside, the passengers cheerlessly talked about the never-ending rain. Li Lung-ti hunched his shoulders in silence, and gazed through the window. The rain crackled against the glass as though striking his very face, close by and thoughtful. He thought of Ch'ing-tzu's black eyes, and a gripping sadness was evoked by gratitude from deep within his heart. Looking out through the blurred glass, he seemed to see Ch'ing-tzu standing behind the show-window of the specialty shop. She repeatedly glanced up at the clock on the wall, desperately hoping and praying that the owner, who had gone home for supper, would return on time to relieve her, so that she could leave. He thought of how she had courageously assumed the burden of supporting their common livelihood. So troubled and preoccupied, his mind stayed on the issue of whether being together meant happiness, although the bus was speeding along like shock troops on the charge.

He had to transfer to the city bus before he got to the theater district, which resembled an unbroken line of mountains. Once there, Li Lung-ti stood in front of the crowd under the marquee, gazing in the direction from which Ch'ing-tzu would appear. The two tickets were already in his pocket. Now he tried to make out, among those swaying umbrellas that one by one approached, one with a golden handle and a design of red jasmine flowers on nylon material. Then he suddenly thought of something. He opened his umbrella and dashed across the street. There, in front of a bakery window, he inspected the various kinds of bread, trays and trays of which were being displayed. Finally he went in and asked for two loaves of raisin bread. He stuffed them, in their paper wrappers, in the pocket of the green raincoat, which he had been carrying all along in his left hand. Shielding himself with the umbrella from a torrential downpour, he rushed back and stood, as before, in front of the crowd. The spectacle of a city at night revealed itself before his eyes.

The sound of the theater doors opening made Li Lung-ti turn his head, and he saw the waiting crowd begin to wriggle in a certain direction. The people under the marquee, so many of them only moments before, soon flowed away like water, leaving only a woman hawker of oranges harassing passers-by and a little girl selling flowers. The little girl came again to where Li Lung-ti was, and begged him in piteous tones, shaking him by the hand which held the raincoat. At first he had thought that flowers were not as important as the bread. But now it was a little past seven, and Ch'ing-tzu would appear any minute. Acting on impulse, he took out a coin, bought a flower, and carefully put it in the breast pocket of his coat.

The gates of the theater closed with a creak. Li Lung-ti turned around, only to see the shadows of the theater staff disappear one by one behind the automatic doors, which when open showed the pitch darkness inside. His right hand gripped the umbrella handle tightly. He stood in the middle of the sidewalk, embarrassed, and stared perplexedly down the street at the rainy, hazy distance. Finally he lowered his head and walked away sorrow-stricken.

He sat quietly in the city bus, its wheels spattering water as it moved along. Several young fellows turned around in their seats and climbed close to the windows, and, hearing the noise of the splash, were so excited that they cheered aloud. Inside the bus, laughter and pleasant conversation drowned a few sighs. Li Lung-ti stared across him at a pale workman, barefoot and in rags. The man had a handsome face with vacant eyes and a black, over-grown beard. The two nostrils under his thin, straight nose seemed to be expelling drafts of tiredness and depression. His arms were strong and lean, like wooden cudgels pared and asymmetrical. Several men in thick fur coats, with the appearance of grizzly bears, were seated together and enthusiastically discussing rainy day pastimes. Just then the happy young fellows began to include in their boisterous conversation some dialectal swearwords that were too gross for the ear.

Li Lung-ti got off the bus to a street full of water; his shoes were swamped. He hurried over to the specialty shop, where Ch'ing-tzu stationed herself day and night for the sake of their livelihood. All the shops in sight had already closed for the day and their doors were only half open. He saw, somewhat surprised, the owner of the specialty shop with rag-mop in hand and fat body painfully bent, stand in the open doorway trying to block the flooding water. Li Lung-ti went over to him and said, "Excuse me, sir—"

"Yes? What is it?" the owner glanced contemptuously at him.

"Is Miss Ch'ing-tzu still here?"

He shook his head coldly, and said, "She left."

"What time did she leave?"

"About half an hour ago. When I got back from supper at home, she looked very unhappy. Just picked up her things and left in a hurry."

"Oh, so nothing happened?"

"She had a quarrel with me, over—"

Li Lung-ti hung a stiff smile on his face as he watched the fat middle-aged man throw out his chest and continue, "Her temper—she simply didn't treat me like the boss; if she wasn't a pigeon lovely enough to attract customers, I'd . . . Well, I had a few words with her, and she flared up, cursing on her way out. I don't know what important business she had. Just because it was raining so hard I came back from home a little bit late, and she got so mad. As if my delay robbed her of her happiness. Frankly, if I had the money, I'd have no problem hiring a prettier girl."

Li Lung-ti thought for a moment, and then said, "Sorry to have bothered you."

The fat man stood up straight again, and it was only then that he took a careful look at Li Lung-ti's intellectual air. "Anyway, you relatives?"

"I'm her husband."

"Oh, pardon me . . ."

"That's all right. And thank you."

Li Lung-ti was back on the street, where the heavy torrents were still pouring down. The sky was like a burst dike letting loose upon the city untold quantities of water. The buses moved only with difficulty, some even halted abruptly in the middle of the road, instantly blocking traffic. The street turned into a river, and it had come to the point where walking too was difficult. The water reached Li Lung-ti's knees. In this city, which sudden disaster had caught unprepared, he was losing sight of what he had been looking for. His hands were so numb that he couldn't hold the umbrella anymore. It had been protecting him, but by the time he managed to fight his way to the downtown area, with next to no hope left in him, he was drenched through and through. The throngs of people were running in all directions, jostling each other in their flight for life. The expression on their faces and the way they screamed infected Li Lung-ti with the panic of collective catastrophe. If at this point he could still see his wife Ch'ing-tzu, what a kind favor from on high it would be! In his anxiety and resentment, he thought that if death was inevitable, a person should at least be holding his loved one. But in the face of such an unprecedented situation, his hope became so forlorn that never before had he hated mankind more for existing in such numbers. The currents were becoming rapid. What was more, the flustered mass of people interfered with his line of sight, preventing him from making out his goal.

He saw that now the people were clamoring to put up ladders and climb to the rooftops, all of them crowding with unparalleled selfishness and violent jockeying, pushing away and stepping on others. Li Lung-ti supported himself against a large stone pillar, panting. Tears came to his eyes. He thought indignantly, "How shameless people who fight for survival like this are. I'd rather stand here and cling to this pillar, and just die with it." The umbrella, which he held in his right hand, could no longer bear up under the rain; it fell into the water, and was lost. The icy-cold raindrops struck his face and body, and he gradually came to himself and calmed down. He privately mourned that in this world of nature death wasn't even worth mentioning. What harm, then, could human tribulation do to cold, unfeeling, Nature? Face to face with this invincible force of natural destruction, how would the values which were a man's conviction and what he lived by achieve enduring existence? He was glad that the ill-defined faith that he had established in earlier days now turned out to be of use. It was helping him confront this frightful attack with fortitude. If in ordinary times he had been the type to fight for power and self-interest, how could he have endured seeing those things swept away now by natural forces? Some wanted to recover valuables. Others grieved over the fact that people who used to be at their beck and call now fled for their lives, never to return. Were all of them now not forlorn, and falling into the water? Their eyes help-lessly followed those things adrift in the current and those people in flight. They raised their hands as though bidding them painful farewell. A man's existence, then, was the relationship between himself and his environment in the here and now. Under these circumstances could he first identify himself, then love himself? Was he now coextensive with Godhead?

The water level had risen above Li Lung-ti's waist. He was still holding high his left hand, which held the raincoat. Apparently he was much calmer than before. This man-made city, in the great calamity, instantly lost its splendor. Before him all was pitch-black and indeterminate. The situation was growing worse by the min-ute. A crowd pressed by him, and, hastily putting up a long lad-der, scrambled to climb up. He could hear the heavy splashes from falls into the water. Groans, pleas. And he saw the shadow of a frail girl at the lower end of the ladder looking up, struggling to climb but too weak to make it. Li Lung-ti waded over to steady her, and then carried her on his back—such frail girls did not weigh too much—up to the roof, step by step. When he set her down, she had, owing to shock and physical exhaustion, passed out. He wrapped her soaked and freezing body in the green rain-coat, and holding her, seated himself gently on the ridge. Lowering his head, he took a good look at the pallid face of this stranger he was holding in his arms. Her lips trembled senselessly, and her eyes were sunken, with dark circles under them. Her hair was a soppy mess all tangled up. He realized that she was sick.

In the waiting and muted prayers of the night, as it happened, the deluge stopped. But below the roof water was continually and rapidly flowing, rising. People could only sit on the ridge up high, worried and anxious. Li Lung-ti saw the dark shadows of countless people sitting dumbly on top of the opposite building, and from time to time one of them would cautiously and slowly approach the eaves, and then go back, to issue in a lonesome monotone a report on the water level. Since evening, there had been intermittent wailing from all over. As it gradually became lighter in the east, Li Lung-ti could see the people around better. So a night's cleansing had succeeded in turning them haggard. But at the same time they had become calm and good-natured, receiving kindly the attention accorded them from what might as well be the opposite bank of a river. Li Lung-ti confusedly met the gaze of a pair of very familiar eyes at the opposite roof. The rays of the abruptly rising sun clearly lighted her up. He cautioned himself against showing either alarm or joy. He felt the girl he was holding stir. When the woman across the water suddenly jumped up and joyously hailed him, Li Lung-ti dropped his head, to meet a pair of black eyes like those he knew. The girl in his lap was trying to get free, but he held her all the more tightly, and said to her softly but seriously, "You're sick. We're in this misfortune together. You must do as I say." Then he looked down at her, and smiled gently.

Deep down inside he wished she were somehow already dead, washed away by the currents or trampled to death by the crowd. "Don't show up at this time, in this way, Ch'ing-tzu. You appear on the opposite bank, but I'm over here, with an impassable gulf between us. I recognize, without having to say anything about it, that as long as this situation remains unchanged, if I should hail you, I'd simply have to cast off my present responsibilities. My conviction is to stand and wait for circumstances to change. If I were like those pessimists, who quietly sit or stand like stones, or if I jeered at current affairs and rejoiced at the entire world's being in troubled times, as those unfeeling optimists would, I'd have lost my existence."

He kept hearing Ch'ing-tzu's call from the other side, but he lowered his head and looked at the girl in his lap. He did, however, answer her in his thoughts, "Ch'ing-tzu, even if you've chosen to be angry, that's your business; you should be able to see that, now that this huge and treacherous gulf has come between us, you shouldn't think of our past relationship."

The girl in Li Lung-ti's lap moved as though feeling uncomfortable, and her eyes shifted to look at the bright sky. Hoarsely she said, "Ah, it's stopped raining—"

Li Lung-ti asked, "How do you feel now?"

"You're holding me, I'm embarrassed." She struggled to sit up by herself, but could not because of a dizziness. Li Lung-ti would only let her lean against him, keeping her steady between his knees.

"I want to go home . . ." Tears rolled from her eyes as she spoke.

"We'll all be able to go home after this disaster is over, but until then there's no way we can get out of it."

"I want to go home, no matter what it takes," she stated her wish obstinately. "Has the water gone yet?"

"I think it's gradually going away," he said, comforting her, "but it could rise again, and drown us all."

Li Lung-ti at last heard Ch'ing-tzu curse after her calling had produced no results. Except for him, everyone who heard her thought she had gone insane. The girl in his lap lowered her tired, weak eyelids, and in a failing voice, muttered, as if to herself, "Even if the water doesn't come drown me, I'm going to starve to death."

Li Lung-ti had been listening carefully. He put his hand into the pocket of the green raincoat covering her, and took out the bread, which was wet. As he was turning over the raincoat to get the bread, Ch'ing-tzu yelled wildly, "That's my green raincoat, mine! That's my favorite raisin bread! We made plans yesterday to meet at the theater . . . Everything that girl has now is mine!"

Li Lung-ti tenderly told the girl, "Although this bread is soaked, the water has been filtered by the raincoat."

He broke off a small piece of bread and placed it in her mouth, which was open and waiting for him. As she ate she heard the mad cries of the woman on the opposite roof, and asked, "She talking about us?"

He nodded.

"Is she saying that you're her husband?"

"No."

"Is the raincoat hers?"

He shook his head.

"Why do you have a woman's raincoat?"

"I picked up this raincoat in the water. That's before I got to you."

"Why is this the same kind of bread, like she said?"

"Just coincidence."

"She really isn't your wife?"

"Of course not."

"Well, then, where's your wife?"

"I don't have a wife."

She finally believed him, and decided that the woman over there was out of her mind. She said with satisfaction, "The bread's wet, and that makes it easier to swallow."

"As Heaven brings ruin to us, so does it help us." And he repeated this solemnly. Deep down, Li Lung-ti was weeping. He now saw that Ch'ing-tzu had stopped her outrageous cursing, and was resting on the roof, sobbing. Several people came over to ask him what was happening, but were driven away by his denials. Because they had since the previous night seen and heard of people going mad—even to the point of leaping into the water—over the calamity, all who heard Ch'ing-tzu's cursing took her to be insane, and so no one paid any attention to her anymore.

"You say I've betrayed our relationship, but under the circumstances how can we put it back together? The one thing that makes you angry isn't my betrayal, but the jealousy in your heart; you can't bear to see the rights you used to enjoy taken over by another. As for me, I must choose, and choose in the present situation. I must be responsible for what I live for, I didn't come into the world to reap its benefits for nothing. I must take up a duty which would make me proud of my existence, no matter what. This gulf makes me feel that I'm no longer really your husband. Unless there comes a time when this gulf disappears—only then could I come back to you. May God have mercy on you; you're in bad shape . . ."

"Why aren't you eating?"

As his face was stroked by a cool hand, Li Lung-ti came back to himself as though waking from a dream. He looked at the girl and smiled at her. "I'll eat after you've had enough. I'm not hungry yet."

He went on feeding the girl, putting piece after piece into her mouth. As she ate, she asked him, "What's your name?"

"Ya-tzu-pieh," *the words rushed out of his mouth.

"That woman says you are Li Lung-ti."

"Li Lung-ti is her husband's name, but I am called Ya-tzu-pieh, and I'm not her husband."

"If you were her husband, what would you do?"

"I'd put you down, and risk my life to swim across."

Li Lung-ti looked up, and noticed that over on the opposite side, Ch'ing-tzu was pleading with a rescue crew to ferry her across. But when told that she was insane, they promptly ignored her. Li Lung-ti lowered his head, and asked, "If I leave you in the lurch, what would you do?"

"I'd just lie here on the roof and die slowly. I'm alone in this city, and I'm sick too."

"What kind of job do you have in the city?"

"I'm a prostitute."

"What were you going to do, right before the flood?"

"I was on my way to the railroad station, to take the train back to the country, but I never thought I wasn't going to make it."

* These are meaningless syllables.

"Why did you want to go home?"

"I lost all interest in the life I've been living. I got to be so discouraged I was going to go back home."

Li Lung-ti was quiet. Ch'ing-tzu sat over there talking to herself about the past. His head down, he listened carefully.

Yes, everyone had a past; pleasant or not, everyone had such experiences. But people often used past circumstances as the basis for making demands in the present, and when they didn't get what they asked for they were hurt, and felt bitter about it. Men were frequently shameless enough to keep deceiving the present with the past. Why was it that they couldn't look for a new meaning for living at each moment of the present? Life was like a stick of burning firewood: although the ashes at the burning end still retained the outward shape of the wood, it couldn't stand being touched, nor could it burn again; only the other end was firm and bright.

"I love you, Ya-tzu-pieh." The girl suddenly raised her body, took Li Lung-ti's head between her hands, and kissed him. He let her kiss him passionately. Suddenly there was screaming on rooftops on both sides of the street, and the sound of something falling into the water made them break from their kiss. Li Lung-ti saw Ch'ing-tzu, the bitterest of hatred on her face, in the water trying to swim across. But she was washed away by the swiftly receding currents. A lifeboat, responding to a call, pursued her closely. Soon both woman and boat disappeared.

"Why are you crying?"

"I'm sorry that people have to die." Tears tracked down Li Lung-ti's cheeks, but they did not spoil his handsome looks. The girl stretched out her arm, and with her fingers tenderly wiped away his tears.

"Never mind me. My weeping, like my caring for you now, is part of my nature."

He gave her the last piece of bread. She put it in her mouth with the fingers which had touched his tears. Feeling something, she said, "I just ate tears; a little bit salty."

"That shows that they're healthy, and it's all right to eat them," Li Lung-ti said.

In the second night they were stranded, Li Lung-ti thought,

"Now that you can't see me anymore, your heart will find peace. I hope you're still alive."

In the dark the people on the roof were now all wriggling about, and there was a bustling clamor all over. So the water had receded. The calamity had come swiftly, and it left just as swiftly. At daybreak, there remained on the roof only Li Lung-ti with the girl tightly in his arms.

They came down from the roof and walked to the railroad station. On the platform, the girl was about to take off the raincoat to return to him, but Li Lung-ti told her to just wear it home. Then he remembered something, reached into his breast pocket and took out the flower. As it had been kept moist it was still fresh in bloom, with no sign at all of withering. He stuck it in the girl's hair. The train left, and slowly he walked out of the station.

Li Lung-ti thought of his wife Ch'ing-tzu, and he was concerned about what had happened to her. He thought, "I must go home and tell Aunt about all this, and tell her that I'm totally exhausted. I need a few days' good rest. I've got to lie down and recover my strength. In such a big and chaotic city, to locate Ch'ing-tzu is a job a worn-out man can't handle."

Wang Chen-ho (1940–), a Taiwanese, received his education from National Taiwan University and was from 1972 to 1973 Visiting Artist at the University of Iowa's International Writing Program. Like Ch'i-teng Sheng, he had most of his early stories published in *Wen-hsüeh chi-k'an,* including "An Oxcart for Dowry" ("Chia-chuang i-niu-ch'e," which appeared in No. 3, 1967). With this story, he has distinguished himself from other Taiwanese writers by using a local dialect largely made up by himself to achieve a comic effect for his characters. To be sure, other Taiwanese writers such as Ch'en Ying-chen and Huang Ch'un-ming have from time to time used local expressions to give an authentic atmosphere to the locale of their stories, but never as profusely as Wang does in this particular story.

In the author's own translation, the names of the characters are "rendered" into English equivalents rather than transliterated. Thus, Wan-fa becomes "Prosperity," Chien becomes "Screw," and Ah-hao is "Nice." He has also taken some liberty with the original. For the sake of consistency and total faithfulness, I have romanized the personal names and retranslated some sentences.

During the past few years, Wang Chen-ho's interest seems to have shifted from fiction to dramatic writing. His latest effort, "Hoping You Will Return Soon" ("Wang-ni tsao-kuei"), a one-act play, was published in *Wen-chi,* No. 2, 1973. His early stories are collected in *The Red Lonely Palace-flowers* (*Chi-mo hung,* 1970).

An Oxcart for Dowry–

WANG CHEN-HO

Translated by the author and JON JACKSON

*There are moments in our life when even Schubert has nothing to
say to us . . .*—HENRY JAMES, THE PORTRAIT OF A LADY

The villagers all laughed at Wan-fa behind his back. Even right
under his nose they curled their lips in contempt, without fear of
arousing his anger. It may be that their insolence was due to his
near-deafness. But Wan-fa was not quite deaf. More often than
not, their offensive words came thumping into his ears. To him,
this was the truly unfortunate thing.

When Wan-fa came home from his carting job he would go to
the *ryoriten* [1] for a good meal. He had finally come to own his
own ox and cart. With his oxcart he got as much as thirty dollars
for a single hauling job. Things were going rather well for him, of
late. Compared with the past, one might say the present was quite
comfortable for Wan-fa. He no longer needed to support his family, so he could spend everything he earned on himself. And this
after being released from prison! He had not expected it, certainly.
It was strange, was it not?

Whenever there was money in his pocket, he soon found himself sitting in the *ryoriten,* tasting the duck cooked in *tang-kuei* [2]
wine. He had never had a chance to taste such good food before.
All the villagers laughed at him, and teased him unmercifully.
And it was worse that his two nearly deaf ears were not quite able
to ward off the villagers' scorn completely. Had he been generous
enough to let his ears fail completely, he might have felt less uneasy among the villagers. He might also feel much better now

[1] A Japanese-style restaurant.
[2] *Ligusticum acutilobum,* an aromatic herb the root of which has medicinal
uses.

75

about holding the bottle of beer in his hands, a free beer, given him by that guy named Chien.

No sooner had he taken a seat than the manager rushed over to welcome him with a flood of courteous words, none of which quite reached Wan-fa's ears. No, not even a single polite word. It was like watching a silent film: Wan-fa saw only the two dry lips of the manager making the open-and-shut motion over and over, with no notion of what was being said. Sometimes the man's mouth moved so slowly he seemed to be yawning; again so rapidly that it was like a hungry dog gnawing at a meatless bone. These incessant lip movements made the manager ridiculous in Wan-fa's eyes. Thinking that he had at last found someone that *he* could ridicule, Wan-fa felt his spirits lift. As if to whisper a secret, the manager put his mouth right up to Wan-fa's ear and shouted what he had said before in a thundering voice issuing quite incongruously from such a tiny, skeletonlike body.

"A plate of fried snails and a bowl of Tainan noodles," Wan-fa ordered, his gaze fixed on the keeper's greasy bald head.

"How about drinks? We have some ten-year-old Red Dew wine."

Shaking his head as monotonously as if it were operated by an electric motor, Wan-fa pompously set out the bottle of beer given him as compensation by Chien.

Two tables away sat five young villagers. They were having a feast and noisily playing the finger-guessing game. Catching sight of Wan-fa, one of them opened his mouth in speech. The other four broke off their game and turned their heads in unison, almost as if they were performing a "Right face!" in response to a drill sergeant, except that their faces all wore a nasty look of contempt and were quite devoid of any military solemnity. Then another villager stood up, his mouth flapping. He had hardly finished when he doubled up with a great roar of laughter that was so contagious that the other four also burst into guffaws that had the effect of distorting them from head to toe. One villager, whose head seemed larger than his expanded chest, suddenly extended his hand to silence the others, nervously glancing at Wan-fa. The one who had first noticed Wan-fa jumped to his feet clutching one ear and exclaimed, "Don't worry! He's stone deaf. Do you think this scandal could ever have taken place otherwise?"

Each word rang against Wan-fa's double-locked ears like a brass gong. There was a time once, when he had just been released from prison, that such words would have made him flush with embarrassment. Now, his face would not color at all; it was as if he were beneath this mockery.

The five young men put their heads back together and resumed their wild carousals.

Having opened the beer, Wan-fa poured himself a cup. As he was about to drink it, he felt in his throat a surge of nausea, a taste he would find in every cup of Chien's beer.

Yes, it was Chien who had turned his beer to gall.

Perhaps in his former existence Wan-fa had been a bad debtor, and that is why he had always been troubled by money matters in this life. He married one Ah-hao, but instead of his life improving, it got worse and worse. From his father he inherited a small plot of land on which he and his wife tried to plant vegetables and herbs of all sorts, but no vegetables and herbs would grow. One year they cultivated the "pneumonia-cure grass"; the grass grew fast and promised a good harvest. Then, with a storm came a flood that not only washed away all the "penumonia-cure grass," but alas, even the very soil. Not long after, they were fleeing from bombing raids. Wan-fa got an earache at that time. It must have been caused, he said, by some "unclean water" splashing into his ears when he took a bath in a river. He had not gotten immediate treatment, for it was very hard to find a doctor during war time. Only when the pain became unbearable did he find a doctor—one who specialized in female disorders. The doctor treated Wan-fa with his rich knowledge of ovaries and uteruses. The result was a hearing loss of only eighty percent. It was not so bad, technically speaking, but on account of this eighty percent, Wan-fa no sooner found a job than he was fired from it. People grew tired rather quickly of having to shout at him as if in argument. They moved from county to county, district to district, until finally they settled in this village. He and his family made their home in a tiny hut near the graveyard, two miles out of town. He was hired by an ox-cart owner and was able to barely keep his family from starvation. If only his wife Ah-hao had not been too fond of gambling. Whenever she got up to her ears in debt, she would sell off a daughter, and one by one, all three daughters were sold. For some reason (perhaps to propagate more offspring), she did not sell either of her two sons. Relentlessly, their life retreated toward the primitive state.

By the path leading to the graveyard stood their little hut, low and drooping; it was like a shabby old man who could not walk with his back upright in the frigid air. They were not alone out there. About three yards away was a dilapidated shanty in which some people had once lived. But these people had left the year before for some other place; they were perhaps too frightened by the ghostly atmosphere of the cemetery. Like a resort for spirits and ghosts, the shanty was now completely without living occupants.

Only Wan-fa and his family lived by the graveyard now, with only spirits and ghosts for company. So it was natural that Ah-hao, when she spotted someone moving into the empty shanty, should be so ecstatic and immediately rush to break the hot news to her husband.

"Some people moving to that shanty. No need to fear evil spirits will do us harm at night anymore. We have a neighbor now."

However, this message did not impress Wan-fa. Not a bit. Half of his life he had lived in a silent world; to him, neighbors made little impression.

Wan-fa took his undershirt down from a bamboo pole and covered his bare chest with it. It was his only undershirt. At night he took it off for washing; by noon next day it was dry enough to wear outdoors. Once, he had owned another undershirt, for rotation. But his oldest son had "borrowed" it when he had gone to town to look for a job. "To be hard up on the road is worse than hard up at home." So Wan-fa, like any father, sacrificed something for his son's sake.

Putting his wide rain hat on his head, Wan-fa went straight out to work, with no intention of visiting his new neighbor. Ah-hao followed him to the door, hands on hips like parentheses to her bamboo-pole figure. "Aren't you going to visit our new neighbor? Maybe you can give them a hand fixing something," said Ah-hao, her mouth cracking open from ear to ear.

Pretending he had heard nothing, Wan-fa sped away without a word.

At dusk he came back. Sitting on the ground in the doorway, he leisurely smoked a cheap cigarette. Still he had no mind to call on his neighbor, although it would only have taken him a minute to go over. This evening Ah-hao's tone in regard to the new neighbor was not nearly so delightful as it had been that morning. She was complaining now.

"*Kan!* [3] He has no dependents at all. He is all alone and single. He is from Lu-kang, you know. Talks just like any Lu-kangnese, like with a heavy cold. So hard to make out his babbling. *I-niang!* [4] I thought there might be some womenfolk for company."

Puffing on his cigarette, Wan-fa did not respond. Presuming he had not heard her, Ah-hao was prepared to repeat her remarks, moving as near him as possible. But Wan-fa declined her efforts, saying, "Don't be repetitious, will you? I am not deaf at all."

"Oh, you're not deaf? Don't make me laugh." Again cracking her face open wide from ear to ear (Ah-hao could have swallowed Wan-fa in one mouthful), she added, "Shame on you. You are like the hog who doesn't know he is filthy."

Neither the next day nor those that followed did Wan-fa visit the Lu-kang man. He was afraid that with his sickened ears he might make a bad impression on the stranger. And he could not understand why the Lu-kangnese did not drop in to say hello or to borrow a hammer—he simply has to nail something on a wall, having just moved in. As if for fear of the she-ghost, the Lu-kang man bolted his door very early in the evening. Although he had yet to meet his new neighbor, Wan-fa was nonetheless familiar with his neighbor's history—at least elementarily. Day in and day out, Ah-hao supplied a bundle of information about the Lu-kangnese for Wan-fa's study and research. The man was thirty-five, almost ten years younger than Wan-fa, and his last name was Chien. Chien was a clothing peddler. At present, he peddled clothes of all sorts in the village. And he rented the shanty from its owner. Wan-fa could see no advantage for Chien in living so near the graveyard. With all the information he had gained from his wife, Wan-fa began to think that he was already on friendly terms with Chien, though they had yet to meet.

[3] A profanity.　　[4] A Taiwanese profanity.

"Does he cook for himself?" asked Wan-fa concernedly.

"I didn't pay any attention to that matter," said Ah-hao with her head turned and her eyes looking sidelong toward Chien's shanty. "Yeah, I think so. Or who would prepare meals for him? I-*niang!* He both sells clothes and cooks meals single-handedly. He is great, isn't he?"

At last Wan-fa and Chien encountered one another.

Watching Chien approach with his mouth opening and shutting repeatedly, Wan-fa had no idea whether Chien was munching food or speaking. Like a crane, Chien hopped near him. Ah, he stinks horribly, muttered Wan-fa under his breath. But he did not cover his nose with his hand, out of politeness. Both of Chien's hands rubbed deep in his armpits again and again; it appeared that whole families of ringworms had been living in Chien's underarms for some time without paying rent and now he was determined to send them packing. The more he rubbed his armpits the worse he stank. Now Chien spoke. Wan-fa was not able to follow what he was saying, only catching a string of sounds—ah, ah, ah—as if the man's mouth were plugged with a big piece of steamed bread. However, Wan-fa forced himself to smile a broad smile of understanding. Soon he felt that he was unable to close his mouth, having forced so many grins. Occasionally, Wan-fa would say something, but each time he spoke Chien would look utterly at a loss. His answer must be beyond the question again. The hell with them ears. The hell with them! All of a sudden he took a dislike to Chien. Ah-hao came out of the door and waved a needle and thread at the peddler.

"This is Mr. Chien," she said to Wan-fa. "He has come to borrow a needle and thread. He said he should have come to see you earlier, but he is just too busy with selling clothes. You know, he has to go out to his business very early in the morning." She raised her voice to top volume, as if speaking to thousands.

Turning to Chien she spoke softly. With a finger pointing to her ear, she shook her head incessantly and with great exaggeration. Obviously, she was informing Chien of Wan-fa's deafness. She must have told him so, otherwise Chien would not bear on his face such a look of amazement, as if he had come across something in the dark that would surely startle the universe. Now he gave a long look at Wan-fa, apparently trying to see what had been missing in his face. Wan-fa was not embarrassed. In the past he would have been very upset, even irritated at having his shortcomings made public.

"How is your business doing?" asked Wan-fa with a forced smile.

"Well, so-so," Ah-hao repeated Chien's reply in a shout. "Mr. Chien asks what line you are in."

"Oh," crossing his hands on his chest, Wan-fa gave Chien another smile with a hint of self-mockery and answered, "I just move goods with a rented oxcart from one place to another for other people."

"Is it good?" inquired Chien. Like a current of electricity traveling up his spine, Chien's hands dived into his armpits with a violent jerk. He must itch badly. Even his mouth was twisted into an ugly grimace. At any rate, this simple inquiry was heard distinctly by Wan-fa so Ah-hao's assistance was dispensed with for once.

"Just enough for us to live hand-to-mouth. If I owned an oxcart, I would certainly make more."

Ah-hao repeated Chien's next question: "How much will an oxcart cost?"

"Well, a used one is around three or four thousand dollars. What are you saying? Me? Purchase a cart? Oh no, where can I raise the money? I'm going to turn fifty; I'm no longer young. Can I not save? Don't you know the old saying: If you have not saved enough by the time you are forty, you will toil and suffer until you breathe your last."

In the wake of this meeting, a congregation of the same sort occurred almost every night at Wan-fa's, with Ah-hao sitting between the two men and serving as a hearing aid. Chien still stank horribly. Still scratching himself in public with an easy conscience. Time and again Chien and Ah-hao would chat pleasantly together, ignoring the presence of Wan-fa altogether. Since Chien had traveled a lot, Ah-hao would urge him to tell her of the gaiety and pomp of city life, her voice falling into a low and soft whisper. At such times, Wan-fa would go to bed with his youngest son, Lao-wu,[5] leaving Chien and Ah-hao to spin yarns until all hours.

Ah-hao went over to chatter with Chien quite often now. She

[5] Literally, "Old-fifth"; one way of referring to the fifth child in a family. Here used as a proper name.

also helped him with washing and sewing. By his own account, Chien had lost his parents in childhood and since then had gone a-roving. No one, he often said to Ah-hao, had ever cared for him as much as Ah-hao. From time to time he would have Ah-hao take home all those badly damaged clothes which the customers refused to buy. Thanks to this generosity, Wan-fa no longer had to worry about his one-and-only undershirt drying in time for him to cover his nakedness the next day.

Perhaps, in order to express his gratitude, Wan-fa began to frequent Chien's shanty. And he was getting more and more used to the heavy odor of Chien's armpits.

Chien's business seemed to be doing very well. He always seemed to need help. He made Ah-hao fully aware of his new plan. Hardly had she heard the joyous news than she raced home to relate it to Wan-fa, in a high-spirited mood.

"I have a piece of exciting news," she said, going near to where Wan-fa lay on his mat and touching his shoulder. "I have a piece of exciting news. With his business Chien always has more than he can do. So he asks us a favor: Let our Lao-wu help him selling clothes. Besides providing meals, he will pay our son two hundred dollars a month. I-niang! Where can you expect anything better than this? Kan! What you make each month is no more than this. Well, what do you say? Will you accept his offer: Lao-wu is fifteen now; time for him to see the world."

With this additional income they could surely improve their lot. It made no sense at all to turn it down. Wan-fa sat up and said, "Tell Mr. Chien to take good care of our Lao-wu." Then he lay down again, a smile of joy shining around the corners of his mouth.

Seating herself on the mat, Ah-hao said, "When I have Lao-wu's pay in my pocket, I shall buy some piglets to keep. We can feed them with the sweet potatoes we plant on the mountain slope. We won't need to buy fodder and we can save a lot. You must have heard how the price of pork is soaring every day. We will surely make a lot if we keep pigs."

Lao-wu went to help Chien the next day. He and Chien pushed a rickshaw full of clothes of all sorts to the village. Spreading the clothes on the mat near the market place they began their sale.

Usually Ah-hao did not go to the village very often. Now she made a point of accompanying Chien and Lao Wu almost daily. If they were too busy with their selling, she would give them a hand. Sometimes she would bring an armful of taro leaves, to sell to the porkmongers and fish dealers to sack their goods. Once she had sold out and had money in her purse, she would go gambling. No matter how secretly she went to the gambling house, she could not escape the eyes of Chien. Not that she was afraid that Chien might disclose her wrong-doing to Wan-fa: with his Lu-kang accent Chien could never make himself understood by Wan-fa. What's more, Chien was no less inveterate a gambler than Ah-hao. It was not long before the villagers observed Ah-hao and Chien going together to the gambling house.

And it was not long either before the villagers started passing around a joke which, they all agreed, was even funnier than the slapstick of Laurel and Hardy. Oh would you believe that Chien has started screwing Ah-hao? Somebody had even watched Ah-hao and Chien while fervently engaged in love battles in the graveyard, behind the pig pen. . . . By no means would they declare a truce, even when it rained cats and dogs. Would you believe they undressed each other in the pouring rain and struggled in the mud until they had their pleasure? As the saying goes, those who love to wrangle over nothing at all don't give a damn for anything, not even their own life. Those who abandon themselves to pure lust don't worry about falling sick.

"I'm not lying," someone would say, "Ah-hao is at least ten years older than that peddler. She's old enough to be his mama. Well, I could understand it if Ah-hao, that old hag, looked like a human being, but then she's ugly as hell, isn't she? She weighs no more than four ounces, but has a yap big as a toilet bowl. And a chest like a washboard! It must be painful to press one's chest against it. I can't imagine what part of that old hag could arouse the lust of that silly Lu-kangnese." Thus did the villagers amuse themselves with the scandal.

A month and a half had gone by before the well-guarded ears of Wan-fa began to clearly hear the gossip. At first, Wan-fa was shocked out of his wits, which was not odd at all since he had never met with such a situation before. Then, a kind of excite-

ment began to swell in his breast. More than once he had complained that Ah-hao's ghastly looks had been the cause of his miserable fate. But now, a much younger man than Ah-hao was
having a love affair with her. From this point of view, it appeared
that the ugly looks of Ah-hao must mean something to a man after
all. Then he considered that Chien's behavior with his wife was an
insult to his lost virility. All at once he recalled the unpleasant
odor of Chien's armpits and worked himself into utter hatred of
the man. As his fury mounted, he determined not to let Chien off
too easy. But, as the saying goes, "If you want to convict a thief,
you must catch him with the loot; if you want to lay a charge
against the adulterers, you must catch the two of them in bed."
Thus Wan-fa said to himself, "All right, Chien, you just wait and
see."

At last, he began to think that it must all be his imagination.
Yes, he must have heard wrongly, for Ah-hao and Chien still
talked and laughed happily in his presence, entirely without any
intention to avoid suspicion. Or . . . might they not be pulling
the wool over his eyes just by pretending to get along as usual, as if
nothing had happened? If they had stopped seeing each other all of
a sudden, wouldn't that have aroused his suspicion? Although he
was stormed with question after question, he had yet to make any
powerful protest or declaration against Chien. He merely quit
calling at the peddler's shanty.

The Lu-kang man usually closed his business around six in the
afternoon. Then he had supper with Lao-wu at a village food
stand. When they returned home, Lao-wu would go to sleep in
the shanty and Chien would come over to Wan-fa's to talk. On
the pretext that his hearing had failed, Wan-fa seldom said anything to Chien, keeping silent mostly, as if he held a grudge
against the Lu-kang man. Or he just wanted to show Chien that
he was not so dumb as to know nothing at all.

In the meantime, the undershirts and the khaki trousers, gifts
from Chien, reminded Wan-fa of the peddler's generosity towards
his family. He hated to be called an ingrate. So on some occasions
he would break the ice and respond a little to Chien's conversation. But never more would he allow Ah-hao and Chien to be

alone together. He would stay wide awake through the night until Chien turned back to his own shanty. Then he would retire with Ah-hao. He would lay with his hand across her chest, not yearning for love, but to prevent her slipping out. "Better late than never." Now he would oxcart goods one fewer trips per day in order to return early in the afternoon. He must have been reminded of the story of P'an Chin-lien and Wu Ta-lang.[6] And it might be from this story he learned to do business less and watch his wife more.

Every night he kept an eye on Ah-hao and Chien. Every night he watched over them attentively, save one night—a night with a full moon hanging in the sky.

With the first payment of Lao-wu's monthly salary in her pocket, Ah-hao showed no inclination to buy piglets to raise, as she suggested. Wan-fa was lenient enough to let her have her own way, realizing that she neglected her promise on purpose. After deducting cigarette and lunch bills from his own monthly wages, there had been only about two hundred and forty dollars in actual take-home pay. With such sparse wages he and his family had had to live a whole month, so that it was all but impossible for them to have even modestly passable meals. All the year round they had eaten nothing but gruel, with more water than rice, and a few cheap dried turnips. But now with Lao-wu's income Ah-hao had made several rich suppers and breakfasts, and Wan-fa was so happy for so many days that he dropped the idea of checking Ah-hao's accounts.

On the night of the full moon, Ah-hao prepared rice, carp soup, and fried bamboo shoots. Almost in a single breath Wan-fa had consumed five bowls of rice with lots of soup and bamboo shoots to go with it. Taken aback by his wolfish appetite, Ah-hao could not help making a strange sound in her throat—ah, ah, ah, ah, ah—as if she were belching.

Pouring the last spoonful of soup from the small cooking pot

[6] P'an Chin-lien, better known to Western readers as Golden Lotus, is a notoriously licentious woman in the two popular Chinese novels *The Water Margin* (*Shui-hu chuan*) and *The Golden Lotus* (*Chin-p'ing mei*). Wu Ta-lang is her husband, whom she eventually poisons to death.

into the empty soup bowl, Ah-hao said with a shrug, "Shame on you, eating like a tiger. Like you haven't eaten anything for ages. Oh, you still want more rice? Eh?"

When Wan-fa finally finished, his cheeks were hot and shining, as if from too much wine. "Getting drunk from gorging" seemed to be a truth. Wan-fa felt tipsy enough to drop off, though it was still only half past seven. Don't go to sleep! Here comes Chien! Don't go to sleep!

Chien squatted on his haunches opposite Ah-hao, as if he were going to relieve himself, and started to talk. Silently puffing a cigarette, Wan-fa dozed off several times. His cigarette slipped from his fingers and fell to the ground. Ah-hao leaned over to him, nearly to the point of sucking his ears, and said twice, "Go to sleep, will you? You look exhausted."

With a start, Wan-fa opened his eyes and saw, to his great surprise, that Chien was still there. Not gone yet. And he seemed to have no desire to leave soon.

Saying, "Don't stop your conversation," and "Pay me no attention, please," Wan-fa bent over and retrieved his cigarette butt. It had gone out long before. He lit it again and resumed puffing. Through a mist of tobacco fumes he watched Ah-hao and the clothing peddler talking and laughing together affectionately.

The moon was bright and as full as on the first or fifteenth night of the lunar month. Outside the hut there were no chairs. They squatted on their haunches or sat on rocks: it was like enjoying the moonlight at Mid-Autumn Festival. Through the smoke Wan-fa saw the two gesticulating with hands and feet, their mouths opening and closing. He did not understand a word they were saying and he was unable to enter their world: he seemed to be listening to a *tête-à-tête* between a man-spirit and a woman-spirit in a spirit language.

He must have dozed off again.

Getting up, Ah-hao yelled in his ear: "Go to sleep, will you?" She yelled it twice, as usual. She wore an extremely loose Western dress which was a milky yellow, but became rat-gray in the moonlight. Above all, it was made from a foreign material. She had gotten it from a church after she had attended worship and listened to a sermon given by a man with a high nose and blue eyes. She could not remember now the reason why she had gone to the church. Without making any alterations on the skirt, she shortened it by sewing the lower part a few inches up. To the bodice of the dress was attached an ornament which bore a strong resemblance to a double lock with an iron chain. There was another lock with an iron chain on the shirtwaist. These locks and chains gave an impression that they were safeguarding the secret parts of the female.

"Go to sleep," said Ah-hao. She sat down on a rock again. She resumed her talk with Chien. They were sitting in the doorway with moonlight shining on them.

Yawning, Wan-fa went into the house to sleep. His daring to leave the two alone may have been encouraged by the locks and chains embroidered on the dress.

When he awoke, the moon seemed fuller and brighter, almost beaming with smiles. Reaching out his hand to the other end of the mat, Wan-fa felt for Ah-hao. But Ah-hao was not there. He jumped out of bed as though bitten by a snake. He was out of his sleeping quarters so fast that his cold sweat hardly had time to start. In the dark he kicked over a wooden box, making a noise that would scare any ghost in the graveyard to death. He slapped his forehead with his hand, cursing his clumsiness. They might have heard the noise. They must have. And if they did, what would be the use of his search?

And they had heard him. In the doorway was spread an old broken mat. The door was open and the moon shone in. Ah-hao sat on the mat, her face pale in the moonlight, as though it had been drowned for quite some time. Chien sat up too and turned his head toward the noise. There was perspiration glistening on his forehead.

With a sharp, cutting "What are you doing there?" Wan-fa came up to them, both his hands made into fists. Like efficient recruits obeying a command, both Ah-hao and Chien stood up in a split second. They spoke in the same breath, each trying to speak louder and faster than the other, as if it were a recitation contest between grade school students. But Wan-fa could only make out sheer sound, sound, sound. Sweat poured from the body of Chien. His nipples grew firm and readily apparent through the shirt which stuck to his skin. Ah-hao pushed Chien to a corner, telling him not to speak any more. Perhaps she was unable to bear the sight of his mobilizing his energy so intensely. She took the floor with every word carefully calculated. But all that Wan-fa heard was: "We only . . . That's all . . . nothing else . . . Isn't it? Isn't it?" It was to Chien that she directed the "Isn't it? Isn't it?" glancing at him from time to time.

Don't believe her, Wan-fa warned himself. He had been married to her for thirty years. What else could there be that he did not know about her? She would talk anyone to death, seeming to be gifted with two ready tongues in her great mouth. She could talk flowers from the sky. Don't believe her. And the locks and chains on her dress seemed to be all gone. Tightly she clutched at the bodice of her dress, as if afraid that the garment would slip down. Don't listen to her! But she kept on talking and talking, her mouth open wide from ear to ear. And she began to use nasty words and dirty phrases. She must have been very upset in her inability to talk Wan-fa around.

"I-niang! Did you hear what I said? I talk almost half a day and you don't even open your mouth to speak. Say something, will you? I-niang! Are you mute, now, as well?"

All of a sudden, Chien stepped forward, bringing an odorous whiff of armpits. His face shone with joy, as though he had thought of a way out of the situation. Patting Ah-hao's shoulder, he pointed at a corner of the house where the moonlight did not reach. It seemed someone was sleeping there. Ah-hao's eyes lit up at once. She exchanged a few hurried words with Chien, then went to the corner. Yes, someone was sleeping there. She shook the sleeper awake with both hands.

"Wake up, Lao-wu. Wake up. Wake up and be your Uncle Chien's eyewitness. Wake up, do you hear? I-niang! You dropped dead sleeping or something?"

When Wan-fa climbed back into bed, hoping to resume his sleep, Ah-hao continued her harangue. Her mouth kissed his ears again and again, as if she loved his ears very much: "You're a real brute, without the slightest idea of what common courtesy demands. You should know better than to call a good fellow like Chien to account. You're just impossible. Lao-wu woke up at midnight to go out for a piss and saw some shadowy form moving in the graveyard. He was frightened and began to cry.

"Chien was unable to calm him down, so he brought him over here. And after Lao-wu went to sleep, I asked Chien to sit down for a cup of water, to show my thanks for his kindness. Then you came out with your long devilish face. Well, the thing is just as simple as that. *Kan*, your imagination has really gone too far. I tell you, everything is as simple as that. You heard Lao-wu's testimony yourself, didn't you? Then you must believe there is nothing between me and Chien; but why were you still angry with Chien? Why? Why?" She repeated these lines over and over, and the more she repeated them, the more furious her tone became.

Wan-fa could find no way to escape the harangue; he wished sincerely he could have been as deaf as a stone.

"Who says I got mad at Chien?" he said.

"Then why didn't you say something? Why didn't you say a word? Do you think it was polite to close your mouth like a dead clam, when the situation demanded you say something to ease his nerves? Tell me, are you jealous of Chien? Are you? You can't even get it up, how can you be jealous?"

An awkward silence fell on them.

As if suddenly recalling something quite important, Wan-fa broke the silence: "By the way, what happened to those locks and chains on your dress?" He tried his best to make the question sound casual.

Well, she has nothing to say now. Or maybe my ears just failed me again and I didn't hear. Tired, and having a slight headache, Wan-fa dropped the idea of pressing his wife for an explanation.

"You're asking about the locks and chains?" said Ah-hao, purposely talking in a low, inaudible tone. "Chien said they're not nice to look at and he tore them off my dress."

"What did you say?" asked Wan-fa. Oh—my ears—my ears always escape the words they should hear distinctly.

"Lost! I said they were lost!" Ah-hao yelled into his ears. "*I-niang!* You're deaf enough to be a stone."

Pressing her body against his, Ah-hao poked him here and there with seducing fingers. She had not been so interested in him since that time he could not get an erection. Wan-fa looked out the window. The moon hung in the sky, round and full like the laughing face of an obese girl. He recalled some lyrics of a popular song: "Miss Moon laughs at me because I am a tomfool, even cheated by the wind." [7]

Maybe he was just that tomfool.

As he was on the verge of sleep the scene came back to him of Ah-hao and Chien sitting on the mat in the doorway. Then the odor of Chien, more irritating than usual, again floated under his nose as he watched again the unlocked parts of Ah-hao's dress. Maybe Ah-hao had played him false. Maybe it was sheer imagination. With question after question in his mind, he lay tossing for hours and could find no sleep.

But he was not to be afforded time to get to the bottom of the matter. Only a few days later, the oxcart owner announced that the ox would be let for ploughing. Wan-fa might as well stay home for a while. At the same time, Chien declared that he must go back to Lu-kang to visit, then on to Taipei for a new supply of clothes. He said he might be back in a month. Did he really mean to come back? In order to avoid any further venture into troubled waters with Ah-hao, he might be going for good. But one thing was certain: during his absence Lao-wu would draw no pay and had to return to live with his parents. This was truly bad news.

Wan-fa had no job now. At first, he went to the mountain slope to dig sweet potatoes to sell in the market. With this he could manage to stave off two-thirds of his hunger. When there were no more sweet potatoes, he set out to climb mountain after mountain in search of taro leaves to sell. Although he could only conquer half of his hunger this way, he had to put up with all kinds of ill remarks from the village women who earned their allowances by plucking taro leaves to sell. They complained that Old Deaf Wan-fa collected all the taro leaves and left none for them, and because of Old Deaf Wan-fa they were bound to have fewer new dresses this year. To hell with that Old Deaf Wan-fa!

[7] The song is titled "Wishes in the Springtime." It tells of a girl who, sitting alone in her room as the spring breeze whistles by her face, begins to dream of her love. Then she hears some noise outside. Thinking that it must be her prince charming calling on her, she rushes to open the door. But no one is outside. Looking up, she sees the moon bright and full, as if mocking her for being fooled by the wind, which has caused the door to make the noise.

Then came the day when there were no more taro leaves. And still he had to fill his empty stomach, which was, as the saying goes, "a hole as deep and bottomless as the sea." What could he do? At the end of his rope, he went to help dig graves to get some pennies for food. The job did not come up every day. Not every day did a man die. Sometimes he had to wait two or three days for a corpse. Ah, it was a pity that people were not generous enough to die sooner. And then, even when he was lucky enough to hear of a death, more often than not some fast-leggers had already won the job before him. He came to realize that if he wanted to live on grave digging, he must do something more than just wait. So he changed his waiting policy. Day and night he searched the whole village for a family with dying people. If he found one, he would hasten to apply for a position as the grave digger, or coffin bearer, even though the dying one was not yet deceased. Soon, when he showed up at a dying man's home the door would be slammed in his face. He was looked upon as the fearsome messenger of Death.

To Wan-fa, a single day seemed to last a whole year. He could hardly get the upper hand on even a tenth of his formidable hunger.

One day, Ah-hao thought her oldest son, who was working in town, might do something for them. In hunger she walked four hours on sandy roads to get to town. When she got back, she brought only a catty of pork and fish. Nothing more. Life in town was not easy either.

Someone recommended Ah-hao to do cooking and cleaning at Dr. Lin's clinic. If she was accepted she could draw, apart from room and board, one hundred dollars per month. On the day of the interview there was not a grain left to stop her hunger. Stealing some sweet potatoes from a farmer's vegetable garden, she put them under heated ashes and baked them. They were her only lunch. Sweet potatoes. Trouble-making sweet potatoes.

When Dr. Lin inquired how many children she had, she volleyed five big, loud farts before she could open her mouth. Her stomach had given her no warning.

Dr. Lin grinned, trying to inject a sense of humor into the situation, and said, "You have five children?"

To her shame, the gas in her stomach started to cannon one

after another, consistently and rhythmically. Her chance for the job was gone with her wind.

Wan-fa and Ah-hao often quarreled now. Almost every minute they found themselves engaged in a battle of words. It looked as though they were venting their disappointments in life by offending each other bitterly. Well, for them to shout at each other was not so bad as it sounded. At least it showed they were still alive— they were not yet totally beaten down by poverty. However, they never fought physically. They were both so emaciated that they were all bones and no flesh. Obviously, it would hurt one's hand very much to beat a bony body like theirs. So there was no pleasure to be gained in it.

Then, Chien came back after forty days' absence.

"Chien is back!" Unable to hide her secret joy, Ah-hao stammered out the news. "He has bou-bought so-so many clo-clothes to-to sell. And you know, he-he is e-even fatter." She stopped for a moment, unable to continue.

Then she added, "He wants our Lao-wu to help him tend his business tomorrow. Do you agree to that? Do you?" There was a brightness in her eyes, betraying her joy at Chien's return. "Oh God, I thought he would never come back."

With Lao-wu's income, they might stop their hunger a bit— hunger like an alarm clock out of order, buzzing and crying at any time or place. No, Wan-fa warned himself, I must not let her know I am pleased to see Chien back. And I can't let Chien feel he is doing us a favor, either. He was surprised to find himself so calculating all of a sudden. But, after all, he told himself, a poor man is not poor at all in self-respect.

Receiving no reply from Wan-fa, Ah-hao reiterated her question in a voice close to shrieking.

Wan-fa ran his fingers through his hair again and again, causing a shower of dandruff on his shoulders. "If you wish Lao-wu to help Chien, go ahead," he replied, in a manner aloof enough to make a person feel cold.

"You don't like Lao-wu to help Chien?"

"Why not?" Even he himself was astonished at the ice-cold tone.

Ah-hao did not say anything. But as she left she said something quite indecent to Wan-fa. Then she was gone like a whiff of wind. Wan-fa had not heard distinctly and did not know what rubbish she had said.

When Wan-fa returned from a coffin-bearing job that evening, Ah-hao had already cooked him a pot of rice.

"Did Chien give you rice?" His eyes fixed on the steaming pot, Wan-fa suddenly felt unable to bear hunger any longer.

As soon as the name of Chien was mentioned, Ah-hao's voice became unnatural, with a lot of "eh" sounds, as if she had taken too much sickly-sweet food and had to clear her throat before she spoke. "Eh, . . . you know we've not eaten a bowl of decent rice for years, so, eh, . . . I just borrowed some rice from, eh, Chien. Eh, . . ."

Wan-fa quickly swallowed the saliva that had filled his mouth and seized the opportunity to speak. He would not let Ah-hao see how hungry he was. "Listen, don't bother Chien any more with our troubles, understand?"

Ah-hao did not reply, as though too exasperated to speak.

Thereafter, whenever she mentioned the man from Lu-kang, her tone would suddenly become serene, somber, and cautious, as though she spoke of some god. The Lu-kang man had hardly come to call on Wan-fa since his return. He must still remember vividly the embarrassment of that night of the full moon. Or perhaps he was only too occupied with his business.

Now that Lao-wu was helping Chien again and bringing home the whole of his pay each month, Wan-fa and Ah-hao began to live more like human beings. Sweet potatoes were growing on the mountain slope again. Taro leaves were green and large everywhere. Wan-fa had no need now to go hunting for corpses each day. He had more time to stay at home and keep an eye on Ah-hao and Chien. He made up his mind to never allow them an opportunity for further physical contact.

Then the situation changed abruptly. The owner of the shanty in which Chien lived wanted it back, so Chien asked if he could move in with Wan-fa.

"What do you say to Mr. Chien's proposal?" Sitting between the two men, Ah-hao relayed what Chien had said, each word circumspectly coined to get the meaning just right, like announcing a communiqué. "If you have any objection, Mr. Chien will find some single room in the village. After all, it is more convenient for him to live in the village. Well, what do you say?"

Chien went on smoking and smoking, not looking at Wan-fa. The weather had turned cool and the odor of Chien's armpits, once so familiar to Wan-fa's nose, no longer fouled the air. Wan-fa had a sudden feeling that he had lost his way in a strange land and was totally bewildered about what to do: the feeling a newcomer usually has when he works his first day in a strange firm.

"I'll think it over."

"You'll think it over? I-niang! What airs are you putting on? Mister, may I tell you one thing? Your affectations make you stink like a poor sick dog all your life." Gritting her teeth, she glared at Wan-fa.

Don't talk back to her when she is so inflamed, Wan-fa warned himself, or she'll try her best to vomit out something filthy. By giving out a loud "oh," to indicate he had not heard her reproach, Wan-fa managed to escape the further resounding tantrum. It was nice to be able to utilize deafness for the best, wasn't it?

"How much will he pay?" Wan-fa put his lips to Ah-hao's ear as soon as Chien had gone.

Jumping up, Ah-hao exclaimed, "How much do you expect? He will pay four hundred and eighty dollars a month for room and board. You think that's not reasonable? He is used to living here, otherwise he wouldn't even look at your tumbled-down shack. I-niang! The rent for a nice single room in the village is no more than two pecks of rice! So four-hundred and eighty dollars is still less than you expect? I-niang! You'll think it over? Think it over? You try to spoil everything nice. You're just a bad hen that lays no eggs but filth. All filth. You good-for-nothing deaf-mute!" She screamed at the top of her lungs. Like a rooster's morning crow, her tirades could be heard clearly for miles.

So, Chien moved in, to live and eat with Wan-fa and his family under the same roof. At night, Wan-fa and Ah-hao slept in their own quarters while Chien slept with Lao-wu on the mat in the doorway. Chien's goods were stored in the back of the hut.

Soon a new rumor swept the village: "I-niang! Old Deaf Wan-fa and Chien and Ah-hao, all three of them, sleep together in one bed. You don't believe it? I-niang!"

Unless he could absolutely not help it, Wan-fa would not go to the village. The mockery of the villagers and their white eyeballs of disdain made him all the more embarrassed. With four hundred and eighty dollars from Chien, Wan-fa and Ah-hao could buy enough to eat now. Lao-wu's pay was kept in Wan-fa's pocket—this was one prerequisite for allowing Chien to share the same roof with him. He no longer needed to go to the village for work. By day, with the help of Ah-hao, he worked on his sweet potato farm. By night, he devoted mind and might to keeping Ah-hao out of Chien's reach. He followed her like a shadow everywhere she went. He even trod on her heels when she went out to relieve herself in the cemetery. Naturally, he was polite enough to stand off always when she was defecating.

One night, Ah-hao got mad at his spying.

"What do you mean by this, *I-niang*, shadowing me all the way here? Want to watch me urinate? I warn you, if you ever come a step closer, I'll piss right in your face!"

The cold war between Wan-fa and Chien was hottest at dinner time. Usually, Wan-fa ate in silence while openly watching Chien and Ah-hao. He ate so soundlessly that he did not seem to chew his food at all. In spite of everything, he would be the last to leave the dining table, so that every tiny contact between Ah-hao and Chien would not escape his watchful eyes. Occasionally, Ah-hao and Chien would lower their voices in the middle of their pleasant chatter, so that Wan-fa could hardly hear a sound. Then he would cough harshly, in warning. Sometimes, they ignored his warning and kept on whispering with smiles on their faces. Deaf and mute, are they? Wan-fa cursed under his breath. They are even blind to my presence. What an insult! I won't stand for it. With a loud crash, he put down his bowl and stalked away in anger. It looked like a hot war was just around the corner.

But, in less than twenty-four hours peace was made without a battle. Each time Wan-fa got angry and rushed out of the house, he would generally go to the cemetery and unfasten from his belt a long purse from which he would take all the coins and bills to count. He counted them forwards and backwards. Ah! Still not enough to buy an oxcart. Still a long way to go. Then he would say to himself: It's not right to be so hard on Chien. After all, he is my god of wealth and it would be stupid to send this god away.

Then he would close one eye to the doings between Chien and Ah-hao for a few days.

In the old shanty there now dwelt a pickle vendor who seemed to be a relative of the landlord. Day in and day out he was drying cabbages, carrots, beans, and what not, causing a great influx of flies. He called at Wan-fa's when he was free. He always came with a swarm of flies around him. Once he sat down to talk, his little rat's eyes peered eastward and westward, looking for some secret to gossip about in the village. The features of his face were harsh and mean. And he smelled as sour as a pickle. Wan-fa did not care for him at all. He remembered the old saying: "He who calls has nothing to offer but trouble." But Chien and the pickle vendor got along quite well; perhaps they liked each other's odor.

One evening, in a cloud of dirty flies, the pickle vendor came to visit. Chien had gone to the river to bathe. Wan-fa, still indoors, could tell from the visitor's excessively nasal twang that it was the pickle vendor. Ah-hao was busy washing dishes in the kitchen. Lao-wu was playing marbles outdoors. Wan-fa could not clearly hear what the pickle vendor and Lao-wu were saying. Then the vendor raised his voice to a high pitch, apparently intentionally. "Where's 'Screw-your-mother' off to?"

Wan-fa could not hear Lao-wu's reply.

"I mean Chien. Chien, that Chien who screws your mother. Where is that 'Screw-your-mother'?"

"God damn you!" Wan-fa shouted, dashing from the hut. He shivered all over with exasperation. Seizing the pickle vendor with one sweep, Wan-fa violently beat him, kicked him, beat him, and kicked him. . . . The flies were frightened away in all directions.

When Chien returned from cleansing his body in the river, he found all his belongings—clothes, shoes, socks, cooking utensils, overnight bags—scattered here and there in front of the hut. It looked like there had been a fire and everything in the house had been hastily removed for safety's sake. The Lu-kang man named Chien had a feeling of being hollowed out.

Wan-fa stood at the door. As soon as Chien, bearing a wash basin, approached the door, Wan-fa rushed up to him waving his fists menacingly before him.

"*Kan!* Goddamit! Get out of here! *Kan!* Get out! I feed a rat to bite my own sack. *Kan!* You think you can pull the wool over my eyes just because I can't hear very well? *Kan!* You must have swallowed tiger balls! You take advantage of my deafness, huh? Fuck your mother! You think I'm blind? You think I can't see what you're trying to hide? *Kan!* I feed a rat to bite my own sack . . ." Almost every line was punctuated with an abusive word, scaring Chien nearly out of his wits.

Chien borrowed an oxcart and moved his belongings to the village the same night. He dared not give Ah-hao a farewell glance, let alone say good-bye.

Then the villagers commenced their gossip. They said Chien had refused to give Wan-fa money, so Wan-fa had got mad and thrown him out the door. Quite a few people came to visit Wan-fa with the intention of digging up some dirt. Wan-fa disappointed them all, saying his ears were completely out of order.

Again life was hard on Wan-fa. Some farmer leased the mountain slope from the Municipal Government, where Wan-fa had planted sweet potatoes. The unripe potatoes were dug up. Wan-fa received only one hundred dollars for his loss. To dampen his courage even more, Lao-wu fell seriously ill with acute diarrhea. All the coins and bills he had saved to buy an oxcart were spent to save the child. As he paid the bills to the doctor, tears came suddenly to his eyes. He might have been feeling the pain of losing his savings; or he might have been lamenting his ill fate.

At last, his former employer, the oxcart owner, hired him again. But a week later, an accident happened. The ox assigned to Wan-fa suddenly went wild and struck down a child, killing it. For this accident, Wan-fa was sentenced to quite a long period of imprisonment. Although the oxcart owner was not jailed, he was fined a big sum of money. At the time that he paid the fine, he uttered in agony, "Heavens! Heavens! Heavens!"

In prison, Wan-fa worried about Ah-hao and Lao-wu. He wondered where they would find the money for rice. He could hardly sleep at night, for worry. One day, for no reason at all, he suddenly regretted having driven Chien away. Thereafter, he spent a few moments each day blaming himself for being rude to Chien. Sometimes, he imagined Chien might have come back to room with Ah-hao in the hut. According to the opinion of his fellow prisoners, a wife had a right to divorce a husband if the husband was in prison. With Chien's help, Ah-hao might have already divorced him. If so, what could he do about it? He probably could ask for money from them, as his prison mates suggested. It was reasonable to demand money when one submitted one's darling wife to another man. After all, he had paid a considerable dowry when he married Ah-hao, so it would not be too much for him now to claim some compensation. It's ridiculous that I'm afraid to lose my wife, while I'm unable to keep her. Huh, ridiculous, indeed!

The fact that Ah-hao had not come to see him lately as often as before led Wan-fa to believe that she and Chien were together again. One day she paid a visit and he asked about her life. At first, she evaded the question by talking about something else. After Wan-fa kept asking the same question several times, she lowered her head and said, "Chien is back."

She smoothed the edges of her skirt. "Well, we're fortunate to have him to take care of us, aren't we?"

Wan-fa did not say anything. In fact, he had nothing to say. He thought of her face blushing red as a peach when she told him. Yes, it's nice to have someone take care of my family while I am in prison.

On the day he was released, Ah-hao and Lao-wu came to meet him at the prison door. Lao-wu had on new clothes. Wan-fa saw no sign of Chien when he got home. In the evening, Chien came in, bringing two bottles of beer to welcome him home. Chien was talking to him in his heavy Lu-kang accent. Wan-fa could not make out a word he said.

Ah-hao came in and joined them. "Mr. Chien has bought you an oxcart, from tomorrow on you can earn more with your own oxcart."

"He has bought me an oxcart?" Wan-fa was quite astonished. He had dreamed of owning an oxcart all his life, and now the dream had come true. For a moment he was pleased and delighted. Then he felt disgusted with himself. What a disgrace! I exchange my wife for an oxcart. What a disgrace!

But, in the end, he accepted the gift. Reluctantly, of course.

Once a week, Chien sent him into the night with a bottle of

beer. With the beer he would go to the *ryoriten* and have a regular feast. He was considerate enough to stay out quite late into the night. Sometimes, when he got back a little too early, he would wait outside the door patiently until Chien had finished and had come out of Ah-hao's bedroom to sleep on the mat with Lao-wu in the doorway. Then, and only then, would Wan-fa enter the house, with a look of aloofness on his face as if he had not seen Chien at all, nor had smelt the unpleasant odor of his armpits.

Only once a week did Chien give Wan-fa a bottle of beer. Never more than once a week. This Chien believed in moderation in all things.

Among the villagers, the prevailing axiom was improvised: "You need only a wedding cake to marry a virgin, but an oxcart to marry an old married hag." It spread far and wide and lasted a long time.

The five young villagers finished their revel in the village *ryoriten* and stood up to pay their bill. As they were leaving, the one whose head seemed larger than his expanded chest spat toward Wan-fa. The deaf man narrowly dodged the flying gob.

Cup after cup, Wan-fa emptied his beer. Thinking it was still too early to go home, he slapped the table and shouted, "Hey, bring me a bowl of duck cooked in *tang-kuei* wine, please."

He did not understand why the five young villagers who had just left had turned back again. They stood outside the door, their eyes flickering toward him. They were talking and laughing: it looked as if they had discovered that Wan-fa's ass had grown on his head.

Yü Li-hua (Mrs. Helen Sun) was born in Shanghai in 1931. After receiving her B.A. in History from National Taiwan University (1953), she came to the United States to study journalism at the University of California, Los Angeles, where she received her M.A. in 1956.

A prolific writer, Mrs. Sun has to date published five novels and five collections of short stories. A story which she wrote in English, "Sorrow at the End of the Yangtze River" (*Uclan Review*, March 1957), was the winner of a Samuel Goldwyn Creative Writing Award.

Long regarded as a spokesman for the "rootless generation," Yü Li-hua is most at home as a writer when she deals with the various problems confronting the exiled Chinese in America. The first usage of the term "rootless generation" appeared in *Again the Palm Trees* (*Yu-chien tsung-lü, yu-chien tsung-lü*), a novel which won her Taiwan's Chia-hsin Award for the best novel of 1967.

In addition to creative writing, Yü Li-hua has occasionally tried her hand at translation. Some of the American writers she has translated include Edith Wharton and Katherine Ann Porter. She is presently teaching Chinese at the State University of New York at Albany. The English translation of "In Liu Village" ("Liu-chia chuang-shang," in *Ch'un-wen-hsüeh*, I, No. 6, 1967) first appeared in *Literature East & West*, XV, Nos. 2 & 3, 1971.

In Liu Village –

Ü LI-HUA

Translated by the author and C. T. HSIA

1. *Ts'ui-o, the woman*

On an early afternoon in Liu Village, the late-July sun, like a tongue of fire, licked its roofs, its river bank, its bare and cracked rice fields, and its vast courts where peasants had spread their grain to dry. Not a single person was visible under the scorching heat. Even the playful water which had wandered away from the Liu River to form a small pond in front of the Liu Mansion was baked into a sleepy stillness.

The back door of the Second Master's mansion was open. Ch'en Ts'ui-o, sister-in-law of the Second Mistress Liu, née Ch'en I-fen, sat just inside the door facing the pond. With her head bent, she was doing embroidery in preparation for her daughter's wedding. On the lilac satin encased in the embroidery stand was a sketch of a pair of mandarin ducks in pink chalk, one slightly behind and below the other but following closely. Two or three wavy lines by the chalk stood for ripples beneath the ducks. Ts'ui-o's needle threaded up and down through the satin. To embroider the petals, leaves, or ducks was not too difficult, but to get those ripples right demanded her full attention. She had to heed each stitch, even though now drowsy from the fierce heat of the late-July afternoon.

A drop of perspiration fell on the lilac satin. Adroitly, she lifted from the embroidery stand a white towel with "Good Morning, Sir" printed on it in red and pressed it against her brow. Lifting up her head, she exhaled deeply. It was so blindingly bright outside that for a moment she could not distinguish the water in the pond from the path alongside it. Though not directly under the sun, her face was suffused in heat. No sooner had she dried her forehead, than tiny beads of perspiration oozed out again. Wrapping the

101

towel around three fingers of her right hand and holding its tail by her left, she pressed it against her forehead two more times. The towel was brought back by her husband, I-fu, from Shanghai when he last came home nearly a year ago. At first she wanted to save it, but eventually the old one with green stripes had become so threadbare that it pricked her skin every time she washed her face. She then took out the new towels, one for her son Ta-ch'i, one for her daughter Yün-jui, and this one for herself. It smelled of camphor when she rubbed her face against it.

With a slight squint, she searched the path on the other side of the pond. Not a soul. It was a heavy and still afternoon like this when her husband last came home, under a burning sun. Her father-in-law was running a fever after a heat stroke and his bowels were loose. Her mother-in-law, in great agitation, thought he would die and sent a message to her son in Shanghai, urging him to return. I-fu came home and stayed for seven days until his father was "out of danger." Ts'ui-o, though blaming her mother-in-law for her needless alarm, secretly exalted over the unexpected reunion with her husband. From morning till night, I-fu stayed with his father, massaging his back and legs, giving him medicine, and caring for him in every other way. But at night, he was all hers. I-fu dreaded the heat. After their love-making, he would immediately turn away to avoid touching her body. She would lie on her side and fan him to sleep. His body odor fanned her nostrils, made her happy and content even though their bodies were not touching.

Now, he wouldn't come home again until their daughter's wedding. She put the white towel back on the embroidery stand. The drop of perspiration on the lilac satin had faded into a large ring, like a waning moon on the western horizon at dawn. Cocking the small finger of her right hand, she selected a mauve silk thread. Whenever the embroidery needle went through the taut satin, it gave out a faint sound "pang." As she plied the needle, she recalled the morning of her own wedding day, twenty years ago. At dawn, her mother urged her to get up. Murmuring her accord, Ts'ui-o nonetheless lingered on her warm bed and drifted back to sleep. Vaguely she heard her mother mutter, "Ts'ui-o,

Niang [1] will let you stay there a while longer. By tomorrow this time, you'll have to get up early, to serve your parents-in-law tea. Hasn't your uncle told you time and again that the Ch'ens are a highly respectable family, and their rules are strict? You have to be extremely careful, my child. Rise early and retire late; when wronged, no matter how badly you feel, don't show it on your face. Your uncle said that their son is kind and self-respecting, try to be a good wife to him."

Someone shook her suddenly and she became wide awake. It was their neighbor, Chang Ta-ma. "Congratulations, Ta-ku-niang.[2] Today is your big day, why aren't you up yet? Hurry get up, I'm here to open your face."

Putting her mother's old quilted jacket over her brand-new pink underwear, Ts'ui-o sat by the window facing the light. Chang Ta-ma fetched a bowl of cold water and soaked a foot-long thread in it. Then, grabbing its two ends tightly in her hands, she pressed the thread against Ts'ui-o's forehead. With her teeth, she pulled it away, then let it spring back to Ts'ui-o's forehead. It hurt her everytime the thread hit her face and she winced. With the thread in her mouth, Chang Ta-ma said, "My Ta-ku-niang, if you think this hurts, wait till you become a daughter-in-law! You have to endure something much more painful than this."

When the face was opened and made smooth and lustrous, Chang Ta-ma spread wet powder over it. She then wet a pencil with her saliva and applied it on Ts'ui-o's eyebrows; mixing some rouge with water, she further reddened Ts'ui-o's lips with it and spread the rest of it on her cheeks. Then she went behind her to coil her ebony hair into two round buns and inserted pearl pins into them. Her job done, she looked at Ts'ui-o through the mirror and said, "I'm not boasting, Big Sister Li, but in the whole village, nobody could surpass your Ts'ui-o in looks! Why else should the Ch'ens send their matchmaker all the way to this mountain village to seek your daughter's hand when there are plenty of marriageable girls in their own village?"

From the mirror, Ts'ui-o watched her mother spread out her

[1] One form of address for one's mother.
[2] *Ta-ku-niang* is one way of addressing a young woman.

wedding garments on the bed—a lined jacket of cherry-red brocade, a pink blouse studded with sequins and matching pink trousers, a pair of slippers embroidered with pearls in a phoenix design. She didn't lift up her head to respond to Chang Ta-ma's
praise of her daughter, but dabbed her face with the corner of her
worn quilted jacket. Deeply touched by this, Ts'ui-o also wanted
to cry. But since her face in the mirror looked taut and smooth
with the wet powder, she bit her lips to hold back her tears.

"Ai-ya, Big Sister Li, are you still moping? Marrying into such
a family, Ts'ui-o need not worry about her food and clothes, and
you have a rich relative to visit from time to time. If I were you, I
would laugh so much that my lips would split! And look at you,
crying away like that!" She rushed over and straightened her up.
"Come, help me put the wedding dress on your Ts'ui-o; the sedan-
chair will be here any minute now."

The embroidery needle threaded through the ripple and pricked
her finger underneath the satin. Ts'ui-o uttered a low cry and put
her finger in her mouth to suck. Inserting the needle slantingly in
the case, she massaged her neck and sat up to rest. Out there,
white vapor floated on top of the pond, like smoke rising from a
large pot of seething oil. A hot breeze coming from across the
pond caressed her face and penetrated her gray pongee blouse. She
grabbed the open collar and shook the blouse to cool herself. After
making sure that there was no one around, she unfastened a few
more buttons with her right hand to bare her neck and part of her
chest. When her fingers touched the chest, the skin felt as silky
and cool as it was twenty years ago.

Suddenly she felt giddy and supported herself on her right arm,
the hand cupping her jaw and the elbow on the embroidery stand.
Her eyes, afire as if she were drunk, gazed sideways at the path
across the pond while her mind went back to the time of her
wedding night when her husband implored her to take off her underwear. Stammering like a fool, he confessed that in all his
twenty-two years, he had never seen a naked woman. With her
face as red as the wedding candles, her hands as shaky as the
candle lights by the bed, she took off her underwear. Against the
crimson silk bed covering, her skin looked whiter than snow. Half
in fear, half in embarrassment, she bent her head low, her eyes

fell directly on her porcelain-white breasts just as her husband's tremulous hands were to touch them. Eager to feel her smooth skin all over, his hands soon fell away from her breasts and slipped down to her waist. . . .

A month after she married him, he went back to his dry goods store in Shanghai, leaving her to serve his parents. Her father-in-law, sporting two brushes of gray mustache, sat from morning till night by the octagonal table in the drawing room. He hardly spoke more than eight sentences all day, but made his presence known by constantly knocking his jade-mouthed long pipe against the blue porcelain ash bowl on the tiger-skin rug, *ting ting*. He never looked at her person when speaking to her. In the beginning, she never could remember to bring him a glass of salt water with his morning tea. He would look at the courtyard outside the drawing room and say in his normal flat voice, "Forgot again?" It was not spoken in a harsh tone, but still, she was in awe of him.

Her mother-in-law was cruel. She had a purplish-brown face and triangle-shaped eyes. Whenever reprimanding the bondmaid whom she had bought when the girl was barely three years old, she would point a long lit spill to her face. Not infrequently, it touched her face and burned her skin with a faint sizzling noise. The bondmaid dared not breathe, to say nothing of crying out, while Ts'ui-o's whole body cringed in pain for her. Her mother-in-law was not that mean to her, but, when she surveyed her body with her sharp-edged eyes, Ts'ui-o often wished that she were a wooden board and not a fair-complexioned woman with firm breasts, a small waist, and well-rounded hips. Her eyes were bearable when I-fu was not home, but when he was home, her mother-in-law would look at her so fiercely that Ts'ui-o thought the blood would spout from the sockets.

I-fu came home three times a year, during the Ch'ing-Ming, Mid-Autumn, and New Year holidays. On each occasion, he would stay from ten days to two weeks, so that each year, she would be very happy for at least thirty days. Even then, though, she could not be with him all the time. He had various duties to perform while at home: worshipping ancestors and visiting their graves, collecting rents and calling on relatives, repairing tools and doing other assorted jobs around the house. Not a moment was idled away. And she still had her daily chores of supervising the servants in preparing meals and serving morning and evening teas. And on New Years holidays, when people came to convey their good wishes, she had to serve tea and sweets, many times a day. Sometimes she didn't get to talk to her husband all day, not even at mealtimes, since he always ate with his parents while she waited on them, then ate with the servants in the kitchen.

Whenever I-fu was home, her mother-in-law would rack her brain searching for extra work for Ts'ui-o to do, such as making shoes by stitching together many layers of rag, edging the quilt covers, putting linings on jackets, and darning the socks. The two of them sat in the still drawing room, her mother-in-law sucking at her water pipe and blowing at her spill while she did all these extra chores. Ts'ui-o's secret anger could almost shoot up through her head and ascend to the ceiling as a stream of hot vapor, blending with the smoke emitted from her mother-in-law's water pipe.

So they would sit until her father-in-law called in his low and weary voice from his room, "Let her retire, it's late."

Carrying the octagonal wind lantern, Ts'ui-o would leave the drawing room, walk across the courtyard and through the dark hallway. Though her heart leapt forward to meet her husband, she had to walk very slowly, step by step, for she knew without turning her head that her mother-in-law, with her hand holding back the heavy door curtain, was watching her.

Picking up her needle once more, she selected a mint-green thread and started to embroider the four characters "Harmony in Hundred Years." Although she had only a few years of schooling, she recognized these characters and understood their meaning. Her daughter's betrothed, Shun-te, seemed to be good-natured. She hoped that they would be happy after their marriage. In the twenty years she had been married to I-fu, he had never said one harsh word to her. He stayed home only thirty-odd days a year, and they were together no more than two years in all their twenty years of marriage, but they were happy and loving when they were together, every moment of it. At night, in bed, inside the gauze mosquito net, she was in seventh heaven a hundred times over. Unconsciously, she rested her needle on the character "Hundred" and cupped her jaw with her hand. Partly because of the scorching heat, partly because she was thinking of those nights, her eyelids felt heavy, her chest burning, and her whole body robbed of all strength.

No matter how much she was berated by her mother-in-law, I-fu, a filial son, would not say anything against her. One night, when they were in bed, his fingers happened to touch a smooth scar on her chest. He asked her about it, she said that she had burned herself. How had she burned herself, he wanted to know.

"I was frying pork fat in a deep fryer. Nai-nai [3] came to the kitchen. She tasted a piece of the fat sediment. It was not crisp enough, she said, and threw the piece back into the fryer, causing the seething oil to splash all over me."

Actually, because of the tremendous heat from the stove, Ts'ui-o had opened a few buttons of her blouse. After throwing the sediment into the fryer, her mother-in-law had muttered, 'Your man isn't home, what's the sense of exhibiting yourself?' But Ts'ui-o, in relating to him the incident, had omitted this part.

In the dark, her husband said nothing, just kept on feeling the scar with two fingers. It felt like two ants crawling on her flesh. The sensation caused her to curl up her body with her knees pressing against his thighs. Unexpectedly, he pulled her to him, straightened her body and held her tight against his body.

"After Yün-jui is married off, Ta-ch'i has got a wife, and after my parents pass away, I'll take you with me to Shanghai to live, just you and me. Shanghai is a wonderful place, all sorts of places and things for one to enjoy. I'll take you to see moving pictures."

"What's that?"

"I have gone with other salesmen at the store, several times. Those foreigners, they do all kinds of things in front of people. The first time I went, I dared not look. They called me a bumpkin, the other salesmen."

"What did those foreigners do?"

He demonstrated to her. She tittered in the dark. The two brass bed-curtain hooks knocked loudly against the mahogany bed posts.

[3] One form of address for one's grandmother or the mother of one's husband.

She said, in a tone of affectionate disbelief, "You are fooling me, because I'm a country woman and have never seen the world."

"When did I ever fool you?" Gently, he touched the scar on her chest. "I'll take you to Shanghai someday, just you and me."

Ts'ui-o gazed at the path across the pond hopefully. Which direction led to Shanghai? Could one reach there from this path? I-fu had told her, "Pass the village, climb over the Mountain of Myriad Gods and walk twenty *li* to the County Seat. From there, take the steamship; after one day and two nights, you are there, in Shanghai." Such a faraway place! Would she ever have a chance to go there in her lifetime? True, her parents-in-law were old, but they were in good health, and rarely ill. "Ah!" She sighed. Resting her jaw in her palm, she continued to stare at the path. The only thing she hoped for now was for I-fu to come home early for Yün-jui's wedding and to stay a few extra days with her before he went back to Shanghai. Her hand slipped down to her throat, to her bare upper chest. The burn had long since gone, but if she looked close, she could detect a faint mark of pink. Recalling the sensation she felt when I-fu caressed the burn with his two fingers, Ts'ui-o became so intoxicated that she could hardly keep her eyes open.

Still, she could see a man standing on the path across the pond. How long he had been there, she could not know. At first, she thought I-fu had come back unexpectedly as he did the last time. She was so overjoyed that she had to press her hand hard against her heart to contain its violent thumping. When she collected herself and looked again, she saw that it wasn't her husband. The man had his silk shirt open at the front. Under the blazing sun she could see the two tufts of hair on his chest and his navel directly above the loosely belted silk trousers. He stood akimbo, his rolled-up sleeves exposing two jutting veins on his forearms. Automatically, Ts'ui-o let her hand fall from her chest and sat straight. How could it be anyone but Liu Ch'ang-ch'ing, that notorious rascal of Liu Village!

That year, after her husband's village—Ch'en Bridge—had been occupied, the guerrillas hiding there staged an attack one night and killed a dozen Japanese. The enemy went insane with rage and started to burn down the whole village. The bondmaid of I-fu's house, getting up in the middle of the night to use the out-house, saw the fire in the barn and screamed, waking up the whole family. Even though there was no man in the house (I-fu was in Shanghai and Ta-ch'i was attending high school in the county seat), Ts'ui-o was fortunately equal to the crisis as a girl brought up in a mountain village. She half carried and half dragged her parents-in-law to the front gate, one after another. Then, with the help of her daughter, the bondmaid, and the old servant, she rescued some of their clothes and jewelry. That night they had a hard time walking to Liu Village to seek shelter with her sister-in-law, the Second Mistress Liu.

Liu Village was already in the hands of the enemy. When the Japanese first invaded it, Liu Ch'ang-ch'ing had assembled a few elders of the village to the market place to welcome them, though the womenfolk had either gone into hiding or disguised them-selves, afraid to be seen. Liu Ch'ang-ch'ing was a ne'er-do-well when young and his mother, unable to control him, had let him follow some villagers to different ports. He was gone for twenty years. When the war began, he returned to the village out of nowhere, and gave the impression that he had made some money. Day in and day out, he wandered about the village with a cigarette dangling at the corner of his mouth, his shirt unbuttoned and his hands at his waist. Everyone in the village shunned him. Then, when the enemy entered the village, he, making use of his inade-quate Japanese, became a person of importance overnight. He went from door to door to collect food, wine and silk to be sent to the enemy camps. The Japanese were so pleased with him that they made him the village head. After a few days of feasting, the enemy returned to the headquarters in the County Seat, leaving only a few soldiers to guard the village. As soon as they left, Liu Ch'ang-ch'ing acted as if he were ten feet tall. Those who ordinar-ily turned their heads upon meeting him and called him "the ras-cal" at his back now behaved demurely in front of him, addressing him by his new title. With a cigarette perpetually at the corner of his mouth, his hands at his waist, he would barge into someone's house unannounced whenever the whim took him. When in a bad mood, he would just roll his eyeballs skyward while spoken to.

Ts'ui-o's sister-in-law, I-fen, had married Liu Shih-chun, the second master of the Liu Mansion, the most prestigous Liu branch of the whole village. Though the second master had died some years ago, his branch remained prosperous. Formerly, should a person like Liu Ch'ang-ch'ing venture across the doorsill of the Liu Mansion, the servant would, without a scruple, chase him out with a stick as if he were a dog. Since he became the village head, however, he had barged into the second master's house several times, and stayed on for dinner. I-fen had to order the servant Chang-sao to warm up the wine for him.

After Ts'ui-o moved here, Liu Ch'ang-ch'ing's visits to the Liu Mansion became more frequent. Each time he saw her, his eyes nailed on her body. Like a dog, he followed her about and kept on calling her Ch'en Ta-sao.[4] When he was gone, her mother-in-law would say, pointing the spill to her face, "Your own man isn't here, so have some self-respect! That man is a born rascal, what evil deeds will he not do! Do you have to swing your hips so much? When speaking to him, do you have to smile that way? How can you act so cheaply when very soon you are to be a mother-in-law yourself?"

Even I-fen could not take it. She said: "Niang, in all fairness, it was for the sake of all of us that Sister-in-law tolerated him, she didn't do anything out of step. Wasn't I talking to him and laughing with him? What else can one do? As the saying goes, 'It's easier to face Yama than to deal with the guards at his Gate.' The lives and properties of the whole village are in his control. Anyone who doesn't court him is definitely looking for trouble."

Now, this Liu Ch'ang-ch'ing, with a cigarette dangling at the corner of his mouth, his hands akimbo at his waist, the hair on his chest shining under the sun, was hooking his eyes on her face. Hastily, she averted her eyes and lowered her head. In a flurry, she couldn't find the embroidery needle and squatted down to the floor to look for it. Suddenly, a shadow fell on the sunlit oakwood floor. She looked up, her eyes meeting the intent gaze of Liu Ch'ang-ch'ing who had come to the door. His eyes, which contained more white than black, shifted from her face to her neck

---

[4] Ta-sao is literally the wife of the oldest brother; use is often extended to unrelated women to whom one wishes to show respect and mild affection.

and to her chest. His mouth all at once hung open, and his cigarette fell to the floor.

"Village Head Liu, you are not in your house taking a nap in this hot weather?" Ts'ui-o said. Covering the chest with one hand, she pressed the embroidery stand with the other to get up.

"I long for you so much, Ch'en Ta-sao, that I can't go to sleep. *Hsi-hsi.*" He snickered.

"Village Head is so fond of joking! Ah, please sit down, I'll go and get the bondmaid to bring you tea." Unaware, her palm was pricked by the embroidery needle on the stand. She uttered a short cry and rubbed the palm with her other hand. Her blouse came open again.

Liu Ch'ang-ch'ing strode froward, caught her wrist and turned her hand toward the light. "Let me see, let me see. Does it hurt? I can cure it for you, I guarantee." He straightened her fingers and placed her hand flat against his chest, so that her palm felt his hot flesh and the bristly hair. A shiver ran through her body.

"Village Head Liu, Village Head Liu! Please let go of me. Should anyone see us, how do you expect me to live?" She struggled. She had no strength, but she kept on struggling.

"Who can see us? The old man your father-in-law and old woman are both napping, your sister-in-law I-fen has gone to the Third Master's for a game of mahjong and your daughter is visiting in the next village, who can see us?" He thrust his face forward from across and above the embroidery stand. "Ch'en Ta-sao, ever since you came to our village, I haven't had a night of peaceful sleep. Your man is blind to leave someone like you behind to hug the pillow night after night. I know, I can tell you don't dislike me. Confess, is my guess correct?"

"Village Head Liu, what kind of talk is this?"

"Just call me Brother Ch'ang-ch'ing. What kind of talk? Ah, intimate talk, of course. *Hsi-hsi!* Ch'en Ta-sao, today I have come especially for you."

Ts'ui-o finally summoned some strength to free her hand. She pushed her chair backward and turned to go. From behind her, Liu Ch'ang-ch'ing roughly encircled her by the waist, his hands turned upward, tightly cupping her firm breasts with his ten fingers. The hot breath from his dilated nostrils, the odor of to-bacco from his open mouth tickled her nape and settled on her chest. She couldn't breathe, nor could she call out for help. Thus captured, she was dragged from the back court to the hallway, to the west-wing chambers, up the stairway, and into a room.

Formerly it was Second Master's study, where he used to smoke his opium, look over his accounts, or browse through his books. After he passed away, the room served no particular purpose though in one corner there were a few trunks and other sundry articles of household use, but the bed was still there. In times of peace, when there were overnight guests, this extra bed had proved useful. Some time ago, when Liu Ch'ang-ch'ing came to the house demanding some bolts of cloth to be sent to the Japanese headquarters, he had come up to this room with the servant Chang-sao to fetch the goods. He had not forgotten it since.

After entering the room, he shut the door with a back-kick of his left leg. The room was as hot as if it were filled with ten caldrons of boiling water. Liu Ch'ang-ch'ing forced Ts'ui-o to the middle of the room, released her and turned her around. Before Ts'ui-o could open her mouth, he had smothered it with his own, while his fingers blindly searched for the buttons of her blouse. Impatient, he then brusquely tore it off from the open collar. The tearing of the sleeveless undershirt required even less effort. As soon as he saw her white, silky bosom and the erect nipples, he gave out a hoarse moan. Throwing her onto the rattan bed, he began to suck her, all over.

Half delirious, Ts'ui-o was dimly aware that the rattan wicker-work uncovered by any mattress was very resilient. Each time after Liu Ch'ang-ch'ing had pressed her down, it sprang her back. It gave her the illusion of being in a boat. She felt dizzy, and to steady herself, she held onto his shoulders. He was breathing hard and in short jerks, puffing hot air onto her face. She had to shut her eyes. Once her eyes were closed, her mind flashed back to the mid-July of last year when her husband came home unexpectedly. It was hot like this also. The room was so hot now that she felt she was in a steamer and was confused about last year and this year. Her body was soaked in sweat, as was the body on top of hers.

Both bodies were so slippery that she had to hold onto him still tighter.

"As I said, you wanted me too, am I right? I can tell, you were starved to distraction!" As he gasped out his words, the spittle from his mouth trickled down to her face and into her mouth. A tremor spread through her body; then she lay, paralyzed. Slowly she opened her eyes and saw, with an excruciating clarity, that the person on her was not I-fu.

She wanted to cry, but all the moisture in her had been drained. She lay there, soft and weak, hands over face. Liu Ch'ang-ch'ing crawled down from her. The cigarettes and matches in his shirt pocket had tumbled all over the bed and onto the floor. He picked a cigarette up, tucked it at the corner of his mouth and searched for a match on the floor. When it was lit, the room seemed hotter. He belted his trousers, muttering;

"Mother's, the weather is hot as hell!"

He picked up the cigarettes from the floor and the bed and put them back in to the flattened cigarette case. With utter indifference, he poked the inert person on the bed. "Ch'en Ta-sao, how was it? Was I comparable to your husband? Eh? *Hsi-hsi!* I'm going. You had better put on some clothes before you catch a cold. *Hsi-hsi!*"

Giving the collar of his shirt a shake and not bothering to button it up, he walked toward the door. Suddenly Ts'ui-o pushed herself up from the bed with her elbows.

"Liu . . . Ch'ang-ch'ing, take me with you, I beg you!"

With his left hand still on the doorknob, he turned around. Taking the cigarette from the corner of his mouth with his right thumb and forefinger, he sent the ashes flying to the far corner of the room by a snap of his little finger. Then he smiled crookedly, pulling his lower lip sideways; "Didn't I tell you so? Once you have tasted the sweets, you can't bear to leave me, can you?" His eyeballs with their large portions of white surveyed her naked body. "My Ta-sao, are you asking me to abduct a decent married woman? How would I dare commit such a crime? Rest assured, I shall appear on the path across the pond every now and then. When you want me badly, wait for me by the back door, all right?

Now I really must be going, hee, hee!" Sticking the cigarette back to his mouth and letting it dangle down, he walked out of the room with perfect ease, not even bothering to close the door behind him.

The room seemed hotter, but Ts'ui-o felt cold. The chill came from the middle of her feet, from her legs and from the bare stomach. She half sat up and picked up the underpants from one side of the bed. Except for her shoes, she had been stripped bare. Standing on the floor, she put on her trousers. The sleeveless undershirt and the gray pongee blouse were so torn that she couldn't put them back on. In hot weather, she disliked to wear the white cotton undershirt that bound her chest as other village women did, so her husband had brought her the sleeveless undershirt made of genuine silk from Shanghai. It felt cool and smooth and never clung to her body. I-fu, except that he couldn't take her to Shanghai with him right away, had done everything in his power to make her happy and content.

I-fu! She squatted on the floor, gathered the torn clothes in her arms and covered her face with them. Heaven above, how could she ever face him? She might as well be dead! Her body had been trampled upon by the rascal, how could she bear to have her husband touch it?

She twisted the torn shirt into a cord, stood up, and with fixed eyeballs, searched for a place to hang herself. The transom was too high and there were no posts around the bed. She tiptoed toward the door, holding the cord tightly in her hands. She remembered that there was a transom by the staircase. A shadow flitted across the doorway, Ts'ui-o stopped short, pressing the cord-clutching fists against her chest and uttering a short gasp.

"It's me, mistress," ssaid the bondmaid. Her flat, pumpkin-shaped face thrust toward the open doorway. The eyes, popping wide, fixed on Ts'ui-o's bare upper body. "The old mistress is looking for you."

"The old mistress is up already?" Ts'ui-o was shivering with cold and pressed the shirt tightly against her bare breasts.

"She has been up for some time now. I went looking for you all over, to the house of the Third Master, to the back door, to the pond. There was no sight of you. When I came back from the backdoor, I bumped into Village Head Liu. He told me that you were here." Her eyes moved from her body to her disarrayed hair, to the dark gray pongee blouse on the floor, then to the bed. "Mistress . . ."

"Hurry, go to my room and get me a blouse. Go, go!"

She was gone for a good half hour. Ts'ui-o kept biting her lips with impatience. "You stupid slave, taking so long to get a blouse!" She cursed when the bondmaid finally came back.

"It wasn't my fault, mistress. The old mistress waylaid me. She asked me if I had found you, I said . . ."

"What did you say?" Ts'ui-o grabbed the blouse, but she was shaking so hard that she couldn't put it on.

"I said I went looking for you all over, to the house of the Third Master, to the backdoor, to the pond. When I came back from the backdoor, I bumped into Village Head Liu . . ."

"You stupid slave!" Ts'ui-o wanted to strike her, but her trembling arm was caught in the sleeve of the blouse and she couldn't get her hand out. "Who told you to repeat all that, eh? Are you out of your mind?"

"You didn't ask me not to repeat it, mistress." Half in confusion, half in fear, she looked down at her own feet.

"What did the old mistress say?"

"She didn't say a word for a long time! Then she told me to get the old master and the second mistress from the house of the Third Master. The second mistress couldn't find anyone to take her place on the mahjong table, so she didn't come back, but the old master has come. Now they are talking in their room."

After buttoning up her blouse, Ts'ui-o picked up the fish-bone hairpin from the bed, pinned her loosened hair back in place, and gathered the torn clothes from the floor. Then, averting her eyes, she asked the bondmaid, "Did the old mistress want me?"

"No," she answered. "But are you going?"

Ts'ui-o was impatient to wash the filth off her body. "I'm going back to my room first. If the old mistress asks for me, tell her I'll come directly." She walked to the door and turned. "Just say 'I don't know' to whatever question she might put to you, do you hear? Have I ever been mean to you in the past, eh? Later on, when you get a chance, put away my embroidery stand by the backdoor."

In the red wooden tub, she washed and scrubbed herself and put on clean underwear. Though her body was now clean, she didn't feel clean inside. But she had dismissed the idea of killing herself. How could she not be there to take care of her daughter's impending wedding? Nonetheless, the ugly incident was eating at her heart. How could she live on? How was she to raise her head high in front of others? Besides, would her mother-in-law let go of her so easily? When her husband came back, how was she to . . .

"Ts'ui-o!" Her mother-in-law pushed aside the pearl-strung door curtain, her purplish-brown face dark with menace. "You did a great deed! In broad daylight, you committed such a scandalous crime and put the Ch'ens to shame three hundred generations back! Yet you have the face not to kill yourself!"

"Nai-nai, I . . . that Village Head Liu . . . he forced . . ."

"Phew!" Her mother-in-law spat on her face. "You think I am only three years old? Eh? Generally, you are strong enough to carry two buckets of water, why didn't you have any strength when you saw that rascal? I have known long ago that you are nothing but a tramp! Whenever your man comes home, you make yourself up like a harlot. You think that I am blind? Let me tell you, have some self-respect, gather up your belongings and get out of here as soon as it's dark. Otherwise, I'll call in a few husky men in the village and beat you to death! We the house of Ch'en can't have a tramp such as you!"

"Nai-nai . . ."

"Who is your Nai-nai?" Pushing aside the curtain, she was gone, leaving a roomful of sultry heat.

Ts'ui-o sat in her room, wiping off in turn her tears and perspiration. Get out of the house? All right! Her only worry was how to explain everything to I-fu. The sun was going down, splashing its golden rays into the room. Ordinarily around this time the servant, Chang-sao, would come calling for her if she was in her room. "Mistress Ch'en," she would say, "how should I cut the pork? Dice or shred? How would you like the bean sprouts? With pork bones?" Now she didn't call for her, the whole house seemed so quiet. Did it mean that they really wanted to get rid of her? Where could she go? Her mother had long passed away. If her uncle found out the reason for her dismissal, would he take her in? He wouldn't. Her mother-in-law demanded that she should get out; she might as well have asked her to kill herself.

Continuing to wipe away her tears and perspiration, she walked over to the dresser where she had on display all the things her husband had brought back from Shanghai: the Beauty Brand cologne, the powder case with the picture of the movie star Miss Butterfly on the cover (whenever she opened the cover, the case gave a musical tune), the sandalwood fan with rose-colored silk tassel, and the small box of rouge. When he was home, she would always sprinkle herself with cologne after a bath and put some rouge on her face before getting into the bed. Turning away from the dresser, she walked toward the bridal chest on which was piled Yün-jui's trousseau: quilts with multiple-colored silk covers, embroideries, jade pendants, and fine silk and brocade. Then she turned to the bed covered by a mat. A thin, summer quilt with a lake-blue silk covering was placed at the corner. Side by side at the head of the bed were two pillows covered also with mats. One mat had a dark ring at the center because her husband liked to use a lot of pomade.

No, she couldn't die, she wouldn't. The more her mother-in-law desired her to die, the more she wanted to live. She must take care of her daughter's wedding; then, when her son went to Shanghai to attend college after the summer, she had to do the packing for him. On top of that, her husband intended to take her to Shanghai to see the world. She couldn't kill herself. Nor would she go back to where she came from. Liu Ch'ang-ch'ing was a villain, but also a favorite with the enemy. Who in the whole village would dare to offend him? How would she dare to resist him? She must explain the whole situation to her parents-in-law.

Picking up the torn blouse and undershirt, she walked out of the room. The sun had set. Though the courtyard was still bright, the dusk had set in the hallway and as she walked toward its end, her pace slackened. Fear gripped her. How could she tell everything in front of her father-in-law? How could her mother-in-law see her side of the picture? Undoubtedly, she would point the spill at her and say: "If you really wanted to resist Liu Ch'ang-ch'ing, you could have killed yourself by knocking your head against the leg of the bed!"

When she reached the door to the room of her parents-in-law, she stood stock still with no courage left to lift the door curtain.

Someone was talking in the room. It was her sister-in-law, I-fen.

"Niang, think it over. By driving her out, you might offend that villain. Then what wouldn't he do once he is angry? He might kill, he might set the house on fire, he could do anything! Assuming he ignores your act and doesn't retaliate, how are you going to explain yourself to I-fu? They have been a loving couple; would he believe you? And if he does, with his bullish temper, would not he want to fight the rascal until one of them is dead? If he doesn't believe you, would he forgive you for driving out his wife? Besides, once Ts'ui-o is gone, how are you going to explain yourself before Ta-ch'i and Yün-jui?"

"I-fen is right. If I were you, I wouldn't do anything. We are living on our son now, it's best not to meddle in any of their affairs." It was her father-in-law talking.

"I have yet to see a father like you! Your daughter-in-law has committed a shameless crime, making your son a cuckold, and you say it's best not to do anything! So you don't care a thing even after she has blackened the name of Ch'en!"

"Niang, keep your temper down and take my advice. Tell the bondmaid not to breathe a word to Chang-sao, who has a leaking mouth. If we don't say a word, nobody will be the wiser. When I-fu comes home, we could tell him the whole thing after Yün-jui's wedding. He, like us, cares for his face and Ts'ui-o is his wife; it's up to him if he wants to punish her or to get rid of her. You don't have to do the punishing. Tieh,[5] am I not right?"

"Most certainly. I told her before not to meddle."

"Then, Niang, I'm going to tell Ts'ui-o that she can stay. I'll just say that you said these things in anger and she shouldn't take them to heart. Anyway, Niang, it will be only a month before I-fu comes back. You must have patience during . . ."

[5] One form of address for one's father.

Ts'ui-o ran the whole length of the hallway back to her room with a thumping heart. Thrusting the torn clothes under the bed, she sat on the bed getting her breath back. Anyway, it would be only a month before I-fu came back. She would explain everything to him herself. I-fu would know whether she was a cheap woman or not.

But the following month was the longest one she had ever lived through. A second was like an hour, an hour like a day, a day a year. She was like a stick of fritter being fried over and over in a pot of scalding oil. Her father-in-law wouldn't look at her. Reviling her daily by alluding to the incident, her mother-in-law was almost tempted to call her a whore in front of Yün-jui. In the past, Ts'ui-o had always served the old couple morning and evening tea; now they wouldn't let her touch their cups. At meals, the bond-maid took her place in filling up their rice bowls and in handing them the face towels. Automatically, Ts'ui-o descended to the rank of a maid and spent most of her time helping in the kitchen. Chang-sao, who had been very cordial to her and addressed her "Mistress Ch'en," became distinctly cold toward her either because she had got wind of the rumor, or because she just wanted to kick a "fallen dog." When asking a question, she would do so curtly, without addressing her.

"What do you want to do with this fish, steam it or fry it with soy sauce?" Or she would say, "How do you want the spareribs prepared?"

The kitchen faced west. Late in the afternoon, with the fire in the stove, it became unbearably hot. In the past, Ts'ui-o would sit in the hallway with her sister-in-law while Chang-sao washed and cut up vegetables and meat in the kitchen for her to cook. Now her sister-in-law was nowhere to be found and she had no courage to sit in the hallway by herself, so the kitchen became her sanctuary. And whenever she walked in, Chang-sao would slip out gleefully to the back door to chat with passers-by near the pond.

All this punishment, all the insult and humiliation from her father-in-law down to Chang-sao, she endured without a murmur. The thing she dreaded day and night was that some rumor might reach the ears of her daughter, or that the disdainful attitude of her mother-in-law might arouse her suspicion. If this should happen, she really would not want to live on. Luckily Yün-jui was still young and she was too preoccupied by the preparations for her wedding to notice the changed attitudes of the whole household toward her mother. Occasionally she caught her grandmother looking at her mother with utter contempt, but she attributed it to the fact that her grandmother had never liked her mother, and so was not troubled. Only once did she feel uneasy when she overheard the conversation of two tailors temporarily stationed in the house to make her wedding outfits.

"The way she fixes her eyes on her nose, her nose on her heart, she appears all virtue. Who would imagine her to be carrying on with that rascal Liu!"

"You are a blockhead! Don't you know that women with light bones always put on a mask of virtue? Just take a closer look at her slanted eyes, then you'll know she is the kind of woman not satisfied with her regular meals!"

Yün-jui didn't pay much attention until her ears cocked up at the words "slanted eyes." Just then her mother came to the backroom to discuss something with the tailors, and as they stopped talking, Yün-jui caught them exchanging a look full of significance. Being heedlessly young, she at once asked her mother upon retiring to their own quarters that night, "Niang, does that Liu come here often?"

Ts'ui-o instantly turned deadly pale. Fortunately, the kerosene lamp on the table was not too bright and she was sitting on the bed away from the table. Immediately, she turned her face away towards the bed feigning to look for her fan. With the fan, she first chased the mosquitoes off the bed and lowered the net. By then, her heart had returned to its normal beat, and so she answered;

"Which Liu? In this village, everybody's surnamed Liu."

"Liu Ch'ang-ch'ing, that rascal."

"Ah, that one. He hasn't come around here for some time now. Except for visiting your cousin the other day when you spent the night there, you have been home all the time, why ask me?"

"Does he have a . . . have a mistress?"

The fan fell to the floor. Ts'ui-o didn't pick it up. Instead, she poured herself a glass of cold water from the teapot and drank it down hurriedly. Then she picked up the fan and fanned herself with vigor as if she couldn't be bothered with questions.

"You are not married yet, why do you ask questions like that? Your *niang* is home day in and day out, how am I supposed to know what is going on outside?" She loosened her hair, which fell on her moon-pale thin blouse, black against white. "From whom did you hear such gossip?"

"The tailors. Tailor Chang mentioned a woman with slanted eyes . . ."

"Ah, I remember now. Chang-sao once mentioned that woman to me. She is a widow from Li Bridge Village, if I am not mistaken. Well, a properly brought up girl like you must quickly forget this kind of gossip. Have you finished embroidering the slippers yet?"

"Almost."

"You had better speed up a little, it's nearly the end of August. I can't wait for the quilting cotton which the Hsin-hsing store is supposed to have delivered to us by now. I have to make two more quilts!"

"Niang, you ought to take it easy, you have lost quite a bit of weight lately. The weather is so hot, what does it matter if I take fewer things over there? They won't mind. Grandfather got a letter from Father today saying he will go to the County Seat to pick up Brother first. Nai-nai told you, of course?"

The fan fell again. She didn't pick it up this time but looked at her daughter with dazed eyes.

"Niang, what's the matter? You didn't know about the letter?"

"Eh? I know, of course I know. Go to bed now, you have to get up early tomorrow."

Around midnight, Yün-jui was awakened by the heat. In her room which was next to her mother's, every window was open yet there was not the faintest sign of a breeze. The gauze mosquito net hung heavily as if it weighed a ton. No sooner was she awake than she heard the sound of weeping. She sat up and listened, trying to tell its location. When she knew it was her mother, she got a fright and ran barefoot to her room. She lifted the net after shaking it a few times to scare away the mosquitoes and hopped into her mother's bed as she used to do when she was a little child. Clutching a thoroughly soaked handkerchief, her mother was lying on her side facing the wall, her body bathed in perspiration. Yün-jui clung to her mother's shoulder, frightened, "Niang, what is it? Are

you ill or something? Having a heat stroke? I'll go and tell Nai-nai
you are unwell."

Turning around, Ts'ui-o held her daughter tightly and cried
even harder. Her breasts were now pressed upon the latter's
shoulder like two hot balls, making her uncomfortable. "My girl, I
am all right. You go to bed." She said this without releasing Yün-
jui from her embrace.

"Niang," the bewildered girl gently unfastened her mother's
arms, somewhat suspicious. "Let me get down to bring you a
towel—you're all wet. Where is the match, Niang?"

"Don't light the lamp, I'm afraid of the light. Don't bother, I'm
going down to wash my face."

After her mother had got off the bed, she noticed a black lump
and picked it up. By the pale moonlight from the window, she
recognized it to be her father's black hair net. Somehow she felt
immensely relieved. He was coming back soon. "Niang, you were
thinking of Tieh, right?"

Ts'ui-o was calmer now. She rinsed her mouth, had a drink of
cold water and came back to the bed. With her legs crossed
Buddha-fashion, she sat in the middle of the bed, placed Yün-jui's
hands on her lap, and caressed them gently. "When I married
your *tieh* twenty years ago, I was sixteen. All these years, though
he was seldom home, I have had nothing to complain of. Should I
again be a woman in my next life, I'd still want to marry your
tieh." It was getting hot inside the net. She released her daughter's
hands and took up the fan and fanned them both. "In a few days,
you will be a married woman, belong to another family. All these
years, you have brightened my lonely hours. When you are
gone . . ."

"Niang, I will only be three *li* away, I'll come to see you two or
three times a week."

"I thought the same way when I left my mother to marry your
tieh. But after I was married, I put my whole heart into making
your *tieh* happy and gradually I forgot my mother. Therefore, I do
not expect you to come to see me too often. I want you to have a
good life with Shun-te, that's more important. I want you to be
happy with him, the way I have been with your *tieh*."

"Niang, beg Tieh to take you to Shanghai for a couple of years,

I can take care of Yeh-yeh [6] and Nai-nai. Besides, there is Auntie. When Tieh comes home, I'll talk to him. You have not had an easy life all these years, Tieh won't refuse."

To her puzzlement, her mother started to cry again; her tears falling on the mat sounded like raindrops beating against the eaves. "My dear child, go to bed. I'll talk to your *tieh* myself. Go to bed. Remember, after you have married Shun-te, try to make a happy life for both of you, then I'll rest easy."

Her mother had said these words time and again in the past, but never with tears in her eyes. She was puzzled for a long time after she got into her own bed, and then fell asleep.

In a few days, both her father and brother returned home.

2.   I-Fu, The Husband

When I-fu and his son Ta-ch'i reached the market place of Liu Village, their backs were dripping with sweat. I-fu with his son at his heel, walked toward the Ch'ang-hsing rice shop. On his way home from Shanghai it was his custom to come to the shop to rest his feet and to drink a cup of tea. The proprietor was formerly the bookkeeper at the Liu Mansion. After the three Liu brothers divided up their property, bookkeeping was no longer needed and he, with the money he had saved while working at the Mansion, opened the rice shop at the market place. From his past connections with the Lius, he got to know a lot of people, which helped his business immensely, as did his amiability. The Lius and their friends and relatives were all his customers. I-fu also got along with him well after his family had moved to the Liu Mansion.

"Brother Ch'ang-hsing, business good?" He stood by the door and greeted the proprietor behind the counter working out his account on an abacus.

"Ah! It's Mr. I-fu!" He brushed the abacus back to its normal position, pushed it away and walked eagerly over to welcome them. The slits of his white cotton gown opened wide, flapping against his legs. "Come in, come sit down, have a cup of tea. You come back for your daughter's wedding, right?"

---

[6] One form of address for one's grandfather.

"Yes. I should have come earlier, but the store was too busy to spare me. Greet Uncle Ch'ang-hsing, Ta-ch'i."

Ta-ch'i addressed the proprietor with a low 'uncle.' He resembled his father, the same swarthy complexion, heavy lips, and bright eyes. I-fu's nose was larger, and he had a scar the size of a thumb on his left eyebrow, acquired when he was small after he had fallen on a piece of broken glass and suffered a deep cut. Whenever he lost his temper, the scar would turn purplish dark and the left eye would blink faster than the right. It always frightened Ta-ch'i and his sister. But I-fu had tremendous self-control and never lost his temper unless unduly provoked. He was of medium height but sturdy: his rolled-up sleeves revealed strong arms. Ta-ch'i was taller by half a head and much broader in the shoulders. His whole body seemed to be made of blocks of muscles.

"Is this your Ta-ch'i?" the proprietor exclaimed. "Why, only a year's time and he has shot up so much! About time he gets a wife too, I gather?" He pulled out two chairs from the table, invited them to sit down, called for tea, went behind the counter to fetch two fans made of palm leaves, and brought out a dish of watermelon seeds and a dish of peanuts. Before sitting down himself, he passed a cigarette to I-fu and lit one for himself.

"Ta-ch'i is thinking of going to college. I figure I can support him for a year or two since I will have Yün-jui married off and so I have given him my permission. You know, brother Ch'ang-hsing, the times have changed; the more stuff you have in your head, the less you will be made a fool of."

"I couldn't agree with you more. Mr. I-fu, what good luck you have, a son so industrious, a daughter to be married into a good family."

"You are being very kind," I-fu said, his face stretching wide with a smile coming straight from his heart. "How is everything in the village, peaceful?"

"Not so good, nor too bad. The Japanese don't come here often, but the evil-doers, the traitors under their protection, come to bother us frequently, wanting money and other things."

"What about that Liu, what's his name? Yes, Liu Ch'ang-ch'ing, what about him?"

The proprietor was startled into silence. He couldn't be sure if I-fu had heard any rumors about Liu Ch'ang-ch'ing and his wife since reaching the market place. If he had, how much did he know? And how much did he believe? Was he trying to get more news from him by asking such a question? He took a deep draw at his cigarette and said, "What do you mean, what about him?"

"I mean does he oppress people?"

He appeared to know nothing then. "I don't know exactly," the proprietor said. "There are rumors that he does. He . . . But one can't rely on rumors."

"Tieh, let's go, Nai-nai must be impatient with waiting."

On their way home I-fu was puzzled. The last time he came back, the proprietor of the rice shop had cursed that rascal with harsh words, accusing him of raping and looting and committing all kinds of crimes. Also he had prophesied that someday the rascal would fall upon a thousand knives. But this time it seemed that he was reluctant to say anything against him, even protecting him a little. What had happened? Had he become an ally of that rogue? Had he taken a bad turn? But he didn't seem to be one without principles or backbone! Then why was he trying to hold something back? He would certainly ask his sister I-fen about it when he got home.

As he approached the pond, his feet suddenly became lighter. Last year, he made a special trip home after his father had a heat stroke. When he reached the pond, the first person he saw was Ts'ui-o, squatting there by its edge and washing clothes. From their reflection in the water, he saw her hands, which had retained their milky softness after years of kitchen work. They were as white as the rest of her body. When by chance she lifted up her head and saw him there, the joy, as if it surged straight from her heart, spread over and softened her whole face. Those twenty years, serving her parents-in-law in the country, raising the children, taking care of the chores in and out of the house, had not been easy for her. True, he came home occasionally, but every time he stayed only a few days, so short. And the nights were even shorter, because she always had to get up at dawn to prepare tea for his parents in the kitchen.

That Wang, a fellow employee who also slept in the store at night, had told him again and again that he wanted to introduce him to the voluptuous delights of the Fourth Avenue of Shanghai. He never went with him though. When he thought of Ts'ui-o's silky skin, he had not the slightest desire to touch any other woman. Now that his parents were living with his sister, who could certainly take care of them, he must sound his mother out this time to see if she would let Ts'ui-o go to Shanghai. Even if he could only have Ts'ui-o for a few months with him in Shanghai, it would be enough for him to have a taste of a normal family life. The very idea of putting up and taking down the bed planks at the store sickened him, to mention nothing about sleeping alone eleven months out of a year. Maybe his mother would sympathize with his hardship and let Ts'ui-o go. Besides, Ta-ch'i was going to Shanghai to attend college, and he could stay with them if Ts'ui-o were there. That way, they could save money. His mother always gave in to any money-saving scheme.

"I'm planning to take your mother to Shanghai for a while. Your sister will be married, Auntie could take care of your *yeh-yeh* and *nai-nai*. This way, you don't have to stay in a dormitory."

"Pa, I must stay in a dormitory or else part of the meaning of being a college student is lost. But I agree a hundred percent with you about taking Ma to Shanghai. It has been very unnatural that you and Ma haven't lived together in the past. Now that Sister is getting married, they have no reason to keep Ma from going with you to live like a normal husband and wife," replied Ta-ch'i.

He talked differently from the rest of the family. Not only didn't he use the village dialect, but also he addressed his parents "Pa" and "Ma," in the fashion of Mandarin speakers. He also used words and sentences beyond the comprehension of his family. His father, though he understood very little of what he said, felt immensely proud of him in secret.

"I agree with you, but I don't know what your *nai-nai* will say to this."

"She shouldn't interfere. I'm going to tell her so."

"Ta-ch'i, this concerns the grown-ups, I don't want you to interfere. Don't think that because you have read a few more books than others have, you can brush aside respect for your elders! Why should you talk to your *nai-nai* about my plans for your *niang*? Confucius said, 'When the parents are living, a son should not travel afar.' It's with great reluctance that I traveled to Shanghai to make money; do you think I wanted to leave them? A daughter-in-law's rightful place is with her parents-in-law, how could you say it's unreasonable? When we get home, don't talk this kind of nonsense to your *yeh-yeh*, do you hear me?"

Ta-ch'i paused a long time before muttering his assent. Then he slackened his pace to maintain a slight distance from his father in order to avoid further conversation. When they were near the Liu Mansion from across the pond, I-fu let out a sigh of relief.

"Finally, finally! It feels much cooler here in the village than in Shanghai!"

Both of them quickened their steps and reached the path. Chang-sao, who stood by the backdoor chatting with the servant from the Third Master's house saw them and yelled, "Master Ch'en and the young master have come home! Master Ch'en is back!" And she ran inside to spread the news. I-fu and Ta-ch'i came down the path, turned and came to the back door. I-fu, who was hoping that Ts'ui-o would rush out to welcome him, saw only Yün-jui skipping and running toward him, followed by I-fen and his parents. He felt a bit let down, but put on a smile to greet his parents and sister.

"Only in three more days you will be married, how can you skip and jump like that? Shame on you!" Ta-ch'i teased his sister. "I bet you can hardly wait to skip to the house of Ch'ang!"

As Yün-jui chased after him to give him a beating, he dashed through the door and ran to the other end of the hall, asking, "Where is Ma?"

Just then, Ts'ui-o appeared at the kitchen door, still wiping the perspiration from her face and turning back her head to give a last instruction to Chang-sao: "Be sure to let it simmer, high heat will spoil the taste of bream with scallions." The moment she turned her head, she saw her husband. She was wearing a suit of jade-green pongee pants and blouse. The blouse, wet with perspiration, clung to her body. Her face was red with heat, and beads of perspiration were on her forehead. The collar was open and turned down, exposing her white neck. Upon seeing I-fu, the red on her face spread over to her earlobes.

"You are back!" Then she saw the eyes of her mother-in-law,

like a pair of poisoned arrows, shoot at her from the back of her husband. Hastily, she turned up the collar and buttoned it up. "You go and rest up in Yeh-yeh's room. I will bring in the water for you to wash up." Then she turned back to the kitchen. I-fu involuntarily lowered his gaze upon her full hips wiggling with her thin green pants.

The day before I-fu's return, his parents and sister had decided at a secret conference that they would not say a word about the ugly incident until after the wedding. So, after dinner, they only went over with him about Yün-jui's wedding plans, then urged him to retire after a long day's journey. Yün-jui, who always slept in the backroom of her mother's quarters to keep her company while her father was away in Shanghai, now returned to the eastern wing of the house and shared a double room with her brother.

When I-fu entered their bedroom, Ts'ui-o had the warm water ready for him in the red-paint wooden tub. While he was taking his bath, she went to the kitchen to see if everything was in order, then to her parents-in-law's room to inquire if they needed anything, then to Ta-ch'i's room to gather his soiled clothes and listen to his rambling chats about his school. By the time she got back to her room, I-fu was already in bed cooling himself with a fan, waiting for her.

"Ts'ui-o." Whenever they were alone, he spoke low, his voice somewhat husky and urgent. "What took you so long to get back? I'm so hot waiting here!"

Although her heart was filled with apprehension, she couldn't help giggling, "Squatting there like that, how can you not be hot? Get up and cool yourself by the window."

"I'm waiting for you, hurry!"

She went to the backroom, using the water he had just bathed in to wash her body clean. After drying herself, she sprinkled talcum powder all over her body and dabbed her underarms and neck with cologne. Then she washed her face and put on some powder. I-fu called her so urgently that she didn't have a chance to put on any clothes before getting into bed. Then, before she had a chance to lie down, he had seized her. Afterwards, their bodies were soaked in perspiration. Ts'ui-o got down from the bed to wash herself again and put on her underclothes, at the same time going over for the thousandth time the words she wanted to say to I-fu. She wouldn't omit one detail of the whole incident. She had to let him know about her true feelings towards him, whatever his decision about her future.

She went back to bed, but to her disappointment, he was already snoring away.

The next day he went to the market place. He needed men to carry the sedan-chair and trousseau-case, drum and gong players, and six men to walk by the chair. It took him all day to find and hire them, to bargain over their pay. Then he brought them back to the house, gave them food and wine, set a time for them to come on the wedding day. After they had left, he went to his parents' room to discuss the details for next day's pre-wedding banquet, itemizing its costs. Then, with an account book in hand, he made an inventory of the trousseau in his daughter's room. By the time he got back to his own room he was dead tired. After his bath, he fell asleep before Ts'ui-o got back from the kitchen.

The next day, the pre-wedding day, was a busier day for him. Relatives and friends bearing gifts and good wishes came and didn't leave until dusk. Three tables were laid out to entertain and feast them. Though Ts'ui-o had not a free moment in the kitchen, she forbade Yün-jui to help her on her last 'maiden day.' After the last guest had departed, her feet were so swollen that she could not even take her shoes off. Yet she had to help Chang-sao clear up the kitchen, and she had to watch the bondmaid tidying up the large dining hall. The lights in her parents-in-law's room were off by the time she was finished, and she went to her daughter's room.

Yün-jui, still in the pink soft brocade dress with short sleeves which she had worn that morning, was sitting by the lamp and listening to her father's instruction. Ta-ch'i was in his own room, practicing his harmonica. Its tune created a desolate atmosphere for the quiet night. Ts'ui-o burst into tears as soon as she sat down by her daughter. She was tired, and remembrance of her wedding twenty years ago had rendered more poignant the uncertainty of her future days.

"Ts'ui-o, Ts'ui-o," I-fu called her gently. "What is the meaning of this? I have finally convinced Yün-jui not to feel bad. Are you going to make her cry again? Shun-te is a nice boy all around.

Yün-jui doesn't have to worry about a thing living with him. In these uncertain times, where can one find as good a son-in-law as he?"

"I know, I know. It's only because I have come to depend on Yün-jui so much. Whenever I need her, I only have to call 'Yün-jui,' and there she is. When she is married, I won't even have anyone to talk to. When I think of this, I can't help feeling sad."

"Niang, I'll come to see you two or three times a week. You can be sure of that."

"I have already decided to take your *niang* with me to Shanghai after you are married. Maybe I'll keep her with me until peace comes. There is Auntie to take care of your *yeh-yeh* and *nai-nai*."

"Ah, how wonderful! I was just talking to Niang about it the other night. Have you talked it over with Yeh-yeh already?"

Abruptly Ts'ui-o held back her tears, waiting for him to answer.

"These days I have been so busy with your wedding preparations, where do I find time to talk to them of anything else? As soon as you are off on your sedan-chair, I'll talk to them. They won't object. Your *niang* has never had an easy day in the past twenty years; now that you and Ta-ch'i have grown up, she should start enjoying her own life a little."

"Exactly!" Yün-jui took her mother's hand and said affectionately, "Niang, now you won't feel so bad, will you? Maybe Shun-te and I will come to see you in Shanghai; maybe we'll move to Shanghai too, and live next door to you. Wouldn't that be marvelous?"

"You silly girl! The whole thing is still up in the air; you talk as if you have caught it in your hands already!" Ts'ui-o couldn't help smiling through her tears. She touched Yün-jui's arm, "Why, your arm is cold! Go to bed, you have to get up early tomorrow. The Third Mistress is coming over to open your face. Where are the wedding clothes I put out for you?"

"Over there."

"Remember what I have been telling you? Always be patient even when you are taken advantage of; don't forget to keep the smile on your face. When you are a daughter, you are a bird; you get fed when you are hungry, then you fly away to enjoy yourself. But when you are a daughter-in-law, you become an ox tending a mill. You push from morning till night; whenever you slow down, the whip comes down on you. I'm not talking of the real whip, but the kind of hardship a daughter-in-law has to endure is worse then being whipped. Be careful in every way, be alert to the expressions on others' faces. Never talk back to your mother-in-law. Even though you are in the right, you must endure her accusation. The word for a daughter-in-law is forbearance."

"I know, Niang. You have been busy all day long, you must be tired and ought to rest too."

"Shun-te's mother is a reasonable and sensible person. She won't mistreat Yün-jui, you can rest easy." I-fu comforted his wife and then turned to Yün-jui, "Go to bed now. Tomorrow will be a tiring day for you and you must get enough sleep tonight. Your brother is following the sedan-chair to Shun-te's house. He and Shun-te were schoolmates, if they invite him to stay over the night, I'll tell your brother to accept, so that you'll feel better knowing your own brother is there with you. Go to bed. Ta-ch'i, stop playing. You know what time it is now?"

Back in her room, Ts'ui-o sat down on the bed, placed her feet on a foot stool and started massaging them. I-fu, kneeling down by her, helped her to massage. Hastily, Ts'ui-o withdrew her feet, saying, "You are more tired than I am. Go to bed now. Ah, by this time tomorrow, Yün-jui will no longer belong to us! Be it son or daughter, they all vanish in the end." Her voice trailed off and she pulled out the handkerchief from her jacket sleeve.

"Ts'ui-o, Ts'ui-o, here you go again! Even though the children all leave you in the end, you'll always have me. You come to Shanghai with me and we'll rent a small apartment near the shop, like my fellow employee Mr. Kuei. I go to work during the day, but in the evening I'll take you out. Shanghai is so colorful and exciting, the Sincere Department Store alone will make your head spin. All kinds of delicacies to eat, all sorts of places to see, as long as you have the money! You have been married to me for twenty years now, and we haven't had a day completely to ourselves. This time, no matter what happens, I'm taking you to Shanghai with me. And I guarantee, two days after you reach Shanghai, you'll forget all about Yün-jui."

Ts'ui-o bent down to pull him up and made him sit by her.

Holding his hands tightly she asked, "Do you really mean to take me to Shanghai with you?" She always referred to him as "Ta-ch'i's *tieh*" while talking about him to others. But when they were alone, she never addressed him. In twenty years, she never once called him "I-fu." "This time, you are set to take me with you?"

"Of course, I thought of nothing else on my way home from Shanghai."

"Nai-nai won't consent." She let go of his hands to massage her feet again.

"I'll talk to Niang myself. Tieh is reasonable. He will help me convince Niang. You don't have to worry. After Yün-jui gets on her sedan-chair, you can start packing."

"Nai-nai won't consent." She didn't raise her head.

"I know Niang is a bit stubborn. And she is so used to you serving her all these years, it's only natural she doesn't want to let you go. But I'll convince her and tell her that you are heartbroken on account of Yün-jui, that I'm taking you to Shanghai to take your mind off her and you will be back in a month or two. She can't very well stop you from going if you are only to be gone for such a short time. Once we are out of here, you can stay away for six months or a year. She has no way to pull you back."

"Nai-nai won't consent. She will say something to stop you, I know."

"Ts'ui-o, I know you and Niang don't get along and I also know Niang is quick-tempered sometimes, but I am sure she is not capable of hurting you on purpose. In the past, she had an excuse not to let you go. Now that Yün-jui is getting married, Ta-ch'i is going to Shanghai to study and they have I-fen to take care of them, she no longer has an excuse to keep you here."

"She has, she has!" Suddenly she grabbed both his hands. "There is something I want to beg of you. In twenty years, I have never begged you for anything, now I am begging you. Whatever Nai-nai or Yeh-yeh might say to you, don't believe them. You must have faith in me. Though I didn't have too many years of schooling, I know good from evil. You have treated me well. I wouldn't do anything to hurt you. You must believe me on this particular point."

He was puzzled and slightly annoyed. "Ts'ui-o, the most Niang can do is not to let you go, she won't say anything bad about you. She isn't that kind of person, you can be sure of that. Sometimes you treat me as if I were only three years old. Do you really think when Niang tells me that the sun rises from the west, I will believe her? Don't you worry, I'll handle everything. To bed now. Look at your feet, if the swelling doesn't go down, you won't even be able to go to the market place, not to say Shanghai." He freed his hands from Ts'ui-o's grip and stretched himself, yawning. Then he started to take off his long gown.

Ts'ui-o's mouth was so parched that the lining of her throat actually hurt when saliva went down. But because she was now extremely nervous, she kept swallowing. "I . . . I have something to tell you. One day . . ."

"Ts'ui-o, I know all about Niang's mistreatment of you, but let bygones be bygones, why talk about them anymore? I give you my word of honor: whatever Niang has to say, I am taking you to Shanghai with me. Are you satisfied?" He was standing in the middle of the room, the left side of his face illuminated by the lamp on the table. She saw his left upper eyelid twitching rapidly and didn't dare to continue as she had no courage to start her confession in the first place. He took off his clothes and went to the back room to wash his feet. Ts'ui-o, dragging her swollen feet to the bed, chased out the mosquitoes with a fan, lowered the net from the net hooks, and went to wash up also. By the time she was ready for bed, I-fu was in there waiting for her. The minute she got in, he held her to him.

"Tomorrow is our daughter's day, let's all pass the day with joy. I guarantee by this time next week, we'll be in Shanghai, just you and me. Ease your mind and go to sleep."

All night long, Ts'ui-o never closed her eyes. At the first crowing of the cock, she got up. Her head felt as if it were placed under a thousand-pound hammer and darkness danced in front of her eyes. She managed to put on her ordinary clothes and, as usual, went to the kitchen to boil water and make tea for the old couple. Then she put the bird's nest soup on the stove and warmed the porridge for breakfast before the bondmaid showed up with heavy eyes to fetch warm water for Ts'ui-o's parents-in-law. When it was time for everyone to get up, Ts'ui-o carried the bowl of bird's nest soup on a silver tray and went to Yün-jui's room. Under the thin quilt covered in silk with a lotus design, her daughter was awake. When she saw her mother, her heart ached and she turned her head towards the wall so as not to look at her mother's face. Ts'ui-o held her own tears back and implored her to get up and drink some soup. Then she helped her to put on her wedding attire. With each new piece of clothing on her daughter's body, her heart grew heavier. When Yün-jui was fully dressed, Ts'ui-o's jacket was stained with tears. She averted her face from Yün-jui.

"I have said all I want to say to you, Yün-jui. In a word, take good care of yourself. Put on more clothes mornings and evenings when the weather is chilly. At meals, don't overeat so that . . ."

"Niang!" Yün-jui threw herself into her arms. "I'll be back in three days!" The words didn't bring herself any comfort and she cried.

Accompanied by several women, Third Mistress Liu came from her quarters to open Yün-jui's face. Hastily, Ts'ui-o dried her tears and put on a smile to welcome them. She called the bondmaid to serve them tea, and went to fetch her sister-in-law to keep the guests company. From then on she was fully occupied with various details in the kitchen until it was time for Yün-jui to get on the sedan-chair. With people milling around, she couldn't say what she wanted to say to her daughter. When the gongs started to clang at the front door, signifying the beginning of the bridal procession, Ta-ch'i, dressed in a new western suit, came to carry his sister to the sedan-chair. Yün-jui held on to her mother's dark red brocade dress and cried, "Niang, Niang!"

With a white-lace handkerchief over her face, and oblivious to the roomful of guests, Ts'ui-o cried with her daughter. All the female guests consoled her, saying, "Your daughter must have been very virtuous and pious in her three previous lives to get married into a family like that!"

"The bridegroom has a square face with large ears, a sure sign of reaching a high position in the future."

"Yün-jui, you mustn't cause your mother more grief by crying so. If the powder on your face gets wet, we will have to do it again. Better hurry and get into the chair, it's getting late!"

Soothed by all these words, Yün-jui finally stopped crying. Her father, who had been in the antechamber entertaining the people from the house of Ch'ang who came to escort the bride, now sent word that it was time. Ta-ch'i tore his sister from his mother, lifted her up, carried her across the hallway and put her down on the seat of the sedan-chair parked by the front door. The guests in Yün-jui's room all followed him to the door, where the musicians again played in preparation for the bride's departure.

Ts'ui-o, in a trance, walked out of her daughter's room into her own and sat down by the bed. It was customary for a mother to lament aloud when her daughter was about to be carried away. So she cried without restraint, releasing all her woes dating back to the day when Liu Ch'ang-ch'ing dragged her upstairs.

Gradually the sedan-chair disappeared, and the din of music became fainter. I-fu and his parents still had the houseful of guests to reckon with. They were invited to sit around the banquet tables in the antechamber. I-fu's mother and sister, for the sake of appearance, went to Ts'ui-o's room and perfunctorily bade her not to grieve too much and comforted her with the truism that every daughter had to get married when she grew up. I-fu made numerous trips to the room during the banquet to give her a hot towel, pour her a cup of tea, or in a gentle voice beg her not to grieve so for the sake of her own health. He also told her that she need not serve the guests in the antechamber, but that she should rest up. He would send the bondmaid in with the food, he told her.

"The guests won't think ill of you if you don't show up. You must lie down after you have eaten something. You have overworked yourself these past few days. If you don't rest, you really will be ill. After I have seen the guests off and given instructions to clean up the place, I'll come in to keep you company. And tonight, I'm going to tell Niang about taking you to Shanghai with me. You just rest up."

Ts'ui-o's shoulders shook from weeping, her handkerchief drenched with tears. After washing her face with the towel he handed her, the powder on her face was gone, showing a yellowish-green complexion and puffy eyelids. She did look ill.

"Nai-nai, she . . . ."

He patted her on the shoulder and stopped her from saying

anymore. "I know, I know. I give you my word everything will be all right. You take a rest after getting something to eat."

The bondmaid carried four small dishes and a small earthen pot of porridge on a shining Fukien lacquer tray to her room. Ts'ui-o, who had not eaten anything since morning, felt hunger when the smell of the food assailed her nose. After the bondmaid was gone, she had a bowl of porridge, rinsed her mouth and washed her face again. The guests were laughing and making loud noises over the fingerguessing game, but she was in no mood to go and join the fun. Besides, the food in her stomach, the accumulated fatigue of the past few days, and her sleeplessness the night before had made her drowsy and inclined her to take a short nap. She would go to see the guests off when she woke up.

But as soon as she lay down, she fell into a deep sleep from which she didn't awake until the room had turned dark. Bewildered, she looked at the small clock on the tea stand by the bed and only then did she realize that she had slept all afternoon. Abruptly she sat up, pushing aside the thin coverlet which I-fu must have put on her. The whole house was quiet. She wondered if I-fu was not in her mother-in-law's room.

In her mother-in-law's room! Her heart beat hard and loud against her chest. It couldn't be, it couldn't be! Vacantly, she folded the coverlet, then, standing in front of the dresser, she powdered her face lightly, combed her hair, and smoothed her wrinkled clothes. When she was about to step out of the room, the pearl-studded door curtain was violently pushed aside and there stood I-fu. She shrank into a ball as if the far-flung curtain had knocked against her heart rather than the wall. In the dusk, I-fu's purplish-brown scar stood out prominently precisely because his face had turned ashy pale, while the upper lid of the left eye twitched rapidly as if he were in an epileptic fit. Involuntarily, Ts'ui-o backed a step, leaning her unnerved body against the dresser. She managed to ask, "Where were you? I was just about to look for you."

I-fu took a large step toward her. Clutching the front of her brocade dress with one hand, he lifted her up from the ground. "You ask where I was, eh? You are scared to death that I might have been to my mother's room, right? You cheap tramp! What a good deed you have done!" He let go of her and she staggered, her back once more pressed against the dresser. "Great! While I'm working like a horse in Shanghai, you steal men at home! Tell me, tell me! How did you manage to hook that rascal?" Taking another step forward, he came near her, his forefinger, like his mother's, pointing at her, nearly touching her face.

"I have wanted to tell you about it, I never tried to . . . to hook him. It was that Liu, he used force to drag me upstairs to . . ."

He thrust his own face forward and interrupted her, pointing the finger at his own nose: "Ha! You think I'm a fool? If you weren't willing, how could anyone do anything to you? Niang is so right, she has always been saying you are cheap, born cheap. Get out of here, the house of Ch'en could not have a tramp like you!"

All at once Ts'ui-o fell on her knees. Holding on to his leg, she said, "Listen to me, please! I wasn't willing, I wasn't! He forced me into it. I'm but a woman, how could I fight him off? If I uttered one lying word, a bolt of thunder would strike me dead this minute!"

"Thunder would strike you dead indeed!" He roared. "Well said! Then why didn't you kill yourself when he was forcing you? Why didn't you knock your head against the leg of the bed and kill yourself?"

"These are your Niang's very words! Yet you told me you wouldn't believe what she tells you!"

He kicked her away. Then he pulled her up, and slapped her hard across the face, so hard that he sent her all the way to the bedside. A thread of bright red blood oozed from the corner of her mouth. "How dare you criticize Niang after what you have done?" With one sweep of his arm, he sent all the cosmetics on the dresser crushing to the floor. The musical powder box began to play a giddy tune in the dusky room. With his foot he crushed out the music. "All these years I have treated you like a decent woman, buying this and that to make you happy. I never dreamed that you would put on powder and rouge to entice men. Tonight, before I return to this room, you must clear out—I don't want to lay my eyes on you again!" As he went out, he again pushed aside the curtain violently so that it slapped against the wall.

Around midnight, when he staggered into the room, Ts'ui-o

was sitting in the same spot where he had left her. On the table against the window a kerosene lamp was dimly lit. He straightaway slumped into the highbacked mahogany chair by the table, and as the table shook, the lamp got dimmer and the room darker. Seeing that he was dead drunk, Ts'ui-o quickly got up from the floor, poured cold tea into a cup and with both hands carried it to him. He gulped it down without turning his face toward her and slammed the empty cup down on the table, which caused the light to go still dimmer. Then he stood up and went straight to the back room. Not bothering to take off his long gown, he threw himself on the bed on which Yün-jui used to sleep when he was not home. Ts'ui-o fetched a thin quilt with a copper-colored covering and went to his bedside. She wanted to cover him but didn't dare lest he should turn savage. She mused there for awhile; then, sighing, she walked away and replaced the quilt on top of the trunk. After turning the lamp's flame even lower, she undressed and lay down on her own bed.

Tangled thoughts made sleep impossible for her. She thought of Yün-jui in her bridal chamber at this hour, enduring the customary teasing and jeering by the wedding guests. She wondered if Ta-ch'i would be able to shield his sister. Ch'ang Shun-te struck her as a smart boy. He should be able to placate the guests and make them leave the room. She wondered if the boy would be gentle to Yün-jui when they were finally alone. In any case, she would not leave the house until she had seen Yün-jui again when she came home with her husband in three days. Could I-fu really be so heartless as to force her to leave right away? She hugged the pillow to her chest to stop the aching of her heart. The mat cover of the pillow on which she laid her head felt wet and cold. She couldn't tell how long she had been crying.

"Ts'ui-o, Ts'ui-o! Bring me some water, I'm dying of thirst!" It was I-fu calling in an extremely sleepy voice. Gladdened, she swiftly got down to pour a cup of cold tea. With the dim lamp and the teacup, she went to the back room, and saw him lying on his stomach, his head hanging down at the edge of the bed. After putting down her things, she deftly turned him over, resting his head against her chest. Then she loosened the collar of his gown and put the teacup to his lips.

He emptied it in a few gulps and said drowsily: "I-fen dragged me to the house of the Third Master Liu to play mahjong. I had a lot of liquor. Um, I am so thirsty! Where are you, Ts'ui-o?"

"I'm right here," she turned up the lamp and smoothed his hair. Lowering her head, she faced him. "Are you feeling better now?"

Gradually I-fu became less sleepy and aware of her. His left eyelid twitching, he sat up with a jerk as if he were under an electric shock. "What are you doing here? Get out! I don't want to see you!" But he saw her all too clearly in her pink pongee underwear, her nipples standing erect under the thin blouse, and her thighs smooth and white below the drawers. Quickly, he turned his head away.

Seeing that the expression on his face was not as brusque as it was in the afternoon, Ts'ui-o threw herself against his chest and wept plaintively: "Do you really have the heart to throw me out? Don't you have any regard for our twenty years of love? You can beat me and curse me and I'll take all this abuse willingly, but I beg you not to throw me out! Have I ever told you a lie? Or done anything to displease you? Have I? Think it over carefully. About that incident, Heaven be my witness, when that rogue Liu dragged me up the stairs, I did think of killing myself. But I was afraid that a person like him would do anything if he didn't get his way—I wanted to protect the family. Think carefully, if I were born cheap as you said, would I have kept my body clean for you all these twenty years?"

Her tearful pleading softened him a little. Turning her around, he looked straight in her face and asked, "Is every word you said true?"

"If I uttered one word of half truth, I'll be destroyed by Heaven and earth! Ah, I remember . . ." Getting down from the bed, she ran barefoot to her room, pulled out a shoebox from under her bed, and than ran back to I-fu and spread out the torn undershirt and dark-gray pongee blouse before him. "Look at these, they are my proof. He tore them . . ."

From the torn clothes, I-fu visualized her naked body and Liu Ch'ang-ch'ing's hands over it. Under her pink undershirt and drawers, he saw not only Ts'ui-o's soft and smooth flesh, but also a thousand hands belonging to that villain. Suddenly, as if he were dead, his face turned the color of a dead fish's stomach. His whole body, as if paralyzed, slumped heavily against the headboard of the bed. Only his left eyelid twitched violently. "Say no more. Take them away, take them away!"

Ts'ui-o went away and came back to him empty-handed. Kneeling down, she hugged his legs. "If you can't forgive me on my account, think of Ta-ch'i and Yün-jui and don't . . ."

"You can stay." He said without any life in his voice. "Tomorrow I will pack my bag and leave for Shanghai."

She looked up at him with fear. "You are not taking me with you to Shanghai? You still don't believe me? I'm clean. I haven't done anything to disgrace you."

"I believe you, that's why you can stay here. I know you have no place to go."

"But you don't want me anymore, is that it?" Slowly she stood up, her eyes nailing his face. "You won't come back?"

He avoided her eyes. "As long as Tieh and Niang are alive, I have to come and see them. But there is nothing left between you and me. I won't throw you out, nor will I say anything to Ta-ch'i and Yün-jui. I'll make sure Niang won't say anything to them either. As usual, I'll send you money every month." Some color returned to his face and his eyelid stopped twitching. "But, there is nothing between you and me anymore."

Ts'ui-o backed away step by step. "I-fu," she said. It was the first time in their married life that she called him by his name. Somewhat startled, because he was not used to being so addressed, he looked at her as if seeing her for the first time. "I-fu," she said, "I understand. Don't say anymore. I only hope you won't regret it." She backed out of the room, leaving him with the dim lamp and the empty teacup on the end table by the bed.

The next morning, he was wakened by the frantic screams of the bondmaid.

"Master, master!" she cried, "Where is the mistress? She can't be found anywhere!"

He sat up with a jerk and his eyelid twitched so violently that he had to put his hand over it. "What did you say?"

"The mistress is gone! The mistress has disappeared! The old master, the old mistress, mistress Liu, Chang-sao, and myself, we have looked all over the place, but she is nowhere to be found!"

He jumped down from the bed, seized her thin arms with both his hands, and shook her violently. "You have looked everywhere? Are you sure?" Suddenly he stopped shaking her and stood dead still; his words came out with difficulty. "Have you looked at the pond?"

Before she could answer, he had pushed past her to Ts'ui-o's room, their room, and nearly collided with his mother and father at the door.

His mother stretched out her arm and steadied him. "Yes, I-fu, we have looked, there is nothing. She won't kill herself, I don't think. She is not the kind."

I-fu looked at his mother as if for reassurance. Then he noticed the contemptuous pull at the corners of her mouth, an expression he knew so well and yet not at all. For the first time in his life, he resented her. "Where could she have gone then, tell me!"

Surprised and hurt by his harsh and vindictive tone, she retorted, "How should I know? She might have gone to that rascal!"

"I-fu's *niang*! What are you saying?!" his father said with annoyance. "Might she have gone back to her people?" He turned to his son.

I-fu looked out from the window to the large empty courtyard made emptier by the bright sun. "I don't know, Tieh, I don't know. She has no one . . ."

His mother sat down on the straight-back mahogany chair by the door and started to put the tobacco into her water pipe. "I certainly would not worry about where she might have gone if I were you. All I can say is good riddance."

I-fu looked at his mother. Her rapid sucking at her water-pipe made two hollows just below her cheekbones and brought out her stern and pointed jaw. More than ever resentful of her malice and indifference, he started to button up his collar and smooth his gown. "I'm going to look for her."

"What?" his mother said, and stopped sucking at her pipe.

"I'm going to look for her, Tieh," I-fu said, his eyes looking deep into his father's as if imploring him to understand him. "When I find her, I'll take her to Shanghai with me."

His mother slammed down the water pipe on the table and stood up. "What are you saying? Are you out of your mind? You are going to take her to Shanghai with you after what she has done to you? After she has blackened the name of Ch'en? Are you a man?"

"I know what she has done, Niang, and she did it for . . . Ah, Niang!" He put his face into his hands. "Has she not been a good daughter-in-law to you all these years? Has she not been a good mother to Yün-jui and Ta-ch'i?" The words came through his fingers and sounded brittle.

"If you want to go and look for her," he heard his father say, "you had better start right away."

He looked up, meeting his father's eyes and holding them for a while, and then he nodded his head. "Goodbye Tieh, goodbye Niang." He took two strides, pushed aside the door curtain and was gone, the sound of his footsteps rapidly receding down the hallway.

"I-fu, I-fu!" His mother rushed to the door.

"Let him go."

She turned her dark and thin face towards her husband and said fiercely, "I only want him to have something to eat before he goes!"

Chang Hsi-kuo was born in Chungking, Szechwan, in 1944. Moving to Taiwan with his family in 1949, he completed both his high school and college education there, graduating with a bachelor's degree in Electrical Engineering from National Taiwan University. In 1966 he came to the United States for graduate studies at the University of California, Berkeley, where he took his M.S. and Ph.D. respectively in 1967 and 1969. He had taught at the School of Electrical Engineering, Cornell University, before he joined the IBM Watson Research Center in New York (1971–1975). He is now an Associate Professor in the Department of Information Engineering, the University of Illinois at Chicago. Dr. Chang is also a Research Fellow at the Institute of Mathematics, Academia Sinica, Taiwan.·

A scientist by profession, Chang Hsi-kuo, with his impressive record in creative writing (stories, satires, science fiction, etc.) is truly a man of "two cultures." His "Earth" ("Ti", in *Ch'un wen-hsüeh*, II, No. 3, 1967) is a unique piece in Taiwan fiction for having vividly portrayed the shifting psychology of the Taiwanese and the mainlander: while the former prefers to make his home in the city, the latter, tired of wandering, yearns for the countryside, where he hopes to be "rooted" with his soil and spend his final years close to the earth. Further samples of Chang Hsi-kuo's fiction can be found in the anthology *Earth* (1973) and *Champion Chessman* (*Ch'i-wang*, 1975).

Earth-

CHANG HSI-KUO

Translated by JOHN KWAN-TERRY

1.

The stone slabs on the threshing floor still glowed yellow in the light of the sun, but standing in the breeze one could already feel a cold nip in the air. At the bottom of the valley stood a cluster of single-story houses, from whose chimneys ascended thin columns of grey-white smoke; whiffs of smoke were also rising from the roof of Kid Stone's [1] thatched hut that stood on the other side of the slope. It was time for supper, but the three Ch'en brothers were still gathered outside, engaged in some interminable argument. Dressed in a cheap suit and dangling a pair of leather shoes in his hand, Lao-ta [2] was sitting on the doorsill. Lao-erh [3] had a singlet thrown over his shoulder, and was puffing away at his cigarette, gesticulating at Lao-ta and muttering an endless stream of reproaches. Lao-san [4] was pacing up and down the threshing floor, his hands behind his back, pursued by a handful of young chickens which were running excitedly round and round.

"Father has just died and here we are talking about selling the land! This is a heartless thing to do. This piece of land came down from our ancestors, we can't sell it just like that," Lao-erh said.

"That's not a fair way of putting it. True, it's not a good thing to sell one's land. But if we don't sell, who is going to farm it? Huo-wang [5] doesn't want to stay and I can't come back either. I have

[1] A nickname presumably given a long time before, in Kid Stone's younger days.
[2] Literally denoting the oldest of the siblings in a family; here used as an alternate proper name.
[3] Literally denoting the second oldest of the siblings in a family; here used as an alternate proper name.
[4] Literally denoting the third oldest of the siblings in a family; here used as an alternate proper name.
[5] Name of the third brother, Lao-san.

my shop in Taipei to look after, and that just leaves me no time at all. Will *you* come back to farm the land?"

Lao-erh puckered up his brow and took a few furious puffs at his cigarette.

"There you are! You don't want to come back either. No one wants to come back, so there's no one to look after the land. If we don't sell it, what are we going to do with it?"

"This is ancestral land. So the only question is: are we going to lease it out or are we going to hire someone to farm it?"

"This is hilly country; the ground is stony and there's not enough water. Who is going to rent it? To hire someone to farm the land is a sure loss. I'm a businessman, I ought to know. Every year, we end up with only a few dozen baskets of kumquats and two hundred catties of low-grade tea. If we did the farming and picking ourselves, we might be able to make a little profit, but it wouldn't be much. It wouldn't even cover the cost of labor if we hired someone to look after the land for us. I'm a businessman, I know these things."

Lao-ta took up his shoes, tapped them on the ground a few times, turned them over, and peered inside to see if they were free of sand. Lao-erh threw away the end of his cigarette and fixed his gaze on Lao-san, who was still pacing up and down the threshing floor.

"You're still the best man to stay, Huo-wang. How about it, eh? You and Father have been taking care of the land all this time, so you should keep up the good work, okay?"

"Oh no, I won't do it. You fellows are leaving me in the hills to dig the ground so you can go off to your jobs in the city and earn tons of money. I already wanted to move into the city the year before last when I left the army. But Father was living, and you said I ought to take care of him, so I didn't have much choice. I've suffered enough here these two years. I'm not going to be the fool again. I don't care which of you stays behind. I'm moving into town to make money and find a wife. Don't expect me to grind away my life in this dump."

"If you want a wife, we'll give you all the help we can. As for farming, there's nothing wrong with it really, is there?"

"If there's nothing wrong with it, why don't you come back

then? This is ancestral land, it is heartless to sell it—it is so easy for you to talk. You know that farming is a hard life; that's why you ran off to find work. And you expect me to like it here?"

"All right, all right!" Lao-erh interrupted angrily. "If you two want to sell the land, sell it and let's be done with it. There'll be money to share, so why should I care? In any case, this family will not be farmers any more."

"It's not that we won't be farmers." Lao-ta pushed a foot into one of the shoes. "Frankly, this piece of land is just no good for farming. To make it pay, we must be ready to sweat our hearts out like Kid Stone. If we can work like that, we can earn our fill of money outside. I suggest we do just that. When we have earned enough money, we can come back and buy another piece of land—good farm land this time, and Father will surely be happy down under."

"Since we've made up our minds to sell, let's find ways to sell it. This plot of land is not that easy to sell, I tell you!"

"What about selling it to Kid Stone?"

"He isn't that rich. Anyway, he was Father's rival all his life. If we sell the land to Kid Stone, Father won't be able to rest in peace."

"The best thing is to go to town and have a look around to see if there's anyone who wants to buy land. . . ."

"Better spend some money to take out a small advertisement in the newspaper then. To do business, you must know a thing or two about advertising. . . ."

"Let's go tomorrow. . . ."

As the evening wore on, the voices of the three brothers subsided into a distant murmur. The sun, hovering uncertainly for a while over the tree-tops on the crest of the hill opposite, suddenly disappeared behind the dark curtain of the woods. Darkness crept rapidly through the valley. From time to time, the houses at the foot of the hills sent out faint glimmers of light, but no light came from Kid Stone's hut. The autumn insects broke into song, a monotonous sleep-inducing chorus. The creek higher up shimmered white in the distance, reflecting from the sky the last rays of the now invisible sun. Further downstream, the area around East Bamboo Town was one broad filament of twinkling brightness.

The night market in the town was just beginning to come to life, but in the valley, one by one the lights went out in the houses. Long before the stream itself became engulfed in darkness, Kid Stone, the Ch'en brothers, and the occupants of the other houses had entered into the land of dreams. Night, then, enveloped the entire valley.

2.

It was past twelve. At Pockmark Chao's noodle stall set up at one end of the bridge, customers trickled away one by one, and now it was almost deserted. On the other side of the bridge, in the plainly-furnished quarters built for enlisted men, people who had been sitting outside enjoying the evening breeze were dragging their rattan chairs into the houses, yawning repeatedly as they struggled lazily to shut the doors behind them. The billiard parlor adjoining the bridge was also closing up for the night. A few army recruits were laughing raucously with the lady markers and helping them to put up the door planks: strip by strip the dull yellow light that spilled from the room was pasted over. In the distance came the sound of a dog barking, and the crisp, resonant tap-tapping of the wooden clapper of a vendor of *hun-t'un* noodles. The regular sound came on and off, and could be heard winding its way along the alley, growing more and more distinct. Pockmark Chao cut up the last pieces of chicken wings and pig's-head meat, sprinkled a few drops of sesame oil on them, and served them up in a dish to his last two customers.

"Captain, try some more, try some of this cold snack."

"Thank you, thank you." The one who was addressed as captain raised his cup. He was middle-aged, tall, and of sturdy build.

"Come on, Lao Chao,[6] stop running about. Sit down and have a drink with us."

"Oh, thank you. I'll go get a dish of shelled peanuts." Pockmark Chao deftly flipped some shelled peanuts from the food cupboard onto a dish and brought a chair over beside them.

"I'm so sorry about tonight. There was slightly more business today, so I've only tiny bits of everything left."

---

[6] *Lao* literally means "old"; often used in conjunction with a surname in reference to a male person, indicating friendliness or mild affection.

"Oh, what does that matter? We're old friends." The other man, who had a swarthy complexion, spoke up. "Come, Lao Chao. Here's to you. I hope that in this trip to the south, you'll get the wife you want as soon as you arrive there!"

Pockmark Chao broke into a broad smile and chuckled. Under the flickering light of the oil-lamp, the pockmarks on his face seemed to stand out even more sharply. "I'll drink to that."

The captain also raised his cup. "Come, Lao Chao. Here's to you too. May the flowers bloom and the moon shine full on you and your bride. May you have an early marriage and a happy union."

Pockmark Chao chuckled again, "May . . . may the land the captain has bought make him a millionaire at once, may everything go the way he likes."

"Well said, well said, let's all drink up."

"Bottoms up, bottoms up!"

Afterwards, the three men flicked the bottoms of their cups toward each other. Swarthy Face took a single wipe at his mouth and said, "Well, frankly, Captain, your luck is not bad either, not bad at all. What a stretch of land you've got, for only forty-five thousand—almost half a hill and a house to go with it too! It's like picking it up for nothing."

The captain laughed quietly. "My wife felt differently, though. She didn't like the idea of spending all our money at one go. What are we going to eat in the future, she said. We'll have half a hill and you worry about what we are going to eat, I said. Even if we can't grow anything but sweet potatoes, we won't have to go on empty stomachs."

"Ta-sao [7] worries too much, but women tend to be more cautious over these things; that's how they are. If I had such money, I too would have bought land and a house. With land of one's own, what need one worry about anything? It is certainly better than pedalling a pedicab for a living here."

"Lao Tung, I'll tell you what. Why not get rid of the pedicab and go with me to the country to help me start the farm? Think of this piece of land as your own. If the venture brings in money in

---

[7] Literally the wife of one's oldest brother; often used as a polite form of direct address for, or reference to, a friend's wife.

the future, we'll split the profits. We're sure to make something. What do you say?"

"Mm . . . well . . ." Lao Tung poured himself a cup of Red Dew wine. "I got my pedicab after I'd almost worn my knuckles to the bone, you know. These Resettlement Quarters that I work are not exactly a goldmine, but still, as such areas go, they are not bad. Frankly, I don't think I can bear selling my pedicab and change jobs."

"I hope you don't mind my saying this, Lao Tung. Look at Lao Chao's noodle stall. It doesn't make big money, but it's a steady job. And if the business is well-managed and the customers keep coming in, it may even be possible to open a small restaurant in the future. That's why I won't try to persuade him to come along with me. But you are different. Though you are just past forty, though you can still pedal your pedicab and earn just enough to feed yourself now, what are you going to do in a few years' time, without any savings to speak of, and still having to pedal for a living? Life can be pretty bleak then. A man who does not worry for the future will live to regret it very soon. Isn't that so? And as the saying goes, of the three ways to be unfilial, the most damnable is not to leave behind a son. You ought to do what Lao Chao here is doing, save up some money and make plans to get a wife. Things will be much better that way, don't you think?"

Pockmark Chao, usually a man of few words, chuckled in agreement. "What the captain says is true, you know."

Lao Tung sighed and said, "I appreciate your kind thoughts, Captain. But at a time like ours, how can a man of my kind talk about plans for the future? Better do as the monks do: say my prayers today and let tomorrow take care of itself. If I have money today, I'll have my fill of food and wine and go for some fun at the pleasure-house. If tomorrow I'm without a cent, well, I'll just stay in my room and idle away the time. Just muddling through, you might say. If I can muddle my way through till the day we fight our way back to the mainland and everyone is able to return to his old home, all is well then. But if I don't live long enough to see it, well, it must be that I didn't do well in my last incarnation and I am fated to the kind of life I have. I wouldn't bear any grudge against anyone."

"Everyone has his idea of what he wants from life. If that's how you feel, I have nothing more to say," said the captain. "As for me, I have been a soldier for the greater part of my life, and although I have a family, my wife and children have been on the move with me everywhere, so all this time we've never really known a settled, peaceful life. And it is I, Li Chen-chih, whose ancestors, for generations, had farmed the land. Farming is a hard life, but after a while, a person seems to grow roots which bind him to the very earth itself. And that's what makes him feel that he belongs, and is also secure. I have been drudging away these many years, so now I really want to have a piece of land where I can settle down, even if it means extra work and extra sacrifice."

Lao Tung emptied another cup of wine. The drink was having its effect on his dark complexion, which had now turned a deep purple. "I still remember the time we were living in Shanghai when I was a child. In those days, my father was a businessman and our family was rather well off. I had an attendant who followed me everywhere I went, and my little sister had a nurse-maid to look after her. So you see, Captain, I come from a good family! One day, my father called me to his room and, giving me a copper coin, said to me: 'Son, spend as much of my fortune as you like. I won't say a word even if you spend all of it. Only keep this copper coin for me, and keep it well. Take the coin out when you turn twenty and promise yourself that from then onwards you'll double it every year. By the time you are forty, you'll have such a sum that you won't be able to use up for the rest of your life.' Captain, my father built the family's fortune with a pair of empty hands. All these years, my father's words have stayed firmly in my mind. I have made a point of remembering them. Captain, those words of my father make a lot of sense, don't they? I'm forty-three this year. If from twenty onwards, I had done what my father told me and doubled the number of coins every year, the first year two coins, the second year four, and so on, I would have collected several million coins by now! Captain, what my father said really makes sense. It's a pity I am no good. I didn't do what my father said.

"Captain, I was a boy scout, you know, the year little Japan invaded Shanghai and the 19th Infantry was locked in battle with the Japanese there. Dressed in a boy scout uniform, equipped with rope, whistle, and a tremendously long dagger—the kind that boy scouts wear—I was scurrying backwards and forwards exposed to the direct line of fire every day, carrying messages, reports, and food for our side. Oh, I was a promising young man then, Captain, one of the select few, you might say. The papers were filled with news stories of how brave we boy scouts were. Yes, we did manage to do quite a bit.

"And then, I don't know how it happened, the 19th Infantry began withdrawing from Shanghai, and quite a few boy scouts started to run with them, without knowing what they were doing. I also followed the Infantry in their retreat, and as a result was cut off from my family for several years. And that, Captain, is how I became a soldier. When at last I returned home, my father had died, the business had gone, the family was in ruins, and I had become a soldier.

"Still, Captain, what my father said does make a lot of sense. If I had followed his words and from twenty onwards doubled the number of coins every year, it would have been fantastic now, wouldn't it? The first year two coins, the second year four coins, the third year eight. . ."

Lao Tung sounded more and more like someone talking in a dream. His words became increasingly incoherent until, his body bent over the table, he fell asleep. Shaking his head gently, the captain stood up, helped Pockmark Chao close up his stall, and got Lao Tung on his feet. Then, with Lao Tung leaning heavily on his arm and followed by Pockmark Chao pushing his stall, the whole party shuffled slowly across the bridge, guided by the unsteady, swaying light of the oil lamp.

"Lao Chao, if you aren't leaving tomorrow, come over to my place for dinner. My son Li Ming is coming back and he said in his letter that he was bringing something for you and Lao Tung."

Lao Chao chuckled with delight. "Thank you, Captain, thank you. . ."

3.

Up on the stage, the four Raymond Brothers were playing their special Beatles number. The young men and women were rock-and-rolling on the dance floor, their bodies writhing in all directions, up, down, backwards, forwards, encouraged by the resonant twanging of an electric guitar. Li Ming was twisting his hips and nodding his head uncontrollably, his eyes fixed on his partner, a dainty, attractive girl with long black hair spread over her shoulders, who was munching a piece of chewing gum as she danced and was speeding up her movements as the beat of the music quickened. She wore a contented smile on her face. As the music reached a pitch of frenzy, the youngsters on the dance floor, as if compelled by some primitive instinct, gave out a yell; the girl's movements became even more frantic, her smile more alluring. There was something infectious about the music and the jerky sharp cries. Li Ming, with sweat dripping down his face, was groaning involuntarily and shaking himself with abandon, as if all the primitive, animal impulses that had been contained in him were shooting off his arms, neck, hips, cranium, and every other part of his body, a sensation which gave him an indescribable feeling of pleasure. The Raymond Brothers finally brought a stop to the primeval din; only the electric guitar remained playing, strumming out a low, ponderous tune. The couples on the dance floor dispersed in different directions to their tables. Slightly dazed, as if just woken from a dream, Li Ming led his partner by the waist back to their seats.

"Hey, Mei, you seemed to enjoy the dance very much, didn't you?"

She gave him a smile. "Sure, didn't you?"

"Actually, I was lost in admiring you, especially the way you danced, as if you didn't have a care in the world. I was watching you all through the dance, you know."

"Cheeky!"

Back at their table, she picked up her glass of orange juice, sucked a mouthful and frowned.

"Ming, order an ice cream soda for me, won't you?"

"Let's eat outside. Things in here are too expensive."

"But I want one."

Li Ming stood up reluctantly. The waiters were hanging about near the door at the other end of the room, so he squeezed his way through, placed his order, then made his way back. Meanwhile, the Raymond Brothers had struck up another number, and his partner was already on the dance floor with a boy, jerking and twisting her body like one possessed, hair tossing in the air, arms flailing up and down. Li Ming knew this was called the "Monkey," one of the most popular dances of the day. He lit a cigarette and glanced at his watch: both hands were pointing at eleven. He was beginning to feel impatient and somewhat bored watching the wild shapes and postures on the floor. These faddish dances, it's fun while you are doing them yourself, but watching from the side-line, you can't help feeling how much they resemble epileptic attacks. The people on the floor began shrieking. A confused babble of sharp cries bombarded his eardrums. He had heard cries like these before, he remembered, several months back, in a cheap, filthy hotel in Yokohama. It was the first time their ship docked at Yokohama. He and the other two apprentice hands on board had immediately vanished like wisps of smoke and turned up in Tokyo to sample those much-talked-about striptease acts. By the time they returned to Yokohama, it was too late for them to get back to the ship, so they put up in this dingy little hotel for the night. About midnight they heard someone entering the room next door; there was only a partition of very thin boards between the two rooms. The man sounded like a foreign sailor, obviously a very drunk one. Once inside the room, he began hollering that he wanted a woman. The woman arrived, and a moment later, from the other side of the thin boards came the sound of panting, punctuated by the woman's cries. They couldn't sleep; the three of them, sitting in the dark, listened the night away. About once every hour the indefatigable sailor would babble for a while, then the panting would start again, rising in volume until there were cries . . .

"His mother's!" Li Ming took a few quick nervous puffs at his cigarette. The Raymond Brothers went on playing number after number without stopping, the dancers went on twisting, shaking, and shrieking. He could no longer see where Chou Mei was; a gentleman sporting a gay necktie and a huge potbelly was dancing at the side of his table and completely blocking his view. He couldn't help cursing again, "His mother's!"

At last the dancing stopped and the electric guitar subsided into a droning, ponderous tune. Chou Mei emerged from the scattering crowd, her brow beaded with sweat.

"Gee, that was fun! Have you ordered the ice cream soda for me?"

"It's been here for ages."

"Thanks." She flopped into a chair, took hold of the long-stemmed glass, and threw him a smile. "You aren't angry with me for dancing with someone else?"

"Of course not. I'm not that narrow-minded."

"I saw you sitting here looking so bored. I thought you were angry with me."

"I wasn't angry . . . . I was only thinking."

"That's swell then." She picked up the small spoon and scooped up a small lump of ice cream. "What were you thinking about?"

"About us."

"Aren't we doing fine? What's there to think about?"

Li Ming looked at her. He could never make up his mind whether she was really that innocent and naive or whether . . . He leaned over and held her soft small hand in his.

"Mei, let's go. I've something to talk to you about."

"But what's the hurry?" She drew back her hand gently. "I want to dance again."

"The Raymonds are going already. There will be floor shows only. You won't like them."

"Do we have to go?" She cast a look at the stage. The musicians were just removing the guitar. "What's the time now?"

"Past eleven."

"Only eleven! The Raymonds will play again at one," she said triumphantly. "They always do, I know. If we leave now, we'll be missing the fun."

"You really like to dance that much?"

"Sure. It's a drag going home this early. Anyway, Mom and Dad are out at their mahjong games and won't be home till past midnight."

"But . . . I have a lot of things I want to talk to you about to-night. Let's go, please. We'll come again another time."

"Bad sport," she pouted, but relaxed into a smile the next moment. "All right, I'll listen to you this once, but only because you are back from a long trip."

At the entrance to the restaurant, a number of taxis were queued up waiting for customers, and a few hippie-type young girls were hanging around, trying to pick up anyone willing to take them in for a free dance. Li Ming stumbled out through an opening in the taxi-line, followed closely behind by Chou Mei. She turned her head quickly and said smiling, "Do you know what I'll do if I become rich?"

"What'll you do? Buy more dolls?"

"Oh, no. If I were rich, I would send someone here every night to get tickets for every girl who wants to dance but can't afford it. How does that sound to you?"

"Great!" Li Ming smiled. "You have the ambition of a Tu Fu."

"You think so? I thought people in ancient times were all long-bearded squares. Tu Fu liked dancing too?"

"Don't be silly. He wanted to build houses for all the poor people of the world." [8]

"Oh, then he *was* a square after all."

"Are you cold? Would you like to have my jacket?"

She shook her head. They were walking along East Nanking Road, and for a while they did not speak a word. It was getting windy. Nighttime in Taipei could be rather chilly.

"Ming, you said you wanted to talk about something? I am listening."

"Oh, yes. What do I want to talk about?" He slapped at his forehead lightly. "I can't remember what I wanted to say just now."

"You are really something. You pulled me out in such a hurry, here we are and now you have nothing to say."

"Don't be impatient. Let me get into the right mood first." He took a deep breath. "Yes, I wanted to tell you that my family bought a piece of land."

"Oh?"

"My family bought a piece of land. Father sold his grocery store and used the money plus the last installment from his pension to buy this large piece of land in the country."

"That's swell. So this is what you wanted to talk to me about?"

"That's not all. I may not be able to work as a seaman anymore. I'll have to help my father get the farm started."

[8] An allusion is made to lines in a work by the compassionate and well-known poet Tu Fu (A.D. 712–770).

"Why? Can you earn more from farming?"

"That isn't the main reason. I . . ." He hesitated. "Let me put it this way. I must have been away for a good half year on this trip, and in that time, I visited many different countries and met many different people. But what was constantly in my mind was the small town I left behind and its people. It is an ordinary little town which you can't even call pretty. And the townspeople, too, are common, humble folk; people that you can find anywhere. Still, I was always looking forward to coming back. The beautiful cities and ports that I'd been to did not strike me as places I could belong to, much less settle down in for the rest of my life. My real home is there, in that small ordinary town. Back there, I feel so comfortable, so completely relaxed. I can never feel like this in any other place . . ."

"You were homesick. You're bound to feel homesick if you are away for so long. After a while back, you'll be itching to go away again."

"Maybe you're right. I used to tell you how fed up I was with that place. It was the most monotonous town on earth, with only two cinema houses and not a single decent bookshop to speak of. Every time I went home to spend my vacation, there was absolutely nothing to do, except share some mindless chatter with friends and play an idle game of chess, or be cooped up at home with Mother and Father, staring at each other without anything to say. In the end, I would almost choke to death with boredom and would give anything to have a brief fling in cities like Taipei and Keelung."

"I don't like living in the country either. Last month, I stayed at my aunt's for a spell. The first few days weren't too bad, but afterwards I was just bored stiff. I prefer Taipei any time. It's such a gay place and so much fun."

"But out at sea, faced with nothing more exciting than the blank walls of my cabin, I had plenty of time to think things over, and I guess I finally managed to work things out. What we describe as commonplace, for example, usually has an attractive side to it. During those months at sea, the things that I used to look back to with a sense of loss were not the wild, gay moments of my life. It was the small, trivial events that kept coming to mind, such as the

time when I and a friend squatted on the bank of a small lake, trying to fish and play chess at the same time. When the game was
over, we pulled in our rods to have a look; they were as clean as
new. We thought we might as well let the fish have a good meal,
so we threw all the bait into the lake. We had a good laugh that
time. Then there was another time, a very hot day during the
summer vacation it was, when I dropped in at my old school to
pay my former teacher a visit. He had just written a poem, and in
a loud and delightful voice he asked me in. He was barebacked
and was fanning himself with a rush-leaf fan. As soon as I was inside, he began chanting and explaining, character by character,
the poem he had written, in classical meter, in praise of snow.
Such simple, mundane incidents came to my mind so vividly that
they seemed to be re-enacted before my very eyes. I think I am just
an ordinary anybody, that's why I fall into such trivial recollec-
tions. And since I am but an ordinary man, why not lead an ordinary life? I'd be happier that way; don't you think so?"

"Sure," she sighed. "You may say what you like, but I still
prefer living in the city. Life is pretty ordinary here too, but at least
there's more chance to have some fun."

"I said just now I'd be going to the country to take up farming.
How do you feel about that?"

"Do as you like. In any case, you always have plenty of excuses
for doing what you want. But I was thinking . . . if you work as a
seaman, you'll get your promotions after a few years; you'll be second mate, then first mate. Didn't you tell me last time that if all
went well, you should become captain in ten years' time? That's
not bad. As for farming, after ten years, twenty years, you'll still be
farming. Right?"

Li Ming couldn't think of what to say in reply. After a long
pause, he ventured lamely:

"What you say makes sense, I guess . . . I'll have to go back
and think things over carefully."

"This is what you've been wanting to talk to me about?"

"Eh, . . . let's forget it, it's not important."

"Fine. I'm so tired from all this walking." She waved her hand
and shouted, "Hey, taxi!" [9]

9 *Taxi* is in English in the original.

4.

Li Ming left his house and followed the lane that led to the school. On both sides of the lane lay paddy fields that, at this time of the year, already looked like a shimmering sea of yellow, undulating in the wind. It was near harvest time. Very soon, one would see the threshing machine set up, the busy comings and goings of men, women and children, the neatly tied bundles of straw standing in the fields. The playground would be taken over by the farmers who would cover its concrete floor with heaps of rice grains, depriving the students, for those few weeks, of their usual game of basketball. But when the sparrows came in flocks to enjoy a feast, the schoolboys, with slingshots ready, would rush to the playground after school to chase the birds. On one weekend Li Ming knocked down more than a dozen sparrows that way. Then if no teacher was around, they would light a fire by the side of the air-raid shelter at the far end of the playground and gorge themselves on barbecued sparrows. During the harvest there would be no reports or complaints of missing bag-lunches. . . .

At the extreme end of the paddy fields stood the low wall of the school house, which Li Ming jumped over easily. He had come this way every day when he was in junior high school. In those days he was a small boy, so he had a few bricks conveniently stacked up at one corner of the wall to help him over. The bricks were still there. Maybe other boys were using them now as he once did.

The students were struggling through the second class of the day. There was nobody in the school yard. Li Ming made his way to the front gate. Lao Ching was not at his usual place in the shed; probably it was his day to be cleaning guns at the armory. The administration building was a single two storey structure painted a somber gray, built not more than three years before, but already the plaster was peeling off in ugly patches. The school motto, "Propriety, Righteousness, Integrity, Dignity," had obviously received countless coats of new paint: somewhere in the process, the character for *dignity* had lost a stroke. The main office was almost empty of people, all the teachers having gone to their classes. Li Ming quickened his steps as he walked past the principal's office. The room farthest back in the building had a black-colored plate on the door with the designation of some section, town, and district. Ever since this section set up its office, it had taken over this corner of the school's administration building for its use. Li Ming went in. The two employees, sitting cross-legged in an ungentlemanly fashion and reading their newspapers, looked up at the same time.

"Hi, Rooster Kung, haven't seen you for a long time."

"Li Ming! Hey, when did you get back?" Kung Chi-chung got to his feet. He was a tall, thin, weedy-looking young man with a lethargic manner. "Day before yesterday I was at your place. Your old man said you were back for a day and had left again. What's the itch this time?"

"I had to go to Taipei to take care of something."

"You mean your girl, don't you?" Kung Chi-chung laughed. "I just can't believe it, an ordinary young girl has come to mean so much more to you than an old buddy of more than ten years' standing. Dear, dear, what are friends coming to nowadays. Oh, sit down, sit down!"

The other employee brought a chair over. Li Ming thanked him and sat down. Kung Chi-chung offered him a cigarette. They lit their cigarettes, then looked at each other and smiled. Kung Chi-chung leaned over and patted him on the knee. "Hell, I thought you would look like a bamboo pole when you came back, but look how you've put on weight instead. You've really set about stuffing yourself. Boy, do you make me sick! The food on board must be good."

"Not bad, meat and eggs every day, American standard. But what have *you* been doing to yourself? You look vegetable-green."

"Oh, well. It's a long story." Kung Chi-Chung gave the other employee a quick look. "This position is not exactly a money-maker, you know. Right now, I'm stooping to get a mere two-and-a-half pecks of rice, not even five." [10]

The two of them laughed. Then Kung Chi-chung gave himself a brisk tap on the side of the head. "How stupid of me. Let me introduce you two. This is Li Ming. We were in grade school and

[10] The poet T'ao Yüan-ming (A.D. 365–427), referring to the meaningless and unfulfilling life of a government official, once remarked that he was stooping for the meager civil service salary of five pecks of rice.

high school together. A graduate of the Marine Institute—now upgraded as a university, I understand—pursuing his career on a merchant ship as fourth mate, otherwise designated as apprentice-trainee. And this is Chin Chao-nien, also from the Department of International Relations, National Chengchi University, but one year my junior. He is now installed in the august postion of Deputy Director of this Office and concurrently Administrative Secretary plus Three-days-a-week Handyman General. His official standing is just slightly below mine, so you might say 'He sits above ten thousand but looks up to only one.' " [11]

"I have heard of the other official titles, but 'Three-days-a-week Handyman General' is a new one to me."

"You dumb ass! Obviously, as Director of this Office, yours truly takes charge for the remaining three days."

The three men burst out laughing. Li Ming looked at Chin Chao-nien.

"When I was undergoing training on Mount Success, there was a gentleman in the camp by the name of Chin I-nien, or 'Hundred Thousand Years of Gold.' Is he, by any chance . . ."

"He's my elder brother."

"Oh, he was a terrific basketball player. He played for the regiment's team."

"That's him all right. He has always loved basketball. He must have an easy time of it in the army, spending his days playing basketball."

"He must be abroad now?"

"No. He's returned to Chung-hsing University as teaching assistant."

"I see." Li Ming paused. "You two brothers have very uncommon names. Don't you have another older brother called Chin Wan-nien?"

Chin Chao-nien nodded.

Li Ming couldn't help smiling. "Isn't there a Chin I-nien or Chin Yüan-nien as well?" [12]

[11] Idiomatic expression referring to the position of a prime minister.
[12] The two names mean, respectively, "one year of gold" and "the first year of the Golden reign." Li Ming is teasing Chin Chao-nien, whose name denotes "one million years of gold." The names of his two brothers are Chin I-nien,

"No. There are only three of us in the family."

"They come from a family that believed in planned parenthood," Kung Chi-chung interrupted. "Three is just the right number: ten thousand, a hundred thousand, a million, that is perfect calculation; one more will break the order, one less will make it meaningless."

"How will one more break the order? What about 'Chin Ching-nien'?"

"What Chin Chin-nien, Yin Yin-nien? What are you talking about?"

"I said 'Ching' as in 'Pei-ching.' Ten millions makes a 'ching.' " [13]

"Oh well," Kung Chi-chung said. "It doesn't have the ring of a name anyway. Three is just right."

"By the way, when you were in the Marine Institute, did you know a Ch'en Ch'i-jen?" Chin Chao-nien asked.

"Oh yes. But we were in different departments. I was in Navigation, he was in Management, so we didn't know each other that well. You know him?"

"He is my cousin."

"He has a very attractive girl friend."

"Yes. Her name is Ho Mei-hui, if I remember correctly. She was supposed to be campus beauty queen, too."

"Ho Mei-hui?" Kung Chi-chung interjected, eyebrows raised. "I know Ho Mei-hui. Come to think of it, I had an interest in her at one time. Are you telling me that actually Chin's cousin had landed her already?"

"That was settled ages ago, so don't you start having ideas."

"So one less eligible maiden for me. What rotten luck!"

"It just seems so incredible," Li Ming said. "In a place like Taiwan, no matter who you come across, if the fellow is about

meaning "hundred thousand years of gold," and Chin Wan-nien, meaning "ten thousand years of gold." The Chinese characters for "one" (*i*) and "hundred thousand" (*i*) are homonyms.

[13] Kung Chi-chung feigns mistaking Li Ming to have said *chin* (gold); hence the joke "Chin Chin-nien, Yin Yin-nien," literally "gold-gold-years, silver-silver-years."

your age, you're bound to discover some connection between you before two words are out: if you are not relatives, then you must be mutual friends of some third person."

"Right," Kung Chi-chung punctuated. The three broke out almost simultaneously, "Taiwan is such a small place!"

"Taiwan is such a small place," repeated Kung Chi-chung. "There's too little room and too many officials, so we end up the way we are. Distinguished graduates in International Relations from Chengta [14]—mind you, Chengta's Department of International Relations is no crummy joint—men with qualifications and ability like us, end up only division-nine officials, worth just ten piculs of rice a year. . . And to get even this much," he added, "you have to have ways and means."

Ever since he was in junior high, Kung Chi-chung had demonstrated his literary and artistic talents. Thanks to him, Li Ming's class used to win every one of the school's display-board competitions. Likewise, in essay competitions, it was Kung Chi-chung who took all the prizes. When he was attending senior high, his articles were already appearing in the literary supplement of the local papers. At one time too, he actively participated in the editing of pamphlets and miscellaneous literature for the local branch of the Organization for the Recovery of the Motherland. He showed all the signs of becoming an outstanding writer. Who would have thought that in the end, all that this experience and competence would lead to was a division-nine post?

"Well, why don't you have a go at one of the special recruitment examinations for diplomatic personnel? If you make it, you can go abroad."

"Why bother? Even if I made it, it would mean two monotonous years in the Ministry of Foreign Affairs before I could even have a chance to be sent abroad. And even if I were sent abroad, would I be better off? At best, it would just be an opportunity to go abroad."

"Don't you even want to go abroad?"

"I am too lazy to move," Kung Chi-chung yawned. "Anyway,

[14] Short for "Kuo-li *Cheng*-chi *Ta*-hsüeh," National Cheng-chi University.

when you have left the country, what then? Look at yourself. Haven't you been abroad often enough? What you gained from it all?"

"My kind of going abroad and what we are talking about are two different things."

"The way I see it, there isn't much difference. You go away to see more of the world, to add to your experience, that's all there is to it. But I am a *hsiu-tsai*, [15] you know, and I am supposed to know everything there is to know between heaven and earth without taking a step beyond the door of my house, so what can I get out of leaving the country? The ancients left home to seek knowledge, the moderns leave home to emigrate. As they said of old, you should attend to your filial obligations and move only when your parents are no longer alive. I have an aged mother to care for, a tender sister to protect. So I stay put."

"Sounds reasonable. If what you say is true," Li Ming said, "Then I'd better give up my seaman's job and retire to the mountains."

"That's a way, too! Anyway," Kung Chi-chung heaved a sigh, "when all is said, no matter what your work is, the idea is the same: just to keep alive. What else could we do? If it weren't for this, I wouldn't have to break my back for a meager two-and-a-half pecks of rice."

Li Ming fell silent. After a brief pause Kung Chi-chung said, "Let's go see Jumbo."

"I thought he'd been sent to teach in Taipei."

"A man of his caliber? You must be joking! As it is, he's lucky after being sent to the south to have been able to get himself transferred here."

"I suppose he got our old principal to help him."

"Of course. As the saying goes, 'A single day of discipleship will foster an everlasting bond between teacher and pupil.' " Kung Chi-chung stood up. "He doesn't have classes in the morning. He'll be in his quarters, so let's go."

Li Ming exchanged some small talk with Chin Chao-nien and then went out of the office with Kung Chi-chung. On the play-

[15] *Hsiu-tsai* as used in this context is one type of traditional Chinese scholar.

ground a class of junior grade youngsters were doing their physical training exercises. The instructor kept blowing his whistle, and the little urchins were vigorously standing up, bending down, standing up, bending down, without being given a moment's rest.

"Rooster, there are many things about this office of yours I won't try to flatter you about, but I must say you have a highly qualified staff. Take the two of you, both university graduates."

"I am here because I had no other way. Chin Chao-nien is here because he had his way."

"How do you mean?"

"His father is a member of some government committee or other. If they don't have their way, who does?"

"Oh? . . . But then what's he here for, in this out-of-the-way backyard?"

"Well, he broke up with his girlfriend and became pretty down in spirit, I suppose," Kung Chi-chung explained in a casual tone of voice. "So he came to this isolated 'backyard' to recuperate. 'Shutting himself off from the world to reflect upon his mistakes, and cultivating the health of his spirit,' so to speak."

Li Ming couldn't help laughing. "He is quite an affable fellow, like some character from one of those pulp novels. The beginning of the tale is promising. Has it got a sequel?"

"Has it got one! The story goes that as soon as our handsome young hero arrived in this rustic desolation, he picked up a 'blooming wild lily growing beside his path, a young and lovelorn creature, with dreamy eyes and cool, delicate hands.' Our heroine, in the proper style of *The View From the Window*, was a grade-twelve student. Various scenes from the *Western Chamber* have been enacted already—'Transfixed on Encountering the Beauty,' 'Serenade for Seduction,' 'Secret Betrothal in the Rear Garden.' The stage is set now, I suppose, for 'The Cross-examination.' "

"Anyway, this is really making the best of one's situation, and the story will have a happy ending this time, I expect."

"The trouble is, it may not. When the girl gets knocked up, you may find it a bit difficult to see a happy ending."

"Then he becomes a cad! Why didn't you talk to him before?"

"Why should I put my nose into other people's affairs?" Kung

Chi-chung shrugged his shoulders. "I'm not sure at all he would have listened even if I had talked to him. As long as it's not my sister that's knocked up, why should I bother? If he had fooled around with my sister, then it would be different, of course; then I would have chopped him up into little pieces. Well, that is Kung Chi-chung's philosophy, for what it's worth."

"You are taking an increasingly cynical view of life."

"If I don't amuse myself with playing cynic, how am I going to pass the long days?"

Jumbo's room was at the end of the second row of bachelor quarters for the teaching staff. Kung Chi-chung knocked at the door. Jumbo poked his head out, gave a delighted laugh, and said, "There you are! When I got up this morning, I broke my tea-cup for no apparent reason. Filled with apprehension, I cast a divination, and drew the Diagram of Earth which reads, 'Friends gained in the south-west, lost in the north-east.' That's how I knew that today I was going to receive friends from distant lands. Uncanny divination, don't you think?"

"There goes our street-corner Taoist with his mumbo-jumbo again," Kung Chi-chung scoffed. "Even if you are right, you've got half of it straight. Friends gained in the south-west, that I can see. But what's the nonsense about friends lost in the north-east?"

"The loss of friends in the north-east has already come to pass. As for gaining friends in the south-west, isn't that materializing at this very moment? Furthermore it is said that the loss of friends in the north-east will bring much rejoicing, which is to say that the said loss is the ill luck that ushers in good fortune. Don't you remember the reports that Lao Ch'eng had stepped on a mine in Quemoy and killed himself? We were even making the funeral arrangements when out of the blue he dropped in on us, as lively as a cricket. That, in short, is the story of how a friend was lost in the north-east." Jumbo guffawed.

"Quemoy is not in the north-east. Who are you fooling?"

Jumbo turned out both palms of his hands in a gesture of defeat: "If everyone were as full of scruples as you, there would be no place for fortune tellers."

"You have lost weight again, Jumbo," Li Ming said. "You don't look like an elephant anymore. You are beginning to look more like a scrawny mule."

"You expect everyone to look like you—with fat head and flappy ears?" Jumbo patted Li Ming on the shoulder. "My clothes are growing in size everday, but I don't waste tears over that."

"Miss Ch'en is well, I gather?"

"Oh, that's over, for more than two months now."

"No wonder you look thin. What happened? You two were on the point of being hitched for life."

"That's where the trouble started. Anyway, this is what happened. We shilly-shallied for a long time. When it came to showing my hand, her parents asked me if I was able to go abroad. I asked them how they expected someone like me—a penniless schoolteacher who had only recently graduated from the Chinese Department of the National Taiwan Normal University—to be able to go abroad. Then they wanted to know if I was financially sound. I replied that I might be in the future. So they said if that was the case there was no point in pursuing the matter further. To make matters worse, she turned out to be a perfect daughter, not the kind who would argue with her parents. So we parted company. After a month or so, she contracted a long-distance engagement with someone abroad."

"How vulgar," Kung Chi-chung said. "Jumbo here can't even conduct his love affair without falling into the rut of the 'Butterfly and Mandarin Duck' school of fiction. You people who dine on the classics every day haven't got the guts to blaze a path for yourselves."

"Well, tease me as you like. I don't really blame her. What kind of a future would she have with a poor schoolmaster like me? To call it quits is the best possible thing to do. Even if it sounds corny, I still say with all my heart that I wish her all the happiness in the world." There was a note of pain in Jumbo's voice. But being by nature optimistic, he immediately recovered his habitual good humor. "Well, Li Ming, let's talk about you instead. How is Miss Chou doing?"

"What a superfluous question!" Kung Chi-chung cut in. "He's just back from his tryst in Taipei, so what do you expect? Of course, things are fine."

"Things are not exactly fine. She's quite good to me, that's true. I was in Taipei for two days and she went to a lot of trouble to get leave from her work so as to keep me company. But . . . somehow, most of the time she doesn't seem to understand how I feel about most things."

"Tut, tut!" Kung Chi-chung teased, screwing up his face. "Just listen to him. Miss Chou took two days off to keep him company, and he still says, 'She doesn't understand me'! You'd better face the truth. It's you who are after her, so it's up to you to accommodate her. It's you who should try to understand her, and you have the nerve to be whimpering about her not understanding you! That's exactly how a booby like you would behave."

"I also think you are being unreasonable, Li Ming," Jumbo added. "Your head is too stuffed with feudalistic rubbish. You may have hoodwinked others, but you can't hoodwink me. She's a high school graduate and isn't as well educated as you are, so you subconsciously feel that she doesn't measure up to you in anything. She can't understand you because you think you are superior to her in every way. Rooster is right, you are a booby to think like this. Actually, Miss Chou Mei strikes me as a very fine girl. She's more than usually fun-loving, I know, but what young girls don't like to have a bit of fun? What really matters is that she is by nature candid and sincere, clear-headed and practical, and not woolly-headed like most girls. It is really not easy to find someone like her these days. What is all this nonsense about understanding and not understanding; what is it but poison spread by all these stupid stories that glut our book stores? Too many of us now have been infected by this sickness! So long as a man and a woman can be on speaking terms with each other, are not separated by too wide a social gap, and can get along with each other well enough to live together, that's all that's needed. And still, here you are, demanding that one understand how the other's mind works. You'd better look for perfect understanding on the moon!"

"You fellows are forcing a cap on me that doesn't fit!" Li Ming protested. "If I had ever looked down on Chou Mei at all, may I be damned in Heaven's name, may I . . ."

"Don't try to trump up excuses," said Kung Chi-chung cutting him short.

"I'm not trumping up excuses. She doesn't understand me, and I don't say this without having perfectly good reasons."

"Well, I'm afraid you'll have to hold over your complaints for a little while." Jumbo looked at his watch. "I have to go to a staff meeting now, so if you'll excuse me. We'll have to postpone our conversation till we meet again."

"It doesn't make any difference one way or the other whether you attend such meetings or not, does it? It's not often we can get together like this, so don't be a kill-joy," Kung Chi-chung said persuasively. "Summon the courage you always had in skipping all the weekly school gatherings; be your old reckless self just this once again."

"The man of character does not look back on the brave deeds of his past," Jumbo said, with a theatrical gesture of the hands. "Talk, that's where my desire lies; meetings, that's where it does not lie. And yet, I forsake talking for meetings, why? Because I've got my rice-bowl to worry about!"

Smiling good-humoredly, Kung Chi-chung stood up. "Well, if you put it that way, let me not spoil your career for you."

"I have an idea," Li Ming said. "My family has just bought a piece of farming land that has a house to go with it. We can get a few of us together and spend a couple of days there this Saturday. We can swim, play chess, or just talk. What do you think, eh?"

"Good idea," Kung Chi-chung said. "I'm not a busy man, so it's no problem for me. What about you, Jumbo, can you get away for a couple of days?"

"I don't have any class on Saturday. I can make it. We can ask Lao Ch'eng to come along as well. He works in the Railway Administration and comes here to see his girl every week. Hank is in T'ao-yüan and most probably can't come. Oh, yes, there's also Hsiao Yü. He's going away next month and said he would make a trip back before leaving. I can drop him a note about this."

"Then there are five of us already, just like that." Li Ming was excited. "Five old friends in one place for two whole days, swapping memories and old dreams before going on each other's way. Won't that be just great!"

"Ooo . . ." Kung Chi-chung stretched himself lazily. "What a reliving of memories and old dreams. Amen."

5.

"I'm back, Captain." Pockmark Chao was standing outside the wire-netting door, a straw hat in one hand, beaming from ear to ear.

The captain took off his spectacles, put down the newspaper he was reading and stood up. "Come in, Lao Chao. The sun is so strong outside, what are you standing there for?"

At these words, Pockmark Chao pushed open the door and stepped in; then he turned around and very carefully secured the door-latch. Li Ta-sao was just coming from the house, and, seeing her, he burst into a grin of greeting, "Ta-sao, I'm back."

"*Aiya*, it's Lao Chao! Have you had your lunch yet? If you haven't, I'll go make you some."

"I've eaten, thank you, thank you. Don't trouble yourself, Ta-sao."

"Sure? With us, you don't have to stand on ceremony, you know."

"Of course, of course." Pockmark Chao was still standing there, grinning foolishly. "Ta-sao, Hsiao-wu [16] is back, isn't he?"

"He's been back for some time now. In fact, he came back the day you left; you left in the morning, he arrived in the afternoon. He asked about you, and he's brought back two bottles of foreign liquor for you and two for Lao Tung. I joked about it to him. It's the perfect gift for Lao Tung, I said, but you should have brought Lao Chao something else. Lao Chao isn't much of a drinker. But he smiled and said he didn't think of that when he bought it. Well, just take these small gifts as his way of saying that he still remembers old friends. We always thought he was such an awkward, muddle-headed child. But after a long trip from home, he has matured a lot and become very considerate. He brought his father a Jamaica-made cigarette holder and a good-quality lighter, an overcoat for me, plenty of cosmetics for his elder sister and a Japanese doll for his little sister, besides things for you and relatives. As for himself, he didn't buy a single thing. I asked him why, and he said, 'The next time, Mother, I'll buy something for myself, but this being my first trip abroad, I ought to get you people the things you like.' He's put himself to so much trouble. . . ."

"Come, Lao Chao, sit down. Don't just stand there as if you were glued to the ground."

---

[16] Literally "Little Fifth," the fifth of the siblings in a family. It is an affectionate or familial form of address, referring here to Li Ming.

"Sure, sure." Pockmark Chao sat down, still gripping his straw hat in his hand. "I must thank Hsiao-wu properly. Is he home?"

"No, he's out again," Li Ta-sao said. "He went to the country with those buddies of his early in the morning. Said they would be staying there for a few days. Last night, he kept pestering me to cook this and that for him. I said, in this hot weather, food can't keep and you will have to finish it in a hurry. He said there were quite a few of them, that the food was not enough to last them even a day, and the next day they would have to do their own cooking. Well, all his friends have big appetites, Hsiao-wu too— they are young people after all. The day before, we made some three hundred dumplings for some guests that Hsiao-wu had over, and the five or six of them cleaned up the lot at one sitting. It makes me happy to see the way they eat. I said, 'Hsiao-wu, when you are away . . .' "

"T'ai-t'ai, [17] go and make a cup of tea for Lao Chao, will you? He must be very hot and thirsty having come all this way."

"It . . . it's all right. Don't trouble yourself, Ta-sao."

"Let me get you a bowl of iced almond bean-curd. I made a pot of it for Hsiao-wu yesterday, but he said it was too watery and troublesome to carry. You'll have a bowl too, Chen-chih?"

"Yes, I think I'll have some. More sugar for me, please."

Swaying this way and that, Li Ta-sao went into the house. The captain looked at Lao Chao, and his solemn face broke into a smile. "How is it, Lao Chao? Has everything gone smoothly with you? Judging from your looks, I'd say it has."

Pockmark Chao chuckled, "Captain, you've guessed right. It's this I've come to see you about." He looked quickly around to make sure they were alone, then leaned forward and said in a low voice, "Thirty thousand for the one with two eyes, fifteen thousand for the one with one eye; which is the better, eh, Captain?"

"What're you talking about?"

"It's the betrothal money I mean, Captain."

"Oh, the betrothal money. You said thirty thousand for the one with two eyes, fifteen thousand for the one with one eye?"

[17] Form of direct address for one's wife.

"Yes, yes," Pockmark Chao nodded with some vehemence. "That's what I mean. I was in the south as you know, looking for someone suitable, and I met these two families that I like very much; there is this girl from one of the families, only eighteen or nineteen, not bad-looking at all, and she can read and write; it's not easy these days to find a girl like her. Her family wanted thirty thousand dollars before they would give the girl away. The girl from the other family is just over twenty, not bad-looking either; the only snag is that one of her eyes is damaged. Her family said that she got the damaged eye from playing with fire-crackers when she was small. She is a very able girl, can do heavy work as well as sew and embroider. Her family said that it's because she has a damaged eye and her looks are spoiled that they are asking for only fifteen thousand as betrothal money. I thought this over for a long, long time, you know. This family is asking for only fifteen thousand. That's a real bargain, but then the girl has only one eye. The girl from the other family is really not bad at all, but then the betrothal money is twice as much. If I marry her, it will mean spending every cent that I've saved all these years. That's a bit hard to take. I've been thinking of one girl, and then of the other, and the more I think the more mixed-up I am. I don't know what I should do. That's why I've come back to ask your advice, Captain. I hope Captain can make up my mind for me."

"Oh, so that's the story." The captain stroked his nose, but stopped talking as Li Ta-sao came out carrying a tray.

"Come, Lao Chao, try this bowl of almond bean-curd. It will cool you. Chen-chih, there's sugar in it; if it's not sweet enough, you can add more."

"Thank you, Ta-sao."

The two men took up their bowls. Li Ta-sao sat down by herself.

"Lao Chao, is it hot in the South?"

"It's hot, very hot. It's too hot even to wear singlets. It's much hotter than here."

"How many days were you in the South?"

"Let me see." Pockmark Chao rolled up his eyes and began counting on his fingers. "I left last Thursday and came back yesterday night. One day, two days, three days . . . eight days altogether."

"So you were around a great deal, weren't you? Found someone you like?"

"Hee, hee," Pockmark Chao chuckled.

"Look how happy you are. You must have found her. What's she like? Everything satisfactory? How much betrothal money did her family ask for?"

"T'ai-t'ai," the captain put down his bowl. "I still have something to talk over with Lao Chao, so could you please clear away the bowls?"

"So that's how it is," Li Ta-sao sounded displeased. "You two want to keep me out of this, don't you? But this is exactly where I can be of help, can't you see? Chen-chih is a man, what does he know about such things? Don't you agree with me, Lao Chao?"

"T'ai-t'ai!"

"All right, all right! I won't bother you, if that's what you want." Li Ta-sao snatched up the tray angrily. "Don't forget that it was I who suggested the idea of going to the South. Now that everything has turned out well, you want to keep me out. What a way to thank people!"

As Pockmark Chao watched Li Ta-sao hurry into the house, his face assumed a look of uneasiness.

"I . . . I owe Li Ta-sao an apology."

"Don't you worry about her. She can't keep anything to herself. If she knows about this, then it won't be long before everyone else knows about it too, and that may not be what we want. We'll let her know when everything has been worked out. What's the hurry?" The captain took out his cigarette holder and inserted a "Double Happiness." "Lao Chao, I've been trying just now to analyze what you've told me, and I've come up with a few points which you might think over. As for deciding what to do, I'll leave that to you. Is that all right?"

"Sure! sure!" Pockmark Chao nodded several times in agreement.

The captain took the lighter from the coffee table, lit his cigarette and then handed the lighter to Pockmark Chao.

"What do you think of this lighter and cigarette-holder? Not bad, eh? They're from Hsiao-wu."

"Oh yes, this is a really classy lighter. You have a very filial son in Hsiao-wu, Captain."

"Hm . . ." The captain blew out a long stream of smoke, without adding any comment. After a pause, he spoke in a serious manner. "Right, I'll go over what you've told me and what I make of it so you'll have a clearer picture of the situation.

"First . . . er, for the sake of convenience, let us call the family that asked for thirty thousand betrothal money Family A, and the other Family B. First, let's examine the question of the money. Family A asks you for thirty thousand dollars, while Family B asks you for fifteen thousand, that is, only half of what A wants. So from the point of view of the money alone, Family B is a much better bargain by far, right? So Side B—I mean, Family B—is one up on that score.

"Point two, the question of expenses. To get married, you have to take care of a number of things besides the betrothal money— decorating the bridal chamber, buying new furniture, the dinner party. These things cost quite a bit, you know. At a very conservative estimate, I would put these expenses at around twenty thousand. Oh, you would get back a decent sum in money-gifts, that's true, but don't forget, Lao Chao, that all our friends are poor folk, and he would have to be a very close friend indeed who will come up with a gift of, say, eighty or one hundred dollars. So, even supposing you can get back fifteen thousand in money-gifts, you still need to have five or six thousand on hand. If your choice is Family A, you'll have to be prepared to spend thirty-five thousand for your marriage. Right? If your choice is Family B, then you might just scrape through with twenty thousand. It's been a hard life for you all these seven or eight years and it's not been easy to come by this kind of money. If, in order to contract this marriage, you not only spend all your money but end up brooding on a pile of debts, do you think it's worth it? So this is where Family B scores again.

"Point three, the question of the girls' looks. You said that the girl from Family A is good-looking, that the girl from Family B has a damaged eye. At first hearing this seems to indicate that Family B is not as good a bet as Family A. But think carefully. You, Lao Chao, are a noodle-stall owner. What does a person like you want such a pretty wife for? I ask you, aren't you just inviting trouble? Take Kao Te-sheng, who married last year. He got himself a beautiful wife all right, a lady-marker at a billiard parlor. Everyone was green with envy at the wedding. And now, look what's happened. She's run away with some bum! Kao Te-sheng abandoned his restaurant to go after her in Taipei. But how is he going to get her to come back? And even if he manages to get her back, what does a woman like her know about contentment and duty? Sooner or later, she would run away again. If you marry this kind of woman, won't you be just asking for trouble?

"The girl from Family B has a damaged eye, but that is precisely what is good about her. It's a guarantee that once she's married to you, she won't have strange fancies in her head, but will stick with you through thick and thin. On top of that, she can do heavy work as well as sew and embroider; she'll be a very valuable helper. What do you need a wife who can read and write like a scholar for? So long as she can look after the family properly, bear your children, continue the line of your family and pay respects to your ancestors, you've got all you want. Doesn't that make sense?"

Pockmark Chao was listening to this exposition with intense concentration, sitting motionless with mouth agape and eyes in a wide stare. As soon as the captain finished talking, he sprang up with alacrity and grabbed the captain's hand.

"Captain, what you've just said is so . . . so very true! Actually, I felt more or less the same way, but after you've explained everything, it's all become perfectly clear to me. I'll go to the South at once and deliver the betrothal money, just . . . just to make sure no one's gotten ahead of me. Hee, hee! Thank you, Captain. Thank you . . ."

6.

They were sitting or standing about lazily in the shade of the trees. Lao Ch'eng and Jumbo picked up a few small stones to keep the paper chess-board down; they were about to continue their mammoth battle of a hundred rounds. Kung Chi-chung was on one side, acting as referee. Li Ming was lying on the grass with eyes closed. Hsiao Yü, seated some distance away, surveyed the distant view of the valley below. The air was heavy with silence. Occasionally, a stray breeze would set the leaves of the trees rustling gently. All of a sudden, Lao Ch'eng clapped his hands and burst into a triumphant crow of laughter.

"Aha! A double-rook check, you're done for!"

"Wait a minute, wait a minute." There was a note of panic in Jumbo's voice. "Where did that rook come from?"

"It was moved from the left flank. It's a straight game, and it's checkmate. Don't you try any tricks."

"Rubbish! Your rook was sacrificed for my knight ages ago."

"That was in the last game. My rook has been moving unchallenged throughout the game, very cleverly camouflaged. What sacrifice are you talking about? Checkmate, checkmate. Rooster, what's the score now?"

"Eighteen to five," Kung Chi-chung announced. "Hey, Jumbo, do you still have the face to go on, after all this? Better get off the hook now and let me have a bash at it with Lao Ch'eng."

"Can't be done. We agreed on one hundred games, so let's finish the hundred."

"What a heel! You sit on the toilet without a single bowel movement, just so no one can use it!"

"It's all right with me," said Lao Ch'eng, "if he doesn't mind being thoroughly licked. Come on, let's set up the pieces once more."

They became quiet again. In the silence Li Ming heard the strains of a folk song coming from the nearby woods. The tune came and went with the falling and rising of the breeze until, after some minutes, the voice of the singer trailed away into the distance, leaving behind the dull tap-tapping sound of a tree being cut down.

"Axe on wood tap-a-tapping,
Birds in the air chirp-a-chirping,
Out of the silence of the dark valley
They move to the lofty trees." [18]

As Jumbo was thus changing, he suddenly broke out, "There! Watch my rook. Check!"

"What's the excitement? A move to the side, that will fix it."

"A move to the side, eh? That won't help you. Check again."

"What check?"

"With my knight of course. Have you gone blind all of a sudden?"

[18] From the Book of Songs.

"No. Forward."

"Once moved away from the palace, the king is either sick or dead."

"No matter. 'To brandish the sword one great pleasure brings: / Do not fail the valiant dreams of youth'!" [19]

"Good. I'll grant your wish then. One more time, check . . . Wait, that won't do, that won't do. I can't check like that."

"You made a move, and that's it. A man of honor doesn't go back on his word."

"But my hand is still on my piece!"

"You took your hand away just now. Don't make excuses. You've made your move, and that's that."

"No, no, that won't do. A disastrous move. I can't make this check."

"Cheat. Hey, referee!"

"Mother's!" Kung Chi-chung gave a big yawn. "One point each: nineteen to six. What sort of a kiddy game do you think you guys are playing anyway? Yelling, fighting, and grabbing each other's pieces . . . What! You dare beat the referee? Help, help!"

"We'll show you, you foreigner's lackey, you turncoat, you comprador, you running-dog!" Jumbo caught hold of one of Kung Chi-chung's legs. "Here, Lao Ch'eng, grab the other leg. Let's give him the treatment, let him taste his 'tortoise straining to look at the moon.' "

"With pleasure! Aha, Rooster, who would have known that your day would finally come?"

Gripping his legs at the ankles, they forced them backwards over his head until the feet touched the ground. Kung Chi-chung was curled up like a dried shrimp, and hollering in pain. It was from some stories of the martial arts that Kung Chi-chung first learned of this form of punishment. And ever since, whenever they were in high spirits, "tortoise straining to look at the moon" had been a favorite trick the old friends played on one another.

[19] The quote is from a poem written by the political figure Wang Ching-wei (1883–1944). The complete text, as translated by Anthony C. Yu, is:
With ardor I sang through markets of Yen;
Calmly I became the captive of Ts'u.
To brandish the sword one great pleasure brings:
Do not fail the valiant dreams of youth.

"*Ai-ya! Ai-ya!* Let me go, let me go. You're killing me."

"All right, we'll ease up a bit. Recovering your breath now? Now, tell us, can you see the moon?"

"No, there's no moon."

"No moon, eh? Partner, give him the works again!"

"Hold it, hold it. I can see the moon now, I really can!"

"What does it look like?"

"Round."

"Round? Look again."

"Crescent?"

"No. Take another peep."

"Hold it! I can see it now. It's square, yes, it's square."

"That's better. Okay, let's spare his dog life this time."

The two of them released their hold. Kung Chi-chung turned over and lay on the ground to catch his breath. Jumbo stood on one side looking down at him and shaking his head.

"You're slipping, Rooster. How come you give in so fast? You used to be able to stand at least five minutes."

"Well, I'm no longer young now." Kung Chi-chung scrambled up. "Even my joints are turning stiff. A few years from now, if we still play this game, you'll have to be ready to dig my grave."

"Probably there's another reason," Lao Ch'eng interrupted. "You've lost your burning enthusiasm to uphold the truth."

"Oh, well, what can I do? Even Copernicus can't face up to it, not to mention a weakling like me." Kung Chi-chung smiled. "Come to think of it, the moon can be square, you know. That will make the poets mad with joy. Just think! Won't it be exquisite fun hunting for adjectives to describe a square moon?"

Hsiao-yü came over quickly from where he had been sitting.

"Hey, Li Ming, get up."

"What's the matter?" Li Ming sat up.

"I have just been watching a farmer working on the hill-slope down below," Hsiao-yü said with a note of excitement in his voice. "You know what he did? First, he dug up the ground to about a meter deep. After that, he turned over the soil, carefully picked up the stones, which he carried to one side, and then he filled the ground up with the soil again. He worked like this all morning. Those large pieces of rock over there were dug up by him just now."

"That's right," Li Ming said. "The land in these hills is dry and full of rocks. It is possible to plant trees, but grain just won't grow. You have to dig up all the rocks first, loosening up the earth, before you can start planting grain."

"Such a clumsy way of doing things! How much soil can he turn over in one day? A few square meters. It'll take years before he's finished."

"Look before you start criticizing. See that stretch of the slope further down covered with terrace after terrace of fields? He carved it all out by himself in that clumsy way you described just now."

"You don't say!" Hsiao-yü stuck his tongue out in disbelief. "He must be a truly remarkable fellow to have cleared such a vast piece of land! Like the legendary old man removing the mountain."

"You see before you the fruit of thirty years' work. All these thirty years, he has lived in that thatched hut over there, every day digging up the rocks and carrying them away, and by sheer persistence clearing up this land for cultivation. People around here call him Kid Stone."

"Kid Stone. A very fitting name," Jumbo said. "Are your folks planning on doing the same thing, Li Ming?"

"Oh, no. We're thinking of planting various types of fruit-trees. Fruit-trees will grow well in this kind of soil as the roots can develop firmly. They're no problem."

"But what about fertilizers? How are you going to get them in?"

"Fertilizers . . ." Li Ming scratched his head. "I can't say, but there must be a way. I'll have to go back and find out more about that."

"I don't understand you and your folks," Jumbo said. "I had the impression that you wanted to come here to start a farm. Now that you've got your land, you don't come to look after it. Won't the land go to waste like this?"

"What do you mean we don't look after the land?" Li Ming was annoyed. "Hasn't Lao Tung been staying up here in the hills for the past two days? He's going down only today to meet my father. As for my father, he'll be here soon enough; when he's bought all the tools, seeds, and fertilizers he needs. And then they'll be living here in the hills all the time. In what way are we neglecting the land?"

"That's fine then, fine," Jumbo said in a conciliatory tone.

"Don't be offended. I asked out of friendly concern, that's all. I feel . . . that farming is not like any other work. You can't take up farming just for fun. To be a farmer, you have to work really hard like Kid Stone, otherwise it'll be no use at all. If you go about it just for kicks you wouldn't make it."

"For kicks? My father's put everything he's got on this one throw; he's sold his grocery store even. Do you call this kicks?"

"No, of course not. I apologize for saying that, all right?"

"Li Ming," Hsiao-yü said. "I am very much with you for coming to these hills to start a farm. There's no doubt in my mind that we are rooted in the earth. If we are away from the soil, it is impossible for us to take roots. Modern man's constant feelings of loss, frustration, and anguish can, I think, be traced to his alienation from the soil."

"That's the way my father feels . . . Of course, he can't put it the way you do, but he has lived those experiences of confusion and rootlessness that you're referring to; that's exactly the way he feels."

"I can believe that Li Ming's old man feels like that," Kung Chi-chung interrupted. "But I don't believe that Hsiao-yü can feel like that. It is true that Hsiao-yü has dwelled long enough in his ivory tower, and he has read widely in philosophy. But does he have genuine feelings for the earth as he puts it? I don't believe he does."

"You shouldn't doubt my sincerity. My feelings are genuine. Heaven is my witness."

"If you really feel like that about the land, then why do you have to go abroad?"

"You think I want to go that much?" Hsiao-yü said. "Then you've got me wrong. Of course, if I said that I don't want to go abroad at all, I wouldn't be honest with myself. All my friends have gone one after the other; you can't expect me to be different. Universities abroad are better equipped, have better facilities and offer a healthier research environment. It wouldn't be true to say that I am not attracted at all. But if it is possible for me to remain here to do research, then I will absolutely not leave."

"There is a graduate program in your department. Why don't you study there?"

"It's not good enough."

"So what are we talking about?" Kung Chi-chung smiled. "We've been talking nonsense all this time."

"That's not true." Hsiao-yü's face flushed. "When I have completed my studies, I will come back to help reorganize our graduate program so that young people in the future can remain here for advanced studies without having to go through what I have to go through, far away from home."

"Bravo! Everybody get this. Hsiao-yü has signed a post-dated check. Let's see if it does cash twenty years from now."

"That's enough. Let's stop this squabbling. Anyone who says another word will meet immediate execution!" Lao Ch'eng barked. "Let's go back and have some lunch. In the afternoon, we can go to the creek for a dip; we need to stretch ourselves a bit."

After a meal of fried noddles, they went down the hill in a group. Halfway down the slope, they passed a pavilion in which were seated several strongly-built men sipping tea. Along the narrow lane outside the pavilion, a few wooden carts were lined up, each loaded with several large tree-trunks.

"Look at that!" Hsiao-yü stuck his tongue out again. "Can you imagine the momentum of these vehicles moving down-hill with that huge load on them? What a time these poor men must have with those carts!"

"They work in the timber yard back there. Every day they have to travel up and down six or seven times and each round trip means five or six kilometers over hilly ground."

"My! My! If I were to do it, I could at most manage a single trip."

"Don't make me laugh," Kung Chi-chung put in. "If you could manage to make a single trip with a load like that, Hsiao-yü, I'd drink up all the water in the creek."

"Ah yes, the aborigines in this area have a legend which tells of how a Frog Spirit once drank up all the water of the creek. In the end the aborigines became so thirsty they couldn't bear it any longer. So they sent their bravest man to kill the Frog Spirit. After the Frog Spirit was killed, his body lay as that hill facing us."

They all looked up, and sure enough the hill they saw was roughly shaped like a frog.

"Phew! I take back my words. It would be no fun to be killed and changed into Mount Rooster."

"You?" Ch'eng teased. "You'd be changed into a heap of mud at most. And as a gesture of our long-standing friendship, we'd formally name it the Fallen Phoenix Mound, offer libations and sacrificial notes."

They reached the foot of the hill and continued on their way past a small paddy field, then across the pebble-strewn floor of a semi-parched river-bed until they came to a small beach, a sandy stretch formed by the curve that the creek made at this point in its course. They changed into swimming trunks and jumped into the creek. The water swirled in eddies around them. Li Ming let himself be carried by the current across to the other side of the creek. He lifted his head and saw a truck far off crawling on its way, like a ladybug, along the ribbon of road stitched around the waist of the mountain facing him. Looking up from the bottom of the valley, he saw the mountains rising to a more breathtaking height and the thick green underbrush seemed to extend to the very edge of the sky to merge with the azure blue of the heavens. He lay down on a sun-baked slab of stone, watched through narrowed eyes the drifting clouds, and listened to the rhythmic sound of running waters beside him. On the opposite shore, Jumbo could be heard softly chanting Li Po's "Early Departure from Pai-ti City":

> I left Pai-ti in the morning swathed in the colored mists of dawn,
> Reaching Chiang-ling in but one day, journey of a thousand miles.
> On the two shores of the waterway gibbons cried ceaselessly,
> My boat sailed swiftly through the folds of ten thousand hills.

Li Ming closed his eyes. He felt happy.

7.

As he stepped out of the station, a blast of yellow dust hit Li Ming in the face so that he had to shut his eyes tight. With knapsack on his back, and his shoulder turned against the wind, he waited till the dust and sand had blown over before he dared open them. Then he walked slowly towards the banyan tree in front of the station. The hot air came in waves. A thick layer of yellow dust had settled on the glass cupboards in the food-and-drink shops that lined both sides of the road. Flies remained glued to the glass without the least sign of movement, and one could just make out a few dim shapes inside the shops huddled up in the shadows. Two pedicabs were standing at the foot of the banyan tree. A man lay stretched across one of the pedicabs, snoring heavily, his shoulders bare, and a cap thrown over his face. The other driver was nowhere to be seen. Li Ming walked over to the occupied vehicle, put his knapsack down on the ground beside it and wiped the grimy sweat from his face.

"Hey, friend, mind taking me to Tung-ta New Village?"

Bare Shoulders stirred, then lifted his cap from his eyes and gave Li Ming a side-long glance. Just as Li Ming was thinking that the face looked familiar, Bare Shoulders jumped up smiling.

"Hsiao-wu! What brings you here at this time?"

"Lao Tung, it's you!" He cried in delight and shook the other man's hand vigorously. "What a surprise. I thought you were with father at the farm. How come you are back here pedalling?"

"Oh, I . . . a friend of mine had to go to Ma-kung, so I offered to stand in for him for a couple of days, to earn a few extra dollars. Why are you here all of a sudden? You should have dropped us a line to let us know beforehand."

"I decided to come back quite suddenly. Our ship was in Japan for some major repairs and we were supposed to be stuck there for a fortnight. Luckily our shipmate's banana boat was about to leave for Taiwan, so I got a passage from him. I landed at Kao-hsiung and came up north by train the same night. That's why I didn't have time to write."

"This will be a very happy surprise for Captain and Ta-sao. No one expects you to be back so soon."

"How are they?"

"Fine, they are fine. Let me take you to your place."

So saying, Lao Tung picked up the knapsack and placed it in the pedicab. Li Ming jumped in. Lao Tung gave the brake-shaft a push and began to pedal along the only asphalt road in the small town. The surface of the road was as uneven as ever, and the pedicab staggered from side to side as it went rattling over the potholes and battled with the occasional gusts of sand-laden wind.

Sometimes Lao Tung had to stand up on the pedals and push with all his strength, making the muscles on his tanned calves stand out like whip-cord.

"What a terrible wind. It's been such a long time since I've been through anything like this. Can't say I'm used to it!"

"You said it. Driving a pedicab for the last two days has been torture. Every day you finish up with hair and face caked with dust or mud. It's no bloody fun, I tell you!"

"Weren't you happy helping my father with the farm, Lao Tung? Why take on all this trouble?"

Just then, they reached a bad stretch of road, so Lao Tung pedalled over it standing up. When the vehicle had steadied, he sat down again.

"Well, Hsiao-wu, to be very frank with you, Captain's farm has folded already."

"What! Folded? Father did write to tell me that the yield was poor, but he didn't mention anything about folding."

"It's folded. We didn't have the experience, and we didn't have enough help. Every time we had to do the picking, we couldn't finish the job, and of what we did manage to pick, half would have rotted before we were finished with the packing. This is for the kumquats. As for the tea, it was worse. We had to pay hired hands to help with the picking, and even then it was hopeless. The tea too, was of low quality and didn't fetch much in the market. We never made any profit. It was loss all the way. When I saw what was happening, I said to myself, well, this can't go on like this, I can't go on dining off Captain's table and living off his pocket. That's how you find me here, pedalling for a living again."

"Where's Father now? Is he still on the hill?"

"No. He's moved down and has opened a grocery store. This time we were really lucky to have a friend like Pockmark Chao. He lent us his savings so Captain could have the capital to open his store and I the money to pay for the deposit for my pedicab. It is in times like this that you know who your friends really are. None of my meat-and-wine friends would lend us a cent, only Pockmark Chao came up with help."

"And the land? Is it still ours?"

"No. It's sold, and a good thing it was. Captain didn't lose much, and the money he got was enough to pay off his debts and to take out a lease on the grocery store."

"Who did he sell the land to?"

"To Kid Stone, the fellow on the other side of the hill who spends the whole day, from morning till night, turning up the soil . . ."

"Yes, I know who you mean."

Lao Tung gave the brakeshaft a pull as the pedicab negotiated a curve. They were now on a mud track.

"Hsiao-wu, when you see Captain in a moment, please try your best not to ask too many questions. If he brings up the subject, just ask a couple of questions as a matter of course. As a result of this business he's been in very low spirits lately."

"I know. Thank you, Lao Tung. I'm so sorry we brought you to this state, with all your money gone . . ."

"Don't say that! I had a pedicab before, and I still have one now! Even if I did lose a bit, what is money after all but a paper game? I didn't have any with me when I came into the world, I can do without any when I leave it, so you can see, it's no great matter to cry over. When Captain asked me to go with him, he was in fact giving me the break of my life; it's I who couldn't thank him enough for his concern. The farm failed, it's true, but it's just our rotten luck that we got this damned piece of rock-land. Otherwise, who knows, we might have hit it rich by now."

The vehicle came to a stop in front of the bamboo hedge of the house. Li Ming jumped down from his seat. Lao Tung was already pushing open the wooden door and shouting into the house.

"Ta-sao, Hsiao-wu is back!"

In a moment, Li Ta-sao had hurried out, her hands still white with flour. After Li Ming's filial greetings, Li Ta-sao held on to his arm, her eyes brimming and lips trembling until she suddenly burst into tears.

"You are thinner, Hsiao-wu," she said between her sobs. "Did you have a hard time at sea?"

"You are imagining things. Every time I'm back, you say I'm thinner. But I've put on more muscle each time."

"Who says Hsiao-wu is thin!" Lao Tung added. "He's darker, yes, but that makes him look ever tougher."

"Where's Father?"

"He's at the shop, not very far from here. Hsiao-wu, your father and I didn't manage to write you in time. Our land . . ."

"Lao Tung told me about it already. You don't have to say anything, Mother."

"*Ai!*" Tears began streaming down her face again. "On account of this, your father has aged by the day, and more of his hair has turned white. It's all for nothing in the end. If he had listened to me at the start, then things wouldn't have ended up like this. Your father thought my opinions were only a woman's scruples. Actually, a farmer's life is not a steady kind of life. I saw that from the start."

"Mother, let's not cry over this any more. Things didn't turn out too badly really, and we didn't lose that much. Though the money is gone, the good thing is that Father no longer has to wear his heart out over his piece of rocky land."

"Hsiao-wu is right," put in Lao Tung. "I'll have to go and make a couple of runs more, Ta-sao. You two have a good talk."

"Thank you for driving Hsiao-wu here. You will come for dinner tonight, won't you? And, yes, since you people must have something to drink, can you bring back some cold snacks on your way here?"

"That's no trouble. No, don't worry about getting the money now, Ta-sao, we'll settle that later. See you in a while, Hsiao-wu!"

Li Ming went to the bathroom at the back of the house and turned on the tap: there wasn't a drop of water. He shrugged his shoulders, then took up a scoop and filled the wash-basin up to the brim with water from the bucket. Li Ta-sao came in softly.

"There's been a drought for the past few days and the Water Department has started rationing."

"Oh." Li Ming jerked down his own towel from the rack. "I haven't seen little sister around. Is she out playing?"

"She ran off to take part in some cavalry-fighting practice or other. She'll be gone for a few days."

"That imp. Aren't you worried?"

"What can we do? She's so excited about it. She just won't listen to anyone."

"Has Fourth Sister been back?"

"She was here last month. Your brother-in-law got a raise and promotion. They were very happy. Hsiao-wu, there's still some dirt at the back of your ears. Come, let me clean it for you."

"It's all right." Li Ming wrung the towel dry. "Have any of my friends been here?"

"Kung Chi-chung and Hsiang Szu-i were here. There were probably others, but I don't remember their names. Kung and Hsiang seem to be doing all right. They got together and started a tutorial class and now have quite a few students. Would you like to ask them over for dinner?"

"Not today, Mother. I don't feel too well. I'd like to have a rest."

"The long journey's probably got you down. Do take a nap. I'll go get you a packet of *wu-fen* pills. You can take them with water."

When Li Ming opened his eyes, the dizzy feeling was still there. It was dark already, and Li Ta-sao came to ask him if he wanted to eat yet. He shook his head, then turned over and lay there, facing inside. Li Ta-sao tiptoed out. He could hear his father's voice outside.

". . . Let him sleep some more. Came all the way like that, he should sleep some more. T'ai-t'ai, you go ahead and save some food for Hsiao-wu." He spoke with a thick drawl; he had probably had more than one or two swigs from the wine-jug.

"Captain," it was Lao Tung's voice. "Don't take what happened between us and Wang Fu-lai last night too much to heart. He came to ask us to help him out with money. Naturally, as things look—you were, after all, his superior officer, and I a comrade-in-arms—we should give him whatever little help we can. But he came at the wrong time. We're just like the clay-molded Bodhisattva who couldn't even keep his own hands from falling apart in the torrent, so how could he expect us to lend him a hand? And it's not that he didn't know about your farm. He did, and yet he came to borrow money. That's not what I would call tactful. We did our best to help him, everything that is humanly possible. If

he is still not satisfied, and wants to speak ill of you, then it is he
who is in the wrong. I wouldn't trouble myself over him if I were
you, Captain."

"Ai . . . How can I hold any grudge against Wang Fu-lai?
We've been like brothers all these years! That year our unit was
cut off in Hsü-chou and I was lying there wounded, he picked me
up and carried me on his back for seventy, eighty miles, that's how
I managed to get out alive. So, when all is said, I owe him my
life. Now he needs help because his wife is going to have a baby
and they have to move. If he can't depend on me at a time like
this, who can he depend on? Ai . . . it's my cursed luck that
things turn out this way. If our farm had been a success, or if the
idea had never occurred to me in the first place, then we wouldn't
have ended up like this now, and we wouldn't have soured our
friendship over this matter of a mere thousand dollars."

"Actually, the way I see it, Wang Fu-lai has no one to blame
but himself. What does he want to move his family for? Why does
he have to go to the south in order to open a shop? Isn't it all on
account of his wife? At the very start when he wanted to marry that
woman, we told him what it would be like. Even if a woman of
her profession could turn over a new leaf and stop monkeying
around with men, marrying her kind would only invite ridicule,
disrespect. Wang Fu-lai was very close to her at that time of
course, so he wouldn't listen to anything we said."

"I wouldn't blame Wang Fu-lai entirely. A woman who paid
for her freedom from her own money in order to marry her man
obviously wanted to make something better of her life. If people
had talked less and let them live their life in peace, there wouldn't
have been so much trouble. After all, from ancient times to the
present, stories of prostitutes returning to an honorable way of life
are not uncommon."

"But Captain, just think. It's not as if she'd been plying her
trade in T'ao-yüan for a day or two only. And the people who
knew her, they're not just one or two either. So how do you expect
everyone to keep his mouth shut? Whenever people began whispering, Wang Fu-lai would roll up his sleeves and threaten to beat
them up. But the more you threaten, the more people will talk,   ·
and things can only get worse that way. And in the end, what hap-

pened? Even friends who'd known him for a long time refused to have anything more to do with him. I don't see how the two of them can go on living together in T'ao-yüan like this."

"Wang Fu-lai has always been a hot-head. He was already like that when he was serving in my unit, and would talk back whenever I gave him orders. Now it looks as if he's become even more short-tempered. He came to see me last night and blew his top before we'd even managed to say two words to each other. Just imagine, if I really had the money, how could I not have let him have it? But since I didn't have the money, we could have at least talked things over. But no, he turned around at once and stormed out. I didn't have a chance to say another word."

"It was the same thing at my place. He came barging in as if I'd owed him these hundred years the money he asked for. People don't usually go about borrowing money like that! Anyway, I turned over to him everything I had on me and I said, believe it or not, this is all I possess apart from this pedicab and the blanket. If you take it, you'll be doing me an honor, if you don't take it, I can't do anything more. He almost burst out crying, I tell you, and said that only Pockmark Chao and I were real friends. So I said to him, you went to the captain's place demanding such an impossible sum. How do you expect him to promise you anything? And when he took a little time to answer, you flared up. Who is being a lousy friend? He didn't have anything to say and refused to stay a moment longer; he left that very night."

"Ai . . . So money is driving him out of his mind too. Even heroes can be unmanned by a piece of silver! We've been through that all right . . ." Bang! The captain struck the table with his fist. "Mother's! All my life I've worked hard, I've suffered, but not one lucky dollar came my way. Then after great difficulties we finally got a piece of land, but the bloody land turned out to be lined with rock. What rotten luck! Here, drink this, let's drink up!"

"Cap . . . Captain." Lao Tung spoke with a heavy slur. "I'll be frank with you. When the farm went broke and I moved down from the hill, a lot of things suddenly became clear to me. We are like, you know what, like the monkey who's learned to play a lot of tricks. You teach the little monkey a trick and he won't take a minute to pick it up. He plays his tricks all his life, you can bet on that, but when you try to teach the old monkey—that's what he's become—a new bag of tricks, he can't, he just can't learn any more!"

"We're old, that's what we are, old."

"Captain, I've fought in countless battles, died countless deaths, what have I not lived through? That I've managed to keep my skin is a miracle already. I should be thankful for that alone. I do not wish for anything more now, except to pay a visit to my ancestral home, to sweep my old man's grave just once before I die. Oh, if I can do that, I'll have lived a full life. I'll have lived without regrets.

"Captain, come to think of it, there's a lot of sense in what my father said. Supposing I had begun at twenty, and every year doubled the number of coins I had, I would have become rich by now instead of pushing a pedicab for a living here. Just try counting, the first year two coins, the second year four coins, the third year eight, the fourth year sixteen . . ."

Li Ming couldn't bring himself to listen any more. He pulled the pillow tight over his ears. Tomorrow, he thought, tomorrow he must leave, come what may. He would not stay here. He would rather drift with the tides to the end of the world, and let loneliness and memories erode his heart away . . .

8.

"Your letters, San-fu.[20] The Company's forwarded them here."

"Thank you." As many as three. Who can they be from? He made out Chou Mei's hand at a glance, deliberated for a moment, then put it to one side. He opened a large envelope first and took out a red card, a wedding invitation. So Lao Ch'eng is finally getting married. Who would have expected it? He looked at the date. It was a few days too late already. What a pity. It would have been fun to tease the bride or let Lao Ch'eng have a last taste of "tortoise straining to look at the moon" on his wedding night. There was nothing much he could do now, except send Lao Ch'eng a belated present.

The remaining letter was an aerogram, addressed in English. Li

---

[20] Third mate; direct address by the title is polite and established practice.

Ming looked at it for a long time, then it suddenly struck him that it must be from Hsiao-yü. He looked at the sender's address; it bore a post office box number of the California Institute of Technology. So dreamer-boy has finally made it and managed to get into one of the top schools in the world. He opened the letter. Yes, the tidy, printed appearance of the script has the unmistakable hall-mark of Hsiao-yü's hand.

Li Ming,

You haven't expected to receive my letter, I am sure. I got the address of the Shipping Company you work for from Jumbo only recently. Jumbo told me that your ship plies between the U.S. and Japan and that you make a round trip every few months. If that is the case, you are bound to call at Los Angeles one of these days, and when that happens, I hope you will be able to come and see me. Just imagine, miles from home in a strange land, and able to have a heart-to-heart chat with an old friend. It will be just great.

It's been almost two semesters since I transferred here from a small college in the Midwest. Life during the first semester was simply hectic. I had to work at a feverish pace, under enormous pressure from the professors and almost overwhelmed by the avalanche of course work and assignments. Needless to say, the standard of the students here is high, so that in this respect the small college I came from is in a different league altogether. At the beginning, I felt I simply couldn't stand the strain, but now gradually I am getting used to life here.

The most dispiriting enemy that a foreign student faces here is loneliness. I am lucky enough to have a fellowship, which takes care of all my living expenses, so I am spared the grief of having to work in a restaurant to support myself. But loneliness is one thing I can't get away from. Usually I am busy with my work, and I don't feel it that much. But on Sundays and other holidays in particular, as I see my American friends rush out to their various activities, while I have nothing to do but pace between the four walls of my room, the feeling of loneliness becomes so unbearable that I have to force myself to go out, to find someone to pass the time with or to join one of those God-knows-what parties. I used to think that these meaningless activities were a waste of time. Not any more. Now I am beginning to get used to them. Fear of loneliness is one factor that accounts for my change of attitude. Attraction towards the opposite sex is another. So it seems that man has not only his psychological needs but also his physiological needs to satisfy sooner or later. And as one gets older, one can only feel the more acutely the animal aspects of human nature.

In the past I considered reminiscence a sin, excusable only among the old for whom there is little hope of an active future. But lately I've found myself quite often lost in recollection, especially of my high school days with my old chums in the small town, in play or study. Those days were the happiest moments of my life. Do you still remember the weekend we spent at your place in the hills just before I left—you, Jumbo, Rooster, Lao Ch'eng and myself? We didn't have anything planned for those few days, but we did have tremendous fun, with our dips in the rivers, our games of chess, our banterings, and, of course, our "tortoise straining to look at the moon"! But, ha, how happy those days were in my memories! Since my arrival here, I have had my fair share of country hikes, long-distance excursions, picnics. On every such occasion, nothing is left to chance: everything is planned in meticulous detail by the selfless organizers: the program of activities has to be varied and inexhaustible, the food has to be rich and plentiful, the sexes have to be balanced in number . . . in a word, whatever is humanly possible is done to make the day a smashing success. But I have no relish for these mechanized picnics of a motorcar culture. Perhaps when we entertained ourselves, we did so spontaneously without forethought, that's why we were able to enjoy ourselves. But this other kind of entertainment is different, it is carefully programmed, that's why the fun is drained out of it.

How are you and your family faring with your land? Have the harvests been good? I really envy you for owning such a large tract of land. During the two years I've been here, I don't believe I have heard a cock crow once. American chickens, you see, are bred and reared under artificial light. From the time they hatch to the time they're dispatched—a matter of two to three weeks—they never see the sun. There is no better symbolization of America's modern technological civilization than these machine-cultured chickens. What is America after all? It is an assemblage of mass-produced cars, artificially bred chickens, and some millions of miles of super highways. How can people take root in such a place? Just think. How can a life spent locked up in a car, whirling the whole day along super highways—how can such a life be rooted? To grow roots, to free yourself from the sense of estrangement and loss, you must live close to the earth.

When Li Ming finished reading the letter, he smiled in spite of himself. Hsiao-yü is Hsiao-yü after all, still surveying the world from his ivory tower. "To grow roots," "estrangement and loss," "modern technological civilization"—so he still clings to his formulas. Perhaps it's time to shake him up a bit? Li Ming took out pen and paper and began scribbling:

Hsiao-yü, I am very happy to have received your letter. Unfortunately, I have this piece of bad news for you. We have sold our land already, to Kid Stone. The land can belong only to people like him. For people like us, a life of wandering and "estrangement" is our lot, we are not worthy to inherit the earth.

At this point, Li Ming put down his pen and glanced over what he had written. All at once the thought struck him—what is the point, what am I doing this for? Hsiao-yü dreams his dreams. Well, he is luckier than most of us then. Why must I go and shatter his visions for him? Would the world be a better place if everybody turned into a Hsiaso-yü? Li Ming's face broke into a smile.

He opened the porthole, rolled the unfinished letter into a ball and threw it into the sea. Then he opened Chou Mei's letter.

Among the "redskin" writers in Taiwan, Huang Ch'un-ming has perhaps the reddest of skins. In sharp contrast to Lin Huai-min, nearly all of his most memorable characters are country folk or the small men from small areas with no intellectual pretensions. Their daily concern is not "Where do we go from here?"—the kind of existential problems with which Lin Huai-min's characters are involved. Rather, what they seem to worry most about is where their next meal will come from. Eking out a marginal existence, they do not have the time to measure out their lives with coffee spoons.

A Taiwanese born in 1939, Huang Ch'un-ming has been a rebel since his childhood. Unable to bear the hardship wrought on him by his stepmother, he ran away from home. He started his undergraduate education at Taipei Normal College, only to be dismissed later because of "misconduct." Then he transferred to Tainan Normal College, but he did not behave himself long enough to finish the requirements. The diploma he finally obtained is from P'ing-tung Normal College. He seldom has stayed at one job for more than a year. Presently, he is unemployed, except for his creative writing.

"A Flower in the Rainy Night" ("Yü-yeh hua") is not the original title of this story. The original is "Days for Watching the Sea" ("K'an-hai-ti jih-tzu," in Wen-hsüeh chi-k'an, No. 5, 1967). With the permission of the author, I have used the title of a song sung by the heroine as a substitute.

A Flower in the Rainy Night –

UANG CH'UN-MING

Translated by EARL WIEMAN

1. The Fish Are Schooling

When the sea water soaks up the sun's first warmth of the year and brews out that special intoxicating salty odor which permeates the fishing ports and dances in the nostrils with the rhythm of the sea—this is the time, in April and May, when the bonito begin to school and come swimming in on the warm currents. In March, small fishing trawlers from all over the island gather in the harbor at Nan-fang-ao, getting ready to haul in the riches that come jumping on the tide. The boats pack both the old port and the new port so tightly that not a crack is left between them; and the population of the village, normally only four or five thousand, swells to over twenty thousand. Most of the increase is seamen—those who wear billed hats and speak in loud voices, those are all seamen. Venders of all sorts come to the harbor also at this time, and there are prostitutes, and red-headed, golden flies—all come with the arrival of the fish. This is the busiest time of the year for the fishing village, a time of madness.

From the day the news came that the first fleet of trawlers had let down their nets into the sea and begun bringing up the fat bonito, the hum of activity in the harbor quickened until there was no longer any distinction between day and night. The lights of the boats bringing back the news were lit at dusk while the vessels were still over ten kilometers from the harbor entrance, and by the time they docked the huge outlines of the mountains had already been swallowed up in the darkness. The only illumination left on the sea was provided by the rolling lights of fishing boats bunched together outside Stone Toad Reef, waiting to navigate the shoal one by one and slip into the trench that they called "the threshold." After passing through "the threshold" the lights formed into a single orderly column as the boats sailed into the inner harbor

195

and continued toward the docks. The clamor aboard the vessels conveyed the news that the fish were schooling, and even before they docked the villagers were struck as if by the clap of a bell. From that instant they spread the news throughout the village, either by word of mouth or by the excitement in their expressions and their actions: "The fish are schooling!"

The poor children of the village took straw baskets and ran with their younger brothers and sisters to the fish market to wait for some fish to steal. This was a regular habit of theirs: as soon as the boats docked and the fish were lifted ashore basket by basket, they would bend down into the baskets right there in front of everybody and snatch some of the fish. To their way of thinking this was a kind of barter; when they bent down to get the fish they would expose their backsides to the fishermen, who would beat and revile them. At first the children had thought of it this way: we take their fish, and they beat us and bawl us out for it, so aren't we even? The fishermen felt the same way: we beat them and curse them, so let them have a few fish. "Your mother's! Little bandits!" But later on neither side had to justify the fish thievery that way anymore; the trading of the scoldings and beatings for the fish had long since become a kind of custom in that village whenever the fish were brought in.

The brothels that had been thrown together halfway up the hillside grew tense as the sound of the boats' engines drew near. Ah-niang [1] stood outside the door watching the fishing boats, which had already entered the harbor, and her heart began to thump with the clanging of the engines. Turning her head she yelled inside, "All right, girls, here comes the money!" The prostitutes came out to look as Ah-niang pointed at the lights of the boats below. "Look! The bonito are schooling! They're earlier than they were last year; it's only the first of the month." Then she called inside again: "Ah-hsüeh, you'd better hurry up and eat; in a little while you won't even have time to sit up!"

2.   A *Flower in the Rainy Night*

Everyone who saw her could tell that she must have been very beautiful once. Even now, despite the wear of time, she still ex-

---

[1] The madam in the house of prostitution.

erted a kind of beguiling attraction for men, though perhaps it was only an illusory remnant of her past beauty. No matter how hard she tried to make herself up to look like an ordinary woman, she could never conceal the self-contempt that she wanted so much to hide. Fourteen years had passed since the time when, at the age of fourteen, she had stood on a stool inside the door of that whorehouse in Chung-li calling out, "Hey, soldier!" All those years of lying in bed letting men have their fun with her had given her a duck walk. And her eyes had spent so much time staring at her little ceiling that they would sometimes of themselves focus at that familiar distance, and then the sound of the quick panting of those animals would return to her ears and drive her almost to distraction. All this, and the feeling that most people had about women of her profession, were walls that kept her rigidly separated from the rest of society.

Although she was used to taking off her only dress in front of strange men in her little room, she was frightened of going out and never did so alone unless she had to. This time, though, she had to go out to visit her family home. True, she could never forgive her foster father for selling her, but in her family the first anniversary of the death of a parent was a very important occasion. Ah-niang had been unwilling at first to let her take a couple of days off when business was so good—especially since most of her customers were so pleased with her that they would ask for her by name whenever they came looking for a woman. Because of this the days she took off were a loss for both Ah-niang and herself. But what else could she do? Whenever this sort of thing had come up she could only promise Ah-niang that she would come back as soon as possible. "Come back as soon as you can," urged Ah-niang over and over as she was about to leave, "and bring some more girls to help out if you can find any." As she left the harbor she bought a few fresh bonito and hurried to Su-ao to catch the 12:05 train back to Jui-fang and Chiu-fen-tzu.

Since Su-ao was the initial station there were plenty of empty seats on the train, and she quickly found one which suited her. The time remaining now belonged to the train and she had two full hours to relax; she had not had a good rest since that day when the fishermen had begun pulling up the bonito. Yes, this was much better than that house on the hillside. She closed her eyes;

whether she slept or not did not matter, so long as she could avoid those cold stares that made her so uncomfortable all over. Leaning her head against the window frame she crossed her arms over her chest, stretched her legs out luxuriously, and crossed her ankles; her whole body seemed to be balanced on a marvelous fulcrum, swaying comfortably with the gentle regularity of the coach as it sped on its way. She dozed; but every time she remembered the string of bonito under her seat she would awake with a start and lean forward to take a look at it. The pool of blood oozing from the mouths of the fish was larger each time she looked, and her concern for public cleanliness forced upon her a feeling of contrite anxiety. But she felt better when she saw that the people around her were showing no concern; and at any rate, what could she do about it?

The train was packed with passengers by the time it had passed through Lo-t'ung and Yi-lan, and as Pai-mei dozed the seat beside her was taken by a middle-aged man. When she awoke he smiled and politely offered her a cigarette; and for a moment, unable to find words, she stared at him dumbly. "You don't remember me, of course, but I know you!" said the man, pushing the cigarette closer. "How I've missed you! Here, try a stick of this." She was enraged by this display of vulgarity. She had heard plenty of words like that used with a double meaning—a "stick" of this, a "rod" of that, a "strip" of something else—but only when she was working, and then she was prepared to humor her customers. Under those circumstances she did not mind such insinuations, no matter how undisguised, how abusive, how obscene they were. But why couldn't these people treat her like anyone else when she was outside? She looked at the fat, greasy face of the man sitting next to her and quickly turned away, paying him no further attention. The man put the cigarette between his own lips and lit it; he seemed to be satisfied with himself, as though he had deliberately wanted to provoke her anger. She laughed; never had she felt such loneliness as this man's abuse had aroused. But no matter how loudly she screamed for help, or how much she called out her own name, not even she herself could hear her pleas. If she were an ordinary woman, she thought after her moment of anxiety had passed, she would have been perfectly justified in slapping the face of that shameless man. Then again, if she were an ordinary woman he wouldn't have taken such a liberty with her. A coldness spread over her, and a sense of solitude made her feel that the world she had seen and experienced was no more than a minute cage, a prison behind whose bars she was nearly suffocating. Then suddenly a familiar, friendly face appeared among the passengers getting on at another station; nothing could have excited her more.

"Ying-ying!"

She stood up; at the sound of her shrill, excited voice, strange faces turned in unison and stared at her.

A mother in the crowd carefully holding her baby turned in the direction of the voice and called out involuntarily:

"Sister Mei!"

The child which had been sleeping so soundly in her arms awoke with a start and she patted him soothingly as she squeezed through the crowd. When they were finally face to face, they were too moved for a moment to speak; they could only let the emotion in their eyes communicate what they could find no words to say. Then Pai-mei saw Ying-ying's eyes turn to the man in the seat beside her.

"I'm going back to Chiu-fen-tzu alone," she quickly explained. "When did you have the baby? Why didn't you even let me know you were getting married?"

Ying-ying answered apologetically, feeling that she had been reprimanded. "I got married last year in T'ai-tung. You were the only one I meant to tell about it; but I heard you were in P'ing-tung, and later on somebody said you were in T'ao-yüan, so how could I have found you?" Her eyes reddened. "So I was all alone at my wedding. It sure would have been a lonely wedding, if not for some of Mr. Lu's friends."

A big, kind-faced man in his fifties, who had been standing to the rear, stepped up beside Ying-ying. Awkwardly he put his right arm around the troubled girl to comfort her, and Pai-mei could see from his gentle smile that Ying-ying's past life was truly behind her. Pai-mei was moved by this as no one else could have been.

"This is my husband, Mr. Lu," said Ying-ying as her eyes brightened. "And this is Sister Mei!"

The two nodded to each other.

"He was a major!" Ying-ying continued. "He knows all about me, and I talk to him about you all the time. He always said he'd like to meet you." She turned to the major. "See? Finally we've found her!"

"Yes . . . yes." The major, embarrassed by his own kind-heartedness, was for a moment lost for words.

And Pai-mei, affected by some indescribable emotion, lowered her eyes bashfully.

Four years before, Pai-mei and Ying-ying had worked in a brothel on T'ao-yüan Street in T'ao-yüan. At that time Ying-ying was also a little girl of just fourteen, and rather frail. On the evening of the second day she worked there a rough, harelipped fellow, half drunk, had taken a fancy to her as soon as he stepped in the door. He had lowered his head and brought his face right up against hers, while she cringed back against the plywood walls of the corridor with such force that the panels squeaked out in protest. She had instinctively put out her hand to shove him away, but the sight of that fearsome face so close to her own had frightened her into drawing the hand back; she had pressed back against the wall even harder as her knees began to go weak.

"What! You don't like my looks? You're just lucky I like yours, you stinking bitch!"

Ying-ying hadn't heard a word of what he said; she was aware only of the forceful motions of his huge, misshapen mouth. A wide split from his upper lip to the base of his nose revealed four big yellow buckteeth on the tips of which saliva continually collected and sprayed out every time he spoke. Ying-ying had rolled her cheeks against her shoulders to rub the spit off and then had dodged away from the man and thrown herself into one of the little rooms, locking herself in and crying in fright. The harelipped man, far from wanting to give up, had chased after her angrily and banged loudly on the door.

"Damn you!" he had cursed. "I'll screw your little cunt to death!"

The bagasse-board door had nearly given way, while inside, Ying-ying had been too scared even to cry anymore. At that moment, Pai-mei had gone over and pulled at the incensed man.

"Sir, you've made a mistake," she had said. "That's our errand girl. She can get cigarettes for you, if you want some."

"I don't want to smoke—I want to have some fun with her."

"If you want her, you'll have to wait a few years," Pai-mei had said rather light-heartedly.

"I don't want to wait, I want it now!"

"You want it now? Okay then, come with me," Pai-mei had said seductively, guiding his hand to her breasts. The man had responded with laughter.

"Mother's! That's real boobs!"

With that the harelipped drunkard had tamely allowed Pai-mei to lead him away into one of the little rooms.

During the transaction of that piece of business in her little cubicle Pai-mei had heard faintly, along with the quick panting of that bull animal, the sound of a whipping and the helpless moans of Ying-ying coming from a back room.

The man had left nearly an hour later, very satisfied. As he walked away he had looked back at the dirty red-lacquered sign-board several times, nodding. Pai-mei's hair, which had been set just the day before, was as disheveled as a bird's nest that had been torn apart by a naughty child. She had squatted by the water jar and brushed her teeth furiously time after time; after ten or twelve minutes of this several of the girls who had been standing out front to attract customers gathered around her.

"Pai-mei, you want to brush your teeth right out of your mouth?"

"That harelipped guy—he *kissed* me!" she had answered disgustedly, bringing gales of laughter from the other girls.

After that, although Ying-ying had gotten a good beating, she was always grateful to Pai-mei for saving her from the terror of that harelipped man. One time Ying-ying had tearfully told the older girl all about her past, and Pai-mei had felt that it was not very different from her own; so they had taken secret vows of sisterhood, and afterwards Ying-ying had always called her "Sister Mei." From then on they had been very close and would take every chance they got to talk to each other; in their endless conversations there would appear at times a ray of hope, which they would try ecstatically to grasp. One day as they were chasing an ephemeral ray of hope two customers had come in together and, as luck would have it, had taken a liking to the two girls. They had taken the men to rooms separated only by a layer of bagasse-board and, as their business was being transacted, they had continued their conversation through the thin wall.

"Sister Mei," Ying-ying had asked, "do you know how to make dresses?"

"I never had a chance to learn when I was the right age," had come the reply from the next room.

"Then can you raise chickens and ducks?" Ying-ying had asked excitedly. "I can . . ."

"I suppose so; that's easy."

As Ying-ying was about to continue, the crisp sound of a solid slap had come from the next room, followed by an angry voice:

"If you're going to take my money, pay attention to what you're doing!"

Ying-ying had listened for more sounds from the next room.

"Sorry, sorry. Okay, I'll pay attention," Pai-mei answered in a brisk voice.

Ying-ying had then heard the man's frenzied panting along with Pai-mei's words of praise:

"Oh . . . You're great . . . You're really great!" The words were followed by the forced sound of debauched laughter.

Ying-ying had wondered how Sister Mei could pay attention to a man who had hit her. She wanted to cry, but then her thought had been forced back to the man weighing heavily on top of her.

"You want to get hit too?" he had asked. "I wouldn't take merchandise like you again even if you paid me!" As he spoke he had worked furiously, though, as though determined to get his money's worth out of her.

As they were washing up after the customers had left, Ying-ying had seen the red imprint of a hand on Pai-mei's left cheek.

"Sister Mei," she had cried out. "It's all my fault . . ."

"It's nothing," Pai-mei had laughed. "I've run into customers lots worse than that."

"I admire you . . . if it was me, I couldn't take it."

Pai-mei had laughed again. "Couldn't take it? Then what would you do? If I felt that way, I would have thrown eight years away for nothing. Just wait eight more years until you're as old as I am, and you'll be just as . . . Oh! No, in eight more years you'll be back home raising ducks and chickens. And that guava grove at the foot of the hills you talked about will be growing fruit just as always, waiting for you to go and pick it."

"That isn't ours, and that old man probably isn't around any more."

"Then his son will be just as kind-hearted as he was, and he won't call you a thief if you pick a few for yourself."

A look of childlike radiance had appeared on Ying-ying's face, but in a moment it had faded as she said sadly, "I know, in eight more years I'll be just the same as now. You've said that fate's a tyrant, and it's no use for women like us to try to change it."

"No . . ." Pai-mei had not been able to find any words of consolation to say to Ying-ying, and as she was trying to think of a way to deny what she had said once, her thoughts had been interrupted by the stern sound of the madam's voice calling from outside, "What're you two washing that takes so long? Have you drowned yourselves?"

With that they had put on the rest of their clothes, straightened their hair a bit, and gone to stand in the doorway again and make eyes at the men passing by.

"Come in . . . My husband's not at home!"

Ying-ying had been, for a fact, immature and unable to control her feelings; she had hid behind the door and cried in pity for Pai-mei, and the older girl had scolded her gently when she found her there, calling her a "fool."

Apparently Ying-ying had learned a lot from Pai-mei, primarily because she had acquired from her a philosophy which allowed her to adapt to that kind of life. If she had not, wouldn't she have been making an enemy of herself, just as Pai-mei had said?

One day Ying-ying, bursting with happiness, had told Pai-mei her secret.

"Sister Mei, I'm in love."

She had been somewhat surprised at Pai-mei's reaction; she had expected a look of happiness and was met, instead, by cold indifference.

"He fell in love with me first!" she continued. "He's crazy about me!"

Ying-ying was a very sentimental girl, and she had wanted to cry when she began to feel the awesomeness of what was happening to her. But the tears would not come.

"Is it that soldier who's been coming to see you so much lately?" Pai-mei had asked coldly.

Ying-ying had nodded, her eyes staring pleadingly at Pai-mei. The older girl had been touched by the longing in her eyes.

"Ah-ying," she had said softly, "you've got to trust me. If things can be arranged, I'll do everything I can to help you."

All that night they had talked; there was no time for sleep. Pai-mei had analyzed the situation for her, and recounted unhappy tales of similar love affairs from her own past. When it was all over they had cried bitterly in each other's arms and Pai-mei had made this conclusion: "In our situation, don't get emotionally involved whatever you do."

Although Ying-ying seemed convinced, Pai-mei had still been uneasy about her. "People in our profession have to keep moving around," she had continued deliberately. "Our prices will go down if we stay in one place for too long, and pretty soon nobody will want us even if we go for twenty dollars; if you want to keep your price at thirty, then you have to keep moving to different places. Men are awful the way they want new girls all the time."

"You want to leave?" Ying-ying had asked anxiously.

"With you."

"Me? How can I leave?"

"Didn't you say you still owe Ah-niang three thousand dollars?"

Ying-ying had nodded.

"I'll lend it to you and you can pay me back whenever you have it."

They had left T'ao-yüan not long after that and kept moving all around the island plying their profession. At first Ying-ying had sorrowed at times because of the wound left by that first love, and when that happened Pai-mei would do her best to comfort the girl.

"Ah-ying, I've never heard you sing before and you've never heard me either. There's a song that I really like," she had said as she began to sing:

A *flower in the rainy night*,
A *flower in the rainy night*,
Blown to the ground by the storm.

No one to see, no one to care,
It sorrows night and day;
A fallen, wilted flower, never to rise again.
A flower in the rainy night.

"I've heard that," Ying-ying had said.

"What do you think about it?"

"It's a sad song, and when you sing it it's even sadder."

"Ah-ying, my tears dried up years ago, and I know how it hurts not to be able to cry when you want to. You still have a lot of tears left; but when you can't cry when you feel like crying, then you might as well sing that song. It'll make you feel a lot better."

Ying-ying couldn't understand what she meant.

"What's 'a flower in the rainy night?' "

"You."

"Me?" the girl had asked, pointing uncertainly at herself.

"Me too."

Ying-ying had felt better then; if she could be like Sister Mei, she wouldn't mind.

"But what does it mean?"

"The situation we're in right now is very bleak, isn't it? It's like a rainy night, and women like us are like weak flowers; we've been beaten and separated from the branch by the storm, and we've fallen to the ground, right?"

Ying-ying had nodded, her tears falling; from that time she had begun to reconcile herself to her tragic fate.

The two girls were together for over two years; then Ying-ying had been tricked away by her foster father and sold someplace else. Separated, they had lost contact with one another.

3. Lu Yen

Mr. Lu and Ying-ying found seats to the rear of the coach, leaving the baby in Pai-mei's arms. The child, only three months old, wasn't able to recognize people yet; so long as it got enough sleep and enough food and so long as its diaper was dry, it would lie contentedly and just look around with its round, luminous eyes. Pai-mei was captivated by the way the little eyes stared at her, and she teased the infant with baby sounds, causing it to gurgle with delight. This was a new experience for her. It wouldn't do to keep making the baby noises, she thought; if she didn't try something else, the baby would get tired of it. But how could she keep it amused? She began to feel anxious and apologetic. By this time the train had just left the T'ou-ch'eng station and was racing along the coast, and the sight of the water gave her an idea; she held the baby upright and faced him toward the window. Pointing toward the sea she began chanting.

"Look! Look! That's the sea!

"Sea water's salty! And there's lots of fish in it.

"Some of them are as big as a train.

"And some are as small as your little thumb.

"Heng-ya, heng-ya! Look!

"There's a boat!

"The seamen on the boat catch fish.

"They catch fish for our Lu Yen.

"Lu Yen says, 'I don't want blue fish.'

"So the fishermen go catch yellow ones.

"Lu Yen says, 'I don't want yellow fish.'

"So the fishermen go catch green ones.

"Lu Yen says, 'You dumbbells, I want spotted ones' . . ."

She sang it out like a song as the child watched the scenery flashing by outside the window, struggling up and down happily and softly calling out, "Yaa, yaa." Pai-mei figured that he was happy because of her singing and she kept it up even more enthusiastically. She forgot everything about her, and she forgot that the baby couldn't understand her as she continued her song, making it up as she went along.

"The seaman's face turns red and he says to Lu Yen, 'I can't catch a spotted fish.'

"Lu Yen says, 'Give me the boat and I'll catch some big spotted ones.'

"Heng-yu . . . Heng-yu . . .

"Lu Yen catches a whole load of spotted fish.

"Lu Yen makes the fishermen kowtow one by one.

"And he gives every one of them a good spanking.

"The fishermen yell, 'Ouch! Ouch!'

"Lu Yen says, 'Dumbbells, will you dare bully my auntie any more?'

" 'We won't dare, we won't dare,' they answer.

"Heng-ah . . . heng-ah . . ."

The baby liked the rhythm of her chanting so much that he struggled to jump up and down. As the train was about to enter a tunnel Ying-ying came up to Pai-mei's seat.

"Have you wet auntie?" she asked, laughing.

Pai-mei turned with words of praise for the baby:

"Ah-ying, look at your Lu Yen. What a smart baby! He seems to understand everything I say!"

"They say a new mother brags for three years. Are you going to brag for three years when you're only the baby's auntie?" Ying-ying smiled. "We're getting off at the next station."

After Pai-mei had given Lu Yen back to his mother, she took out two fifty dollar bills and stuffed them inside his clothing.

"There isn't any red paper for me to wrap this up on the train," she said apologetically, "but I want to give this to Lu Yen for a token; I hope it'll bring him a little brother."

Ying-ying didn't want to take it, and they pushed the bills back and forth for a while. Then Ying-ying got off the train with her husband and baby, and when the train started up again Pai-mei stuck her head out of the window and called to them, throwing toward them the lucky money she wanted to give to the baby.

Ying-ying raised her arm as the train pulled away and kept waving it in excitement, growing smaller and smaller as the distance increased. When Pai-mei couldn't see the girl any more she drew her head back, noting contentedly that at last Ying-ying had picked up Lu Yen's money. She was happy about Ying-ying's having found a husband, and unconsciously she raised her arm and with her sleeve wiped away the tears in her eyes. In her happiness she could still hear Ying-ying telling of her good fortune: "Major Lu's a smart man; he said that if our baby was a boy we'd name him Lu Yen, and if it was a girl we'd name her Lu Yüan. 'Yen' means 'continue' and it expresses a hope that the Lu family line will be continued. And if it was a girl the 'Yüan' would mean 'affinity' and would remind us of the affinity between him, who came all the way from the northern part of the mainland, and me. Since Lu Yen was born he's stopped drinking and smoking; they said that since he never liked to talk he used to just smoke and drink all day long up there in the mountains at T'ai-tung."

Unconsciously she began comparing herself with Ying-ying and a sense of emptiness closed in on her, forcing her to turn and concentrate her gaze on the sky outside the window. There had been men who had proposed to her, and her foster mother had even engaged a go-between to arrange a match for her; but if the suitors weren't ox-cart drivers they were tinkers. Besides, all of them were too old. Her foster mother had talked until she was out of breath trying unsuccessfully to get Pai-mei to accept one of them; finally, in exasperation, she had said, "Take a good look at yourself! What are you, anyway? You ought to be glad that somebody wants you. What right have you got to turn anybody down?"

"You're not the one trying to get married, so what're you in such a hurry about?"

"A woman ought to have a husband! I only wish you were illiterate."

"I know what you're after!" Pai-mei had retorted, somewhat unreasonably.

"What do you mean? What do you mean by that?"

Pai-mei, instead of replying, had burst into tears as her foster mother began scolding her angrily.

"You rotten baggage, you don't know when somebody's trying to help you. How dare you talk that way!"

Finally Pai-mei had poured out everything that had been building up inside her for so long.

"Yes, I'm rotten baggage—rotten baggage that you sold off fourteen years ago. Think about it—what kind of life were the eight of you living then? And how are you living now? Now you have a house to live in. Yü-ch'eng's graduated from college and has gotten married. Yü-fu's going to senior high school. Ah-Hui's married. Do you eat any worse, or wear any worse clothes than anybody else? Where would you be today without this 'rotten baggage?' " The words were accompanied by tears, and the foster mother's anger had dissipated.

"There now, there now," she had said. "We're just thinking about what's best for you."

"And look at my own family," Pai-mei had continued, still unable to restrain her tears. "They're still as poor as ever. And yet what do you take me for? Rotten baggage! If it wasn't for this rotten baggage would Yü-ch'eng be where he is now? His family despises me. They avoid me. They won't even let me get near their children. Yü-fu and Ah-hui aren't any different—they consider me a blot on their reputation. What a waste! How I've wasted myself!"

"There, there, Ah-mei, you've always been a good girl. Don't say any more; mother understands."

"No! Today I'm going to talk until I'm finished. Have you ever heard so much as a single word of complaint from me before? Your trying to get me married shows that you still have a little conscience left . . . It's your conscience that's forcing you into trying to marry me off. But I don't need anybody to worry about me now; I have my own plans."

The foster mother had been so stung by these truths that she had burst into tears.

"Ah-mei, mother knows all that, but I don't know how to make it up to you. I know we've been wrong, but I don't know where we went wrong or when we started to go so wrong. Pai-mei, forgive your mother!"

The soft-hearted girl had embraced her foster mother and begged forgiveness in her turn for the words she had just spoken.

But except for her foster mother there was not a single person in the whole Ch'en family that Pai-mei could forgive. Suddenly she was struck by the thought that she needed a child, a child like Lu Yen. Only a child of her own would give her something in this world to call hers. Only a child of her own would give her someone to pin her hopes on.

"I'm sure I can be a good mother," she thought.

"But how are you going to get married?"

"No, I won't get married. I'm already twenty-eight; and being in this business, anybody who wanted me would either be a dullard or a bum."

"Then who will the child's father be?"

"Good men come to the brothels too."

"Will you tell him you want to have his baby?"

"No. I'll find out what he looks like, what his voice sounds like, and what kind of person he is, that's all."

"Then what will you do when the child grows up and asks about his father?"

"I'll say, 'Your father's dead. He was a great man and he hoped

that his son would be like him; although he's dead, he still expects
you to be a good son.' "

"What about your background?"

"Oh! I don't have to let my child know everything about me. I'll
move far, far away, to a completely new place."

"Are you sure you can do it?"

"Starting from now, I'll do my best."

"Do you really need a child so much?"

"That's the only thing I want to keep living for."

"Is your mind made up?"

"My mind's made up!" She couldn't sit still any more so she
stood up; but she didn't want to go anywhere so she sat back down
again—and she sat with a deportment new to her, purposeful yet
full of gentleness. Ying-ying's voice came back to her: "The 'Yen'
in Lu Yen's name expresses hope." She wanted to hear the rest of
it, but the voice disappeared. Lulled by the clickety-clack, clickety-
clack of the train's wheels racing so rhythmically, so monotonously, so unchangingly over the rails, her emotions faded into
nothingness.

4. Buried

The fishing port that she had left for only three days was already
bustling at the peak of its activity. The wild flowers [2] on the hillside had no time to put on their outer garments now, and even
slipping into a blouse was a luxury that they could not enjoy for
very long. The fishermen came one after another, not having time
enough even to pick out a girl with a figure to suit their fancy. The
scent of fish clinging to their bodies was even heavier than that on
the bonito which they pulled out of the water.

"Dammit," joked a middle-aged man as he buckled his belt, "in
three days' time bonito have dropped from NT $8.60 a kilogram to
NT $1.90. But you women still charge the same NT $30!"

At both ends of that row of temporary houses people were busy
putting up others, and the motorized carts and trucks that trans-
ported the fish were kept busy shuttling back and forth along the

_____

[2] A euphemism for prostitutes.

road above. The drivers never forgot to blow their horns wildly and whistle whenever they passed by the brothels, and some of them even yelled out. If the prostitutes had time they would not let those men get away easily; they would come out and yell, "Come on down! If you don't we're going to dump a bucket of water on your feet!" Sometimes they actually would throw water up at them; the water never came anywhere near the road, but both the drivers and the girls below enjoyed the game.

That morning the craving of the young fisherman Ah-jung had been aroused by the relentless sun; normally morning was the only time when the temporary brothels were not very busy.

The boat that he worked on had taken a huge amount of bonito the night before and, riding too deep in the water when it returned to port, it had scraped its bottom coming through the trench that they called "the threshold." This was a misfortune in which the young fisherman could rejoice; for the past several days he had been too busy to sleep or even to take a rest, so he really could not take it any more. The chance for a couple of days' rest while the hull was being repaired was a rare opportunity during that time of frenetic activity. The first thoughts that struck his mind that morning had been about girls. Although this was no cause for embarrassment, he could feel a vague sensation of restlessness growing within his body. He remembered how every time they set out to sea, as the bow of their boat headed for the mouth of the harbor, the voices of the women would drift down from the hillside and the boat, which would have been charged with anticipation for that moment, would erupt in a frenzy of yelling and carrying-on. After that the crew's talk would be of nothing but women until they reached the seas around the Bonin Islands and the captain's first order to prepare to cast nets drove all thoughts of women from their minds. From the way they lit into their work then it would seem that such a thing as women never existed on this earth. But the instant the boat turned toward port again with a full load after a period of intense activity, the talk would turn naturally, methodically, back to women again. That was the time when the older fishermen, very openly, would pick out a few fat male bonito, cut open their bellies, and take out the white organs that only the male fish have; then they would open their mouths and gulp those bloody organs down. There was not a single fisherman that didn't know this was the best aphrodisiac available.

When one of them saw K'un-ch'eng down a pair of the organs he had joked, "I guess K'un-ch'eng Sao's [3] going to have a rough time of it tonight!"

"No, no . . . I just want those birds on the hillside to sing an even sweeter song."

The rest of them had laughed at that; but they, too, all ate those organs. Young Ah-jung, however, had stolen away alone to the rear of the boat and furtively cut open several female bonito before he finally found a male one; then he had shut his eyes and forced himself to swallow the organs. While his eyes were still closed tightly in distaste his ears had told him that he had been surrounded by his shipmates, as the sound of laughter attacked him from all sides. Flustered, he had jerked his eyes open to look at them as they taunted him.

"Ah-jung's surely a fellow who likes to have his meals alone. What side of the road are you on anyway, Ah-jung?"

"Ah-jung, what've you got to be embarrassed about, taking your tonic in secret back here all by yourself? Mother's! You don't even know the difference between male and female bonito yet, and in such a dark place too—I bet what you swallowed was ovaries!"

"Oh . . . How about that! From now on we won't have to climb halfway up the hillside looking for girls any more. All we'll have to do is look for Ah-jung, right here on our own boat!"

The taunt had come from a young man about Ah-jung's own age; there was not a man among them who did not laugh uncontrollably at his joke.

Ah-jung's face had reddened and he had leaped at his tormentor, and in a moment the two of them had been upon each other. A man was about to separate them but another had restrained him.

"It's all right!" he said. "Don't stop your own dogs from biting each other."

[3] Sao literally is an older brother's wife. K'un-ch'eng Sao is therefore a polite form of referring to K'un-ch'eng's wife.

"Right! Let our own dogs bite each other. Otherwise, they're so full of energy they might knock a hole in the boat!"

They had all gathered around in a circle with the two combatants in the center, as though it were a show staged for their amusement. When they saw that Ah-jung was pressed down on the bottom the onlookers had laughed and said, "Ah-jung really *did* eat fish ovaries by mistake just now!" Then, when Ah-jung had managed to get himself on top, they said, "No, no . . . Ah-jung took the right tonic!" Some of them, as they spoke, had gone over and tried to rearrange the positions of the two young men so that it would look like they were making love, and the rest of them had clapped their hands and laughed. One fellow had run and got a basin half full of water and some pieces of toilet paper to put beside them; this had so disjointed the men who had had experience buying girls that they had nearly split their sides with laughter. The boat had rocked a little and the captain, in his best voice of command, had called out, "Hey! Carry them a little more to the center—the damned boat's listing!" With that the onlookers had lifted up the two young men, who were still locked in combat, and held them. Then Ah-jung and his foe had burst into laughter too, whereupon they had released their holds and Ah-jung, who was on top, had almost fallen to the deck. The fight had been concluded by a remark from K'un-ch'eng:

"Okay, okay; save a little energy. What did you take your tonic for?"

The brothels did their best business in the evening. When the boat passed below the houses, the fear about the bottom scraping the reef had been dispelled in an instant: the fishermen had lifted their faces and looked longingly at the brothels, but all they had seen was fishermen going in and coming out. Not a single prostitute had come out to entice them. Halfway down the cliff, separated from the boat by only a strip of water, they had seen the wads of white toilet paper that had been thrown down from the brothels, fluttering in the gentle coastal breeze like lilies in full bloom.

His courage roused by the well-ripened craving within him, Ah-jung lowered his head and stepped into the brothel; he saw Pai-mei and picked her without bothering to make a choice. Seeing that certain slightly unnatural expression on his face, she knew that this customer would not be hard to deal with. Very politely she led him inside.

"What's wrong?" she asked. "You should be out to sea in such good weather."

"We scraped the bottom of our boat," he said lazily.

"Scraped it?" asked Pai-mei, her eyes widening.

"Yes, we scraped it on the reef last night."

"Anybody hurt?"

"Oh, no."

Pai-mei went outside to draw some water and get some paper.

"You're smart., knowing to come at this time," she said when she returned.

"Why?" asked Ah-jung, somewhat at a loss.

Pai-mei laughed dryly; she was attracted by the young man's ignorance. He seems like a nice fellow, she thought. He wouldn't give anybody a hard time.

"Mmm . . . nothing."

Ah-jung was anxious to get on with the business at hand.

"Are you in a hurry?"

"No; our boat won't be fixed for two days."

"You married?"

"Not yet," he replied. "Why would I come here if I were married?"

"You think married men don't fool around outside? I don't believe it. You men . . . you're all animals." Pai-mei was watching her young customer closely. His muscles were strong and well-developed, and she imagined the pleasure of his arms holding her with all their might until she nearly suffocated. Taking his hand she began running it over her body; he took it up himself and stroked her awkwardly. He had heard his friends say that prostitutes were incapable of being aroused, so he asked her about it.

"They say that after living this kind of life for a long time, a prostitute's feelings for this kind of thing are all gone. Is it true?"

Pai-mei was pleased at this naïve question. Wasn't he just the man she wanted to father her child?

"Why do you ask that?" she inquired.

"I figure that if you don't have any feelings left any more, then all the customers at these places must seem like a funny bunch," he laughed.

"What're you laughing at? You said the customers at these places must be *what?*"

"Do you know about artificial insemination?"

"I've heard of it."

"At home I've watched them get sperm from a boar," he giggled. "The veterinarian tied rice straw around a bench and covered it over with burlap, so that it looked just like that kind of wooden horse that they use in gymnasiums. And then he smeared vaginal fluid from a sow on one end of it, and when the boar was brought out and smelled it he got so excited that he slobbered all over, and he mounted it and worked for dear life . . . ha ha ha . . ." He was laughing harder now. Pai-mei laughed too when she imagined how funny it was.

"You're insulting me. You said that I look like a wooden horse," Pai-mei pouted.

"I'm laughing at myself too. I'm just like a boar," he laughed.

Pai-mei noticed his white, even teeth, his pleasant eyes. She saw through to his good heart, and she told herself that this was the man with whom she wanted to have a baby. It was her period of fertility, and she decided not to take any contraceptive measures afterward. The thought of it gave her butterflies.

"No! You're making fun of me for being like a wooden horse."

Ah-jung was getting impatient with the banter; all he wanted by then was to get on with it, but Pai-mei wanted him to continue caressing her.

"Oh, yes," Ah-jung remembered. "You still haven't answered my question. Do you have any feeling for this sort of thing?" His face twitched with eagerness and he swallowed involuntarily.

"That depends on who the man is," the girl answered, discovering to her surprise that she felt embarrassed. "If we like him, we have feelings like anybody else."

"What if it's me?"

"I don't know," she answered softly. She looked at him intently for a long time, but still she wouldn't let him get started. She was engraving Ah-jung's image on her memory.

"Where do you live?" she asked.

"My home's at Heng-ch'un. My family farms, but I like the sea."

"What's your name?" Her eyes and her voice were filled with emotion.

"Wu T'ien-t'u."

She sniffed at his body and he trembled slightly.

"Your name means 'field-soil,' but you only smell of fish. Your name should be Wu Hai-shui—Wu Sea-water!"

"Okay!" he said, giving her a hug. "My name's Wu Hai-shui then. I'm not Wu T'ien-t'u any more."

He kissed her very sincerely and passionately, and this time Pai-mei herself felt a need for him. She put her arm around his shoulders, giving him the signal he had been waiting for.

"There are holes in the wall," he whispered.

"They're all stopped up with paper, aren't they?"

"Some of them aren't."

"Nobody will look; it's unlucky to look at somebody like this."

"What's your name?"

"Pai-mei."

"Oh . . . Pai-mei . . ." For a moment he felt a strange surge of happiness. He was worried about how she felt and asked over and over how is it? How is it? How is it? When he finished he noticed that her eyes were filled with tears.

He rolled down gently and lay beside her; he saw the muscles of her throat twitching and reproached himself, thinking that he probably hadn't satisfied her. But she had certainly satisfied him; never before had a prostitute made him feel this way, and he had a vague feeling of having misused her. Satisfy her then! The next time he would surely take longer.

Suddenly there was a knocking on the wall, followed by Ah-niang's voice.

"Pai-mei, what's the matter?" The tone of the voice conveyed impatience.

"She wants us to hurry up, doesn't she?" asked Ah-jung in a whisper.

"Don't pay any attention to her," she whispered back. Then more loudly, "My customer wants to go on."

"I don't," said Ah-jung nervously when he heard this. "I . . ."

Pai-mei signalled him with her eyes to be silent.

"Then give me another ticket," said Ah-niang, knocking on the door.

"I'll give it to you later," answered Pai-mei.

"That won't do; I'll forget about it."

"Okay," said Pai-mei, taking a card cut from coarse cardboard from under her pillow and sticking it through the crack in the door. "Here it is."

Ah-niang took the ticket.

"What's that for?" asked Ah-jung curiously.

"When she collects her share of the money, she figures it up by the number of tickets." Then, as if to change the subject, she added, "Are you in a hurry to get back?"

"I'm tired; I don't want to do it again." Actually he only had NT$50—not enough for two times.

"Then lay here with me awhile, okay?"

"I . . ." he stammered, "I can't do it twice, I . . ."

"Hold me." His protestations were stopped by Pai-mei's plea. "Let's just lie like this for a while," she said contentedly.

His mind became clearer as he held her dumbly; yet it was the clarity of ignorance, for his mind was overwhelmed by an emotion he could not understand.

This moment was a very important one for Pai-mei: she hoped that it would mark a new beginning for her. As if from nowhere, a ray of hope had quietly entered her body, whose mystery and the weight it carried only she could fully understand. She frightened Ah-jung so much that he cried in her arms. She wanted more of her feeble hope than for it to remain buried in her body, although it was at the same time buried in this society, in the perverse fate of this foster daughter turned prostitute. She wanted one day to see her hope develop and grow.

5. *K'eng-ti*

After Pai-mei had watched Ah-jung make his way back down the hill, she hurriedly packed her few things as she had planned and said good-by to Ah-niang. The madam, taken by surprise, thought that she had offended the girl.

"If you're mad at me for asking you for that ticket just now, you're wrong," she said by way of conciliation. "That's our rule. And you're the oldest girl here, so you should know that better than anybody else."

"It has nothing to do with that."

"Then I just can't understand why you want to leave."

"No reason in particular." She knew that if she told Ah-niang or anyone else that she wanted to go and have a baby they would laugh at her.

"That doesn't make sense."

"I'm going to get married," Pai-mei lied.

"Why haven't I heard you say anything about it before now?" Ah-niang asked. "With who?"

Pai-mei smiled and shook her head without answering.

"Is it that young fellow who was just here?"

What could she do? All Ah-niang wanted was to get something to gossip about; so to relieve herself from the interrogation, Pai-mei smiled again and nodded her head silently.

"Oh . . . Are you crazy, Pai-mei? I want to advise you for your own good . . ."

All of her talking had no effect; Pai-mei took her bundle and left. The girls, greatly puzzled, all came to the door to see her off. Ah-niang, standing among them, jeered:

"Look! Our Pai-mei's off to get a husband!"

Pai-mei, her eyes filled with tears but her heart full of joy, went down the hill toward the harbor and the bus station, never looking back nor stopping for so much as a second. She had lived by the coast for a long while, but now for the first time she really heard the sound of the sea rushing against the shore over and over, as if it were cleansing her soul. Before long the bus came, and Pai-mei's past was buried in the swirling cloud of dust that it left behind.

It was already evening that day when Pai-mei reached the cutoff leading to the home where she was born, the home where they still called her by her pet name "Mei-tzu." It was one of those places that had not changed during the past twenty years. The little Earth God shrine was still under the tree there at the cutoff, but the top of the stone seat beside it was smoother than before. The potlid grass that they used on infected sores was still climbing all over the slope, the same as always. Pai-mei remembered how once when she was a child she had lost a coin on that slope, a coin which she was going to buy some kerosene with. She had looked for it for a long time and had pulled up all of the potlid grass in the area without success, and had become so worried that she had burst into tears. She had hidden in the Earth God shrine, afraid to go home, for she had known that a good beating was in store for her. To avoid the beating she had broken the kerosene bottle on the stone seat and picked up a piece of the broken glass, intending to slash a hole in the bottom of her foot so that it would bleed, figuring that when her mother saw the blood she would be pitied instead of beaten. She had sat there with the piece of glass in her hand, trembling, lacking the courage to carry out her plan. But courage had welled up when she thought of how her mother would baby her when she saw the bleeding wound. She had thought no more of how fearful and painful cutting herself would be, but only of how her mother would wash her foot, dress her wound, and even feel the pain of it for her. She had been overcome with a feeling of comfort and warmth, but she had cried as the glass cut deeply into the sole of her foot. The blood had spurted out of the slash; she had cut deeper than she had intended. But she had comforted herself with the thought that the deeper the wound, the more her mother's sympathy would be aroused. She had known that she could stop the bleeding with a handful of mud from the field, but since she was looking for sympathy she had decided to let it bleed. Hiding in the shrine she had waited for someone from her family to come and find her, but several hours later no one had come yet and it was getting late. Then she had become scared, for she had heard stories about spirit fire being seen where the road branched off there. The more she thought about it the more frightened she had become; but she couldn't go home by herself, for the cut in her foot had been too deep. Just as she was about to lose all hope her eldest brother had found her and carried her home on his back; she had told him what happened and he had comforted her all the way home. But after they arrived nothing had gone as she had anticipated; instead of pitying her her mother had thrashed her good, and she hadn't gotten so much as a single sweet potato for supper that night. Three days after that a stranger had come and taken her away, and for a long time she had thought that her mother hadn't wanted her any more because she had lost that coin. She hadn't been able to understand at the time why, when she was about to be taken away, her mother had cried so hard as she gave her daughter some last instructions: "Mei-tzu, you're eight years old . . . You're a big girl now, and you've got to be good. It's because we're poor, just remember that. But from now on you won't have to feed on sweet potatoes anymore. It's all because your father died so soon . . ." Still mad at her mother for the beating, she had left with the stranger without a word.

Pai-mei climbed the stone steps up through the terraced paddies for a while and then walked along a path, picking up memories of her childhood along the way. Seeing such a fashionably dressed girl coming up the hill, the workers in the fields—men and women, young and old—all put down their tools, straightened up, and stared. Wasn't that Uncle Lucky working bare-backed in the potato field down the slope? Yes! It was Uncle Lucky! She could tell by the way he stood with his one leg shorter than the other. She waved her hand and called out:

"Uncle Lucky, are you weeding the sweet potatoes?"

The man was mystified and excited by the call.

"Oh! Yes . . . Who are you? How do you know me?" The voice, wafting across the distance, quivered with pleasure. Wanting to increase his happiness she answered:

"You built the Earth God shrine at the cutoff all by yourself. Doesn't everybody know that?"

"Yes . . . yes . . . That was twenty-three years ago. After I sell this crop of sweet potatoes I'm going to fix it up again!" Then he continued even more excitedly: "Hey, lady, who're you looking for at K'eng-ti?"

"I'm Sung the Capon-maker's youngest girl . . ."

"What? Is Sung's youngest girl so big already? Then . . . then you're Mei-tzu?"

"Yes . . . yes, I'm Mei-tzu."

"Ah . . . I didn't recognize you, didn't recognize you. Has Sung been dead so long?" He paused for a while, then continued: "Yes, it's been that long; he died the year after I built the Earth

God shrine. He carried the three hundred and sixty bricks to build the shrine with for me."

"Come over to our place after a while," Mei-tzu said after a period of silence.

"Okay, okay. You hurry on home now; your mother'll be waiting for you."

She hadn't gone far when she heard someone running up behind her. By the time she turned to look the teenage girl was already by her side.

"My father told me to come and help you carry your suitcase," the girl said, reaching for the bag.

"No, no." She shot an appreciative glance over her shoulder at Uncle Lucky, who stood in the distance and indicated with a wave of his hand that it was all right, let the child carry it. The suitcase had already been taken by the girl and hoisted onto her shoulder. They walked on.

"How long are you going to stay home?" the teenager asked.

"I'm not leaving," Mei-tzu answered quietly.

"Not leaving?" the girl asked in surprise. "Why not?"

"I want to take a rest." Mei-tzu, staring at the path ahead, seemed to be talking to herself.

The path stretched along the side of the hill, bounded both above and below by sweet potato fields and acacia groves. A group of village children, six to eight years old, made their way through the trees above the path, following Mei-tzu curiously at a distance of seven or eight feet. They would run for a while and then stop a while to giggle at something or other. Mei-tzu noticed that a boy carrying a bird's nest bore a strong resemblance to someone she remembered.

"Are you Ah-chiao's kid?" she asked.

The child stood in embarrassed silence but the others laughed that yes, he was. And this other one was, too; they pushed out a girl who had been laughing with the rest, scaring her mirth from her.

"How many kids does Ah-chiao have?"

The boy stretched out six fingers.

Mei-tzu saw in another boy's face the image of his father.

"Are you Ah-mu's kid?" she asked.

The child hid himself in embarrassment as the others laughed again.

"Huh? That's funny . . . How do you know? What fun!" one of the children said.

"Okay! I'll guess some more." Mei-tzu looked at their faces one by one; one by one they hid their faces and, laughing, ran a little way up the road. Seeing this group of lively children reminded Mei-tzu that she too would have a child. But she was worried; was it in fact already developing in her body? She must not fail! Otherwise, she would have to start over again. God! Goddess of Birth! You must help me!

Suddenly, on the pathway ahead, her mother appeared.

"Ma . . ." Her voice failed; she could say nothing else.

"Uncle Lucky's kid came and told me—said that you'd come back."

Her mother did not stop to wait for her; she walked down the path as Mei-tzu walked up it, and then the two of them walked side by side.

"How long are you going to stay?"

"I'm not going to leave."

"Not going to leave?" asked the older woman, surprised. "How can that be?"

"I don't care."

They walked in silence for a while.

"How're things at home now?" Mei-tzu asked.

"That'll depend on this sweet potato crop."

"How's big brother's leg?"

"That depends on this potato crop too, whether we can have it amputated." The voice was strained.

"Amputated?" Mei-tzu was shocked.

"The doctor says he won't live long if it's not amputated. Day before yesterday we carried him down there, and yesterday we carried him back again."

Mei-tzu remembered that when her brother had carried her on his back up the hill that time both of his legs had been strong and healthy.

"You won't be able to stand it here. His seven kids'll worry the life out of you."

"I have some money, Ma—let's take big brother down tomorrow morning."

Tears filled the woman's eyes as she said, "Mei-tzu, it isn't that I don't love your brother. They say that even a tiger won't eat its own cubs, no matter how cruel it is. But I don't think there's any hope for him; even the doctor won't guarantee anything. Better to help his seven kids than try to save him."

"Let's try anyway, Ma."

"Don't be so naïve. Next year the government's going to take back all the forestry bureau land that we use for growing our sweet potatoes at K'eng-ti. What'll we do then?"

"Take back the forestry bureau land? What for?"

"It belongs to the government, and they can grow weeds on it if they want to."

Uncle Lucky's daughter, who had been following along silently behind with the suitcase, suddenly broke in with an optimistic observation:

"I heard that a provincial assemblyman's trying to help us out." Mother and daughter turned their heads together; as they looked at the girl shouldering the suitcase with her face to the ground, the expression on her face was extremely different from theirs.

Just ahead, at the stone wall covered with cactus, was the house where Mei-tzu was born. A black dog was rushing toward them, barking fiercely.

"Calm down, Black Ear—Mei-tzu's one of the family!" The words calmed the black dog, and wagging its tail it walked lightly to the girl and sniffed her. "That's a funny dog," the woman continued. "He came here last year and has stuck around ever since; he behaves himself even if we don't feed him. He catches field rats, and when he gets a lot of them we help him eat them. Those field rats eat better than we do; every one of them is fat, usually more than a catty. Black Ear catches rabbits, too."

The dog seemed to know that his mistress was praising him; he ran over and rubbed against her legs affectionately.

"Nuisance, get away from here. I'll step on your feet if you're not careful."

Black Ear bounced away lightly and led them through the stone wall.

Back at the fishing port the next day, Ah-jung went back to the brothel looking for Pai-mei about the same time as the day before, taking five fat bonito with him. He was going to tell her that their boat had been repaired, that he would have to go back to work. But he was met with unexpected disappointment.

"She isn't here," said the madam.

"But she was here yesterday."

"She said she was going to get married with you. Did you get married?" she asked.

"Stop kidding. Where's she gone?" he asked anxiously.

"I ask you."

"Where's her home?"

"I ask you that, too."

Ah-jung searched inside the room hopefully with his eyes, looking at the prostitutes there. Then he turned and left.

"What? Leaving without having any fun? Stay a while—I'll find a tender chicken for you to taste. Such a young fellow like you shouldn't be looking for an old girl."

He walked away helplessly, letting the string of fish slip from his hand; he went on without even looking back at it.

"Hsiao-ch'üeh," called the madam when she saw the fish drop, "go get that string of fish. We'll have fish for lunch!"

6. *Ten Months*

The first thing that Mei-tzu did when she returned to her home was decide to have her brother's bad leg amputated.

The steady moans were interrupted by a sudden shout: "Ah-ch'ih . . . Ah-ch'ih . . . Help me . . . Come chase the flies away from daddy's leg. Ah-ch'ih, you better stay in here! Ah-ch'ih . . ."

Mei-tzu rushed into her brother's room and chased away the flies that had gathered thickly on his decayed leg, sucking up the pus.

"You've got to listen to reason," she urged him once again. "It's your own life; if you don't have enough sense to take care of it, what can anybody else do for you?"

"Ah-ch'ih's changed; that kid think's I'm a bother." Tears flowed as he continued: "I know—the whole family thinks I'm a bother. They talk behind my back all the time, I know it."

"You've got no reason to say that. You know how much Ma's cried over you, and Ta-sao [4] is doing more than her share as a woman, the way she's taken over all your work. What do you think they do that for?"

"What about Ah-ch'ih? I want him to keep the flies away for me."

"What do you expect from a four-year-old boy? I just found him sleeping on the floor and put him to bed. You . . ."

"Oh! The flies!" he called out in pain.

"You'd better listen to me," said Mei-tzu as she chased the flies away. "You've already lost the leg anyway, so you might as well get rid of it. If you don't you're not going to last much longer."

"All I want now is for the flies to stop tormenting me. I don't care, so long as I can die in peace." He thought for a moment and continued: "I probably won't last until this crop of sweet potatoes is harvested."

"You don't have to worry about the money."

"No, no. I won't make you suffer any more. When father died I should have provided a good life for you." His voice was strained with shame. "There's no hope for me. Can you forgive this worthless brother?"

"Nobody did anything wrong. Let's not talk about that any more."

"Oh! Those hateful flies!" Engrossed in her conversation, for a moment Mei-tzu had forgotten to keep waving her hand to scare the flies away and they had caused her brother to cry out in pain again.

"It's settled, then. Tomorrow we'll take you to the hospital." Her voice had a decisive ring.

"No, no. What good will it do for me to live?"

"Have you forgotten? Aren't you good with your hands? Can't you make chairs and baskets and sifters and lots of other things out of bamboo?"

"Yes—that's not hard at all." His eyes brightened. "Mei-tzu, it's not too late for your sister-in-law to plant some bamboo beside the stream; it's best to plant it before the Grave Cleaning Festival, and next year it'll be ready to use."

[4] Mei-tzu's sister-in-law.

Within the first month after she returned to K'eng-ti, Mei-tzu began to have a new confidence in everything. Her brother took her advice and let his leg be amputated; what made her almost unbearably happy, though, was that the time for her period came and passed with no menstruation. She was examined at two different clinics in the town and both doctors reported a high probability of pregnancy. One of them calculated that if she really were pregnant, her time would be up the next January.

The rays of the May sun did not fail to brighten the little piece of land known as K'eng-ti.

Early one morning a middle-aged villager known as Uncle Woody returned from town with news that set the whole of K'eng-ti in an uproar. Grasping a newspaper in his hand he raced up the hill in mad excitement; everyone he met was infected by the madness and ran about wildly through the village.

Standing in a knot of villagers who had not yet heard the news, Uncle Woody loudly told it again:

"The government's not going to take back the slopeland next year. They're going to turn it all over to us!"

"Who says so?" asked one of the listeners suspiciously.

"It's in the paper!" replied Uncle Woody. He showed them the item in the newspaper where the headline had been circled in red by the owner of the general store in town. He jabbed his finger at the article, and the people surrounding him peered intently at the black words inside the red circle.

"Then it's true?" asked one of them as he raised his eyes from the newspaper.

"Then it's true! Then it's true!" echoed the others as they too looked up from the paper. Actually, though, not a single one of them could read.

When Mei-tzu's mother heard the news in the potato field she dropped her rake and rushed home, where she grabbed Mei-tzu and said, "Come, Mei-tzu, we're different now. I'll take you to look at our own land!"

The girl was taken aback for a moment, uncomprehending, until her mother explained it to her. Then the older woman led her over the ridge to look at the sweet potato fields on the slopes.

"Look! From the top of the hill all the way to the bottom of the valley is all ours!"

They walked over to another piece of slopeland.

"Mei-tzu, the land you're walking on now is our own; I bet you never dreamed this could happen! All the way to the bottom's ours. It's true—a blade of grass, a drop of dew, who'll starve to death and who'll get rich, it's all predestined."

The old woman was unusually silent as they started home. "Mei-tzu," she said after a while, "formerly we worried about land and money, but now that we have our land, we've a new problem."

The words were not lost on Mei-tzu, but she didn't want to think further. She remained silent.

"Mei-tzu, don't you think that now that we've this land, we need a man in the house?" the old woman said as she looked at the silent girl. "Besides, you're still young."

As expected, her mother finally had spoken her mind. After a while, Mei-tzu decided to take this opportunity to speak out about her own plans.

"I know what you mean. But I came back for a purpose this time." Her voice was low. "I'm pregnant, and I want my baby to be born in this quiet place."

"Who's the man?"

"That doesn't matter; I just used him to give me a child. I need to have my own child."

"Have you gone crazy? Pregnant without getting married—how can I explain that to the neighbors?"

"Is that more shameful than being a whore? It doesn't make any difference what you are so long as you treat other people right."

"I can't understand you wanting a kid while your own big brother has more than he can take care of. I think Ah-ch'ih would make a good one for you."

"No, I don't approve of separating children from their parents, or mixing them up. If I took Ah-ch'ih to be my son it'd disturb his mind." She noticed the solemn expression on her mother's face and continued. "Ma, I'm not blaming any of you for what happened before."

"Okay then." The old woman gave in, struggling to change her attitude and make the best of the situation. Mei-tzu's already been a great help to the family since she came back, she thought. What more can I ask of her?

"Mei-tzu," she said happily, "you didn't bring good luck only to our own family—you brought it to the whole village!" Her spirits brightened.

Soon everybody in K'eng-ti considered Mei-tzu's return a good omen, that the government's giving the slopeland over to them was a result of the good luck which she brought. That, plus her devotion to her family and her warmth toward the other villagers, earned her much respect in K'eng-ti.

June was when the land repaid the villagers for their labor. When they began to dig up the soil, the huge sweet potatoes that were turned out brought joy to the hearts of all who saw them.

First the villagers carried their hand-carts to the cutoff; then they loaded them with the sweet potatoes and sweet potato tops that they had carried out slung from poles over their shoulders. Early in the morning they gathered to transport the potatoes the twenty miles to town.

There was no man to help out in Mei-tzu's family, but her brother's wife and the three oldest children put on grass sandals like the men wore and went to work hauling the sweet potatoes with the others.

When they returned that day the salted fish which each of the carts carried drew flies from the town all the way back to K'eng-ti.

"Dammit! Handling a hoe's not worth anything at all. Work ourselves to death, and now a hundred catties of sweet potatoes only brings NT $48."

"Isn't that the truth!"

"But we really worked hard."

"Just think—two salted fish cost NT $16: the same amount can buy a whole pile of our potatoes."

Some of the returning men pulled their empty carts side by side and complained along the way. When they got to the cut-off they rested their feet, smoked, and drank some of the branch water.

"Mei-tzu," asked Uncle Lucky, "do you still want to stay in a hard-luck place like this?"

"Yes!" she answered. "I like it here."

All of the villagers resting their feet by the Earth God shrine turned their attention to her.

"Surely you don't think being poor is any fun!" said Uncle Lucky. "Think of it," he continued solemnly. "A hundred catties of sweet potatoes goes for NT $48. Certainly that's no fun."

Mei-tzu hadn't expected that Uncle Lucky's innocent talk would lead to such deep questions, and it frightened her a little. But she herself had gone to the market in town with her sister-in-law and the others that day, and on the way back she had thought about that question. Finally her own ideas, which she was too timid to express freely, were practically forced from her.

"It seems that NT $48 for a hundred catties of sweet potatoes is the price that we asked for ourselves," she said, and the villagers gathered around her.

"Twenty some carts left K'eng-ti this morning," she continued, "and they must have taken ten or twenty thousand catties of potatoes to market—didn't they?"

"More than that! More than thirty thousand catties!" came the answer from the crowd.

"Okay, over thirty thousand catties. Look, around three-fourths of the sweet potatoes at the market by the gate of the Matsu temple were ours." She felt a little awkward in her speech and was afraid that she wouldn't be able to express herself; but seeing the circle of faces waiting expectantly for her conclusion, she continued nervously. "What I mean is, if we could send that many potatoes out over three or four days instead of all at once, maybe we could get a little better price for them. But I don't know," she hastened to add. "That's just my idea."

Contrary to her expectations the villagers took Mei-tzu's idea to heart and then and there, by the Earth God shrine, they arrived at an agreement to divide each day's shipment into three batches which would be taken to market in succession.

And, indeed, the results were apparent the very next day; the price of a hundred catties of potatoes had already gone up NT $24.

July, sometimes, belongs to just one person.

There was no longer any doubt. The first thing Mei-tzu did when she got up in the morning was go to the back yard and vomit. Her mother came up behind her quietly and patted her gently on the back.

"It's for sure then. It's for sure!" The woman's voice showed excitement, but it was mixed with uncertainty.

"I think it's for certain now," Mei-tzu said, turning to her mother with hot tears of joy filling her eyes.

"Yes, it's certain now."

Mei-tzu's face brightened into a shy smile. "Ma, all of a sudden I've got a taste for pickled turnips."

"Pickled turnips?" The old woman rolled her eyes. "Ah—you're lucky—there's a bottle left from last year, but I don't know if they're moldy or not. Don't matter, though; some of them on the bottom will be okay, anyway."

She hurried away and searched through a pile of old bottles, pulling the stopper from each one and smelling the contents, then holding it up and looking at it. A sense of anxiety engulfed her.

"What're you looking for, Ma?" asked her daughter-in-law.

"Where's that bottle of pickled turnips left over from last year?"

"Pickled turnips?" the daughter-in-law asked, puzzled.

"Mei-tzu's baby-sick."

"What? Mei-tzu's baby-sick?"

Mei-tzu's whole body was filled with a feeling of warmth as she heard the crisp, clear clinking of the bottles knocking together.

It seemed to them that August, September, and October slipped by like a cat slinking past.

November was a time of cleansing. Every year, this month never failed to bring deluges of rainwater to wash K'eng-ti.

First the mountain rain fell continuously, and by the middle of the month it was joined by the wind. The villagers were forced to stay inside their houses and almost every woman in K'eng-ti became pregnant at the same time. The stump of Mei-tzu's brother's leg was much better now, and his wife got pregnant along with the rest. But she was most regretful for bringing herself into this situation again.

Mei-tzu's belly was so big now that it constituted something of an inconvenience, and she treated the bit of hope inside her with the utmost care. The baby's clothes and everything else she would need for it were made ready, and her mother had already raised a dozen chickens to strengthen Mei-tzu's health during the first month after delivery.

One night the rain fell more heavily and the wind blew harder than ever. K'eng-ti trembled in the storm's onslaught the whole night through.

"If this keeps up our mud-brick wall won't be able to stand it," said Mei-tzu's brother, as though he had had a premonition that something was going to happen.

"Here, then—let's get under the dinner table," said his wife calmly. His mother, though, started calling out to heaven and earth for protection.

No sooner had the eleven of them crowded under the table than with a thunderous crash the rear wall collapsed, leaving the bamboo-and-thatch roof precariously askew with one end resting on the ground.

Mei-tzu fought back the tears as she comforted her wailing mother: "We can't complain! We're actually lucky—if we'd stayed in the back a minute longer we'd all have been buried alive."

Not only their house but the rest of K'eng-ti too was washed clean during that one night. Mei-tzu didn't complain about the disaster like the rest of them; she was grateful that she had escaped injury so that she could continue safely to nurture her only hope.

December came with a smile, brushing away the dark veil that hung over the countryside.

The people of K'eng-ti felt that their lives resembled someone repairing an old roof: finding a leak here and repairing it with great difficulty, then having to search for and repair another leak that developed there, only to discover still another leak someplace else. They couldn't give up; but to keep on working seemed to do no good either. They were really placed in a quandary.

After the November rains the sun bared its indolent face to watch them cleaning up after their disaster. All of the families whose mudbrick walls had collapsed worked together on the hillside, some cutting rice straw and mud, some leading the oxen which trampled in circles over the piles of mud and straw, some mixing, some firing the bricks. For more than ten days the hillside was the busiest place in K'eng-ti.

"This kind of soft sun with a north wind is the best time for making mud bricks," the adults there instructed their children. "These bricks won't have any cracks."

"But it's even better not to have to make bricks at all," joked a bystander.

"Of course, unless we have to build houses we don't like to have to make bricks."

As they bantered the talk turned to Aunt Sung.

"Aunt Sung," asked Uncle Woody, "Mei-tzu's so big now, when will we get to drink some sesame oil wine?"

Others too voiced their enthusiastic concern: "Yes! When?"

"Pretty soon now."

Mei-tzu's mother was overjoyed by this show of concern by the villagers, and the anxiety she had felt lest the girl should suffer their ridicule vanished.

"It'll be with us in January," she said.

"Oh? So soon!"

"Such a good girl, she should be given a son," said one of the older bystanders.

"Yes, she's the only good girl these eyes of mine have ever seen."

"Oh, it is only because you people're just too kind to her," protested her mother. But of course she rejoiced at the praise.

"Really, our praise doesn't do her justice."

"I think she'll have a boy," said one of the women. "Look at the way her belly points out."

"It's only right for her to get a boy."

"Why'll it be a boy if her belly points out that way?" The question came from a boy of twelve or thirteen who was leading an ox round and round over the pile of mud.

"You've got no business butting in asking questions about childbirth," admonished the boy's father gently. "All you need to know is how to handle the ox."

In the friendly laughter that followed, Mei-tzu's mother heard someone say, "Aunt Sung's a lucky woman." She added two extra bricks to her next load, and even with the extra weight her happiness was such that she felt as if she were floating.

Mei-tzu, though, felt a stab of anxiety when she saw her mother with eight of the mud bricks hanging from the pole across her shoulder. "Ma!" she called, "You shouldn't carry so many; your back can't stand it at your age."

The old woman put down the shoulder pole and answered without even taking time to wipe the sweat from her face. "Mei-tzu," she said, "everybody in K'eng-ti wants you to have a son. You've got to try hard!"

The girl forced a laugh; of course she too wanted it to be a boy, but who could she appeal to for help? She could only try to reassure herself; there would be time enough to worry about it later.

"I think it'll be a boy for sure; it jerks about fiercely already. Both sides can move now, and when it moves it really acts like a boy." Suddenly she stopped talking, feeling the movements in her belly start up again. "Hurry up, Ma—put your hand here!"

The mother pressed her hand on the girl's belly and her eyes rolled up in concentration as though she were eavesdropping on someone in the next room. After a while her mouth cracked open and her pupils darted to the left; after another period of concentration she said, "Ah . . . This is a wild one! Where's it get all that strength if it isn't a boy?"

Mei-tzu was watching her mother's face all the while, and the expression she saw there forced her into a position from which there seemed to be no escape. Her face showed a fervent hope as she repeated, "Is it so? Is it so?"

"It's a boy for sure, Mei-tzu!"

"It should be a boy—it should be a boy!"

"It's a boy for sure. It was just like this when I had your four brothers."

"How about when you had me?" the girl asked.

"When I was carrying you and your sister, I felt like there was a quiet swelling there. Then I knew I was going to have a girl, and I was right—I had you and your sister."

"Then I'll have a boy?"

"Ai! What're you worried about? If it's going to be a boy it'll be a boy; it can't run away, can it?" Her optimism did a great deal to bolster Mei-tzu's confidence. "Hurry back inside, Mei-tzu. Be careful you don't catch a cold. I've got to get back to work. The bricks'll be piling up." As she spoke she picked up her empty shoulder pole. But she knew that no one could tell whether her daughter would have a boy or not. Actually, Mei-tzu had had strong movements too before she was born; she remembered that of all her six children, Mei-tzu had had the strongest movements. What could anybody do about it? I didn't mean to lie to Mei-tzu! she thought. Turning back she saw that the girl had obediently gone inside already; nothing was left there but some wet firewood and some broken pieces of bricks. She felt weak somehow. Perhaps she was getting tired; her legs went so soft that she felt like she was stepping on her own body as she walked down the muddy path. Ahead of her was a place where two mountains came together, forming a huge valley. Looking out through the mouth of the valley she could see nothing, but there seemed to be something there in the far distance that stretched back into the sky, diminishing to a tiny speck. The old woman focused her attention there and suddenly she felt the mouth of the valley brighten; it seemed to her that she stood before a temple of the gods, and her whole soul was in her pleading voice as she uttered her fervent prayer: "God! Give Mei-tzu a son!"

January, they say, is a beginning.

The mountain wind, which made people crowd around their stoves or shrink beneath their covers, slipped down over the ridges of K'eng-ti's houses and squeezed through the mouth of the valley into the town. Had the townspeople been a little more sensitive they could have perhaps felt the heat that had been stripped from the bodies of the K'eng-ti villagers. All of K'eng-ti was like an icebox.

The ache in Mei-tzu's back was not brought on by the attack of the cold front; she knew it was a signal that the birth of the infant in her womb had begun, and it filled her with mixed emotions of happiness and anxiety.

"If it was anybody else but you, Mei-tzu," her mother said, "I'd help with the delivery."

The girl was secretly relieved when she heard this; she had been worrying about it for a long time but hadn't dared say anything. Since all of the women in K'eng-ti had their children in their own homes, she had wondered what she could say when the time came. But now there was nothing to worry about.

"Ma," she said, "with the weather so cold, I think I'd better go into town to have it."

"I think so, too."

That same evening the gripping pains started in Mei-tzu's belly. Her brother had long before rigged up a sedan chair for her; and when the villagers heard that she was going into town to have her baby, a group of them soon gathered to carry the chair for her.

The cold midnight wind pressed them closely and blew the flames of their torches to the side and sometimes below the paper wicks. Black Ear showed the way for them, sometimes running ahead, sometimes behind.

Mei-tzu's brother stood in the wind with a crutch, watching the light of the torches recede into the blackness of the night, shrinking to pinpoints and then to nothingness. Intuitively he felt the seriousness and significance of the sight and could not restrain the chill which ran through his bones.

By the time Mei-tzu arrived at the maternity clinic in town the pains, which at first had come every twenty minutes, had quickened to every five minutes; the doctor said that it would be soon now. A nurse came and gave her a shot of medicine to hasten the birth and said that it would probably be half an hour more. Not long after the shot the pains began to come and go in a continuous stream. Mei-tzu had been put on a delivery table and big drops of sweat gathered on her forehead as she underwent the primal ritual which the Creator had bestowed on womankind. Yet she took comfort from the wracking pains, for the more they hurt the more she felt that her hope had been not only a dream but an actuality about to be realized.

The doctor told her to grip the rails along each side of the delivery table and bear down hard. He stood beside the table giving her instructions, telling her that way was wrong, this way was right. "You're doing very well," he encouraged her. "Bear down like that some more, until the baby is born." The amniotic sac had already broken. Three more hours passed and the sky lightened but still the baby had not come; Mei-tzu appeared exhausted and the doctor had become anxious about her, though he kept his fears hidden from the others. The baby should have been born by now. Mei-tzu had done everything expected of her, and the doctor had seen that she could stand more pain and could put forth more effort than other expectant mothers. Maybe the umbilical cord had become wrapped around the infant's neck? He wondered.

The clinic was a small one and there was only one delivery

table; so when another woman about to give birth came in, Mei-tzu was taken to another room. Two other babies were born and Mei-tzu alone was still left there, trying with all her strength to force the baby into the world.

When she heard the cry of a newborn child in the next room, Mei-tzu saw in her mind an infant red all over and knew that she would have one too. But she had never dreamed that it could be such a difficult undertaking. The doctor took note of her stamina and decided to try the shots again, and the attacks of rending pain that followed the injections prompted the girl to strive with all her might once again, moaning all the while.

"That's right," the doctor said. "That's right. You're doing very well . . . that's the way, don't stop . . . bear down again."

Every time she felt her strength ebbing and her hope fading, those words from the doctor would fill her exhausted body with vitality and she would exert herself again and again and again. With the doctor beside her she had faith.

Sweat appeared on the forehead of the doctor too as he walked over to the glass cabinet and stared vacantly at the operating instruments arranged neatly inside. He couldn't make up his mind; he had the highest respect for this girl who had been so obedient in everything and so earnest, who transformed each attack of pain into strength. She still had the will and the means to go on; he would wait until she was exhausted and then decide what to do. He walked away from the cabinet; glancing at the clock on the wall he shook his head, noting that it had dragged on for six hours already.

"Kind doctor, please help me," pleaded the weak voice. "I've got to have this baby."

"Don't worry," he answered with a forced smile. "You've got the baby."

"I want it to live. It's got to live."

"Of course it's alive," the doctor said, taking her pulse. "How do you feel?"

"Worried about my baby!"

"There wouldn't be any baby without you, would there? How's your head feel?"

"Very clear."

"Good!" He told the nurse to give her another shot.

Mei-tzu was tortured by another long string of sharp pains; but without wasting a single chance, she transformed her painful struggles into strength. She was as soaked as if she had just been dragged out of a river, and now she appeared to be much weaker. It was a little frightening the way her mind remained so clear while her body became so weak; and her mother, who had stayed with her from the beginning, was shedding a continuous stream of anguished tears.

"Ma, why are you crying? Have you found out there's no hope left?"

The old woman could only shake her head.

"Where's the doctor?" the girl asked anxiously.

The doctor wreathed his face in smiles again as he came into the maternity room. "The time has come," he said as he gave her yet another shot. "The way you acted before will be a great help now. Just bear down once more."

The pains which had subsided came on strong again and Mei-tzu did her best, but with each try it was apparent that she had no strength left.

"You know, it's hard on the baby too when it can't come out. It wants to come out too! But nobody can help it except its mother. Come! Try again."

"Oh . . ." Mei-tzu was trying hard.

"Right," the doctor encouraged her. "Once more now."

"Oh . . ."

"Good—it'll be soon now."

"Mei-tzu . . ." Her mother anxiously tried to offer her encouragement too, but every time she opened her mouth to speak her voice broke down and so she closed it again.

"Ah! We can see the baby's head."

"Oh . . ." Mei-tzu tried extra hard that time.

"Try a little harder—we can see its head. The baby's saying, 'Try again, Mommy, try again.' " The doctor groaned along with her: "Oh . . . That's right, that's right." He was filled with anxiety; actually he could not see the baby's head at all, and the amniotic fluid had drained dry. There was not much time left.

"Oh . . ." She bore down again. She felt like an elephant with a heavy load on its back and a stalk of bananas just one step ahead, its stomach crying out for food. It steps forward hoping to get the bananas, but they too move a step forward. The elephant keeps pursuing the bananas but they maintain their distance a step ahead, until finally the animal realizes that it is all a cruel trick. Still it pursues the food desperately, thinking that its will and determination will surely bring it sympathy. The girl tried hard, so weakly now, still not abandoning hope; but finally her exertions became merely a gesture and she lapsed into unconsciousness.

Dreamily she walked into the garden that appeared before her eyes. A man—he must have been the gardener—told her sternly that she must not intrude so casually.

"But I've planted flowers here."

"What flowers?"

"I can't say."

"What kind of flowers?"

"Just that kind."

"What kind?"

"I can't say."

"Do you mean chrysanthemums?"

"No."

"Roses?"

"No."

"Then we don't have the kind of flowers you're talking about here."

"Yes you do! I planted them here."

"I don't know anything about them."

"I don't care . . ." Mei-tzu screamed.

The doctor took her pulse and gave her another shot. "We can't afford to think about the baby any longer," he said to her mother. "She's more important."

"Doctor . . . you don't know—this baby's her very life."

He understood the very special significance of those words.

"Of course, I'll do what I can."

The doctor and nurse put on surgical masks and rubber gloves, and an occasional clink of metal knocking together broke the silence of the delivery room. In her oblivion Mei-tzu felt herself afflicted by a new kind of pain, and when she came to she felt like a novice monk who, having dozed off while chanting scriptures, wakes up and hurriedly resumes his chanting. Ashamed of her laxity, she again summoned her strength and bore down. "Oh . . ."

"That's right, that's right. Very good." The doctor already had the baby's head in his forceps, but he waited for her to bear down again before pulling it out so that she would not feel that her efforts had been wasted.

"Oh . . ."

The doctor pulled. "Ah . . . It's out, it's out . . . It's a boy!"

Mei-tzu's mother and the nurse too let out a sigh of relief as though they had been unburdened of a heavy load. Mei-tzu herself felt no emotion when the thing was taken from her womb; but with the first sound of the infant's crying she felt, finally, that everything in her past was truly finished. She was very calm; her mother, on the other hand, cried with joy. The door of the delivery room was opened, and waiting outside was Mei-tzu's crippled brother with his wife and children.

7. *Days for Watching the Sea*

A compulsion in Mei-tzu was born at almost the same instant as her baby—a compulsion which would not lend itself to even the simplest explanation, although it was her own. She insisted on taking a mental position directly opposed to this compulsion—with no fear, however, of her isolation. She carried on a mental debate with herself:

"I'll go! I'll take the baby and go to the fishing port."

"The fish haven't schooled yet."

"I know."

"Then you can't possibly meet him—the baby's father."

"I know; that's not why I want to go."

"Why, then?"

"I don't know—maybe I'll meet him."

"If you do, then what?"

"I'll tell him that this baby is his."

"You want him to take care of you?"

"Never!"

"Why, then?"

"I know very well that he won't be at the fishing port now,

because the fish haven't schooled yet. He's probably at Heng-ch'un now."

"Then for what purpose do you want to go to the fishing port?"

"For no reason; I know I won't meet him, but I have to go . . ."

"But why?"

"I don't know, so I can't explain what this compulsion is."

From the time that the compulsion began Mei-tzu was at a loss to understand it; she knew only that it was urgent. Her health was fully recovered now and the compulsion was driving her more strongly than ever.

Taking her baby, she bought a ticket and squeezed on a train going toward the port. Not a single seat on the car was empty, but she didn't mind; she was happy enough just to be on the train going in that direction. Before she could find a spot to stand comfortably, two men in front of her stood up at the same time and offered her their seats; she was so surprised and moved by this ordinary event that she stood dumbfounded until a woman came over and led her to her own empty seat. She looked into the woman's face and was met by a warm and friendly smile. She looked at the people beside her and then searched the eyes of everybody she could see; in them she found without exception a warmth that she had never experienced before. Her eyes blurred. The barrier that had always constrained her and kept her separated from the crowd no longer existed, and the world that she saw now was obscured no longer by the suffocating bars of her prison. She had become a part of that world. She treasured the moment as she slowly lowered herself into the empty seat, and as she came into contact with the cushion a sense of warmth flowed over her. "All this is what my baby does for me," she thought as she clasped the child to her and began to cry silently.

The train sped through the long tunnel at Ta-li, and at the other end the broad expanse of the Pacific flashed into view. Mei-tzu stared at it for a moment and then held the baby upright, braced against her arm, and faced him toward the sea. His big round eyes were not able to focus yet but his mother pointed at the sea and said:

"Look, baby that's the sea!"

"Sea water is salty! Lots and lots of fish live in it.

"Some of them are as big as a train.

"And some are as little as your thumb.

"Look! There's a boat!

"Fishermen are sitting on the boat catching fish.

"They catch red ones, and white ones, and green ones, and yellow ones.

"All for my good baby to eat.

"Yes, your father was a brave fisherman.

"And one day when he was catching a big fish in the sea far, far away, he died.

"My good baby, don't you be a fisherman when you grow up.

"You'll go on a big ship across the ocean to study.

"You'll be a great man."

Then, as if in prayer, she continued:

"No, I don't believe that just because he has a mother like me, the baby will have no hope for the future." Her eyes were wet again.

The waves of the Pacific sparkled in the soft light of the winter sun as the train continued its smooth and steady swaying on its way toward the fishing port.

Lin Huai-min (1947–) received his B.A. in journalism from the National Cheng-chi University in 1968. From 1969 to 1970 he took graduate courses in journalism at the University of Missouri and Columbia University. He left both universities without taking a degree. Finding modern dance and creative writing more to his liking, he transferred to the University of Iowa, where he obtained his M.F.A. from the Writers' Workshop in 1972.

"Cicada" ("Shan") was published in *Hsien-tai wen-hsüeh*, No. 37, 1969. This translation of "Cicada," however, is from the version published by Ta-ti ch'u-pan she in 1973. With the permission of the author, some passages that do not render well into English are deleted. In "How Much Truth Can a Blade of Grass Carry?" I have briefly touched upon the characteristics of this story as follows:

> A native of Chia-yi, Taiwan, Lin Huai-min, however, has given little indication in his writings that he is a regional Taiwanese writer. His language is free of local expressions and he shows no particular interest in the fate of small men from small areas. Translate it into English, substitute John and Mary for the proper names, and you have in "Cicada" a story about a "lost generation" drinking coffee, smoking expensive cigarettes (Rothmans, to be specific), listening to Bob Dylan at the Cafe Barbarian in Taipei. . . . The above remarks, it should be emphasized, are not meant to be disparaging. As a story about youthful frustration and spiritual loss, "Cicada" has managed to give us a picture of truth—however partial—while at the same time recoiling from the truth.

Lin Huai-min is at present Instructor of English at his alma mater in Taiwan. He is also the director and choreographer of the Cloud-Gate Dance Ensemble (Yün-men wu-chi), the first modern dance company in the Republic of China.

Cicada-

LIN HUAI-MIN

Translated by TIMOTHY A. ROSS *and* LORRAINE S. Y. LIEU

"Five-five-six-four-eight-nine?"

"That's right. Five-five-six-four-eight-nine."

Chuang Shih-huan accepted the copper coin, damp with sweat, from Kuo Ching-p'ing's hand.

Clang! The coin dropped. Five-five-six, four-eight-nine.

He got a busy signal.

"Busy." He hung up the receiver. The coin returned.

"Wait a moment and try again. Don't forget, if it's her mother who answers, say you want to speak to T'ao Chih-ch'ing. Say you're her classmate and want to borrow her notes."

"School's out; no one would want to borrow notes."

"Her mother wouldn't know about such things. Just say you want to prepare for a make-up exam."

"Go on! You go prepare for a make-up exam. You call!"

"That won't do. Her mother would recognize my voice and then it would be hard for her to get out. Her mother takes most of the calls. T'ao Chih-ch'ing says the phone is right beside her mahjong table."

Chuang Shih-huan took out the coin and put it back in. This time, the telephone immediately gave a throaty roar: "Ring—, ring—, ring—"

Twang! The coin dropped. A man's voice came through hoarsely, as though just awakened:

"Hello? Who do you want?"

"Is this the T'ao residence? May I speak to Miss T'ao Chih-ch'ing please?"

"Wait a minute." The voice raised, "Third Sister! Phone!" The receiver was set down heavily, making his ear buzz. Chuang Shih-huan moved his receiver a bit, but a succession of piano notes still came indistinctly over the line, like large and small pearls falling

243

into a jade platter, although it was difficult to tell what tune it was.

With one hand placed on his hip and the other leaning against the wall, Kuo Ching-p'ing watched him closely.

"It's her brother, he's gone to call her."

"Oh." His smile immediately deepened.

"Really now, is she your girlfriend? Eh?"

"I wish she were. You'll see when she comes. An interesting girl."

A hundred *li* away someone was calling, "Third Sister! Telephone!"

The piano stopped. Someone was coming downstairs—someone was picking up the receiver:

"T'ao Chih-ch'ing. Who's there?" Like the dripping of the eaves late at night when all is quiet, each syllable was distinct and stamped directly on one's heart. "Hello. Who's there?"

Chuang Shih-huan raised his eyebrows and nodded. Kuo Ching-p'ing grabbed the receiver.

"It's me! Saucepan! Ha-ha! Surprise!" If T'ao Chih-ch'ing's mother had been next to her, playing mahjong, she would have heard too.

Chuang Shih-huan stood to one side. Someone wanted to go upstairs and he moved further back until he was leaning against the wall. Kuo Ching-p'ing, at the phone, was chattering away, now asking, now pleading, and now threatening, while his free hand kept gesturing to express his feelings.

Behind the cashier's desk, the proprietress, who had a round face like a Japanese doll, watched them with playful eyes.

During his first year in college, when Chuang Shih-huan had gone to the Star Cafe for the first time with his classmates, the proprietress had been sitting just as squarely behind her cashier's desk, smiling at her old customers. People came and went, and she must have seen enough of such phone conversations.

But this was the first time he had played such a role. Having just completed his final examinations and seen Wu Che off, he was like a convict just let out of jail, exhausted and weary but unwilling to remain in his room. Loafing around, Chuang thought that a cup of coffee wouldn't hurt, since he wouldn't be able to sleep well that night anyway. How could he know that once inside the Star Cafe, he would run into Kuo Ching-p'ing, who would drag him off to make this mysterious telephone call— T'ao residence? My God! Is this fellow called Kuo Ching-p'ing? Chuang Shih-huan couldn't remember clearly. He had seen him only once before. That was the time he took Wu Che to a dance and this Kuo had worn a pale blue shirt with white stripes, looking like a tropical fish. They said he painted. Painters perhaps had special rights to be eccentric. His hair was long, his shirt spotted, and he talked fast and loud.

"*Okay,*[1] all set," Kuo Ching-p'ing hung up the phone. He clapped his hands and with a big smile on his face dragged Chuang Shih-huan upstairs.

"Are you free now? Don't go. Wait a bit and we'll go have a drink."

"Just a second, I'll get my coffee."

There were two people at Kuo Ching-p'ing's table. He introduced them. The man was Chu Yu-pai. The girl was Liu Yü-ling; her short hair framed a round white face.

"This is Chuang Li-huan."

"Chuang Shih-huan."

The girl broke into a smile, her lips parted, and there was a piece of gum. She closed her mouth, chewed a few times, and asked:

"Is T'ao Chih-ch'ing coming?"

"She wouldn't dare not to come. I told her to take a cab."

"Forget it!" Chu Yu-pai said. He had a square face, thick brows, black-framed glasses, a close-cropped head, and he seemed to be in very good spirits. As he spoke, he lit a cigarette.

Kuo Ching-p'ing took a cigarette from Chu's pack and asked Chuang if he wanted one. Chuang shook his head. Kuo struck a match and lit it for himself. He inhaled deeply, removed the cigarette, and smoke issued from his nostrils and lips.

"Nine-forty," Liu Yü-ling said, chewing her gum, "T'ao Chih-ch'ing had better come soon; this place closes at ten." Suddenly she started to laugh and leaned back on the sofa, laughing so hard that her two eyes narrowed into slits. She turned her head and asked Chu Yu-pai:

---

[1] The Chinese original contains many phrases in the English language. However, in order to avoid confusion, none of these have been italicized.

"Do you remember that time we were chatting on the third floor and we forgot the time? When we finally thought to go, it was already ten-fifty. We rushed downstairs and the second floor was all dark. That fat waiter was standing at the bottom of the stairs and he gave you the check without a word. You were so scared that you didn't even want to wait for the change. You just dragged me and hurried away."

Chu Yu-pai nodded.

Liu Yü-ling lowered her head and sipped a few mouthfuls of lemonade, chewed her gum, and continued:

"T'ao Chih-ch'ing had better come soon. With windbags like Saucepan among us, we'll be kicked out as soon as it's ten."

Kuo Ching-p'ing blew out a mouthful of smoke and gestured with his hand:

"When the pub closes, I'll go!" [2]

Chu Yu-pai frowned in disagreement. Chuang Shih-huan followed Liu Yü-ling and began to laugh nervously. Only two swallows of coffee and a small pitcher of cream remained. He emptied all the cream into the coffee and there was half a cup of greyish-brown liquid, like cocoa.

"Do you know?" Kuo Ching-p'ing asked, "I'm going to open a coffee house one of these days."

"There seem to be quite a lot of things that you want to do," Liu Yü-ling said. "Just when did you get the idea of opening a dark coffee house?"

"Not dark, not dark," Kuo said, "as bright as broad daylight. All the walls will be panelled with lucite and lights will be installed behind the panels and there will be lots of colors for the guests to amuse themselves with, drawing whatever they like."

"Drawing on what?"

"On the lucite panels. Thus the whole room will be filled with colors. If you don't like someone else's drawing, you can always wipe it off and draw your own, and you can also write whatever dirty words you can think of. Besides," Kuo Ching-p'ing struck the table, making the cups and saucers jump and settle again, "it'll be open all night long!"

[2] A saying attributed to Sir Winston Churchill.

"I'm afraid only people like you would go to such a place."

"You'll see, just wait till this old boy has some money!"

Chu Yu-pai laughed as the smoke from his cigarette twisted through space.

"Come on now! Wait till you have money? How soon will that be? Oh yeah, how's your business lately?"

"So-so, but anyway I don't have to worry that they won't sell."

"Are you still copying Hu Ch'i-chung?"

Kuo Ching-p'ing shook his head:

"Too many people copy him. Now I'm specializing in painting Van Goghs. For export."

"Oh my God! Are you painting them stroke by stroke too?" Chu asked.

"Ah, it's not hard; we can often finish a Number 3 in one night, and I guarantee you can't tell them from the originals."

"Damn you!" said Liu Yü-ling, spitting out her gum and tossing it into the ashtray. "Van Gogh is going to climb out of his grave and come cut off *your* ear. When are you going to paint seriously?"

"Wait till I have some money!" Kuo Ching-p'ing was not at all embarrassed about his boasting. He crooked his forefinger as if he wanted to say some more, but he paused and his forefinger curled back up into a fist. He raised his eyebrows and said:

"Ah, Miss T'ao is here!"

A slender girl stood at the head of the stairs. When she saw them, she smiled, circled around a row of tables and chairs, and whirled to their table. Her long hair, which fell down her back, was gathered with a ribbon of pale blue satin. She wore a loose pale yellow shirt, and beneath her skirt, which had a pattern of fine yellow lines on grey, was a pair of small knees. She was not tall, but because the lines of her face stood out boldly, she seemed smart and spirited.

"Is Saucepan bluffing again?" The corners of her lips quirked in what might have been a smile.

Chu Yu-pai stood up and made a place for her while Liu Yü-ling took T'ao Chih-ch'ing's hand and made her sit down. But even before she had settled down, she saw that Kuo Ching-p'ing had not responded and she went on:

"Is it because your paintings are selling so well and you feel embarrassed to be so rich? Otherwise, how come you're buying people coffee when you're supposed to be going into the army?" As she spoke, she lifted her head and squinted in a frivolous manner.

Chuang Shih-huan felt that he had seen her before but he could not quite remember where.

Kuo Ching-p'ing could only smile while the cigarette between his fingers burned down to the filter.

T'ao Chih-ch'ing had just sat down when Liu Yü-ling asked her, "Oh, wow, where did you buy such a lovely skirt?"

"Don't bring that up," T'ao Chih-ch'ing said, waving her hand. Just now when I was leaving, I had to argue for a long time with my mother. She insisted I change into something presentable. She said this wasn't a skirt at all but just a strip of cloth that would whirl away at the first breeze. Every time I go out she wants me to get fixed up like—"

"T'ao Chih-ch'ing," Kuo Ching-p'ing said, "this is Chuang Li-huan."

"Chuang Shih-huan."

Liu Yü-ling bit her lower lip, trying not to laugh. T'ao Chih-ch'ing smiled and nodded.

Suddenly Chuang Shih-huan remembered!

"Miss T'ao, I think we've seen each other before."

T'ao Chih-ch'ing lifted her head, brushed away a lock of hair that had crept onto her forehead, raised her eyelashes, arched her brows, and half parted her lips as though to say "Oh!"

"It was some time last month. Here, on the third floor, you were with a friend and you borrowed my newspaper to look at the movie ads. But I think you were wearing glasses then."

"Oh! I remember now. That time you were sitting alone at the window. Right?" T'ao Chih-ch'ing's elbow rested on the table and her hand supported her cheek; she kept nodding and smiling. "I was wearing glasses that day. I wasn't used to these contacts yet."

Kuo Ching-p'ing shoved over excitedly and asked urgently:

"Who were you with that day?"

T'ao Chih-ch'ing pursed her lips and tilted her chin. "None of your business!" Turning to Liu Yü-ling, she said:

"Guess what movie we picked that day? *The Sunflower*. A rotten movie! Absolute trash. . . ."

Kuo Ching-p'ing grabbed Chuang, "Do you remember what that fellow looked like?"

Chuang Shih-huan said he couldn't remember clearly but it seemed the man had been wearing a black sports shirt.

"Stop making a fool of yourself, Saucepan." T'ao Chih-ch'ing shook her head resignedly. "It was Hsiao Fan—³. All this talking, talking! What are you going to treat us to tonight anyway? I've been here all this time and I haven't even seen a glass of water."

"This place is going to close up pretty soon. We'll go drinking at New Park. Yu-pai and I will go first to buy the beer."

"Go right ahead, since I know you can't bear to board the train tomorrow unless you've spent all your money. I want to sit here a while longer. I'll meet you later at the park gate, all right?"

"Saucepan," Liu Yü-ling said, "I want dried beef, the kind with the fruit juice flavor."

Kuo Ching-p'ing agreed and went downstairs with Chu Yu-pai.

Liu Yü-ling jumped up, saying, "Chu Yu-pai's always so absent-minded. Look, he's forgotten the keys to his motorcycle again." Picking up the keys from the table, she went after them.

T'ao Chih-ch'ing shrugged and leaned back into the corner where the sofa met the wall. She stretched out her hand to switch on the wall lamp so that the orange-yellow light spilled across the table.

"Do you know why I like the Star Cafe? I like these little wall lamps, these clumsy marble table tops. They make me feel very secure. My God, it's so hot. Would you tell them to bring me a glass of cold water? Chuang—"

"Chuang Shih-huan." Chuang Shih-huan smiled, rubbing his nose as he spoke.

"How do you write it?" T'ao Chih-ch'ing asked. As she supported her chin with her hands and inclined her head, her eyes held a spirit both strange and serious—could it have been because of the contact lenses?

³ Hsiao means "little." It is a familiar form of address.

Like the rising sun at dawn, the lamplight penetrated the slowly rising mist and fell upon the sheet of Korean grass.

Five people emerged slowly from the darkness, with Kuo Ching-p'ing's voice charging ahead of them.

"Oh, mother, this time tomorrow this old boy'll be a soldier. Assistant squad leader, my my, commanding twenty or thirty men! Screw 'em! Chu Yu-pai attention! What are you laughing at? Showing off your teeth? Give me fifty push-ups!"

Liu Yü-ling hid by Chu Yu-pai, giggling:

"Saucepan is such a silly ass!"

Chu Yu-pai waved his hand. "Stop clowning around, Saucepan!"

Kuo Ching-p'ing went to the revolving door and pushed it with his shoulder, but he had mistaken the direction so he just stood there and refused to budge.

Chuang Shih-huan opened another door and as T'ao Chih-ch'ing went through, she said, "Saucepan has no sense of decency. Just a little beer and he acts as if he's really under the influence."

"T'ao Chih-ch'ing!" Kuo Ching-p'ing leaned against the iron-work fence and called from the other side of the gate, "You still owe me a painting; you agreed to pose for me."

"You cut that out! You still owe me a 'Sunflowers' by Van Gogh." T'ao Chih-ch'ing turned around and yelled, "Don't think you can get away with it just because you're going into the army."

Chuang Shih-huan broke into a smile. As he raised his eyes, he saw the round roof of the City Museum, a mass of pale blue wrapped in fog. Spring had spread itself on the dandelion-filled lawn—what a strange evening!

As they passed the great brass cow at the park gate, Kuo Ching-p'ing caught up; he came striding up, his footsteps echoing in the vast space.

"T'ao Chih-ch'ing, I'll take you home!"

"Thanks, Chuang Shih-huan is seeing me home. You'd better go home and get some sleep. If you don't catch the train tomorrow and report in time, see if they don't catch you and shoot you."

"Then I'll see you home, Liu Yü-ling; don't you ride on Chu Yu-pai's motorcycle, he's been drinking and he's liable to run into a pedestrian island."

Liu Yü-ling smiled but said nothing.

A taxi slowed down. Chuang Shih-huan hailed it and turned around to shake Kuo Ching-p'ing's hand and thank him.

Having gotten into the taxi, T'ao Chih-ch'ing stuck her head out the window. "Saucepan, don't forget to send me a photograph of your bald head!"

The taxi drove off. From behind, Kuo Ching-p'ing shouted, "T'ao Chih-ch'ing! You fool! Officer cadets don't have to shave their heads!"

"Saucepan, why are you so impossible this evening?" Liu Yü-ling asked, giggling.

The taxi started down Kuan-ch'ien Street. Its light picked out the road in the gorge of smothering mists.

"Where to?" the driver asked.

Chuang Shih-huan turned his head and looked at T'ao Chih-ch'ing.

T'ao Chih-ch'ing sat up and sighed, "My God, if I go home now, I can't escape a big fat scolding." Then, turning her head and fluttering her lashes, she said, "Didn't you say that your roommate had gone home?"

"Mm-hmm."

"Then suppose I spend the night at your place? If I go home now I'll have to ring the bell and wake up the whole house."

The slight confusion brought on by the beer was instantly eclipsed; Chuang Shih-huan gaped in amazement and stared at her. Separated from him by the darkness of the taxi's interior, T'ao Chih-ch'ing was regarding him without the slightest confusion; her eyelids and her cheeks flushed, her eyes were pools of water without any hesitancy or trickery, as though she had merely said, "Let's go and get some ice cream."

Chuang Shih-huan rubbed his nose, swallowed hard, and said to the driver, "An-tung Street!"

"Do you have a cigarette?"

Chuang Shih-huan shook his head.

"Ask the driver for one."

"I smoke Chü-kuangs," the driver said. "Miss may not be used to them?"

"Fine. I like Chü-kuangs."

Chuang Shih-huan took the cigarettes and matches and gave a cigarette to T'ao Chih-ch'ing. He lit two matches, but each time the match was blown out. Just as he was going to roll up the window, T'ao Chih-ch'ing snatched the matches over and, laughing, lit the cigarette with a "pop!" Leaning back, she contentedly puffed her cigarette, pulled off her hair ribbon, and tossed her head. The wind blew strands of her hair across Chuang Shih-huan's face and carried her exhaled smoke out the window to blend into the fog.

The taxi sped through the fog-hidden streets. Chuang Shih-huan looked at his wrist watch: one twenty-three. Wu Che should have arrived in Kaohsiung by now. A series of jolts, and T'ao Chih-ch'ing swayed over against him. Chuang Shih-huan stretched his hand over her shoulder and rested it on the back of the seat, but as soon as it rested there, he pulled it back and bent his head to light a cigarette.

Smoking, he watched the fog lit up by the headlights and the darkness behind the fog. The taxi seemed to be trapped in the night fog and no longer moving forward. He hoped the taxi would go on like this forever and ever, never to stop again.

Sssss—ssssss—ssssss—when had it started to rain? Chuang Shih-huan was puzzled. Ssssss—Ssssss. His frown deepened. Eyes tightly closed, he put his hand to block a strand of light. He was puzzled: when had it started to rain? Ssssss—the rain stopped.

Chuang Shih-huan rolled over and sat up, shaking his head to get rid of that light which pursued him and his remaining drowsiness. He had not yet opened his eyes when he smelled the heavy aroma of coffee.

The curtains were not pulled tight and were whirling in the light breeze. A sunbeam curved over the long sofa and spilled onto the floor, where it lay flat. Fine dust particles formed lines swimming toward the window and darting back to the floor. In the corner, the coffee-pot screeched and sent forth puffs of milk-white steam.

Chuang Shih-huan blinked, scratched his head, and went over to open the curtains. A broad band of sunlight grandly thrust its

way in. He drew a deep breath. The wind ruffled his dry, disordered hair. Creak. Behind his back, someone had opened the
door.

"Oh, you're up." T'ao Chih-ch'ing stood in the bathroom doorway with her head wrapped in a water-green towel. The satisfaction of having slept her fill was in her smile and she gave off the
fresh scent of having bathed.

"Half past ten. But I saw you were sleeping so soundly . . ."
She moved slowly into the center of the room, bent her head and
removed the towel, and her black hair fell like a cascade. "Oh, my
God, the coffee-pot is going to blow up!" She hurried over, bent
down, and pulled out the plug. Standing in the misty steam, she
wrung the towel and wiped some drops of water from her neck.
With a jerk of her head, she swung her long hair down her back
and looked at Chuang with a smile.

Chuang Shih-huan looked at his two long hairy legs beneath his
shorts and did not know just what to say. Such underwear! He
thought and thought but nothing occurred to him, so he shrugged
his shoulders and smiled at her. He picked up a pair of trousers
lying over the back of the couch, rubbed his nose, and went
whistling into the bathroom. As he passed T'ao Chih-ch'ing, he
smelled on her body the fragrance of Lux soap and his heart
jumped suddenly—it was Wu Che's scent!

After he had washed, he came out. T'ao Chih-ch'ing was sitting
on the rocking chair beside the phonograph, playing with
Wu Che's guitar, and the towel rested on the arm of the chair,
hanging to the floor. There were two coffee cups on the table and
a plate of egg with a ball of egg yolk resting in the middle of the
egg white: a white lotus with a yellow stamen. He couldn't help
laughing.

"What a waste to live in such a big apartment—the refrigerator
is empty, there's butter but no bread, and the cheese has gone all
green with mold. I searched around for quite a while and all I
could find were two carrots. At least there was an egg, otherwise
you wouldn't have a thing to eat."

Chuang Shih-huan looked at her. This girl, she's really something!

"I've been busy lately with exams and I've been eating out. I've got to hand it to you for finding the egg. The night before last, I couldn't find any."

"It was in the vegetable bin," T'ao Chih-ch'ing patted the arm of the rocking chair and jumped up, "with the carrots. Eat, it's getting cold."

Chuang sat down, poured her a cup of coffee, and poured one for himself. T'ao Chih-ch'ing took the cup, sipped, and said, "Don't you want cream?"

He shook his head and licked his gums with the tip of his tongue; he had just scratched them while brushing his teeth, and there was a faint taste of blood.

"But the cup you had last night at the Star Cafe looked like milk—never mind, I'll bring you some anyway. Otherwise the cream will go sour too."

Chuang Shih-huan poured a great puddle of cream, just like a child playing games. When he looked up, T'ao Chih-ch'ing's lips, with a drop of coffee at the corner, were puckered in a smile. He pushed the cream over to her but she shook her head.

"I don't take anything. Breakfast for me is just a cup of black coffee like this—and a cigarette wouldn't hurt. Last night I was in such a hurry when I left that I forgot my purse."

He brought cigarettes and an ashtray from the study and lighted her cigarette.

"Did you sleep well?"

"Okay!" T'ao Chih-ch'ing knit her brows, lowered her eyelids, and nodded. She said quickly, "And you? Honest to God, I didn't mean to make you sleep on the sofa. Who could have known you had only one bed. I tell you, no fooling, that lotus-blue embroidered quilt is all crumpled out of shape after I've been sleeping on it. I have an awful habit, on summer nights I like to sleep on top of the coverlet. You know, it's cooler."

"I know, I do it myself sometimes."

"And the pillow? Do you like to punch a dent in the pillow and then put your head in it too?"

Chuang shook his head in the negative—it was Wu Che who did that. "I'm just the opposite. I have to fluff it up and when it sinks after I've been sleeping on it, I turn it over."

T'ao Chih-ch'ing shook with laughter and flicked her cigarette ash as she said, "If I made a good investigation of this place, I could really write an interesting essay!" Her eyes roved, trailed by a sly smile. Then she lowered her head to sip her coffee, "Oh, do you know what? When I slept in that room, I felt like I was at home, not in a man's room."

"Oh?" He swallowed the last mouthful of egg, took a sip of coffee, raised his chin, and rubbed his nose with his forefinger, stroking the bridge of his nose to the top and then slipping down, down over his sweaty lips to his chin, and over the whiskers which he should have shaved before.

"How should a man's room be?" For some reason or other, the tone of his voice had suddenly grown low and rough, as if ground out by cog wheels.

"Well, there should be a certain smell."

"What smell? Smelly socks, old shoes, and moldy wet quilts all together?" He took a cigarette, lighted it, and inhaled, but his throat was as dry as tinder and he put it down.

"Maybe, maybe not. Oh—maybe it's just that your room is a little too clean. Even the pillow cases are unnaturally clean, and there's this smell of perfume." Smiling, she added, "And those pictures of Alain Delon and Anthony Perkins on the wall—do you like them?"

He rolled his eyes and heaved a sigh, "Ugh—no!"

"I didn't think you would! But what about that roommate of yours? Gay, or what?" She cocked her head and her hair fell across one eye, leaving the other blinking, blinking . . .

Chuang Shih-huan thought, I ought to pound the table and stand up. His hand swept over the table, picked up a cigarette, tapped it, and the ashes fell outside the ashtray. The cigarette was between his lips but he did not inhale it. He heard the neighbor's canary repeating its song endlessly and the alarm clock in the study going "tock tock tock" like a galloping horse.

"Of course it's just a wild guess . . ."

Chuang Shih-huan put down his cigarette and lifted his cup. The dark brown liquid rippled and reflected the whiteness of the ceiling, the light behind him, his forest-black hair, the smoke swirling above his head, his high nose, the razor-trimmed brows

and the eyes below the brows, the two points of bright light in the
eyes, his glistening cheeks, his half-opened lips on the rim of the
cup. As though frightened by his reflection, he started, closed his
mouth, and bit his upper lip. Oh, Wu Che! He raised his head.
T'ao Chih-ch'ing blew out a cloud of smoke which suddenly
rushed at him. Wu Che!

Wu Che had been a classmate of his in the fourth year at
Tainan High School. Tall, lean, bright, and pure. When the
others finished playing basketball, they were like oxen and only
he, although sweating, still looked as if he had just finished show-
ering, clean and refreshed. During summer vacation, Wu Che's
father moved to Taipei and Wu Che transferred to another school.
When the Matriculation Examination results were posted,
Chuang Shih-huan saw Wu Che's name on the admissions list of
the university by which he had been accepted, in the Department
of Foreign Languages.

Although they were not in the same class, Chuang ran into
Wu Che on the campus from time to time. Is that teacher Chao,
who used to teach us calisthenics still at Tainan High? Are you
busy? Did you come out all right on the exams?—and so forth.
They often greeted one another, nothing more. Once Chuang
Shih-huan happened to hear someone speaking of Wu Che. His
good looks and aloofness were well-known. He never took part in
class activities and was seldom seen in the library.

Not until the day of registration for the second year of college,
when Wu Che cut into Chuang Shih-huan's line, did the two of
them have a chance to talk as they went through the process
together. Chuang mentioned that he was looking for a place to
live. He had arrived too late and the relatively cheap and quiet
rooms near the university were all rented. It was a real headache.
Wu Che eagerly suggested that Chuang move in with him. His
parents and younger brother had moved to Kaohsiung the summer
before and he was now living alone in an apartment with two bed-
rooms and a living room. Chuang Shih-huan went home with
Wu Che. The same evening they used his rickety old bicycle and
moved his things over in two trips.

However! However, he really didn't know that Wu Che was like
that! He didn't know that Wu Che still wanted the light on while

he slept. The double bed was big enough for four people but Wu
Che kept crowding over against him, pushing him against the wall
as if afraid he would run away in the middle of the night. What
Chuang found even more annoying was that Wu Che, upon waking in the morning, would not even open his eyes but would first
reach over and feel if Chuang were there and then, reassured, he
would open his eyes.

One day, he got up first and was shaving in the bathroom. He
heard some shuffling in the bedroom and Wu Che called softly:
"Shih-huan!" He paid no attention and went on shaving. A desolate wail of alarm followed: "Shih-huan!" His hand slipped, and a
drop of red blood appeared on his lip. The next moment, he saw
in the mirror that Wu Che had appeared behind him, his face as
pale as the wall. Chuang grabbed a towel to wipe away the blood
and asked coldly, "What's the matter?" Wu Che, leaning against
the wall, said "I thought you were gone." The blood oozed out
again. He threw down the towel, rushed into the study to gather
his notes, slammed the door, and left.

When he came back that night, there was a letter for Wu Che
in the mailbox. He took it upstairs and laid it on the dining table.
After a while, Wu Che came in and glanced at the letter without
opening it; instead, he picked up his guitar and played song after
song from popular songs to flamenco. Chuang Shih-huan paid no
attention to him and went to bed by himself.

In the middle of the night, he felt someone hanging onto his
arm. It was Wu Che. He was fast asleep, with his right hand on
Chuang's arm. The tip of his index finger was wrapped with a
piece of cloth where a brownish stain of blood had dried; an irritating sight. He gently removed the hand. He turned over, rolling
toward the wall, and a certain disgust wriggled to the surface of his
mind. But in the dimness of half-sleep, matters weren't clear to
him until the next day—

The guitar lay slanted across the rocking chair, with one of its
strings broken and curled like a worm. The letter lay limply on the
floor, wrinkled, as though it had been crushed into a ball and then
pressed flat again. Out of curiosity, Chuang Shih-huan picked it
up. If he had not read it with his own eyes, he would not have
believed such things could exist in the world. That a man could

write such a letter to another man! He began to understand the feeling he had had during the night and made up his mind to move out.

Several mid-terms followed and he could not find a room at once. After the examinations, an old classmate from Tainan High School invited him to a party at his house and wanted him to bring a couple of friends along. Thinking that he should give Wu Che a chance to have more contact with the outside world, he dragged him along.

Wu Che went, sat quietly for a while, and suddenly developed an interest in a freshman girl wearing a red dress. He asked her to dance four or five times in succession, and then the two of them sat in a dark corner, talking and laughing. Later, as abruptly as he had begun, he deserted her, made his way into the crowd of dancers, and told Chuang Shih-huan that he wanted to leave. The old classmate asked Wu to stay but Chuang Shih-huan said, "O.K., if you want to go, then go by yourself!"

When he returned, furious, Wu Che had already gone to bed. Beneath the pale fluorescent light, in the middle of the big bed, Wu Che, his long body curled like that of a child, lay sound asleep. His black hair shone brilliantly against his white forehead, his eyebrows were slightly knitted, and beneath his eyes were pale bluish shadows. His long lashes trembled intermittently, as if some delicate little moths, fanning their transparent wings, were engaged in their last struggle with death. In an instant most of his anger dissipated and his body was suddenly filled with a powerful emotion: a compassion that came from the deepest recesses of his heart. But when he thought of that letter, Chuang Shih-huan looked at Wu Che sleeping and said to himself, I've got to move out.

For three days Chuang Shih-huan looked for a room after classes, went to the library in the evening until it closed, and went to his classmates' dormitory to spend the night. On the fourth day, when Wu Che's class representative stopped him at the school gate and gave him Wu Che's English essay, he knew that Wu Che had not been to class for three days. The hell with him! he thought. That evening, he found a small room, paid a fifty dollar deposit, and was all set to move in the next day.

Wu Che's essay had a strange title: "An Awakening in the Toilet." In the library, Chuang Shih-huan opened his book and the two sheets of typewriter paper floated out. He glanced at them, brushed them aside, and returned to his book. Before he had read many pages, the horizontal lines suddenly came alive—rows and rows of eyelashes trembling, trembling. The hell with him! he thought. But the class representative had said that Wu Che hadn't been to class for three days. He closed his book and picked up the essay. Not a single word registered in his mind; that cursed letter swam before his eyes. Those passionate sentences, which were enough to make a person throw up, renewed his resolve. That letter, Wu Che could have torn it up or burnt it. Wu Che is not blind to his own danger and has in fact struggled against it; you are the only friend who can help him—the hell with him! You're moving tomorrow anyway—but, how hot it is in the library! He went outside for a breath of fresh air. He went out for air three times before it was nine: pacing, smoking, and at last walking across most of the campus to the student union to drink a bottle of cold milk.

He returned with a stomachful of coldness. Before he had sat for a few minutes, he stood up again and went over to the pencil sharpener at the door, where he took a fine new pencil and sharpened it down to the length of his little finger. If he hadn't been to class for three days, where had he been? The hint contained in that unburned letter, Wu Che's pale face as he leaned against the bathroom door, those words, "I thought you were gone" suddenly became a flag signalling for help, so bright that he could not be indifferent—damn it! He pulled out his pencil and returned to his seat—to hell with him! In any case I'm moving out tomorrow! He moved his chair forward a little and had just settled when he shoved the chair back again, swept up his books, and strode out.

The bicycle clattered all the way back as though it would fall apart at any moment. He paid no attention but pedalled recklessly on like an arrow cleaving the wind, as though he were going to put out a fire. When he entered the lane, he slowed down a bit. You're just like a dog trying to catch a rat; maybe he's already brought the guy home with him! He turned and crossed the little bridge. In the whole apartment building, only their place was dark—so he's not there! He's not there after all! Disappointment relaxed his tension.

Two and three steps at a time he climbed the stairs, opened the door, and turned on the light. There was a layer of dust on the floor. In the dishpan lay two bowls which he hadn't had time to wash that day. The contents of the icebox were as before. The quilts were neatly folded and not a wrinkle appeared on the sheet, which was as flat as a beach. The wastebasket in the study was full—that was one of the things Wu Che could not abide. So, he wasn't here all along! Having satisfied himself on this point, Chuang Shih-huan suddenly didn't know what else to do. He went back to the living room, sat down in the rocking chair, got up again, and turned off the light. He returned to the rocking chair. He lit a cigarette.

He had just lit his seventh cigarette when he heard movement outside the door. He inhaled fiercely. It will be beautiful if the two of them come in. I can wash my hands of it!

The door opened with the jangling of keys. Discovering that the door to the living room was not locked, Wu Che hesitated a moment and pushed the door open. Wu Che was amazed to see the fiery tip of a cigarette in the darkness; then he turned on the light.

Although he was mentally prepared, Chuang Shih-huan was still shocked. He had not seen the other for four days and Wu Che was even thinner. Contrary to his usual neat and clean appearance, Wu Che's collar was unbuttoned and his trousers were wrinkled as though they had not been pressed or dried. His hair had not been groomed and looked like a clump of wild grass on top of an air-raid shelter. His eyebrows were mussed. His eyes gleamed, but only as he entered the room; then the light faded. He resembled a carefully carved statue of stone impassively standing there. Abruptly, as if he had collapsed, he sank down onto a short sofa. He lifted his right foot, bent his head, untied his shoelace, and dropped the shoe. He lowered his foot and sat there staring at Chuang with the vacant, stagnant look of a blind man.

Where'd you go? he wanted to ask, but did not; there was no need to ask. Chuang Shih-huan remained motionless, glaring at Wu Che and puffing his cigarette.

Two days later a strange young man came to the door looking

for Wu Che. Without even taking a good look, Chuang Shih-huan felt intuitively that he was "one of those." He was going to tell him that Wu Che was not in, but before the words reached his lips, he changed them to "There's no such person here!" and slammed the door shut.

"Fine! Now they're coming to the door!" He stormed angrily into the bedroom, yelled at Wu Che, and meant to grab him and hit him. But Wu Che just clutched his guitar, curled up his long legs, and shrank into a corner of the bed. His expression said, "One word from you and you'll see me breathe my last!" Chuang Shih-huan sighed, crossed his arms across his chest, and sat down heavily on the edge of the bed near the door.

For a long time they sat there, two enemies staring at each other suspiciously. It was as though they had sat like that from the dawn of creation and would go on sitting so, in this room devoid of life, forever.

The sunlight fell on the dining table as Chuang Shih-huan drained the last swallow of coffee from the bottom of the cup. It was cold and bitter. He set the cup down and said, "In fact, it's nothing; he just needs someone to look after him."

T'ao Chih-ch'ing laughed with a light snort and extinguished her fourth cigarette.

"And you're really good at looking after others, eh? How long do you intend to look after him?"

Chuang Shih-huan lit a match and watched the bluish-red flame slowly consume itself. When it burned down to his finger-tips, he dropped it into the ashtray. It was soon burned out and curled into a thin line of black ash.

How long? He didn't know. He only knew that he was like the circle of protection which Sun Wu-k'ung had drawn for Tripitaka. If he ran away, Wu Che, like a falling star, would quickly plunge out of the normal stream of life.

Someone was cooking downstairs. There was the sound of a spatula tapping against a wok.

T'ao Chih-ch'ing smacked her lips and waggled her jaws from side to side as though she had smoked too much and her jaws ached. But she pursed her lips and took out another cigarette.

"Aren't you going home for the summer?"

"Not just now. I'm helping a professor prepare the index of his book, and when that's finished I'll go home for a while and look for a couple of tutoring jobs."

From downstairs came the sounds of a woman scolding a child and the sloshing of a tap overflowing.

"Ah, I should be going." T'ao Chih-ch'ing rubbed out her cigarette and stood up. "If I don't go, you'll chase me out. Making you sleep on the sofa, getting two cups of your coffee, and forcing your secrets out of you. Shall I call you some time and we can get together one of these days?"

T'ao Chih-ch'ing had gone as far as the door when Chuang Shih-huan unexpectedly seized her elbow and gazed fixedly into her eyes. "Do you often go home to spend the night with a man you've just seen for the first time?"

Amusement seemed to flash in T'ao Chih-ch'ing's eyes as she shook her head calmly and replied: "But I knew you couldn't do me any harm." She jerked free of Chuang's hand and smoothed the hair behind her neck. "There was something strange in your eyes."

"What?" The words were forced between his teeth.

T'ao Chih-ch'ing looked at him and closed the door.

Chuang Shih-huan sat on the balcony railing and watched as T'ao Chih-ch'ing came out of the apartment building and stepped into the street. She raised her head, moved her lips, and waved. He waved to her. T'ao Chih-ch'ing hailed a taxi and got into it, her long hair blowing in the wind. The taxi crossed the bridge, turned at the end of the lane, and disappeared.

The sky was cloudless and so blue that one expected it to drip oil, the king coconut palm in the courtyard across the street was spreading its great shiny green leaves in the breeze, and the sunlight was warm on his body. Strange, that I should have told her so many things for no reason, as though she were an old friend of many years. And stranger still, I don't regret it a bit, at least not now. The thought that he did not regret it gave Chuang Shih-huan a cold shiver.

In the lane, a piece of torn newspaper came whirling along, fell to the ground, and was again whirled away by the wind.

"Hello, can I speak to Chuang Shih-huan, please?"

"Speaking."

"Hey, it's you. I'm Yu-pai, Chu Yu-pai, do you remember me? That day at the Star Cafe—"

"Oh, sure, sure. How are you?"

"Are you free now?"

"Just now I was getting ready to leave."

"You see, T'ao Chih-ch'ing told me to call you and ask you to come out and join us."

"Where are you?"

"At the Yuan-shan Amusement Park. Me, T'ao Chih-ch'ing, Liu Yü-ling are all here, and Hsiao Fan too."

"The Yuan-shan? Great!"

"Are you coming?"

"Well—all right."

"Are you at school? Look here, I'll come pick you up. I'll ride my motorcycle, so it'll be real soon."

"Okay, thanks. I'm on the second floor in the Social Science Building."

"All right, I'll see you."

"Hey, your motorcycle's not bad! Honda? How much?"

"Unh-uh, it's a Vespa. I got someone to bring it in from Hong Kong for just over twenty thousand. Liu Yü-ling chipped in half and the other half I earned myself."

"How did you earn it? Tutoring? Or did you win the lottery?"

"Uh—selling textbooks. A classmate of mine in medical school and I are partners, we get pirated textbooks wholesale from a printer, and each book sold means a net profit of thirty percent."

"Is it really that profitable?"

"You bet, very profitable. But then we sell them much cheaper than the bookstores. Think how many students there are in the medical school and almost all of them have to buy those books."

"Nice set-up. You're really putting your business management study to use."

"Forget it! Since I'm grown up, I can't be always asking for money from home. Do you know what bugs my father most about me? He's angry because I no longer ask him for money!"

Chu Yu-pai stopped for a red light on North Chung-shan Road, lifted his dark green sunglasses, and turned and smiled at Chuang Shih-huan.

A scarlet sports car braked to a stop beside them. The driver was an American. His dark glasses covered half his face and a king-sized Pall Mall dangled from his lips. He watched the flowing traffic in the intersection as he spoke to the blonde seated next to him. They didn't know what he was saying but the girl laughed loudly. The young driver turned his head, chewed his cigarette, and showed a mouthful of white teeth.

The light flashed green and the sports car shot ahead. Chu Yu-pai opened the accelerator wide: "Damn! We'll chase that damned Mustang!"

When the sports car turned up the street leading to the Yuan-shan Restaurant, Chu Yu-pai eased up on the accelerator. Chuang Shih-huan let out a sigh of relief.

"Someday I'm going to have one of those Mustangs for sure."

"Don't they cost a lot?"

"A lot; you could work a lifetime in Taiwan and still not be able to afford one."

"Say, aren't you a junior? How is it you haven't been called up for the service yet?"

"I'm in the second lot, I'll go in September."

"What branch?"

"Signal Corps."

"Telegraph or wireless?"

"Telegraph."

"Too bad if you get sent to Quemoy. They say that you have to go out and repair the wires even during an artillery barrage, in spite of the shells."

"So what? So many men have made it back, naturally I will too."

"And when you're finished with the army? Are you going abroad?"

"It's too soon to tell. Liu Yü-ling doesn't really like the idea of going abroad; she's afraid of hardship."

"Oh."

"We're here. I'll go and park my bike. Liu Yü-ling is up there bowling by herself and I'm going up to see her; T'ao Chih-ch'ing is ice skating."

Chuang Shih-huan pushed open the door of the skating rink and the frigid air, blended with the music of "The Blue Danube," came rushing at him all at once, giving him goose bumps.

In the vast, chilly space, shadows of people in new and beautiful clothes flashed by, cutting lines and circles, going and coming in interlocking patterns like a nighttime rainbow. The noisiest of all were a few youngsters in undershirts who crashed straight into others on purpose and chased one another, stumbling and falling, sprawling flat on the ice and getting up again, stumbling and colliding, and making several girls scream hysterically.

"Ya-ho!"

A brown-haired fellow dashed over recklessly. Just before he would have bumped into the rail in front of Chuang Shih-huan, his legs slid apart and he grabbed the rail and stood firm. His face turned red as he coughed. He panted in great gasps, and puffs of his steamy breath climbed up Chuang's chest. As he turned, he laughed loudly. Bending down, he scraped up a large pile of ice chips with his skates, packed them into a ball, and threw it at the place where the crowd was the thickest. Kicking gently backwards with both feet, he reentered the crowd like a trail of mist.

Following the silhouette of the brown-haired fellow, Chuang Shih-huan saw T'ao Chih-ch'ing.

She wore a loose yellow cardigan which fell to her hips, and a pair of tight dark blue trousers. Smiling unselfconsciously and twisting around, with her black hair flying free, she darted left and right, boring through the crowd. When she reached an empty spot, she leaned her upper body backward, shook her hair loose, and began to spin around, faster and faster, spinning so fast that one could no longer tell if she were spinning to the right or to the left. Her body wriggled upward like a piece of hemp twisting between the hands. Suddenly, she flung both hands up and stopped. A slight pause, then she turned and skated to the opposite rail. She bent her head and talked with a boy in a black pullover and blue jeans. As she leaned against the rail, she looked in Chuang Shih-huan's direction. Chuang waved to her.

T'ao Chih-ch'ing smiled, lifted her head, tossed back her hair, waved her hand, and pointed at the ice. Chuang Shih-huan shook his head, both hands brushing at his arms, which were not covered by his light blue sports shirt. T'ao Chih-ch'ing bent over with laughter, said a few words to the black pullover, pushed off from the rail, and sailed through the crowd, her long hair trailing behind like a kite. As she approached, she tripped and Chuang quickly put out his hand to hold her.

The drone of noise from "The Blue Danube" was shut off behind the closed door.

"Oh, it's so hot!" T'ao Chih-ch'ing put up a hand to block the burning sunlight.

"Hot? I almost froze into a chunk of ice!" said Chuang Shih-huan, teeth chattering.

"Chu Yu-pai's to blame, not telling you to put on more clothes. Will you hold my bag?"

Chuang Shih-huan took her dark red clothing bag. "Sure. Anyway, I won't run away, I don't want to fall down."

T'ao Chih-ch'ing glanced at him and smiled. She removed her hairband, held it in her mouth while she combed her hair with her hands, put it on again, and tossing her head, led him up the stairs.

"Yü-ling is bowling, shall we go there?"

"Forget it, I can't do that either."

"I see you don't know how to do anything. All right, I'm tired too. See, I'm all sweaty; let's go upstairs and have something to drink."

They chose a table near the side from which, looking down, they could see the bowling lanes. Even though they were separated from the bowling lanes by a large pane of thick glass, the landslide noise came through distinctly.

The waiter came over. Chuang Shih-huan ordered orange juice and T'ao Chih-ch'ing ordered a cup of coffee.

"Make it hot and please bring me a glass of cold water too."

The waiter went away and T'ao Chih-ch'ing turned her head to ask, "How's it going? All right?"

"Is what all right?"

"Your professor's book. Didn't you say you were helping him with the index?"

"Oh, let's not talk about that. It's a lousy book, patchwork and plagiarism. He didn't even bother to sort it out, so it doesn't read smoothly at all. Some places simply don't connect. Any informed person can tell at a glance that it's plain plagiarism. What is more outrageous is that this book is written on a grant. My work is so boring that if it weren't for the money I'd have told him to save the trouble of the index."

"Come, come now, don't be so cynical. It's the same everywhere; as the saying goes, all writing is a form of plagiarism."

Their order arrived. T'ao Chih-ch'ing took her cold water and was about to drink it when she put it down and grimaced. She called the waiter back and asked him to bring another glass.

"What's the matter?" The waiter stared wide-eyed at her.

"What's the matter?" T'ao Chih-ch'ing's face stiffened. "How come this glass has fingerprints all over it? Bring me another!"

The waiter went away and she said to Chuang, "Since their prices are so exorbitant, the service ought to be at least a little better."

Chuang Shih-huan rubbed his nose and did not know what to say. He took a sip of his orange juice and looked below. A short-haired girl in a pink shirt took a few short, quick steps and released the ball, which thundered down the alley and knocked over nine pins. The girl jumped for joy and clapped her hands. She turned around and he saw that it was Liu Yü-ling.

The waiter came back with the ice water, followed by the boy who had just been speaking with T'ao Chih-ch'ing at the skating rink. He had taken off his black pullover and his red terry-cloth sports shirt revealed long, bronzed arms. A canvas bag was slung over his shoulder and one hand was stuck into his hip pocket.

"I tripped and my wrist is banged all numb."

"This is Fan Ch'o-hsiung. And this is Chuang Shih-huan."

Fan Ch'o-hsiung nodded. He had a pair of wide, deeply set eyesockets and his eyes seemed clear and transparent; they were not large, but because they were double-lidded, they seemed quite large. His lips were thin and strong but his smile seemed a little sour. He said in a mournful tone:

"Damn! Son of a bitch, that ice is like sandpaper."

My God! Chuang Shih-huan frowned to himself: how is it that

with Wu Che just gone, I run into another fellow who loves to complain?

"Relax," T'ao Chih-ch'ing patted Fan Ch'o-hsiung's elbow. "You won't die!"

The black pullover slumped down beside Chuang and studied his red abraded hand. Chuang Shih-huan saw that he wore long sideburns and smelled the fragrance of a familiar hair oil.

"Do you use Vitalis on your hair?"

"Eh?" Fan Ch'o-hsiung looked up. "That's right, do you use it too?"

Chuang Shih-huan pursed his lips, shook his head, and turned to tell T'ao Chih-ch'ing: "What you smelled that night actually wasn't perfume."

T'ao Chih-ch'ing at first seemed startled, then murmured "Oh" and smiled in comprehension.

When Fan Ch'o-hsiung's lemonade came, he took a gulp and, holding it in his mouth, reached into his hip pocket, took out a plastic bottle, and poured out several little white pills.

"Again?" T'ao Chih-ch'ing asked, frowning.

Fan Ch'o-hsiung swallowed the pills down with the lemonade.

"I'm allergic," he said to Chuang Shih-huan. Then he went on to explain profusely that he didn't know when his skin had become so sensitive. When it bothered him, it was terrible; his whole body would itch so that even if he could have scratched open the skin it wouldn't have helped. He had tried quite a few remedies, none of which had been of any use; the treatments offered temporary relief but did not cure the cause and the doctors couldn't say what was causing it.

"They said, 'allergies have many causes, with some people it's the smell of fish and with others it's pollen.' But maybe it's because some ingredients in the rice or the water don't suit my constitution or maybe it's simply the atmosphere. Damn it! Does that mean I can't even breathe?"

"Can they find out why?"

"They wanted to test my blood and do the tests one by one. It often takes more than six months, and sometimes they just can't find out what it is. I really couldn't care less now, since I won't live long anyway."

"I've told you a hundred times," T'ao Chih-ch'ing interrupted. "It's all in your mind; stop being so hypersensitive and you won't be sick. . . ."

Before she had finished speaking, someone behind her called in a low voice, "Chih-ch'ing!"

The three of them turned around to look. It was a middle-aged man and, although it was a hot day, he was all dressed up in a dark blue suit with a sapphire-blue necktie. His hair was sleek with oil. He got up from a nearby table and came over.

"Long time no see."

Chuang Shih-huan caught a glimpse of a strange emotion which flashed across T'ao Chih-ch'ing's brows; her eyelashes dipped and rose.

"How are you? Have you come to bowl?" she asked without inflection. Her face betrayed no expression.

"No, I just came down from Yang-ming-shan." He stuck out his hand to look at his watch. The flash of his cufflink was dazzling. "It's almost six. Shall we go and have dinner?"

"Thanks, but it's not convenient." T'ao Chih-ch'ing inclined her head and glanced at a fashionably dressed woman seated at the other table.

"That doesn't matter. She's leaving. She has other business." He was most attentive.

"All right," T'ao Chih-ch'ing said, leaning on the back of her chair. "But you see, I've some friends—oh, here come two more."

"It doesn't matter, we'll all go together—Miss Liu."

Liu Yü-ling smiled at him and nodded.

"Where are we going? I said I'd be back a little early." Seeing Chuang Shih-huan, she bent forward: "Hi, Chuang!—My aunt's having her birthday and mama said I had to go."

T'ao Chih-ch'ing patted the back of the chair and said, "Then the three of us will go and after dinner we'll go to the Cafe Barbarian—Chuang Shih-huan, have you been to the Cafe Barbarian? You haven't? Good." She looked up. "Where shall we go for dinner?"

"How about the Blue Heaven?" The middle-aged man asked, bowing slightly.

"Too high-class; who's all dressed up like you?"

"Well—shall we go to the Rose Grill for steak?"

"Forget it! Their steak is like shoe leather."

"Then let's go to the Normandy for Western food."

"The last time I was there, they served ox-tail soup and it made me sick the whole evening," said T'ao Chih-ch'ing.

The other pondered for a moment and said patiently: "Look here, I'll go and pay my bill and call them up to see what the main dish is tonight and then we'll decide, all right?" As he finished, he went off to phone.

When he was gone, Chuang Shih-huan said, "T'ao Chih-ch'ing, are you sure it's okay?"

T'ao Chih-ch'ing lowered her head on her chest and put her hand on his. Chuang Shih-huan could feel it trembling slightly. He waited until she raised her eyes but there was nothing written in them.

"Don't worry about him; he loves to spend money."

"Who is this guy anyway?"

T'ao Chih-ch'ing winked—it was not a joking wink, but a warning wink—and said softly, "I'll tell you some other time." Her eyes shifted. "How old do you guess he is?"

"Around forty."

"I'm afraid more." T'ao Chih-ch'ing lifted one corner of her mouth in a grin.

"When I first got to know him, he asked me how old I was and I told him. He said that in the year I was born, he made his first trip from Shanghai to New York."

T'ao Chih-ch'ing descended the narrow, steep stairs of the Cafe Barbarian and a wave of whistles flew out of the darkness.

"Hey, Hsiao Ch'ing, real pretty today!"

"Hsiao Ch'ing, come sit over here!"

T'ao Chih-ch'ing casually nodding here and smiling there, said to a foreigner, "Hi, Joe."

She went over to a table where a boy in a blue shirt sat alone. Fan Ch'o-hsiung came along behind, surrounded by shoulder-slappings and greetings.

The small underground room was full of the noise of people, the smell of sweat, and the stink of smoke. In the rising clouds of smoke and the dim yellow lamplight, there appeared hair of pitch black and of bright gold, dancing hands, pairs of glowing eyes, and mouths full of shining white teeth. A song, now sung clearly, now in an indistinct mumble, and now as though the singer were oppressed by the weak accompaniment of a guitar, came trickling through the hubbub of laughter and conversation.

Chuang Shih-huan felt that everyone was looking at him as he stood hesitating at the foot of the steps. He felt like a person unfamiliar with the water, standing at the edge of the water while the waves lapped at his feet, unable to decide whether to enter the water or not. T'ao Chih-ch'ing beckoned to him and he went over. Fan Ch'o-hsiung moved a chair over for him, and the hard wooden back of the chair forced him to straighten up. The obscure light, the obscure sounds, overwhelmed him. But once inside, he discovered that there was nothing to be afraid of after all; the water was not as cold as he had feared and it would not drown him.

The table was very small and was crowded with a crude yellowish earthenware ashtray, a saucer of matching design and material, a sugar bowl, a pack of cigarettes, a table lamp, and T'ao Chih-ch'ing's handbag. The lamp shade consisted of a funnel of thin plywood which bore five or six holes burnt out by cigarette butts. There were also inscriptions: the scribbles of fountain pens, ballpoints, and crayons. Chuang Shih-huan moved forward a little for a closer look: "No mistake. This is Friday, July 13th, and it's my birthday, so bless me!"; "Jimmy Liu and Grace C.—July 8"; "I come here every day because I'm bored"; "P.S. I Love You!"; "Hey! Speak a little louder! I can't hear you!"; etc. He turned the lamp around. There was writing on the other side as well and black charred holes. Someone had linked these holes with red ink, creating a lovely flower. He smiled.

"Hey!" T'ao Chih-ch'ing clapped him on the shoulder. "I want to introduce Yang P'ei-te. Chuang Shih-huan, this is Lao Yang." [4]

Chuang Shih-huan hadn't heard Yang's personal name clearly, so he mumbled "How are you?"

The boy in the blue shirt greeted this with a shrug.

"Smoke?"

He took the pack of cigarettes from the table and offered one to

[4] Lao means "old." It is a familiar form of address.

T'ao Chih-ch'ing. They were Rothmans. T'ao Chih-ch'ing took
two and gave one to Chuang Shih-huan. Fan Ch'o-hsiung took
his own cigarettes.

Yang P'ei-te took out his lighter and lit their cigarettes. The
flame shot up high and burned with a hissing sound.

"Watch it! I've singed my eyebrows three times with this
damned lighter."

The four of them laughed. T'ao Chih-ch'ing puffed out smoke
and said, "Don't give Hsiao Fan a light or he'll tell you that there's
no soul in a lighter."

Fan Ch'o-hsiung forced a smile and struck a match.

A tall, lean waiter came over to take their orders.

"I want a Coke," T'ao Chih-ch'ing said. "Chuang Shih-huan,
do you drink beer?"

"That's fine."

"Haven't you any apple cider yet?" Fan Ch'o-hsiung asked. The
waiter put his hands behind his back, smiled, and shook his head.

"I'll go out and get a bottle." Fan Ch'o-hsiung stood up. "I like
cider."

The waiter asked Yang P'ei-te if he wanted anything. The boy
in the blue shirt, gazing fixedly at an abstract painting hanging on
the burlap-covered wall, inhaled and shook his head; his long hair
brushed his collar. The waiter left. Fan Ch'o-hsiung pushed his
way through the close-packed chairs and tables and arms and legs
that blocked the way. Yang P'ei-te sat up straight, rapped his
fingers on the table top, and puffed smoke. The smoke gathered
above the lamp and lingered for a long, long time.

"Lao Yang," T'ao Chih-ch'ing said. "Turn off the lamp, all
right? It hurts my eyes and makes them water. Maybe I'm too
tired."

A short fellow with a pompadour, wearing clothes of pork-liver
red, came strolling in and without a word perched himself on Fan
Ch'o-hsiung's chair. After glancing around, he helped himself to a
cigarette, tamped it a few times on the table, and lit it with a
lighter. Then he crossed his legs and puffed away. The boy in the
blue shirt and T'ao Chih-ch'ing smoked on and said nothing, as
though he were not there.

Yang P'ei-te inhaled slowly and deliberately, then leaned over
and pulled out the table lamp's plug.

As the lamp went out, Chuang Shih-huan caught the thread of a song. Wu Che had the record—it was Bob Dylan, moaning as though half awake and talking in his sleep, singing:

> *. . . the times they are a-changin'.*
> *Come mothers and fathers,*
> *Throughout the land*
> *And don't criticize*
> *What you can't understand.*
> *Your sons and your daughters*
> *Are beyond your command*
> *Your old road is*
> *Rapidly agin'* *

As he sat in darkness, the lights and the shadows of people around him suddenly came alive. That long hair, those shaggy haircuts, those bright and dazzling clothes kept swinging back and forth before his eyes. Light and shadow, flowing and ebbing, came and went upon their faces. Moving, gesturing with their hands, shaking their legs, crossing and uncrossing them. Kicking off their shoes and resting their feet on the chairs. Shaking their heads and nodding. Opening and closing their mouths like fish in the water. Mandarin blending into Taiwanese, into English. The Kuang-hua Express rushed by, one car after another. Conversational partners changed as fast as the topic of conversation. The drone of conversation gave way to laughter. Between the talking and the laughter, a temporary pause sewed their lips shut; they smoked, drank, ate.

The waiter arrived and T'ao Chih-ch'ing threw her handbag down on the floor. Beer, cola, glasses, and the check filled the empty space. Chuang Shih-huan reached into his pocket for money, but T'ao Chih-ch'ing said that she would take care of it and gave the waiter a hundred dollar bill.

"Thank you," she said.

The waiter took the money but did not leave, and said, "Plug the lamp back in, it won't do to leave it off." The boy in the blue shirt poured half a glass of beer, took a swallow, let out his breath, and said, "Oh, let it be, Hsiao Ch'ing's eyes hurt."

"Please, for my sake, turn it on," the waiter said. "Otherwise,

* © 1963 M. Witmark & Sons. All Rights Reserved. Used by permission of Warner Bros. Music.

when the cops come and see it, they'll have something to say."
Yang P'ei-te shrugged at T'ao Chih-ch'ing, put down his glass,
bent over, groped around for a long time, and the light came back
on. No sooner had the waiter left than he pulled the plug out
again. When the waiter returned with the change, his eyes flashed
like those of the Thunder God. The boy in the blue shirt stuck out
his tongue, then put up his hands as though to say "I surrender."
He plugged in the light again.

Chuang Shih-huan felt around in his pockets and pulled out a
wrinkled handkerchief which he put over the lamp.

"Thank you, Chuang Shih-huan," said T'ao Chih-ch'ing. She
drank some cola, looked up, lifted her eyelids between thumb and
forefinger, and removed her contact lenses. After carefully deposit-
ing them in a small case, which she replaced in her handbag, she
looked at Chuang and smiled.

"Ha, ha, ha!" Loud laughter burst from the corner near the foot
of the stairs.

Yang P'ei-te and T'ao Chih-ch'ing seemed not to have heard.
But Chuang Shih-huan turned to see a few young Americans and
a Chinese girl grouped around a long table, all rocking with laughter. A red-haired girl kept beating on the table. "No, no, I can't
believe it!" She sighed and slumped on the table. The others,
standing up, were ready to leave. They were pulling her, calling to
her, and laughing together. The men and women all had long
hair down to their shoulders. One of them had allowed his beard
to grow, but the face behind the beard was surprisingly pink and
fresh. A kid of about twelve or thirteen, with a childish sharp
ring to his laugh, had a cigarette dangling from his hand.

When the red-haired girl had laughed enough, she got up. As
the five or six of them made their way outside, a little girl with
high cheekbones, who wore her hair in a loose braid, glanced
toward their table. Like Columbus discovering a new world, she
suddenly cried:

"Hi, T'ao!"

T'ao Chih-ch'ing forced a smile.

"Hi, Judy!"

The two of them laughed, thrust out their right hands, and
while still three feet apart, moved them up and down in a pan-
tomime of hand-shaking. The girl with the braid waved her

fingers, in a gesture of saying goodbye, and went off up the stairs with her friends, laughing all the way. God! Chuang Shih-huan was startled. Two of those girls had been barefoot!

"Some characters!" Chuang took a drink of beer.

"They're from the American School—actually, the real characters weren't here tonight." T'ao Chih-ch'ing brushed back her hair and lit a cigarette before she went on: "There's an American who's hairy all over. No telling how long his hair is and his beard covers his face. On top of that, he wears a pair of thick glasses and all you can see is his nose. He comes here every night with a box of chessmen. He just sits quietly until he gets someone to play a game with him. If you don't know how, he'll teach you. He sits there until closing time. And there is also this girl. Whenever her mama can't find her elsewhere, she has only to call here. That girl once said something quotable. . . ."

"Are you talking about Gigi?" The boy in the blue shirt had been talking to a blonde American at a nearby table and had turned around to look for a cigarette. Fan Ch'o-hsiung had returned unnoticed and was straddling his chair, leaning forward on the back of the chair. His right hand held a bottle of apple cider and spittle flew in all directions as he spoke in broken English to the American.

". . . really, you don't feel a thing. Drink a few gulps of water and they'll all go down just like that. There's no feeling at all. . . ."

"Yeah, I was talking about Gigi," T'ao Chih-ch'ing said, glancing at Fan Ch'o-hsiung. "My God, he's telling those death-defying heroic tales about himself!"

"What was Gigi's 'quotable saying'?"

"Well, one time a fellow asked her, out of the blue, why she was so fond of hanging around the Cafe Barbarian. She said because here if she wanted to talk with someone, she could talk. If you wanted to talk with her, she would talk if she felt like it, and if she didn't feel like it, she would simply ignore you, and if you still pestered her, she'd curse the hell out of you!" T'ao Chih-ch'ing laughed softly and said slowly: "Gigi also said that this was one of the good things about the Cafe Barbarian. If you were at home and you got mad at your father, you couldn't very well cuss him out!"

"Mother's!" The boy in the blue shirt balanced his chair on two legs and rocked back and forth, laughing. Without knowing why, Chuang Shih-huan felt that his laugh sounded hollow, as though heard in the emptiness of a vast room.

The tape had been changed and a woman's soprano voice accompanied by a guitar floated lightly through the crowded room, breezy and refreshing.

"Hey, Joan Baez," T'ao Chih-ch'ing slapped the table and propped her chin on her left hand. "I really dig her."

The door opened, letting in the light and noise of the street. As it closed again, a boy wearing a pale blue tie came in and approached the American at the next table.

"Hi, Joe!"

Fan Ch'o-hsiung returned to his own chair and the boy in the pork-liver red shirt got up and left as silently as he had come.

"Joe is a University of California dropout; he's in the American army now," Fan Ch'o-hsiung told Chuang.

"Who was that fellow just now?"

"Who knows?" said T'ao Chih-ch'ing nonchalantly.

Chuang Shih-huan saw the boy with the pale blue tie sit down beside Joe. He was clearly a dark-haired Chinese. Once he sat down nearby, Chuang discovered that the boy had blue eyes, and his jaw dropped in surprise.

"That boy's got mixed blood," Yang P'ei-te said with a smile. "His father was a diplomat who married a Caucasian wife. Later, when his father died, his mother found him a Caucasian father. Later on that gentleman died as well and his mother brought him back here to become a Chinese."

"Did he get to be one?"

"God knows." Yang P'ei-te shrugged.

T'ao Chih-ch'ing sneered.

"If he'd gotten to be one, he wouldn't be here."

"You can't say that." The boy in the blue shirt slowly exhaled a puff of smoke. "The Cafe Barbarian is too much a part of the culture of Taipei. Last time Joe said it, it's a sub . . . sub . . ."

"Subculture," Fan Ch'o-hsiung said, as he shook several pills out of a little glass bottle. Just as he was about to swallow them, Chuang Shih-huan asked him: "Itching again?"

Fan Ch'o-hsiung looked at him, gritted his teeth, and said that they were for his stomach but since he had mentioned it, he did feel itchy again.

"My, my, can't one even mention it?"

Fan Ch'o-hsiung shook his head and said, "I get itchy as soon as I think of it." As he spoke, he took out the bottle of allergy pills again.

T'ao Chih-ch'ing's eyebrows rose and she was about to flare up, but she let out a long sigh and made a gesture of resignation with her left hand.

Fan Ch'o-hsiung put the two kinds of pills into his mouth and swallowed them without water. Once they were down, he shakily lit a cigarette. Chuang Shih-huan shook his head.

Several people had clustered around the table where the American students had just been sitting. One boy, wearing a high-collared shirt of deep purple with a pair of tinkling medallions hanging on his chest, was playing the guitar.

"Who's that fellow? How come we haven't seen him before?" T'ao Chih-ch'ing tapped her cigarette.

"I don't know," the boy in the blue shirt said languidly. "I haven't seen him before either."

"Hey, Lao Chuang," Fan Ch'o-hsiung said. "Have you tried this? If you drink apple cider and smoke at the same time, you can get a—um, a very strange feeling, like being dizzy, but not the same. It goes right to your head. Really cool."

Chuang Shih-huan rubbed his nose and said that he had not. Fan Ch'o-hsiung at once demonstrated.

"What the hell is the matter with you? Fan Ch'o-hsiung!" cried T'ao Chih-ch'ing. "Does a little soda make you go crazy?"

"It's like this." Fan Ch'o-hsiung squinted, totally immersed in his feeling of simulated dizziness. He grasped the neck of his bottle of cider with one hand, as though without it he would really faint. Suddenly he asked wide-eyed, "Perhaps the high one gets from smoking marijuana is something like this?"

Chuang Shih-huan asked Yang P'ei-te in a low voice where the washroom was. Yang stubbed out his cigarette and said, "We'll go together."

When they returned, they found T'ao Chih-ch'ing giving a

speech and Fan Ch'o-hsiung listening with his eyes fixed on her.
". . . Really. A classmate of my sister came back in May and I
asked her if she had smoked it. She said there's nothing fantastic
about it and that it just wasn't such a big deal; it wasn't much different from ordinary cigarettes. Nothing special. . . ."

"What's that?" Lao Yang struck his lighter, lit a cigarette, and
gave one to Chuang.

"Marijuana."

"How could it be the same as ordinary cigarettes?"

"Because she's Chinese!"

"What do you mean?" Chuang Shih-huan frowned, swallowed
some beer, and refilled his glass.

"Well—when you smoke," T'ao Chih-ch'ing shrugged and
demonstrated with great realism, clasping a tiny cigarette butt between thumb and forefinger and inhaling greedily.

"When you smoke, you're thinking with all your heart 'Okay,
I'm smoking marijuana' and then you *expect* something to happen." She closed her eyes, as though concentrating hard. "Will
that muscle cramp a bit? Is my head still clear? Oh my God, I'm
actually smoking marijuana!"

Fan Ch'o-hsiung laughed nervously and T'ao Chih-ch'ing
slowly, slowly lowered her hands, slapped her knees, and opened
her eyes.

"That's how it is! With this kind of thing the more serious you
are, the less results you get. If at the same time you're doing it you
feel that you're doing something you shouldn't, that won't do! We
Chinese have never learned to really let ourselves go. Five thousand years of culture weighs down on our backs like a great big
stone. We're so inhibited we can't even breathe."

"The Americans are also inhibited."

"They don't have a history as long as ours; they don't have five
thousand years of culture."

"Things can gradually change," Yang P'ei-te said. "Maybe next
generation . . ."

"All right," T'ao Chih-ch'ing cried. "Here's to the next generation!"

Chuang Shih-huan, laughing with the rest of them, raised his
glass. "Bottoms up!" He saw T'ao Chih-ch'ing wiping foam from

the corner of her mouth with the back of her hand and he knew that she had taken his beer. T'ao Chih-ch'ing put down the glass and suddenly started to cough violently, until tears started from her eyes. Yang P'ei-te stood up, waved his hand, and snapped his fingers to summon the waiter. "Another beer!"

The little group of people that had gathered around the guitarist were humming softly, whistling along, and singing a song called "Michael." When they got to the "Hallelujah" part, their voices were loud and high, as if they were singing an army song. The more they sang, the more excited they became. Gradually everyone in the basement room was caught up in it and started to sing along with them.

"Turn off the tape player!" someone called out.

"Turn it off! Turn if off!" cried a thick nasal voice.

Joan Baez was singing sadly:

If I had listened to what my mother said;
I'd 'a been at home today. . . .

Then suddenly "ah—" and she became mute.

The table lamps cast a dim yellow glow on the smoky atmosphere. The boy in the purple sports shirt holding the guitar sat down on the long table. He lowered his head and at his casual strumming, a light and melancholy tune dripped from the strings. The boy craned his neck and a thick lock of black hair slid over his brow. He brushed it away with two long thin fingers. Looking ahead into the smoke, he sang slowly word by word:

If you miss the train I'm on;
You will know that I am gone;
You can hear the whistle blow a hundred miles. *

The sound of clapping came from the west end of the room. But it was hard to be the only one clapping and the sound soon died away. The smoke rose in swirls and the whole basement room was so quiet one could almost hear cigarette ashes dropping. There was only the boy's rather husky and low voice floating along with the stream of guitar notes.

Listening to the metallic strings Chuang Shih-huan thought, This fellow isn't up to Wu Che's standard. But he has a knack of being casual which Wu Che lacks. Any song in Wu Che's hands becomes a melancholy tune, as though his ten fingers had been cursed by black magic so that whatever he touches, whether it's gold or silver or anything sparkling, turns at once to rust and dead ashes. Why am I thinking of Wu Che? I should be happy now that he's gone home! But God knows what will become of Wu Che in Kaohsiung!

Stop asking for trouble! Chuang Shih-huan inhaled his cigarette fiercely and puffed all his feeling of depression out with the smoke. He looked about. Lamps on each table swam about in the murk like so many stars. The lamplight made each face stand out in high relief. Those faces, those quiet faces, so sincere, so innocent, so good—God, how I like these people! Chuang Shih-huan thought, I'd really like to go over and hug them and chat with them and listen to them talk about their lives and their dreams and let them tell me the secret formula for happiness.

The boy in the purple sports shirt switched to a fast, lively pop tune. He got off the table and walked among the crowd, fingers snapping and hair flying. A girl stood up in the aisle and began to writhe like a snake. Some hummed and others whistled along. Gradually, nearly everyone was responding by clapping their hands, stamping their feet, shaking their heads, and rapping on the tables as they sang. T'ao Chih-ch'ing and Yang P'ei-te sang loudly and Fan Ch'o-hsiung hummed softly. One tune followed another like a stream of water swirling by. The thick atmosphere grew still warmer like the steam of boiling water rushing through the neck of a whistling pot.

Chuang Shih-huan had never heard most of the songs before. The few songs which he had heard he could not sing, so he might as well have been dumb. After he had rubbed his nose a few times, he could only sit and smoke his cigarettes in silence. Happening to turn around, he saw that Joe, seated at a nearby table, was also silent. He was listening with his mouth slightly open. The cigarette between his fingers burned with a curl of smoke and a length of ash dangled from it. Joe turned his head and saw Chuang. Their eyes met and the two men exchanged a bitter smile of understanding; Joe's cigarette ash dropped onto his lapel. Lowering his gaze, Chuang Shih-huan saw that Joe's jeans were frayed and through the shaggy fringe showed half his profusely hairy calves. He wore a pair of brown sneakers.

Beside the pair of sneakers stood an empty cola bottle whose surface reflected a blurred light; it stood as straight as a writing brush, its dark shadow repeated on all four sides. Joe crossed his legs and a shadow crossed the bottle. The singers lost their unison; they were like a bunch of recruits learning army songs, off-key and out of rhythm.

Joe shook his leg and the shadow of the bottle disappeared and reappeared. The noise of the singing went from bad to worse, like chestnuts roasting. Chuang Shih-huan looked at T'ao Chih-ch'ing, Yang P'ei-te, Fan Ch'o-hsiung, and every one of those flushed faces streaming with sweat, twisted, and distorted; they were the faces of strangers. His head began to ache with a burning sensation, his ears were hot, and his temples throbbed. And the smoke! That smoke, a primeval fog, clouded his eyes and made them ache and nearly suffocated him! He looked at his cigarette, from which he had only taken a few puffs, and put it out. He swallowed hard and realized that his throat was rebelling too—he had smoked too much. Chuang Shih-huan leaned back in his chair and shut his eyes; inwardly he groaned. What was the matter? Had he no share at all in these warm runaway emotions? Was it because he did not belong to them and didn't belong here? Or—or was it because of Wu Che? Did Wu Che separate him from all this? He opened his eyes, frowned, and gazed vacantly at those mingled human shadows; beneath the table the shadow of the bottle disappeared and reappeared. Joe lowered his leg. The bottle suddenly leaped out of the darkness. Silently, with a gleam like the eye of a dead fish, it regarded him coldly!

For a long, long time they sat there, two enemies staring at each other suspiciously. It was as though they had sat like that from the dawn of creation and would go on sitting so, in this room devoid of life, forever.

That room, that room he shared with Wu Che: it was like a transparent cocoon, a thick membrane which separated him from the sound and light of the world outside. Wu Che seemed satisfied to voluntarily imprison himself and to be imprisoned, even to the point of agreeing to sleep with the light off as long as he could be sure that Chuang was there breathing in the same room. And Chuang was always assuming the burden of a million worries, for he didn't know when Wu Che might open the door and sink into the bottomless abyss outside.

For what? Chuang Shih-huan! Why do you have to shoulder this heavy, coarse cross? Why?

"Ah—!" T'ao Chih-ch'ing sighed and leaned back lazily against the wall. Without any reason she started to cough and coughed so hard that she grew red in the face. When she was finally able to stop, she yawned. Pressing her temples, she faced Chuang with a smile:

"I'm so tired; shall we go?"

She raised her glass, tilted her head, and drained it at a gulp. She bent over to pick up her handbag and her long hair flowed across half the table. Chuang Shih-huan stood up.

"Why leave so soon?" Yang P'ei-te asked. "Help me finish this bottle of beer and then we'll go."

"I can't." T'ao Chih-ch'ing stood up, smoothing down her dress. "I'm tired enough now!"

The manager turned on the tape player again. A group accompanied by tambourine and electric guitar was screaming and yelling. The smoke in the basement room grew thicker and someone called out to turn up the air conditioner. Amid the drone, the high-pitched voice of a girl cried, "Hell, no!" Then a man's deep voice burst out, "I'm not kidding! For seven thousand five, they'll even change the cylinders!" At a table beside the air conditioner, a couple murmured to each other across the lamp. A black man came in and Joe said to him:

"You missed a whole concert! These kids know more pop songs than we do."

Fan Ch'o-hsiung sat quite still, his eyes fixed on an abstract painting in violent reds and pale greens which hung on the wall.

"Let's go, what are you staring at?" T'ao Chih-ch'ing said. "If we don't go, my aunt will be calling me up pretty soon asking about you."

Fan Ch'o-hsiung reluctantly swept up his bottles and cans and stood up.

"I've been looking at that picture and thinking . . ."

"Thinking! You're always thinking!" T'ao Chih-ch'ing curtly interrupted him. "Your trouble is you think too much! Who wants you to think? All you're supposed to do is study and study! You went through all those cram courses in grade school so that you could pass the exams and get into junior high, and you did the same thing to get into high school and finally college. Who wants you to think?"

Yang P'ei-te sighed. Tugging at T'ao Chih-ch'ing's dress, he asked half-jokingly, "And after college?"

"After college?" T'ao Chih-ch'ing thought for a moment and shrugged her left shoulder. "To Cafe Barbarian!"

She brushed off Yang's hand, said "Bye-bye" casually to Joe, and walked toward the stairs.

Beside the stairs, a longhaired boy was doing a sketch of a girl with glasses. Seeing T'ao Chih-ch'ing, he smiled and nodded.

"Saucepan's friend," T'ao Chih-ch'ing said to Chuang as they went upstairs. "Saucepan caught me here and insisted that I let him do my portrait, a Number 6. My God, sitting there all day long and you can't even move. I went once, but I couldn't stand it."

"Hey! Chuang!" Yang called.

Chuang Shih-huan went back. Yang had crossed his legs and stuck both hands in his pockets; he was leaning back and smoking. Without giving Chuang the slightest glance, he indicated the handkerchief over the lamp with a nod of his chin. Chuang took the handkerchief, thanked him, and left the Cafe Barbarian. Outside in the arcade, he caught up with T'ao Chih-ch'ing and Fan Ch'o-hsiung. Fan was buying cigarettes.

"Three dollars worth," Fan said and the old cigarette vendor gave him six Longevity cigarettes.

As they walked along, T'ao Chih-ch'ing, as though she had just thought of something, said to Chuang, "Chu Yu-pai and Liu Yü-ling are going to Changhua next week to see Yü-ling's grandmother. We're going together to Hsi-t'ou and maybe Sun Moon Lake too. Do you want to come along? Have you been to Hsi-t'ou? They say it's quite a place."

During the previous year's winter holidays, Chuang Shih-huan and a few classmates from the Forestry Department had spent a couple of nights at Hsi-t'ou. As he gazed at Hsi-men-ting's dazzling rainbow of lights, madly rushing traffic, and bustling people, thoughts of the white fog of Hsi-t'ou, of the greenness of the trees in the white fog, and of the little cottage filled with the colors of fairy tales suddenly rose in his heart.

"Hey, I asked if you had been to Hsi-t'ou?"

"I've been there—of course I'm coming along!"

"Will it really be fun? They say it's very cold. Is it as cold as Mount A-li?"

They crossed the street and followed the pedestrian traffic up a bridge. Chuang Shih-huan gave a dramatic description of the beauty of Hsi-t'ou. When they had climbed the steps, he realized that T'ao Chih-ch'ing seemed distracted.

"Are you listening to me?"

"Listen!" T'ao Chih-ch'ing grabbed him by the arm and her eyes suddenly grew bright. In a voice so excited that it trembled slightly, she said, "There's a cicada singing, I heard it. Listen!"

"What?"

"A cicada! A cicada that can sing! A cicada has crawled up out of the earth!"

Chuang Shih-huan strained his ears and listened for a long time, but he heard only the sounds of people, cars, horns, and the humming of records which drifted up from the China Commercial Building. The neon rainbow dyed the night a cruel white, a poisonous red, a fearful green—he shook his head.

The light in T'ao Chih-ch'ing's eyes suddenly went out.

"Perhaps I heard wrong," she said, letting go of Chuang's hand.

Fan Ch'o-hsiung sniffed his collar, frowned, and said, "Every time I come out of the Cafe Barbarian, I smell of cigarette smoke all over."

"But you'll still go there anyway!" T'ao Chih-ch'ing nodded heavily and went on ahead.

A few paces farther on, Chuang Shih-huan called out breathlessly, "I heard it!"

T'ao Chih-ch'ing turned about and smiled softly, with an ambiguous expression in her eyes. The gentle breeze of the summer night stroked her hair lightly.

"What did you hear?" Fan asked.

"A cicada!"

"There can't be any cicadas in Hsi-men-ting!"

After that T'ao Chih-ch'ing tossed her head and said quietly and slowly, "You'll never hear one your whole life, because even before you make an effort to listen, you've made up your mind that there can't be any cicadas in Hsi-men-ting. You'll never hear one your whole life."

Chuang Shih-huan heard nothing of what they said.

The cicada's song was as momentary as the fluorescence of the firefly between the blades of grass on a summer night. Now far and now near, strange and yet familiar. So fine and delicate, yet so clear and crisp. Abruptly it stopped. After a while, it came floating up again amid the clamor of Hsi-men-ting at night like a fine strand of silk, giving off a soft and dim light, slowly and persistently poking its way farther and farther out of a tangled mass of threads. Swirling about in the emptiness, it circled ceaselessly, like the notes of a violin, rising and rising, surpassing the sound of an entire symphony orchestra, flying about during a slow interval, cringing and shivering. . . .

When he first heard it, it sounded a little mournful. After he had listened more carefully, he felt that the sound, which fluttered like a pennant, actually came from some luxuriant forest, writhing about until it penetrated a cleft in the rock, spread over the fallen leaves, and soaked the green grass, making a clear spring which came hurrying to him from far, far away, briskly and coolly trickling into the chambers of his heart. . . .

A cold shiver ran down his backbone. Chuang Shih-huan stood still on the crowded bridge, suddenly engulfed by an excitement and happiness he had never before experienced.

> *There's a fog upon L.A.*
> *And my friends have lost their way*
> *We'll be over soon they said*
> *Now they've lost themselves instead.*
> *Please don't be long, please don't you be very long*
> *Please don't be long. . . .*

"Liu Yü-ling, what's that sutra you're chanting?"

"A Beatles song, 'Blue Jay Way'; haven't you heard it?"

"Beatles? It doesn't sound like them! It sounds like monks

chanting a sutra and I thought the Beatles only made a lot of noise."

"I didn't used to like them either, but their latest songs are very easy to listen to and there are a lot of good things in them."

"What things?"

"Life, living, God knows! They were really taken with Indian music and some critics say they're the greatest talents since Beethoven. Frankly, I don't think about it too much, but now that I've listened to some of their songs, I can't understand why one person can be so deeply affected and another not. Even if you are, you can't express it. When someone sings it out for me, I'm so moved I could cry. It doesn't make sense." She shook her head, chewed on her gum and resumed humming.

"There's a fog upon L.A.—Chuang Shih-huan, is there always this much fog at Hsi-t'ou?"

The air held the chill and damp of green grass, decaying wood, and the autumn countryside. The sunlight struggled to penetrate the mist among the tree tops, fell upon the green, dark water, and broke into several ripples of light, which captured the yellow leaves on the water's surface.

Chuang Shih-huan, pillowing his head on his arms, reclined on a stone chair in the summer house, with his feet crossed on top of a stone post, and said lazily, "Perhaps there is."

Each word was wrapped in a puff of light mist, and his heart, for no particular reason, was filled with contentment.

"Please don't be long don't you be very long. . . . Oh, they have another song called 'A Day in the Life.' It's very interesting; I'll recite it for you:

> Woke up, got out of bed,
> Dragged a comb across my head
> Found my way downstairs and drank a cup,
> And looking up I noticed I was late.
> Found my coat and grabbed my hat
> Made the bus in seconds flat
> Found my way upstairs and had a smoke . . .

Chuang laughed, nodded, and recited, for no reason, to Liu Yü-ling:

The necessity of being gentle
The necessity of being positive
The necessity of a little wine and the cassia flower
The necessity of carefully watching a girl going by. . . .

The words flowed like water dripping down:

The necessity of going for a stroll
The necessity of walking a dog
The necessity of peppermint tea

 . . . .

The necessity of the evening paper
The necessity of wearing flannel trousers
The necessity of a lottery ticket
The necessity of inheriting Auntie's fortune
The necessity of the verandah, of the sea, of a smile
The necessity of being lazy

When taken as a river, the river must continue to flow
The world has been, and always will be, like this—
Bodhisattva on the distant mountain
Poppies in the poppy fields [5]

Liu Yü-ling stared at him and cried out:
"What's the matter with you? Chuang Shih-huan, you're chant-ing sutras yourself! What Bodhisattva?"
"Don't you read modern poetry? You haven't?" Chuang laughed. "Never mind—say, how did you discover the Beatles' tal-ents?"
"Um—, I've never liked Chinese pop songs. Chuang, do you know that every time I'd ride the Zero-South bus and we'd stop by the record shops, with their 'cups full of bitter wine' and their 'blue dreams,' I'd feel that the students on the bus were just like caterpillars, all restless, and I couldn't wait for the bus to start up again?" She paused. "Once at a party, we danced to soul music and it was really strange but good listening. I looked at the record—Oh, wow! The world turned upside down! It was the Beatles! I went out and bought a whole stack of them, and the more I listened to them, the more excited I got. Chu Yu-pai says I must be crazy."

[5] These lines are from Ya Hsien's "Rhythms Like Songs"; see his collection, *The Abyss.*

Liu Yü-ling sighed, and rattled on like a machine gun.

"But, and this is strange, once people change, they change, and they've really changed. I'm talking about the Beatles; you know they used to scream and shout, signs of boredom and rebellion. But their latest record now, 'Revolution 1,' has this line: 'when you talk about destruction, don't you know that you can count me out.' Perhaps they've grown up, matured, and besides, they've made enough money and are afraid that others will come and revolt against them—pooh! I'm babbling again. T'ao Chih-ch'ing is always saying I'm not very smart and that I love to give lectures. But I don't see what's wrong with not being smart. You know, T'ao Chih-ch'ing . . ."

"You really aren't going to see the Sacred Tree? If you want to go, you can still catch up with them if you leave now."

"Forget it! Two days by bus, and tossed around all the way up the mountain. The Sacred Tree is just a big unreasonably thick tree; it's no more than a rotten old stump and can't be anything worth seeing. . . . I'm telling you, Chuang Shih-huan, and you can scold me for being a busybody if you like, but I have to tell you, Chuang Shih-huan, you really ought to be a little nicer to T'ao Chih-ch'ing."

Chuang Shih-huan crossed and uncrossed his legs; he couldn't get them arranged satisfactorily, so he was forced to pull them back and put them on the floor. He sat up and rubbed the end of his nose.

"Do you have any more gum?"

Liu Yü-ling, chewing, shook her head.

"No, this is the last piece. Hsiao Fan took all the rest. Do you want some chocolates? Never mind! I'm telling you the truth—T'ao Chih-ch'ing has always been incredibly stuck-up toward boys, but she seems to treat you in a special way. Oh, Chuang Shih-huan . . ."

Chuang Shih-huan stood up and looked out of the pavilion. A lean, ash-white bird skimmed the water surface and was gone in the twinkling of an eye. A bamboo bridge, like a cat stretching itself, arched across the pond. On the bridge, a couple were taking a picture of their son. The shadows of the people and the bridge lay meekly upon the surface of the water.

Leaning one hand on the stone pillar and rubbing his nose with his thumb, Chuang said, "Let me ask you, who is that man Yen?"

"Which Yen?—Oh, oh, oh, you mean that one you ran into last time at the Yuan-shan, the one who asked you to dinner? How did the dinner go that night? Did they serve ox-tail soup?"

Chuang Shih-huan turned his head and gave her a look.

"No, but something like it, beef tongue. T'ao Chih-ch'ing ate a couple of pieces and then put it aside. That Yen fellow talked the whole time we ate, and his pipe never left his hand. T'ao Chih-ch'ing took every opportunity to make stinging remarks to him. When I asked her who he really was, she would only say that she met him at a funeral parlor."

Liu Yü-ling burst into laughter, her head shook, her foot stamped, and the gum sprang out of her mouth, to be mashed beneath her feet. When she had laughed her fill, she leaned against the pillar, scratched her hair, threw back her head, and laughingly said, "Met him at a funeral parlor! Lao Yen was a friend of T'ao Chih-ch'ing's aunt in America. Last spring, her aunt died and Lao Yen was also at the funeral, so that's how they met. When we left the funeral parlor, he insisted on seeing us home. That 'seeing us home' started all the trouble. I wore my tongue out warning T'ao Chih-ch'ing not to mess around with a middle-aged man." Liu Yü-ling wrinkled her nose and made a gesture with her hand.

"But at that time, she didn't listen to anyone! I guess she must have suffered a great deal on his account." She raised her eyebrow. "Did you know that T'ao Chih-ch'ing used to give Chu Yu-pai a lecture whenever she saw him smoking? But now see how she smokes!"

A dried red mulberry leaf came fluttering down to the water.

"The fog's coming," Chuang said.

A streamer of thick fog rose gently from the mountain valleys, twisting and mingling with the vapor rising from the green water, turning the entire woods as white as a Turkish bath, but much cooler.

Liu Yü-ling's black hair, two paces away, was barely visible. Immersed in the green-shadowed fog, Chuang lit a cigarette, took a puff, and let it burn.

"So, I say," Liu Yü-ling said seriously, "Chuang Shih-huan, you certainly ought to be nicer to her!"

The fog clung about him as though someone were putting out hands to seize him and hold him, as though there were someone there yet not there, but he couldn't move a finger. A transparent cage—be nicer to her? Why not? He was only afraid that it might not be as simple as that. Or was it because of Wu Che? Then it's the same as with Wu Che and me . . . sympathy—he took a puff and inhaled deeply; the thick smoke mingled with a bitter smile as he exhaled it from his mouth and nostrils.

"Do me a favor, Chuang Shih-huan." Liu Yü-ling's face swam closer. "Help me eat a few pieces of chocolate; otherwise I won't be able to control myself, I'll eat them all up and when I go back to Taipei, I'll have to go on a diet."

"Diet? You're not fat!"

"Everybody's standards aren't as liberal as yours." She came over and gave a bar of chocolate to Chuang.

Chuang Shih-huan threw his cigarette away and asked with a smile, "Is Chu Yu-pai really that strict?"

"Huh—him?" She smiled slightly. "He's a tyrant! With him, it's like this," said Liu Yü-ling, making a horizontal gesture with her hand. "Flat! No highs or lows. Still, two people are always better than one."

"Of course."

The bamboo bridge creaked as the couple and their little boy descended.

"Mama, is it going to rain?"

"Little silly," the man smiled, "that's fog."

He was running about and the leaves piled on the ground crackled as they were crushed.

"Don't run!" the woman said. "Why are you so naughty? Slow down, I tell you! Just wait till you fall down, then you'll cry your heart out!"

"How many children do you plan to have?"

"Chuang Shih-huan," Liu Yü-ling stared at him but smiled. "What do you mean?"

"Aren't you going to have any?"

"Oh, oh! You! Naturally we're going to have some. I'm no T'ao

Chih-ch'ing. She vowed never to have a child! How many? Who thinks that far ahead? Ask me again in ten years."

"Chu Yu-pai said that you don't want to go abroad." Chuang Shih-huan wadded the tin foil from the chocolate into a ball and flicked it away with his middle finger.

"He's full of big ideas. I say that if you don't go abroad, you can still make a living. He says he's not satisfied with just that. Studying is only a secondary consideration. He says that if you don't go abroad, you can work yourself to death for ten or twenty years and get nowhere; but once you go abroad, you can return after five years at the most, and having studied abroad, become a junior executive at the least. Moreover," Liu Yü-ling tossed a piece of chocolate into her mouth and glanced at Chuang, "do you know what? His greatest dream is to buy a Mustang. That man thinks only of swallowing an elephant. Sometimes I get so mad, I really want to quarrel with him, but I can't get started; you can't rattle with a single coin. But one day, we figured a bit; if we stayed here and both of us worked, we'd make about five or six thousand dollars a month. And we'd have to eat and have a place to stay, so that going to Hsi-men-ting to see a movie or eating at a restaurant would use it all up!" She shrugged and shook her head. "Let him go! At least I won't be the one who has to wash dishes! Oh, what are you going to do, Chuang Shih-huan?"

"Me? Live!—If I had the money, I wouldn't dare buy a Mustang. I'd be sure to drive it too fast and I'd get into three accidents the first day, and if I had any luck, when I got into the third, my soul would return to heaven!"

"Oh," Liu Yü-ling gave him an exasperated look, "I'm talking seriously with you."

Chuang Shih-huan watched the fog slipping into the green pool and smiled unselfconsciously.

"If I had the money, I'd invite everyone to Hsi-t'ou and I'd build a music hall so everyone could listen to Wagner."

Liu Yü-ling picked up a stone, playfully tossed it up and down in her hand while she waited for Chuang to finish what he was saying, and idly threw it into the water. "Plop" came the sound, like punctuation. The rippling water pushed the floating leaves up and down, up and down . . .

"Chuang—Shih—huan! Liu—Yü—ling!"

"It's Hsiao Fan! Why are they coming back so soon?" She rushed ahead out of the pavilion and dashed onto the bamboo bridge.

"Coming!"

Chuang Shih-huan crossed the bridge to see Fan Ch'o-hsiung, the collar of his red jacket wide open and his dark glasses pushed back over his hair, panting to catch his breath.

"T'ao Chih-ch'ing isn't feeling well; she wants Yü-ling to go back to the guest house with her."

"Stop making a mountain out of a molehill, Fan Ch'o-hsiung! I won't die!" T'ao Chih-ch'ing, accompanied by Chu Yu-pai, rounded the corner. Despite her tough talk, she slumped down on a gnarled tree trunk.

"What is it?" Liu Yü-ling felt T'ao Chih-ch'ing's temples. "You don't seem to have a fever."

"My head really aches; I'm too tired." She began to cough. "Come on down with me, all right?"

"We'll go down with you," Chuang Shih-huan said.

"It's no big deal, just let Yü-ling come with me; I'll be fine after I lie down for a while." T'ao Chih-ch'ing smiled a disappointed smile.

"You go and enjoy yourselves, otherwise you'll soon be blaming me for asking you all to come to Hsi-t'ou but not getting to see a thing."

"Do you want some aspirin?" Fan Ch'o-hsiung suddenly became very attentive.

"Never mind," T'ao Chih-ch'ing waved her hand and stood up. "I don't want any of your stuff! Yü-ling, let's go."

The two girls went off. Chu whistled silently and Fan Ch'o-hsiung pulled down his glasses. Chuang Shih-huan thrust his hands into his pants pockets and kicked at the damp leaves on the ground. Suddenly he raised his head and said, "Do you want to go? I know a river . . ."

Bare and black, the little path stretched on with no end in sight. Rocks, varicolored and rough, stuck up from the path and green moss climbed over the rocks. Moisture-laden creepers grew beside the moss and, from time to time, water silently dripped onto the grass so that, at each step, one trod upon a suddenly shocking coldness.

Monotonous rows of pines lined the path. A light mist twined about the forking branches. The topmost branches moved gently in the dim light. When one looked back, the path was only a vague gray strip. And beside one were only trees, and beyond the trees, trees, trees, and more trees.

There was no wind, there were no sounds of insects, and the junglelike leaves scrubbed at their bodies as they wound along in single file. A bird, deep in the gloom, gave a chilling low-pitched cry: "Ah-wo—ah-wo—!" The thin mist rose and in the mist swam tiny, pale, purple flowers. The path was often hidden behind the trees. Dark willows and bright flowers would appear suddenly and pleasantly, and then an unlimited vastness . . .

"Aren't we almost there, Lao Chuang? We've been going for almost half an hour."

"Ah-wo—ah-wo—!" Chu Yu-pai imitated the bird.

"We're almost there."

Just as they were gasping with exhaustion, a thread of delicate sound came bubbling up out of the darkness. Behind another line of trees, the river moved with formless steps; the sound of its light footfalls reached the little path, enticing the hikers.

"Yahoo!" Fan Ch'o-hsiung shouted, waving his red jacket about as he rushed madly ahead, racing through the ranks of trees. At last, the river's heroic song shook the mountains!

The cloud-white foam rushed between boulders as big as houses. The boulders were piled up as far as one could see, upstream and downstream. And the water, swirling up but unable to catch the white rocks, rolled heavily back and fell, crashing down upon itself, singing a loud, captivating song as it sought its way through the crevices. Farther down it slowed and gently formed a belt of blue and a belt of green, making a clear and quiet pool from which issued a chilly mist.

"Let's go down and take a bath, eh?" Chu Yu-pai stuck out his thumb and gave Chuang a couple of playful pokes in the ribs.

"Why not?"

"I dare you! I dare you!"

"Let's find a quiet pool that's a bit larger and maybe we can swim."

"Swim, hell!" Fan said. "You'd freeze to death!"

"Don't come if you don't have it in you!" Chu Yu-pai called out as he scrambled onto a large rock.

Having climbed up and down and gotten moss stains all over themselves, the three stood firmly on a dry, flat boulder. The force of the water was restrained by the great cliff blocking its path. The water, edged with white foam, had carved the limestone below, and green threads of moss grew in the cracks. The green grass and ferns along the bank shivered endlessly as they were splashed with drops of water. A withered tree, bending its old brown trunk, extended countless thin, bony roots into the water.

"This will do!" Chuang Shih-huan said.

"Hey, are you really going in?" Chu Yu-pai rubbed his hands together.

"It wasn't my idea," he said, taking off his dark blue pullover sweater and bending over to untie his bootlaces.

Chu Yu-pai looked all around and found that, except for the trees, the water, and the stones, they were absolutely alone.

"Damn! Watch this old boy take a bath!" He hastily stripped, placed his glasses on his clothing and, holding onto the rocks around the pool, stuck one foot in the water. It felt as if it had been scalded and he instantly drew it back.

"Oh, Mama! A hundred degrees below zero!"

Fan Ch'o-hsiung squatted down barefoot, lowered his eyes, and gazed at the smoking water.

"It could give you rheumatism," he said ruefully.

"Nobody's holding a gun on you!" Chu Yu-pai pushed off with one hand and hurled himself into the water like an exploding bomb. The drops of water, followed by heart-rending shrieks, fell upon the rocks and dampened the piles of clothing.

"Yahoo!" Chu Yu-pai leaped wildly about in the water, shaking up a pool of white froth. "Hsiao Fan! Hsiao Fan, come on in, it feels so good!"

Chuang Shih-huan rolled his eyes and shook his head.

"Fan Ch'o-hsiung, don't pay any attention to him. If you don't want to go in . . ."

"Of course I want to!" Fan hastily took off his trousers.

Chuang Shih-huan threw aside his undershorts and slid into the water. As his feet and ankles entered the water, a stab of cold struck upwards from his toes—like the mercury rising in a thermometer when it is plunged into boiling water—and poured into his brain. His whole body shivered involuntarily and his very marrow grew numb with cold. He stopped for a moment, gritted his teeth, caught his breath, braced his muscles, and slowly went into the water. When the water rose to his chest, he seemed to hear a sound: "Cold!" Chuang Shih-huan could no longer control his jaws . . .

Fan Ch'o-hsiung stood naked and stunned. Suddenly he turned around, putting his back to the water and the two white faces which were turning blue. His two hands cupped his lips as he looked up and gave a long cry, "Ah-h-h—!"

"Stop howling, Fan." Chu Yu-pai said in a trembling voice.

Fan continued howling nonetheless.

"Ah ah ah—ah-ah!" He was so excited that he stood on tiptoe, and his limp hair trembled. He couldn't catch his breath and with mouth agape, he sat down, burying his head on his knees. After some time, he suddenly sat up so violently that his black hair fell over his forehead. Raising his forefinger, he cried:

"Listen! Listen! Listen!"

Among the bubbling sounds of the water, a thread of clear sound circled back and returned. Fan Ch'o-hsiung froze in position and his eyes gleamed as he laughed.

"Look at you! Happy as a dog!" Chu Yu-pai laughed. "Hurry up and come in! Sitting up there with a bare ass, even iron would freeze!"

Just as Chu finished speaking, Fan Ch'o-hsiung suddenly sneezed twice. Chu Yu-pai laughed.

A big cloud of pasty-white mist drifted from between the withered tree branches, sank, and entered the water like ink, a thread, or a line of dangling silk. The water flowed smoothly along. From deep in the woods, a bird called: "Ah-wo! Ah-wo!" Pillowing his head in a hollow of the rock, Chuang Shih-huan smiled and closed his eyes, relaxing and allowing each needle of cold to penetrate his body. A red sun began to rise from the bottom of his heart.

Let me become water . . . water . . . water without form or

substance, without responsibilities; water so young, forever young. . . .

"I quit!"

"How disgusting! Trying to cheat again, eh?" Liu Yü-ling scowled severely. "T'ao Chih-ch'ing! You've no sense of decency when it comes to playing cards!"

"I'm giving you a break and you're complaining!" T'ao Chih-ch'ing turned her cards over on the tatami, pushed with her feet, and slid into a corner, tossing her head so that her long hair fell over her shoulder. "If you lose any more, you won't have a single piece of dried beef left."

"Tsk-tsk-tsk, what big talk!" Liu Yü-ling chewed a mouthful of dried beef as she fanned and tapped her hand of cards.

Chu Yu-pai laid his cards on his lap, grabbed the cigarette pack, and took one. "Lao Chuang?"

"Thanks, I have some. I don't feel like smoking right now."

Fan Ch'o-hsiung bent over, propped himself on his elbow, and flipped over T'ao Chih-ch'ing's cards. He looked up to smile at Liu Yü-ling.

"Bad cards, right? Oh, T'ao Chih-ch'ing . . . ." Liu Yü-ling's sharp voice blended with the rock and roll music from her transistor radio.

Fan Ch'o-hsiung shook his head, coughed twice, and announced in a loud voice, "Three queens, two big tens!"

Liu Yü-ling threw down her cards and stretched out on the tatami. She studied the five cards for a long time. Then she sat up, shook her cropped hair, swept off the melon seed shells which clung to her elbow, and shouted, "Big deal! When you make a mess, you make a mess of everything! When your cards are bad, you won't play, and when your cards are good, you quit. Isn't this kind of unfair to the rest of us?"

T'ao Chih-ch'ing, leaning against the wall, chuckled.

"It's no fun. Besides, I'm really tired." She frowned and shook her head, covering a yawn with her hand. "Let's go to bed a little early; you still have to go to Chang-hua tomorrow." She lowered her head, held her eyelids apart with one hand, and cupped the other hand under her chin as she took out her contact lenses.

"Don't mind her, Chuang Shih-huan. You can take her place. We'll start again."

"I told you, I don't know how to play poker."

"Then what can you play?"

Chuang Shih-huan thought a moment and said, "I can only play Go Fish."

"Fine, we'll play Go Fish then. Come on, Hsiao Fan, hand over the cards. And you too, Chu Yu-pai."

Liu Yü-ling was shuffling the cards with a riffling sound when suddenly the light went out.

"Oh—it's T'ao Chih-ch'ing up to her tricks again!"

"I'll go ask them for a candle." Chuang Shih-huan stood up but a hand stretched unexpectedly from the darkness and caught his trouser leg.

"Chuang," T'ao Chih-ch'ing said softly, "sit down, I've dropped my contacts."

"Serves you right!" Liu Yü-ling laughed. "What? Your contacts? Chu Yu-pai, hurry and get a flashlight! T'ao Chih-ch'ing . . ."

"Stop acting like an Alfred Hitchcock movie, Yü-ling. Just don't run all over the place. Wait until the light comes on and look for them." T'ao Chih-ch'ing let go of Chuang's trouser leg.

Chuang Shih-huan seated himself against the wall and just as he was getting settled, a mass of soft hair spread across his shoulder. His right arm was wedged between two people and it felt uncomfortable. He deliberately stretched out his hand but stretched it too far and it bumped into Fan Ch'o-hsiung's ear. When he pulled it back, he found himself hugging T'ao Chih-ch'ing's shoulder—such a skinny shoulder! His cheek snuggled close to her cool hair and vaguely he remembered the clear depths of that afternoon's pool: he had slid into the water, his whole body in the harsh, freezing cold, but his heart had been filled with ripples of warmth.

"And now the news," said the woman's unhurried voice on the radio. "From Saigon: the American Air Force in Vietnam this morning carried out dawn raids, bombing locations thirty miles south of Hanoi. . . ."

"Turn it off, all right, Yü-ling?" said T'ao Chih-ch'ing. "Please?"

"Let's listen to the news."

"Turn it off." Chu Yu-pai said.

The woman suddenly raised her voice as she announced how many bridges had been destroyed and lowered it to announce how many granaries had been bombed. With a "pop," her voiced stopped.

"Do you want some dried plum seeds? They're from the Wild Water Chestnut Shop and they're not bad!"

"How much money did the Wild Water Chestnut Shop give you?" Chu Yu-pai asked impatiently, "since you've been promoting them all the way from Taipei?"

"You people are getting harder and harder to get along with," Liu Yü-ling cried.

T'ao Chih-ch'ing slowly and heavily turned her head and said softly, "My God, I'm so, so tired!"

He could feel her breathing against his right arm, and her hair scratched his neck. Chuang Shih-huan asked in a soft voice, "Did you really drop your contacts?"

Fan Ch'o-hsiung struck a match.

"Don't smoke! Fan Ch'o-hsiung!" T'ao Chih-ch'ing didn't stir but each of her words carried the force of command. "You're already coughing!"

Fan Ch'o-hsiung stood up and went to the window.

"Is it raining?" Chu Yu-pai asked. "I hear something."

"It can't rain," Liu Yü-ling said. "If it does, you won't have much fun going to Sun Moon Lake tomorrow."

Fan Ch'o-hsiung said nothing but pushed open the frosted glass window and the moonlight swirled in through the fog, bathing his face with a blue radiance. Fan struck another match and lit a cigarette. As the match flame illuminated his eyes and nose, Chuang Shih-huan glimpsed the muscles beneath his eyes jerking strangely.

"So much for your rain, Chu Yu-pai!" Liu Yü-ling laughed.

T'ao Chih-ch'ing and Fan Ch'o-hsiung sneezed explosively, one after another.

"But I clearly heard the sound of rain."

That sound, so light and delicate, its every note struck clearly and crisply in the quiet, dark night, came splashing onto the windowsill lake water.

"That's not rain," T'ao Chih-ch'ing said quietly. "An insect is singing."

It was not an insect, it was not rain. Chuang Shih-huan's left hand covered his mouth and nose, and with his middle finger he lightly rubbed the bridge of his nose. A patch of peaceful, peaceful sunlight spread across his heart.

—That is my river, across the woods and the night fog, summoning me with a secret language known only to you and me.

The lake, drenched in the night rain, looked like a big piece of black silk, but its blackness was not unrelieved, for distant mountains and nearby trees flickered like shadows. Invisible hands held the silk at the four corners, pulling and shaking it from time to time, revealing patches of radiance of different shades and colors. Chuang Shih-huan, leaning on the balcony railing, stretched forward to peer out. The black silk was extended evenly, making him feel that he could jump and yet avoid death.

"Chuang!"

Although he had just been thinking that he could jump down and not die, this piercing call startled him. Chuang Shih-huan shuddered and turned around.

"Do you want to come over? There are still a few cookies and we can brew some tea and finish them off."

T'ao Chih-ch'ing stood on the next balcony, with her back to the light and her long hair falling about her shoulders. She clasped both arms across her chest. A white robe with a blue pattern moved in the slight breeze, now falling unevenly and now rising. . .

Without knowing why, Chuang Shih-huan felt the black water in the lake behind his back rising in the darkness. After a long time, he said, "Good! I'll go get Hsiao Fan."

Fan Ch'o-hsiung was barefoot and had hung up his red jacket in the wardrobe.

"But I'm just running myself a bath."

"Didn't you say you wanted to hear the bell?"

Fan took his jacket out, hung it back up, took it out again, and flung it on the bed.

"All right, I'm coming."

Chuang Shih-huan closed the French windows from outside,

stretched his leg, and straddled the low brick wall to reach T'ao Chih-ch'ing's balcony.

T'ao Chih-ch'ing turned on the balcony light and carried out the tea tray. Her waist was loosely circled with a dark blue sash and the corners of the robe whirled in the breeze. Just as the robe was about to touch the water on the floor, it would be whirled upwards again.

"Oh, so you're wearing a kimono."

"This is a yugada; it's a combination robe and nightgown, and very comfortable. My uncle, Hsiao Fan's father, went to a conference in Japan and brought it back."

T'ao Chih-ch'ing's breath smelled mildly of wine.

"Anyway, it's Japanese clothing!"

"So what? Doesn't the Taiwan Tobacco and Wine Monopoly sell foreign tobaccos and wines? Besides, it was our dress originally during the T'ang Dynasty—like coal, the compass, and mahjong, it's another example of the Chinese people's altruistic spirit of extreme generosity!"

Chuang Shih-huan rubbed his nose until it reddened. The rattan chair was a bit damp, but he paid no attention to it and sat right down, stretching his feet to the railing.

T'ao Chih-ch'ing poured the tea.

"Eat the cookies."

"What! Didn't we just finish dinner? I'll drink some tea."

"I'm not hungry either. But there are a few left. I've carried them from Taichung to Hsi-t'ou to the Han-pi Guest House and I just won't carry them back to Taipei. If I'd thought earlier, I'd have given them to Yü-ling and let her get as fat as a cookie!"

"But she's not fat!"

"She thinks she's fat." She glanced at Chuang and smiled. "If you say she's not fat, she'll say you're making fun of her; if you say she's fat, it annoys her." She spread her hands in a gesture of helplessness. "What can you do?"

T'ao Chih-ch'ing kicked off her slippers, curled her feet under herself on the chair, and hiccupped. She took matches from the secret pocket in her sleeve and lit a cigarette. Chuang Shih-huan crooked his forefinger to rub his nose. He picked up his teacup, lifted the lid, blew away the tea leaves, and drank a mouthful.

Someone knocked lightly at the door.

T'ao Chih-ch'ing frowned, put her feet down, and fished for her slippers.

"I'll go."

T'ao Chih-ch'ing blocked him with her hand and continued hunting for her slippers. Chuang Shih-huan bent over, discovered the slippers by the legs of the tea table, and put out his hand to pick them up for her. To his surprise, she stepped into them at the same moment.

"Thanks!" Dragging her slippers, she shuffled over to open the door.

"Oh! So it's you! What are you doing sneaking around?"

"You call coming in by the door sneaking around?" Fan Ch'o-hsiung complained as he went over to the balcony. "Lao Chuang, have they rung the bell yet?"

"I haven't heard it."

"But that nun at the Hsüan-kuang Temple this afternoon said they ring it at seven-thirty and it's almost eight now."

"There are only two kinds of people who can hear the sound of such a bell." T'ao Chih-ch'ing sat down and picked up a cigarette. "Those who are especially sad and those who are especially pure in heart. Which kind are you?"

"I'm neither kind," Fan said. He leaned on the railing and then drew back. "Damn! It's wet!" He pulled a chair over and sat down.

The three of them were silent for some time. Beyond, the rain soughed. Occasionally a few threads of rain and chill air were blown in by the wind.

Fan Ch'o-hsiung coughed. He took his wristwatch, the sunglasses which were clipped to his lapel, and the paper tissues, the handerkerchief, the nail-clippers, the eye drops, and the aspirin from his pockets, and piled them on the tea table.

"Bring them all out again?" T'ao Chih-ch'ing cried. "Someday you'll lose them all!"

"It's more comfortable with it all out," he said, and brought out yet another plastic bottle from which he poured a few small white tablets.

"What is it this time? Aspirin?"

"No, I don't bother about colds; they get better by themselves.

These are allergy tablets." He raised his head and stuffed all the tablets into his mouth.

"I can never figure out what kind of medicine you take," Chuang Shih-huan said, drinking some tea. "What is it like when you itch?"

"Um—," Fan Ch'o-hsiung's brows drew together and two wrinkles appeared on his smooth forehead, forming an inverted "V." From his deep-set eyes beneath thick eyebrows shone two flashes of cold light.

"Itching! Just itching! I can't really describe what it's like. Sometimes I'm asleep at night and I haven't the energy to scratch, I just rub myself against the wall. Um— It feels a little like ten thousand ants crawling on my bones."

"That's right!" T'ao Chih-ch'ing blew out a breath of smoke. "The trouble's in your bones! If we could split open your bones and wash them out, then you'd have no trouble!"

Fan Ch'o-hsiung said nothing. Chuang Shih-huan rubbed his nose three times in the space of half a minute. T'ao Chih-ch'ing swallowed a mouthful of tea and smacked her lips.

"Fan Ch'o-hsiung, do me a favor and ask them to send up a cup of coffee, will you?"

As though he had just received a generous pardon, Fan Ch'o-hsiung jumped up with alacrity and dashed into the room to make the telephone call.

"If you drink coffee at this time of night, aren't you afraid you won't be able to sleep?"

"It doesn't matter, it's just like a cup of milk before going to sleep, and besides, I just drank a little wine." She tapped her cigarette.

Seven or eight June bugs flew around and around the lamp, leaving streaks like free-style calligraphy on the semi-transparent shade. As Chuang Shih-huan lifted a cookie to his mouth, an insect's wing fluttered down into his teacup. He sighed and put down the teacup. T'ao Chih-ch'ing smiled.

"When I was little and it rained at night," he said, "my father would often amuse us by opening the window on purpose to let the June bugs fly in, and he'd put a plate of water under the lamp so that they'd fall in the water. My mother would get so mad. . ."

"Yeah," T'ao Chih-ch'ing said. "The first few years after we came to Taiwan, we lived in a Japanese style house and we did the same thing. Funny, I still don't know what your father does."

"I don't know what yours does either."

T'ao Chih-ch'ing shrugged her left shoulder, tilted her head, and said with a smile, "Then we're even!"

"Ssshh!" Hsiao Fan put his hand on the back of Chuang Shih-huan's chair. "They're ringing the bell!"

Dong . . . Dong . . . The sound, passing through the rainy forest, seemed not to come from the temple on the opposite bank but rather to come bubbling up from the water: an ancient bell in a lost lake, covered with moss-green verdigris, swaying with the waves, and sending forth its low-pitched, gloomy sound. It pressed upon the balcony, caught the railing, and wound about incessantly. Dong! . . . Dong! . . . Dong! . . . Dong! . . . Suddenly the waters of the lake boiled up, causing the sunken bell to toss wildly to and fro: Dong! . . . Dong! . . .

"Nine quick and nine slow, the nun said," said Fan Ch'o-hsiung. "She has to ring it a hundred and eight times."

Someone rang the buzzer.

"The coffee's arrived!" Fan Ch'o-hsiung went to open the door.

"Please, bring it out onto the balcony, all right? Oh, Hsiao Fan, do you have any loose change for a tip?"

"You can put it on the bill," the waiter said.

"Thank you!"

The waiter left and closed the door behind him. Hsiao Fan started: "Damn! I was running a bath! It must be full to overflowing!" In two or three paces, he stepped over the wall and was gone.

The rain grew dense. The sound of the bell faded away until only a last thread of it remained: a fine and gentle thread of silver which lingered in the mind. Suddenly it was gone, becoming a gush of coolness which flowed through one's whole body.

He really wanted a smoke! Chuang Shih-huan felt the pack of Chü-kuang cigarettes on the tea table but it was empty. Reluctantly, he cleaned out his pockets and then gave up.

T'ao Chih-ch'ing cleared her throat and began to cough, great noisy coughs. After she had done this for some time, she stopped and drank some coffee.

"Wouldn't it be better for you to go back inside for a while?"

T'ao Chih-ch'ing shook her head and set her coffee cup down on the saucer.

"Say, how's that roommate of yours?"

He withdrew his hand, which he had just raised to the bridge of his nose, and rested it on the arm of the rattan chair.

"I don't know," he mumbled.

"Hasn't he written you a letter?"

"He hasn't written anything." His hand began to fidget slowly on the arm of the chair.

"Oh, that sort!" T'ao Chih-ch'ing suddenly turned. She blushed, blinked, and her eyes flashed dangerously.

"In fact, it's not bad having a fairy for a boyfriend, you know." She gestured, and the cigarette butt fell from her fingers to the damp floor, where it hissed and died. "A girl—well, in fact men and women are the same; they go out together a few times and they begin to calculate: marriage material! Only fairies can be true friends. . ."

Resting one hand on the arm of the rattan chair, he stood up and gazed at the chilly rain beyond the balcony.

"Pardon me, you're mistaken!" Chuang Shih-huan said coldly.

She heard Chuang Shih-huan step over the low wall, pull the French windows open and shut them again. T'ao Chih-ch'ing sat numbly. She smoothed her hair, then bent down, picked up the wet, blackened cigarette butt, and dropped it in the ashtray. She looked at Fan Ch'o-hsiung's things on the tea table, picked out the cigarette pack, found that it was empty, and crumpled it into a ball. She picked out the longest cigarette butt from the ashtray and, although it was slightly damp, she got it lighted with the second match. Smoke, mingling with the coffee fumes, swirled in the moist, close air, greyish-blue, thickening but refusing to dissipate. . . .

Many things about the Han-pi Guest House were old-fashioned in their Chineseness but the arrangements of the rooms were completely western in style. Chuang Shih-huan came out of the bathroom and prepared to go to bed. He saw that the milky yellow blanket was tucked under the mattress on three sides and one corner was turned back. The blanket was trimmed with red silk: an extraordinarily irritating sight—a shroud! And sticking to the mouth of the shroud, the last drop of fresh blood! Hadn't he been too long in the company of people who weren't right in the head, so that such weird associations came to him? Never mind, so it's a shroud, so what? Didn't the Monopoly sell foreign tobaccos and liquors too? He lifted the corner of the blanket and burrowed in. Just as he was reaching to turn off the light, he saw that Fan Ch'o-hsiung didn't look as though he were ready to go to sleep. Forget it!

Fan Ch'o-hsiung, shirtless, leaned against the headboard, hugging a pillow and reading a book. His lips moved constantly. He looked up and tossed over some gum.

"No, I'm going to sleep."

"Have you counted how many times a minute you chew a stick of gum?"

"Huh? I haven't. Why?"

"For you, I guess about twenty or thirty."

"Did you count?"

"I guessed." Fan Ch'o-hsiung raised his eyebrows. "Because you walk slowly; I thought your rate of chewing would be in direct proportion to your rate of walking. An impatient fellow like me gets about sixty to the minute."

"Don't you have anything better to do?" Chuang smiled.

"It's just for fun—oh, what time is it?"

"Your watch? Oh, you left it next door." Chuang Shih-huan took his hand out from under the blanket.

"When you were bathing, I went over and got it. It is on the table and I'm too lazy to go look."

"It's nine-thirty." He couldn't help asking, "Has T'ao Chih-ch'ing gone to sleep yet?"

"No, she was still sitting on the balcony, pulling a long face and not saying anything—I don't know how I offended her."

Fan Ch'o-hsiung threw away his book, picked up a piece of silver foil and wrapped up the gum he had spat out. He threw it at the wastebasket but missed. He shrugged. "Basketball—no score!" Then he picked up a small yellow bottle from the bedside table and poured out a few pills.

"Didn't you just take some?"

"No, these are sleeping pills."

"Sleeping pills?" Chuang Shih-huan sat straight up in bed, frowning. "Are you taking those too? How many?"

"Four." He said it as though he were talking about four bowls of rice.

"Don't you want to live? You can't go on like this!"

Fan Ch'o-hsiung shrugged and tossed the pills into his mouth.

"How long have you been taking them?"

"I don't remember. Not very long. Let me see. Last summer when I almost drowned. . . I don't remember. At first I didn't take much, half a pill, a pill. . ." He turned to glance at Chuang and shrugged.

"What does drowning have to do with sleeping pills? Do you mean that time you almost drowned in the Tamsui River?"

"Yeah, have you ever nearly drowned?"

"When I was little, four or five; I've forgotten what it was like. Really, can't you swim?"

"Sure. During summer vacation in my second year of senior high school, I took part in water sports at Tso-ying. But during this last year or so I've only dared to paddle around in the swimming pool. To tell the truth, it doesn't hurt much to drown. You swallow a few gulps of water and then you sink and you don't know anything. Afterwards you don't feel anything . . . but after a long, long time has gone by, there's a terrifying feeling that often mysteriously arises to grip you by the neck; on the bus, in class, at the movies, or when you're taking a walk, that feeling suddenly comes. Later on it gets worse. When you're in bed and want to go to sleep, you just close your eyes and it comes. . ."

The expression in Fan Ch'o-hsiung's eyes slowly darkened. He stared woodenly at the ceiling, the dressing table, the mirror, the floor.

"Later on I'd take a pill and nothing would happen. The more I took, the more I'd be wide awake, the more I couldn't get to sleep, and the more that fear would grip me. Later on I'd take the pills and read a book, read with all my concentration, read until the pill took effect, until I could no longer hold my eyelids up, until my head spun and I'd sleep. Goddamn it! That's why I read these books!"

"Isn't that cheating yourself as well as others?"

Fan Ch'o-hsiung's hair hung over his eyebrows and, as he stared at Chuang, with his lips half-parted and his face immobile, the muscle beneath his left eye began to twitch again.

"What can I do? You don't know how it feels! It's like—um— it's like you're surrounded by a great crowd of people beneath a blazing sun and they're watching you slowly being swallowed up by quicksand. . ."

His head turned mechanically back and forth and suddenly he threw away the pillow he had held to his chest and jumped off the bed. His breath came raggedly and he ran barefoot to the window. There was a brushing sound as he pulled the curtains together. He turned around, picked up the gum, and threw it into the wastebasket.

Looking at Fan Ch'o-hsiung's back, Chuang Shih-huan had the feeling of being gripped by the neck—the well-proportioned body, the broad shoulders, the narrow hips, all the shining muscles. What a handsome fellow! How could. . . ? Then what about Wu Che? Hastily he grabbed a stick of gum, unwrapped it, tossed it into his mouth—chew it sixty times per minute. He couldn't help rubbing his nose. This won't do! Won't do!

"This won't do! Fan Ch'o-hsiung, you can't go on like this! Maybe, maybe you ought to go see a psychoanalyst!"

Fan Ch'o-hsiung came back to the bed, fluffed up the pillow, and placed it behind his back. Holding onto another one, he rested his chin on it and said tonelessly, "Yeah, that's what T'ao Chih-ch'ing has said. But . . . no! Not me! I'd rather die than go to them—you know? There's a famous hospital which has a big reputation but can't do anything. Sometimes they just send an intern to get rid of you. Afterwards, perhaps the next week, the story circulates all over campus. Dreadful. I myself know of someone who was a victim of all this." He gulped and continued, "In fact, I'm the best analyst, I understand myself better than anyone else. Only, I just can't help. . ."

"Take it easy, don't think about it too much."

"Moreover, I know I already have too many crutches. I'm not going back to look for another set to hold me down!"

Fan Ch'o-hsiung finished talking, sat still for a moment, sighed, and bent his head to read.

Chuang Shih-huan said nothing, chewed a bit, frowned slightly, and spat out the gum.

"What are you reading?"

"*The Heart Is a Lonely Hunter* by Carson McCullers." Fan's interest was aroused. "Have you read it? No? Then did you see the movie? They called it something like *Red Tears on Remnant Frost*, a rotten name. It played for three days last year at the Losheng Theater and this year for four days at the Yüan-tung Theater. The movie wasn't as good as the book, but Alan Arkin . . ."

"Who's Alan Arkin?"

"You know him. Didn't you see *Wait Until Dark*? The villain who scares Hepburn and finally gets killed by her."

"Oh, I saw that movie; he's not bad."

"In *Lonely Hunter* he played the mute and finally," Fan Ch'o-hsiung pressed two fingers to his temple, "he killed himself! His acting was fantastic! He was nominated for an Oscar. Didn't you see it?"

"Someone told me it was pretty good but I didn't go see it."

"Why?"

"Someone told me it brought up the racial question and I don't like blacks."

Fan Ch'o-hsiung opened his book, read a few lines, and asked, "Why?"

"Blacks are lazy and dirty! I've got a bad impression of them."

"Aren't Chinese about the same?" Fan Ch'o-hsiung said without looking up.

God! A wave of hot blood came flooding up, making his whole belly blaze with rage at himself; why couldn't he say even a single rough word? Damn you? F—? Your mother's—? F— your mother? It wasn't that he didn't know the words, it was that he didn't know how to use them naturally enough. After pondering a long while, Chuang Shih-huan said "Ugh!" He felt that it sounded sonorous but Fan Ch'o-hsiung made no response. He rubbed his two hands, itchy and moist, desperately on the sheet; his body was dripping sweat as he got into "the shroud" . . . ugh! Thank God the two pillows were piled up, for with their support he could sleep comfortably! . . . Ugh!

After a time, Fan Ch'o-hsiung suddenly trembled, looked up

from his book, and called softly, "Lao Chuang . . . Lao Chuang!"

Chuang Shih-huan remained still. Fan Ch'o-hsiung hesitated a moment, then put out his hand to turn down the light so that there remained only a circle of dim yellow light around him on the bed.

In the vast landscape, every color, so clear and light, seemed to be brewed out of the thick, dew-moist grass, which emitted an elusive fragrance. The sky was blue, the water was indigo. Between water and sky flowed the peppermint-green mountain peaks, and light clouds spread among the peaks, like strands of new silk just emerged from the wash to face the violent winds. The rising sun sprinkled a thin layer of gold dust over all. A motorboat's white wake upset the cloudy sky reflected in the water. The triangle traced by the two ripples of the wake was lotus-green, and the water beyond the triangle was sea-blue. Beyond the milky-yellow railings were two white birches, as straight as writing brushes, and their transparent leaves danced in the gentle breeze.

As he pulled the apricot-yellow curtains open, Chuang Shih-huan trembled inwardly. For a long time he didn't dare to breathe, as if afraid that he might crumple this mirror-like serenity. Mustering all his strength, he released the curtain.

Fan Ch'o-hsiung's hands were drawn up to his chest clutching the blanket. His head lay aslant against the corner of the pillow. A lock of black hair spilled across his right eye. He was fast asleep with rosy cheeks. Chuang Shih-huan took a couple of light steps, crossed the room, opened the door, and went out.

The clerk at the reception desk said that T'ao Chih-ch'ing had not gotten up yet.

"Thank you. When she does get up, please tell her that I've gone out for a walk."

Downstairs, he leafed through a copy of yesterday's newspaper and went out to walk around. When he returned to the hotel, he was about to go upstairs when the waiter who had brought the coffee the previous night stopped him and said, "Miss T'ao is waiting for you in the dining room."

A cloud-white tablecloth covered the table by the window and in the center of the tablecloth was a square lavender napkin. On this napkin a few sprays of yellowish orange day lilies rested in a shiny black vase. Drenched in the green light which leaked through the screened window, T'ao Chih-ch'ing wore a square-necked white dress. The loose sleeves opened up around her elbows and her long hair was caught into two braids, bound at the ends with dark blue ribbons, which fell over her shoulders. She wore a light application of dark red lipstick. The fatigue beneath her eyes was not disguised; it looked as though she had been beaten a week ago and the bluish bruises hadn't yet disappeared.

"Morning."

"Morning." T'ao Chih-ch'ing drank some coffee and lit a cigarette.

"The noodles with shredded pork here isn't bad. I've ordered you some. If that's not enough, then order something else."

"How did you know I'd come?"

"I saw you coming back from the window."

"Oh—Hsiao Fan . . ."

T'ao Chih-ch'ing opened her left hand and waggled her fingers loosely.

"When you take sleeping pills, you can't get up, eh? But don't ask me how I slept! A power drill did a night's work inside my skull."

Chuang Shih-huan laughed and pulled his chair closer to the table. The sore in his heart was suddenly scraped clean.

"Where did you go just now?"

"Nowhere. I looked at the paper and I went for a stroll."

"Anything new?"

"Oh, another student riot at Columbia."

"They're really devils for fighting!" T'ao Chih-ch'ing said with a slight sneer. "They've got food to eat and books to read. So why all the riots? Are they tired of living?"

"Enough!" He didn't know where his anger came from but it suddenly flared up. "Complaints! Complaints! You don't do anything worthwhile! You just complain! Yesterday Fan Ch'o-hsiung said Chinese are dirty and lazy just like black people."

T'ao Chih-ch'ing did not quite laugh and exhaled a long puff of smoke.

"You can't be always complaining and blaming this or that," Chuang Shih-huan scowled. "The main thing is—you've got to do something!"

"Well," two streams of gray smoke curled from her nostrils, "for instance?"

"For instance—for instance . . ." His hand grasped at space. "For instance!" Suddenly he grabbed the cigarette which T'ao Chih-ch'ing was lifting to her lips.

"Don't smoke so many cigarettes! All this coffee and cigarettes, and half a bottle of Shao-hsing wine at dinner last night; it'd be strange if your head didn't hurt!"

He stubbed the cigarette out in the ashtray, then twisted it and shredded it until it was quite dead. His hand relaxed and suddenly tensed. How he wished to turn into a puff of smoke and dissipate at once.

T'ao Chih-ch'ing's chin lifted, the corners of her mouth drew up, and two teardrops swam in her eyes, ready to fall at the slightest provocation. The one hand Chuang Shih-huan rested on the table was held loosely in a fist, while the other hand, under the table, had rubbed his thigh hot with friction.

The waiter brought the noodles, turned, and left. The two of them, without a word, picked up their chopsticks and buried their faces in their noddles.

Chuang Shih-huan was just wiping his lips when Fan Ch'o-hsiung came swaying into the room, trailed by six or seven middle-aged people dressed in bright clothing. They were all talking at once, as if they feared people would not notice them; it sounded as though every home in a country lane had turned on its radio to a different station, all going at once.

Fan Ch'o-hsiung pulled up a chair and sat down. Without looking up he called the waiter, "Bring me a cup of coffee first!" He puffed his cigarette back to life and suddenly came back to life himself. He raised his head and said, "Do we really have to go today?"

"What are you up to now?" T'ao Chih-ch'ing took a cigarette out of habit, "Didn't we agree to take the noon Golden Horse bus down the mountain?" Her forefinger tapped the cigarette filter and she put it back in the box.

"Besides, Chuang only asked for time off until tomorrow. . . ."

"If we don't go," Chuang said, tossing his napkin onto the table, "I'll be forced to become a waiter to settle the bill."

T'ao Chih-ch'ing smiled, turned her head, forced a smile at Fan Ch'o-hsiung, and said, "What? Don't you want to go?"

"Uh—I thought we'd stay a couple more days and then go back, since there's nothing in particular to do at home anyway."

"It's up to you, I don't care." T'ao Chih-ch'ing half-lowered her eyelids. "But, you'd better make a long distance call first to fix things up; don't expect me to be able to speak up for you with your aunt." She picked up the napkin, folded it neatly on the table, and turned her head to the crowd of gaily dressed men and women.

"Gosh," she said, "I really wonder what kind of language the Cantonese would use at romantic moments?"

"Do you want me to call a cab?" The waiter opened the big glass door.

Chuang Shih-huan looked at T'ao Chih-ch'ing.

"No." She broke into a smile. "Thank you!"

The tree-shaded, winding concrete road, like a neatly and delicately carved peeling of a pear, wound its way down the hill.

One of T'ao Chih-ch'ing's hair ribbons was gone and her hair fell loosely behind her shoulders. She shook her head and sighed, "Oh God, I'm dying. . . ."

"If you're so tired, why not take a cab?" Chuang Shih-huan took her red bag and slung it over his shoulder. With his right hand he picked up the pale blue suitcase and he put his left hand around her waist.

"We've visited Sun Moon Lake, and taken a boatride, and we haven't walked a single step." T'ao Chih-ch'ing leaned her head on Chuang's shoulder. "Oh, God, I'm dying. . . ." Something small and black, trailing its last notes, flashed past their eyes.

"A cicada!"

"A cicada?" T'ao Chih-ch'ing's eyes flashed; she glanced about and put her head on Chuang's shoulder again. "My God, I'm really going to die!"

It was quiet on the hillside. Unexpectedly a sound like tearing silk came out of the forest . . . and stopped. The clumps of grass beside the road began to wriggle hesitantly. The green silence grew larger, higher, deeper, broader, until one could hardly draw breath.

"Chuang."

"Eh?"

"Next year, if we come again next year, will there still be cicadas?"

"Of course, but they'll be a new crop of cicadas."

"How do you know he really took his own life?"

T'ao Chih-ch'ing, absently gazing at the rain dripping on the window, did not move. The left corner of her mouth suddenly quirked upward and a few tiny wrinkles appeared at the corners of her eyes.

"Didn't all the papers say so?" she snorted. She leaned back against the sailcloth-covered cushion of the rocking chair and began to rock.

Chuang Shih-huan rested his elbow on the arm of the sofa. His chin rested on his thumb and he brushed at his nose with his index finger.

"I don't believe it."

After saying this, he suddenly realized how inconsequential his words were, as weak as if spoken in competition with a fast, noisy record. He moved his hand, relaxed his body, and rested his head against the back of the sofa. Dimly, he was beginning to be able to distinguish between Prokofiev and Rachmaninoff, but at this point, Chuang Shih-huan couldn't help getting angry with himself.

"I know he couldn't have killed himself!" he cried. "I know it! The night before we came down the mountain . . ."

"Those reporters said so: he killed himself; melancholy fiction murdered him!"

"To hell with those reporters! Just because he was reading *The Heart is a Lonely Hunter* and one of the characters killed himself?! They don't understand a fart! If it hadn't been made into a movie, which one of them would ever have read it?!"

"They also dug out an essay he'd written for the school magazine called something like 'Cotton Candy and Others' in which he said that life is like a stick of cotton candy. Those who sell it say it's good and it does look good. When you taste it, it's sweet, but in fact there's nothing there and in the end there's nothing left but a stick of dirty bamboo. Damn! But . . . But why, why in hell he . . . ?" T'ao Chih-ch'ing wrinkled her brows, deliberately brought a cigarette to her lips, inhaled fiercely, and exhaled slowly.

"What the hell did he know about life? He hadn't been hurt, he hadn't suffered; a blank sheet of paper burned to ashes before anything was written on it . . ."

Chuang Shih-huan closed his eyes, grasped a lock of his hair, and pulled his head down. The thunderclaps of sound on the record pealed on as before, like clashing swords. His hair slipped through his fingers. He straightened up and said, "I put in a good many calls to you but none of them got through."

"The night I got back to Taipei, we went to Yang-ming-shan. Besides, the telephone was taken off the hook throughout those few days. Those reporters! They never told me; it was when my aunt could no longer stand it and came crying to our door that I knew. She doesn't say so directly, but the way she acts, it's as though I murdered her son! God! You don't know, she controlled him so strictly. He was twenty years old but she inspected every letter he received. She watched him like a hawk but it wasn't until after he was dead that she found out he took so many kinds of pills!"

The music suddenly soared, drawing the waves to a high crest which scattered millions of bubbles as it broke and swirled back.

"Chih-ch'ing, is it true that . . ." Chuang hesitated. "I felt that Hsiao Fan seemed to like you."

T'ao Chih-ch'ing snapped her head around, her frown relaxed, and she gave him a chilling glance. Stunned for a moment, she was saddened, and then said very quietly, "Perhaps . . . no, he didn't like anyone, except himself, and he wasn't my type. I don't like the kind of person who's always leaning against the wall and can't stand firmly on his own! Perhaps I was a bit short with him but I always thought he should be trained to control himself. Hunh! How much stronger than he am I?" she asked with a cold smile.

"But he wasn't as weak as you thought. The night before he died, he told me he didn't want so many crutches."

T'ao Chih-ch'ing tossed her head violently and suddenly realized that she had cropped her hair short. She trembled slightly and ashes dropped onto her lap. Her hand moved slowly to her ears and felt her naked neck. She brushed her temples, pressed her cheeks in towards her nostrils, and thrust her head toward Chuang.

"Late that night he telephoned me in my room and said that he was troubled and couldn't get to sleep." She glanced at Chuang. "You know, I was upset myself that night, and tired, so I told him irritably that if he wouldn't think too much and would quit being so spiritual and would let himself believe that he wasn't itching and would stop being afraid of water, then he wouldn't have any problem." The fingers on her face slipped one by one over the end of her nose and lips. "Perhaps he didn't kill himself but I'd rather believe that he did." She opened her mouth and held her index finger between her teeth.

"You know yourself that he didn't kill himself!" Chuang Shih-huan roared. "It was an accident! Chih-ch'ing, there's no reason for you to suffer like this!"

After yelling a few words, he discovered that T'ao Chih-ch'ing hadn't heard a word and an irrational feeling suddenly seized him: it seemed that they were a pair of conspirators, anxiously seeking a pretext for their crime in order to plead for themselves. Or else they were shipwreck victims, cast ashore on a desert island, supporting one another back to back, with two different views before their eyes. He shut his mouth but his heart was struck cold.

Several kinds of instruments combined and alternated in an heroic motif, waves surging upon waves, wave after wave boring into the sand bank and washing back—the record came to an end and the needle revolved in the last groove: ka!-ka! ka! . . .

Chuang Shih-huan went over, bent forward, and put out his hand to lift the needle, but he saw the reflection of his own brownish-yellow hand swimming in the spinning black ripples. The cold feeling in his heart suddenly dissolved; his hand stiffened.

Chuang Shih-huan hooked two fingers and lifted the needle and that pool of spinning ripples instantly froze into a circle of deep black—Wagner's "Overture." How could he have thought it was Rachmaninoff? He shut off the record player and turned his head to look at T'ao Chih-ch'ing's two feet on the floor. They were moving, now together, now apart. He stood up and went into the bathroom.

A few drops of the half cup of milk that had been spilled that morning remained and a black mass of ants had gathered on the white porcelain wash basin. He turned on the faucet and washed away the ants, except for one in a corner which wouldn't move. He turned the water on harder and the ant fell into the whirlpool, swirled about, and was washed away.

As he turned off the water faucet, Chuang Shih-huan discovered his own countenance inverted in the water bowl. Gripping the cold water handle tightly, he hesitated. He sighed heavily.

Wu Che! If you want to die, help yourself! But going on this way, both of us are going to go under!

Having wiped his hands on the towel more than ten times, Chuang Shih-huan came out of the bathroom. T'ao Chih-ch'ing was holding a lighted cigarette and looking about; he went into the study and brought her an ashtray.

"Thanks." T'ao Chih-ch'ing ground out the cigarette, looked up at him, and slowly turned her head away.

"It's late, let's go out and eat dinner."

T'ao Chih-ch'ing seemed not to have heard, for she didn't stir. Her disordered, cropped hair only half covered her ears and her ear lobes were nearly a dead white.

—God, how could she cut her hair? How can she be so thin, so tiny, so ugly? Chih-ch'ing, turn your head, you'll find that there are still the two of us!

As though she had heard what he was muttering to himself, T'ao Chih-ch'ing did turn her head. She chewed her lower lip while regarding him fixedly. Then she let go her lip and opened her mouth, but said nothing. She looked away again and gazed at the rain outside the window. After a time, she said evenly, "Last month my sister helped me get admitted to Sarah Lawrence. Before, I didn't know if I wanted to start over again as a sophomore, but now . . ."

Chuang Shih-huan drew back the hand he had stretched out to

T'ao Chih-ch'ing's shoulder and followed her gaze outside the window.

The rain pattered down, washing against the king palm tree across the way until it hung its head in a melancholy way.

Seen from the balcony, the twilight-filled living room darkened to deep gray. T'ao Chih-ch'ing sat in the rocking chair, and as she rocked toward the light from the window, the traces of the rain on the glass were all at once reflected on her pale face. Chuang Shih-huan abruptly waved his arms and started to speak. But from outside the window only the sound of the rain could be heard.

Beyond the balcony, a string of raindrops hung from the electric lines. They flowed together and fell to the ground, into the mud and sand beside the road, chiselling out holes the size of beans. The water in the ditch rushed noisily into the little stream at the mouth of the alley. The water of the stream rose violently, plunging forward with a battle cry, as though it wanted to destroy not only the bridge, but the whole world.

The thick glass ashtray was the only bright object on the cluttered table. In the corner were a stack of *Genesis* magazines and several volumes of modern poetry: *In Dreamland, The Abyss, Associations of the Lotus, Homage.* . . . A thick layer of dust had settled on the books. In the center of the table was a heap of foreign books, large and small. An English dictionary held down a stack of *Time* magazines. The book's cover was open and showed on the flyleaf two crude letters: S.H. The green ashtray bore the name Lufthansa in white letters, with a small circle containing a white crane beside the letters. In the center of the ashtray was a pile of black and white cigarette ashes. On top of the ashes floated seven or eight cigarette butts of varying lengths. A cigarette with a long ash occupied the lip of the ashtray and sent up a long thin curl of smoke. The smoke rose up the white-washed wall to the level of the calendar and made the airplane on the calendar look as though it were, in reality, flying through broken clouds.

Two rough fingers reached out to the ashtray, hesitated a moment, and pushed the butt into the ashtray. The hand, flying over the ashtray, picked up the dictionary and placed it on top of a pale blue air mail envelope. It didn't cover the envelope completely; half of the letter showed from under the dictionary.

Scratch! Someone pushed back a chair. The rustle of clothing and the sound of footsteps. "Bam!" Someone shut the door.

Perhaps because the door was slammed violently, or perhaps because of the breeze from the window, the letter flapped against the dictionary. The dangerous heap of ashes on the ashtray were blown by the breeze. After a while, the breeze stopped and the puff of light smoke was once more drawn straight as a line. The letter fluttered slowly and then lay flat once more.

Chuang:
I've been dreaming a lot these days and last night I happened to dream that I was walking along Shui-yüan Road with you on our way to Yung-ho to eat bean curd (but we'd never gone to eat bean curd!). You said when we got across the bridge we'd be there, but that bridge was so long, we could never get across it. Afterwards I woke up very angry and quarrelled with my husband first thing. I don't know what could have caused such a dream, maybe it was because last week at a party, I accidentally heard one of your former classmates say that you'd found a better job. (Perhaps he wasn't really a classmate of yours; I forget his name. There are quite a few Chinese here and they gossip a lot.) Generally I'm busy, although I don't know what I'm busy at, but I'm busy enough that I really haven't the time any more for idle thoughts, especially since the children (a boy and a girl).

But I'm not complaining about anything. I think it's wrong to always feel that one is suffering. Besides, when one is really suffering, it's not for others but for oneself and for the lifestyle one has chosen. Before, when I was at home, I seldom did anything except amuse myself; now, except for going every other week to study Peking opera, I simply haven't a second for relaxation. (Believe it or not, I am studying Peking opera! As soon as the Chinese here meet you, the subject of mahjong or poker comes up, and you know that I'll never be interested in those pastimes.) Frankly, I've hardly thought of you these past six years. . . .

Hsi-men-ting in the July twilight. The smells of people, of sweat, of earth, of tobacco mingled together in the hot evening, spreading a sticky rotten smell. Only when the wind blew did a scent of magnolias waft from beneath the marquee of the Hsin-sheng Building, to make people feel a little more comfortable.

"Wait a minute, I want to buy a spray of magnolia."

"Eh! Magnolia scent is too strong." He rubbed the end of his nose. "Why not buy jasmine?"

"All right, one spray of jasmine!"

The short-haired girl took the spray of jasmine with a pliable wire, fashioned a circle from the wire, and placed it like a ring on her finger; when she waved her hand, it accidentally met the tall young man's nose. He took a deep breath, smiled, and hugged her around the waist as they went up the bridge. The warm breeze ruffled his hair and he smoothed it down with his hand.

That bridge was so long, they could never get across it.

But I do think often of Hsiao Fan, particularly when I'm especially happy or especially bothered. After this long, I still prefer to think that he took his own life. When life gets me down, I think that Hsiao Fan was luckier than us; by going as he did, he saved himself ever so much bother and pain. But there are even more times when I think that by making an end of himself so early, he missed many things which deserve to be called occasions of human satisfaction, such as family and children. (Are you married yet? That classmate (?) of yours didn't say. I really can't imagine what your wife could be like. Do you keep in touch with that roomate of yours, Wu? He's over here too but doesn't have much to do with the Chinese. But this is only hearsay, perhaps it's not him at all.) In fact, we needn't think too much. There are many things which we think may happen and which we fear but in the end they do not happen. On the other hand, things we'd never have dreamed of keep happening one after another like waves, and in both cases we keep on living. In fact, we shouldn't think of anything; then we can go on living. And after we've lived, we won't need to think of anything, we won't have to think. . . .

—One year in the summer, I met a bunch of people. After that summer, I never saw them again, nor was I ever able to hear the cicada again.

Ding, ding, ding, ding . . . A train chugged out from under the bridge. Ding, ding, ding. . . .

At six o'clock on a summer afternoon the color of the sky is as it was in the early morning, and the rainbow of Hsi-men-ting keeps company with the signal bells at the crossing and the wave of music flying up from the China Commercial Building. Rotating blue, yellow, green, white, red, in flowing beauty; and the people on the bridge are just like that, an eternal river flowing on.

Spring, 1969

Yang Ch'ing-ch'u, born in Tainan, 1940, is the only writer in this anthology without a formal college education. He is also the only one who is not associated with any of those magazines mentioned in the Preface. His stories are mostly published in literary supplements of newspapers. Though he has a large audience and his books often run second editions, there has yet been no serious discussion of his works. The only critical notice his much-anthologized piece "Virgin Boy" ("Tsai-shih nan," 1969) has received is negative. Yen Yüan-shu considered it a "vulgar and obscene story" (see *The Literary Experience* [*Wen-hsüeh ching-yen*], 1972).

In one respect, Yang Ch'ing-ch'u resembles Huang Ch'un-ming in that his fiction is populated by big-city people of humble origin: bar girls, petty officials, clerks, and hawkers. Besides "vulgarity and obscenity," his writings also carry an edge of violence reminiscent of Nelson Algren's early tales of Chicago. Because the characters are taken outside the city, and are situated in pre-1949 Taiwan, "Enemies" ("Yüan-chia," in *Hsin-wen-i yüeh-k'an*, No. 172, 1970) is an unusual product of this Taiwanese writer. It belongs to that category of writing labelled as "The Japan Experience in Taiwanese Fiction" (Yen Yüan-shu, in *Tamkang Review*, IV, No. 2, 1973).

Enemies ~

YANG CH'ING-CH'U

Translated by JEANNE KELLY *and* JOSEPH S. M. LAU

The night soil collector at the public toilets next to the temple scooped up a dead infant in the soil pit. The entire village rose in a clamor. Many quit their farm work, running over to take a look at the dead infant. A thick wall of people blocked the pit on all sides.

"Mother's! Got to be some widow or unwed girl so man-crazy that she can't help taking a lover. And then getting rid of the bastard."

"You don't by any chance know of a family with an unmarried woman who was pregnant?"

"She must have tied her stomach up tight to keep it from getting big. Such a tiny thing, it probably doesn't weigh more than three catties."

"After giving birth you think she could make it without taking a rest? Once she takes a rest, we'll know who she is."

"It must have been someone like Tzu-fu's wife. Even when she's pregnant you can't see her stomach, and then she gives birth faster than a hen lays eggs. A hen still has to let out a cluck when it lays an egg, but with her, the midwife has hardly finished tying up the cord when she's up cooking the pigs' feed."

The crowd buzzed in a raucous clamor. My small size made it easy for me to squeeze in. One foot boring in after the other I drilled all the way next to the pit. The stench assaulted my nostrils and my stomach churned. The dead infant was laid on top of the pit cover, pale and bloated. It lay on its side with its arms and legs bent up, its body covered with yellowish flecks of excrement and wriggling maggots. From the stomach hung a small section of something long, like a pig's intestine. The on-lookers said that was the umbilical cord. I didn't know what an umbilical cord was.

"*Ai!* I've lived all these years and though I've heard people talk

321

about having illicit children, I've never seen it before with my own
eyes. Is there really such a thing? This world is really getting more
depraved every day. More depraved every day!" Han-shan Po-
kung,[1] his white beard flowing over his chest, shook his head and
sighed.

The footsteps of three inspectors approached, their knee-high
leather boots echoing menacingly—two Japanese four-leggeds [2]
and one Taiwanese. Behind were two others in *kimonos.* The
inspectors ordered the temple-keeper Wai-niu Po [3] to go fetch
water from the pond in front of the temple and wash off the dead
infant. Taking a stick, they then turned the body over this way and
that to examine it. The conclusion was that it had been given
birth to in the toilet, then dumped into the pit, where it drowned.

The two inspector four-leggeds cast a sharp, piercing glance
toward the temple-keeper. "You were in the temple all day. Did
you hear the wailing of a baby?"

"No," Wai-niu Po shook his head timorously.

"How did you ever become temple-keeper?" The officer's face
tensed up into a fearsome expression and, raising his hand, he
slapped him across the cheeks. "Someone delivers a bastard in the
toilet next to your temple and you don't even know it?"

Wai-niu Po's trembling cheeks turned two colors. The left
cheek swelled up into red finger marks, while the right paled to a
bloodless white.

The officers instructed the *pao-cheng* [4] to nail together a
wooden crate and find someone to carry it out to the public cemetery for burial. As they were leaving, they took Wai-niu Po off to
the yamen with them.

The crowd moved over to the front of the temple to cool off

---

[1] *Po-kung* is a form of address for a paternal granduncle who is older than
one's grandfather. Also commonly used in polite and respectful address for an
unrelated person of that generation.
[2] Derogatory Taiwanese term for the Japanese during the Japanese occupation
of Taiwan, the implication being that they are like dogs.
[3] *Po* is a form of address for a paternal uncle who is older than one's father.
Also commonly used in polite and respectful address for an unrelated person
of that generation.
[4] A guarantor having responsibility for the actions of the village members and
acting as an intermediary between the Taiwanese and the Japanese.

under the banyan tree by the side of the pond. The tangled roots
of the tree were soon fully seated with people. Inclined slightly
toward the west, the noon sun filtered through a few streaks of
sunlight from behind the weeping willows.

"It must have been Chin Hua who did it. There're monkeys [5]
that always sneaked into her room in the middle of the night to
sow seeds.

"Barely over thirty—right at the desperate age, sexy and loose:
she's ripe for the plucking! So it's got to be sure fire."

"Who else could it be? Shameless slut."

Back and forth, one picked up where another left off. From a
suspicion, it went through a round of speculation, and the more it
was discussed, the more it rang true. Everyone reckoned it to be
the work of the widow Chin Hua.

If somebody is going to have a child, why not have it at home?
When Mother had my little brother, he was born right at home.
They said something about taking a lover and getting a bastard.
Taking a lover must be the biggest disgrace of all. At dinner Po-
fu,[6] Father, and Shu-shu [7] all talked about the incident. Po-fu
swore angrily, "Mother's! Shameless woman. Got the guts to take a
lover but won't accept the responsibility of having the child. Once
this woman is found out, she ought to be shoved into the soil pit
herself and stuffed to death with shit."

"Father, why does a pregnant woman sneak into the soil pit to
deliver the baby?" I asked.

"Shut your trap!" Po-fu's eyeballs were like copper bells as they
glared at me and rang out, "Kids don't understand. Any more
questions and I'll slap you in the face."

I lowered my head and kept at my rice, not daring to utter a
sound. There wasn't a single one of us in the family who didn't
fear Po-fu. People said he was good at heart but had a mean look.
He was a big, tall man. Naturally curly hair coiled up against his
head in ringlets, and his eyes protruded slightly. When he spoke,
his eyes blinked rapidly; otherwise his lips were always tensely pursed. In the village he was a man whose words commanded atten-

[5] Dialectical slang referring to an adulterer.
[6] Form of address for a paternal uncle who is older than one's father.
[7] Form of address for a paternal uncle who is younger than one's father.

tion. No one dared offend him; at the slightest provocation he would grab a hoe and fight it out to the finish.

"Ti,[8] were you afraid when you saw the dead infant?" Erh-chieh [9] asked in a low voice, pulling me into her room after she was done with the dishes.

"No, I wasn't." Actually I was.

"What sort of thing did the people say?"

"They all said Chin Hua took a lover and something about seeing monkeys sneak into her room in the middle of the night to sow seeds. Erh-chieh, what does it mean, 'Sow seeds'? Is it like the way we plant beans? A monkey sneaks into Chin Hua's room and buries the seeds under the bed, then she gives birth to a bastard? Can a monkey sow seeds? Where'd the monkey come from?"

"I don't know." Erh-chieh turned away from me. The reflection of her face on the wardrobe mirror appeared pale and forlorn under the oil lamp. She bit her lip in deep thought.

"What's the matter, Erh-chieh?"

"I have a headache. You go on out. Let me take a nap and it'll be all right." Erh-chieh pushed me out, shut the door and bolted it.

Erh-chieh and Ta-chieh,[10] who was married, were both Po-fu's children. She hadn't been feeling well lately and her face was quite pale. Po-mu [11] told her to see the doctor, take some medicine and rest at home, but she wouldn't, saying she just had a mild cold which would be over in a few days. She still went with the others to work in the fields, as usual.

The temple-keeper, Wai-niu Po, spent the night at the yamen and, on returning, cursed right in front of the temple all the women who have ever borne bastard children. He pulled up his clothes to show people the dark lash marks all across his back. Chin Hua was also summoned for a night's questioning. After she came back home, she hid in her room and cried the whole day. In

---

[8] Literally, "younger brother"; often broadly used as a mildly intimate form of address for younger males, related or otherwise. It is used here to address a cousin.

[9] Literally, "second elder sister"; used here to address a cousin.

[10] Literally, "eldest sister." In this case she is Erh-chieh's elder sister.

[11] Wife of one's father's older brother; i.e., wife of a po-fu.

the course of the interrogation, the officers had tortured her by filling her up with water, so they said.

Then the officers came to investigate Wang Hsiang-chu. The
coquettish, enticing Wang Hsiang-chu, like a cat in heat, was out
on the prowl all day long. In all corners of the fields, wherever she
happened to run into a young fellow, she would glibly flirt and
tease, throwing lingering looks and chattering on for the whole day
with no intentions at all of going home. Once while picking *lung-
yen* fruit by the side of the stream in the back hills, she got into a
quarrel with Ah-yung. Unable to get the better of her, Ah-yung
gave her a brush on the breasts to vent his anger. She ran home
and got together her brothers to go to Ah-yung's to seek redress,
and made him pass out cigarettes to passers-by at the cross-roads in
front of the temple. Ah-yung's mother was quite a woman. She
stood on the road yelling at the passers-by, "Hey! Come here,
come here! Come get a free cigarette. My son stole a feel of
Hsiang-chu's breasts and has to give out cigarettes for punishment.
Come smoke one! Smoke a breast-feel cigarette. Come on! Smoke
a breast-feel cigarette." Hsiang-chu was furious, because this
amounted to having the incident broadcast at the roadside. She
wouldn't have him pass out cigarettes anymore. One day as Ah-
yung was passing by the stream, before he knew it he was pushed
by her into the stream. When rescued, he was already uncon-
scious from the intake of water. With this her ruthlessness became
notorious. And only such a ruthless woman could have the brutal
guts to dump an illegitimate child in a soil pit to drown.

One time she was seen going into the sugar cane field with a
young man from Chin-ts'o. She also had been seen with the
Wang bum, carrying on under a haystack. All three of them were
ordered off to the yamen for a night.

The officers also investigated the foremen at the farms. Many of
these foremen took advantage of their authority to lead the prettier
female workers into the cane fields alone to "work." Half a year
ago, when the village girl Ah-yü was working on the farm, her
foreman granted her many special favors. Often after the others
had left for the day, he took her into the cane fields to work. She
ended up getting pregnant and raised such a fuss that he compensated her with a sum of money and sent her off. Pregnant as she

was, Ah-yü was given as a wife to a man close to forty whom no one had so far wanted to marry.

The Japanese inspectors also came to our house to investigate Erh-chieh. The very sight of four-leggeds was enough to upset Po-fu. In a very annoyed tone he said, "We ourselves keep a strict watch over Feng-ch'un. There's nothing to be investigated. If you don't believe it, you can go check with our neighbors."

Erh-chieh was a very well-behaved girl. She wasn't talkative and unless she had business, she wouldn't go over to the neighbors, not to mention the fact that Po-fu watched over her like a hawk. The officers asked a few questions about everyday life and left.

Mother was sitting on the edge of the bed unfolding the blanket, getting ready to retire. She asked Father, "Officials came today to investigate Feng-ch'un. I've seen her and the Hsieh boy, Erh-lang [12] stealing around on the hills. The Hsiehs have a grudge against us, but despite that they are sending someone over to discuss a match. Could it be that Feng-ch'un has slept with Erh-lang?"

"Not likely," Father replied. "Feng-ch'un is such a good girl she wouldn't do anything that would bring disgrace upon the family. How could someone who hardly even speaks be involved in such a relationship? In fact, if I-lang [13] and Feng-ying's marriage hadn't been broken off, Erh-lang would have made a good match."

The day the Hsiehs came to discuss a possible marriage, it had just grown dark when I went to hide in Erh-chieh's room in the midst of a hide-and-seek game with the neighborhood boys. Erh-chieh had changed into a new dark green dress and was standing in front of the mirror on her dressing table, looking at herself from the front, then from the side, giving her clothes a pull here and a tug there, continuously pulling at them as if she would never pull them straight. She combed her long hair over and over again, parted it into two and threw it over her chest. With her side to the mirror, she knotted her hair into a braid. Under the bright oil lamp, Erh-chieh, her face slightly tinged with make-up, bore a trace of dejection in the midst of her youthful charm. For that trace of dejection, which make-up could not disguise, she was

[12] Literally, "second son"; here used as a proper name.
[13] Literally, "first son"; here used as a proper name.

often scolded by Po-mu: "At such a tender age, there is nothing to mope so much about. You're degrading yourself!"

"Where are you going, Erh-chieh? Take me along!" I asked, as she looked like she was going out.

"No, I'm not going anywhere."

By the time I'd run out and then back in again, Erh-chieh was out of sight. Just then the back door creaked. She must have left by the back door. How come she didn't take me along? I ran out in pursuit, crossing the dense leafy shadows of the pumelo orchard. The full moon hung on the treetops of the hills, spreading the fields with a dim, milky light. The wind whished, the insects hummed. Erh-chieh cut across the mounds of a potato field in the direction of the hills, on which grew bamboo, mountain apple, *lung-yen*, and mango. In the bamboo groves perched swarm after swarm of egrets. I often came here with Erh-chieh to pick nuts and fruits and wild mushrooms, catch cicadas, and collect egret eggs. The entire route through the hills was very familiar to me. I followed Erh-chieh, hiding as I went, with the intention of giving her a surprise.

Circling past the big mango tree, Erh-chieh tripped over the roots and stumbled a few steps, but did not fall. When she reached the old *lung-yen* tree, someone met her and took her by the hand. The two walked hand in hand through the shadows of the bamboo groves and sat down on an old banyan tree. I opened my eyes wide and, with the aid of the shadowy moonlight beneath the leafy screen, took a look at him. Aha, Erh-lang!

"My father wouldn't think of letting me marry you. I told him if he insisted I was going to kill myself. That scared him into compromising. That's why he finally sent a go-between to your home. Did your father agree or not?" Erh-lang asked.

"My father gave the go-between a piece of his mind. He said he'd sooner chop me up to mix with the pigs' droppings than have me marry into your family." There was a sound of sobbing from Erh-chieh.

"You could plead with him that you want to marry me."

"You think I dare open my mouth? The minute I mention it, I'll be beaten to death, that's for sure. For a girl . . . it'd be so shameless."

"If my brother hadn't broken off the marriage to your sister, our marriage would have no problems at all."

Erh-chieh kept on sobbing.

I couldn't hear clearly what they said next. I circled round the *lung-yen* tree and hid behind the trunk of the mountain apple tree in front of them. Erh-chieh lay in Erh-lang's lap. He wiped away her tears, lowered his head and bit her lips. When Mother kissed me it was always on the cheek, but they were biting each other's lips. I dashed up to them and gave a yell. That noise must have awakened the slumbering mountain and woods. The egrets flew off amidst the sound of flapping wings. Erh-lang abruptly pushed Erh-chieh aside and sat upright, both of them staring dumbly, rooted to the spot.

"Erh-chieh, aren't you ashamed of yourself? Old as you are and you still lie in Erh-lang's embrace, biting each other's lips."

"Ti, how come you're here?"

"I followed you. It's all because you didn't take me along."

"Erh-chieh will give you some money, then you go on back and don't tell. If you do, Po-fu will beat Erh-chieh to death. Would you like to see me beaten to death by Po-fu?"

"All right, the money, then!" I stuck out my hand. Erh-chieh groped in her waist pocket, got two coins, and gave them to me.

"Don't tell, seriously. In a few days I'll give you two more coins," Erh-lang begged me.

"Huh, I don't want your money. I bet you're Erh-chieh's lover. You got a woman, a lover. Shame on you!"

"Ti, you—" Erh-chieh was shocked by what I said.

I got set to take to my heels, but she pulled me close and held me. "You insult Erh-chieh like that! Just go back and say that, and I'm dead for sure . . ." She began to cry in her agitation.

"All right, I won't say anything."

I ran to the village store in one breath to buy some candy, then ran over to play hide-and-seek with the other children. When I got home, Po-fu grabbed hold of me and asked, "Have you seen Erh-chieh?"

"I don't know."

The back door creaked; it was Erh-chieh coming in. Po-fu

stared at her with blinking eyes. "Where've you been? A girl shouldn't be out prowling around this late."

"No." Erh-chieh bit her lips, her face a grey-green. "I was out for a walk."

"The Hsiehs are shameless enough to send a matchmaker over to propose. Your aunt says she saw you and Erh-lang all by your-selves in the hills. Now don't forget I-lang broke off his marriage with your sister. Not a single one of the Hsiehs is any good. If I see you with him again, I'll tie you up and throw you into the fish hatchery for feed."

"I just happened to run into him while passing through the hills," Erh-chieh furtively raised her head to give Po-fu a glance, but just at that instant his burning eyes met hers. She lowered her head at once and slipped into her room.

When it was suggested that the marriage be broken off, our fam-ily spent days discussing how to respond. Everyone said since I-lang had made the promise, he shouldn't have taken up with a girl in town and broken off the marriage. The conditions laid down by Po-fu were that the money paid to the bride be confis-cated and the sum be paid once over as a fine. Also, the services of a band complete with gongs and drums, firecrackers, and red streamers for the door should be provided, so that the family's good name may be preserved. On top of that tobacco was to be distributed to the entire village as public apology. The Hsiehs maintained that confiscating the money to the bride should settle the matter and they would not accept the other conditions. Po-fu threatened that if they didn't accept them, the minute I-lang came back from town, he'd be stopped halfway and beaten dead. Scared out of their wits, the Hsiehs accepted all the conditions. Afterward I-lang married the girl from town and Ta-chieh married someone else.

The Hsiehs had a paddy field adjoining ours. That piece of land had no waterway, so they had to draw water for irrigation from our field. After the marriage was broken off, Po-fu would not allow the Hsiehs to dig at our field to draw water. They called in someone to negotiate, saying that Po-fu was being unreasonable. They paid the same water taxes yet weren't allowed to draw water.

"If it's unreasonable, then let it be unreasonable. Was it reasonable for them to ruin our good name? I'll be damned if I let them dig at our fields to get water. If they have any doubts, try it and see. One move and I'll chop off their heads," Po-fu declared with cutting finality.

That section of the Hsiehs' fields became arid land.

The *pao-cheng* informed Erh-chieh of a meeting in front of the temple at one in the afternoon for labor service. When I went to the front of the temple to play, Erh-chieh had arrived there also. There were about twenty-odd people gathered, all marriageable girls. The inspector led the girls inside the temple, and all idlers were driven off. I went around to the rear window of the temple and peered in. The officer yelled, "Beat it, kid!" and closed the window. I backed up a few steps, hid awhile, then scurried up to crouch against the sill and peer through a crack in the window.

"It isn't for labor service that we've assembled you all today. In order to investigate the case of the illicit birth we've gotten you all together to squeeze breasts for milk. As your name is called, you will remove your top clothings and step forward. Those not obeying will be seized and detained in the yamen for three days," announced the officer to the girls, his face stern and grim.

The girls, aghast, shrank to a corner, staring at each other.

One of the two officers sat at the table, turning over the register as he called the names. The other stood and waited.

"Hung Hsiu-ch'ou."

Hsiu-ch'ou timidly hung back.

"Come on, move it!"

She cringingly moved her feet, and slowly, reluctantly came over.

"Unbutton your blouse!"

Her head lowered and her cheeks fiery red, she stood motionless. The officer jerked her forward, and with one rip, the buttons of her blouse broke loose. He then pulled open her underclothes to bare her soft, white tender breasts, from which protruded the nipples shaped like mountain apples, delicate and bursting with life. A lecherous smile flickered across the stern face of the officer. With his hand on the tip of the nipple he gave it a few pinches.

Then, opening both hands, he grasped hold of the entire breast and squeezed with force. Hsiu-ch'ou was shaking all over, and her nipples wobbled as though about to pop off. The left side having been squeezed, he went to the right side. The girl grit her teeth in hatred. Tears were squeezed out from her and she began sobbing in short gasps.

After one was through being squeezed, the next one followed. Once before the officer, all the wrappings that concealed the precious jewels were peeled away layer by layer; and they were pinched, fondled, and squeezed at will. Then, in utter disgrace, each buttoned up and withdrew to one side.

"Huang Feng-ch'un." The eighth to be called was Erh-chieh.

Erh-chieh, her face a deathly pale, her eyes fixed in a vacant stare, stayed where she was, as though she hadn't heard.

"Huang Feng-ch'un, come on out here!" stormed the officer as he strode forward and pulled her out. "Take it off!"

Erh-chieh turned her head away, ignoring him.

The officer pulled her around and tore at her blouse and underclothes. She dodged right and left, shielding the bust area with both hands; but her clothes were ripped open anyway. Erh-chieh's breasts were firm and full, like newly-ripened pomelos.

"Hey, hey, your boobs are the biggest of them all!" The officer gave one cruel squeeze, and Erh-chieh's nipple spurted forth trickles of milk, dribbling down like early morning dew shaken from a tree. The milk stunned every one of the embarrassed faces.

"So you gave birth to that illegitimate child?" The table resounded. Even the officer's feet underneath the table jumped.

"No."

"No? And your breast could have milk?" The officer squeezed Erh-chieh's other breast. The milk dribbled out as before. "You see, you see! What's that?"

Erh-chieh flung his hand aside and pulled up her clothes to cover her breasts. Smack! Smack! The officer brutally slapped her twice in the face. Erh-chieh backed up to the doorway, turned suddenly, and fled from the temple. The officer took to his heels in pursuit. Bam! He tripped over the doorsill and rammed against the wall. Erh-chieh rushed headlong through the hall and dashed out the rear entrance. By the time I had gone round there, she was just slipping into the sugar cane field behind the temple. The two officers gave chase into the field.

"Erh-chieh! Erh-chieh! Even if you aren't caught and beaten to death by the four-legged officers, when you get home you're going to get it from Po-fu anyway!" I was so distressed I burst into tears.

Before long, the officers came out of the field, without Erh-chieh. The inspector came to our house to demand her from Po-fu. Po-fu glared at them, too infuriated to reply.

"You motherfucker!" The inspector clenched his fist and struck him savagely in the chest. "Your daughter takes a lover and gets a bastard, and you don't know about it? Off to the yamen!" The inspector twisted Po-fu's arm to his back and led him away. A flash of horror passed through me. Before my eyes came the picture of Po-fu stripped and hung from the beams. Below, two four-legged inspectors were holding canes, lashing as they cursed, "You asshole! Start talking!"

Po-mu hired a search party of more than ten, going through the sugar cane fields section by section, over a stretch of several miles. By sunset they still had found no trace of Erh-chieh. Father got together three men to tie up a bamboo pole over twenty feet in length and went out to the fields poking into the wells one by one. He even hired two people who could dive to search under the dammed-up water near the source of a river at the neighboring village.

Some of the neighbors said they had not noticed either Erh-chieh's being pregnant or symptoms of morning sickness such as vomiting. They'd only seen her moping around all day, saying nothing. How could she have given illicit birth? Others said there was something funny about Erh-chieh's stomach. It did protrude slightly, though not unnaturally enough to give the impression she was pregnant. And she was always wearing wide, loose fitting clothes, too. When Po-mu came across five strips of white cloth, measuring about five inches wide and four or five feet long, at the bottom of Erh-chieh's clothing chest, it became obvious that she had tied her stomach up tightly to keep it from getting big.

If throwing up meant morning sickness, I had seen her having dry heaves. Food rationing had been in force. Since Po-fu wasn't about to turn over our entire yield of rice, which had taken us so much pain and effort, to the Japs for military provisions (it would have meant starving ourselves), he held some back every harvesttime to supplement the insufficient rations. Erh-chieh would get up every morning at four. After getting me out of bed to recite my lessons, she dug up the rice stored in the back room. Under the lamp I used for my reciting, she ground it with a brick. All the extra rice needed by the family for the day was ground this way by Erh-chieh. There were these days that, while grinding the rice, she threw up. But it was only some saliva. Sometimes halfway through her grinding she would lie on the bench and doze off right up until time to cook breakfast. Then she would finally pull herself together.

It was getting dark. The clock struck six, seven, eight, and still Erh-chieh was nowhere to be found. Po-fu hadn't returned either. Po-mu went to the *pao-cheng*'s place three times, begging him to bail our Po-fu. The *pao-cheng* just kept beating around the bush until on the third visit Po-mu gave him some money. It was only then that he finally agreed to do it.

When Po-fu came back, his face was ashy and he limped along like a man with one leg shorter than the other. As he strode over the doorstep of the hallway, a mouthful of blood spurted from his mouth. Po-mu hurried to support him, tears gushing down as if from a burst dam. "Oh, no! He has internal injuries!"

Po-fu leaned against the wall and gasped. There was a swell of rage in his disconsolation, "I'll kill him! I'll kill him!" He grabbed a hoe by his side and was about to hobble off. Po-mu caught hold of him, but he flung her hand away. Like a bull going berserk, he limped across the fields heading for the Hsieh place. Po-mu became frantic. She hurriedly sent for Father. "Your brother has gone to the Hsiehs. Hurry up and catch up with him. And make sure nothing happens to him!"

I followed Father. He called out as he gave chase. Without even turning his head, Po-fu half hobbled, half ran on one leg into the Hsieh compound. The main living room was lit by oil lamps, and milling with people. Hoe in hand, Po-fu stood in the yard and yelled, "Hsieh Erh-lang, get out here. I'm out to kill you today. You've brought ruin to our family's honor and left us in disgrace.

Come on out! Get the hell out here if you are a man!" With that Po-fu spit out a lot of something.

"Let's go home, Brother. You're hurt. We'll settle it later," Father urged him in a low voice.

Po-fu kept his gaze glued on the movements inside the living room as though he hadn't heard anything. People inside stood immobilized as though cast in a spell. Po-fu yelled again. Slowly an old man with a long flowing beard emerged; it was Han-shan Po-kung of the Wang family. He was learned and highly regarded, a person Po-fu had always showed great respect for. "They have all gone to look for Erh-lang," said Han-shan Po-kung. "He was working in the sugar cane fields behind the temple in the afternoon and hasn't been back since. Maybe the two of them ran off together. What worries me most is that they might have . . . The important thing now is to find them. We can't afford to make things worse. No good will come out of it, only grief—it's bad for both families. Let's try to bear with it."

"The way things are, how can I face people without shame from now on?"

"The important thing is to find them. Let's worry about other things later."

Po-fu numbly let Han-shan Po-Kung and Father drag him back home. It was eleven o'clock at night. The searchers all came back to our house. The wells in the village had all been probed with a bamboo pole. The woods in the hills had all been gone over with flashlights, and someone had been put to work groping around underwater in the ditches and the pond next to Huang-ts'o Village. Still no one was to be found.

Po-mu's tears had run dry. With that look of desolation, her face appeared severely shrunken. Taking two flashlights she dragged Mother and Shu-shu out again.

"Feng-ch'un—come back—" The sound came from the woods in the back hills like thin strains from far, far away, so mournful, so helpless, so full of despair, as if a spirit were calling for its soul from the very depths of the earth. "Come back—Feng-ch'un—" The cry gradually turned to the sugar cane field behind the temple.

"Erh-lang—come back—"

"Erh-lang—" From the dike on the east side of the Hsiehs, near the end of the village, cries could also be heard. They wavered as though coming from the groves of ancient tombs. Rising from the east side and falling to the west, the calls echoed. The cries from both places gradually drew together, mingled into one, then gradually receded toward the wilds. "Erh-lang—Feng-ch'un—come back—" It was impossible to tell if the voices were ours or the Hsiehs. Both families were calling together.

Five policemen groped through the dark and burst into our house. Three guarded the front and rear doors while two came in to make the arrest. Po-fu told them no one had been found yet. Unconvinced, they turned on their flashlights and searched everywhere—under the bed, in the closet, the kitchen, the cattle shed, the haystacks.

"Feng—ch'un—Erh—lang—come on back—" Both families called together. One couldn't tell whether the voices were ours or the Hsiehs.

Not one of us went to bed. Instead, everybody waited in distress, as if Erh-chieh would return only during the depths of night, when everyone was dead asleep.

Pai Hsien-yung, publisher of *Hsien-tai wen-hsüeh*, was born in Kwei-lin, Kwangsi, in 1937. Upon graduation from National Taiwan University in 1961, he came to the United States and studied at the University of Iowa, where he earned an M.F.A. from the Writers' Workshop. He is now Associate Professor of Chinese at the University of California, Santa Barbara. His published stories can be found in the following anthologies: A *Celestial in Mundane Exile (Tse-hsien chi,* 1967); *Wandering in the Garden and Awakening from a Dream (Yu-yuan ching-meng,* 1968); *Taipei Residents (T'ai-pei jen,* 1971); and *The New Yorkers (Niu-yüeh k'e,* 1974).

A paragraph in my article, "How Much Truth Can a Blade of Grass Carry?" has thus characterized some of his stories:

Among the second generation émigré writers, Pai Hsien-yung is generally considered the most gifted. His father being the late General Pai Ch'ung-hsi, Pai Hsien-yung has since his childhood, thanks to his unusual family background, had occasions to observe firsthand the unguarded lives of many of the most privileged men of Kuomintang China now living in reduced circumstances. . . . Characteristically, though most of his celebrated characters are Taipei jen, they have little in common with the kind of Taipei jen depicted by the native Taiwanese writers. . . . His Taipei jen are moving, well-etched characters, but they are not as much a part of Taipei as Joyce's Dubliners are a part of Dublin. . . . They are the "last aristocrats" of an ancien regime—the generals without soldiers, ministers without portfolios, Helens without Troy—whose paradise, once lost, can never be regained except in memory.

Winter Nights –

PAI HSIEN-YUNG

Translated by JOHN KWAN-TERRY *and* STEPHEN LACEY

In Taipei, winter nights are usually cold and wet. A chill gust of wind was blowing again this evening and then, without warning, the rain fell, pitter-pattering onto the pavements. The alleys around Wen-chou Street already were under more than an inch of water. Professor Yü Chin-lei made his way to the entrance of the alley where he lived, and looked around. On his feet were a pair of wooden clogs and he held a torn, old-fashioned umbrella made of oil-paper; through the gaping hole the raindrops dribbled down onto his bald head. He was wrapped in his customary thick, padded gown, but even this was no protection against the bone-chilling cold of a Taipei winter night. He hunched his shoulders and shivered.

The alley was shrouded in a hazy gray mist. Not a shadow of a creature could be seen anywhere. The heavy silence was broken only by the sound of the rain which fell like a faint shower of fine-grain sand on the tiled roofs of the low houses that stretched far and near. Professor Yü stood stiffly in the cold rain, his two hands propping up the torn umbrella. After a while, he turned around and plodded back to his house in the alley. He was lame in his right leg, and in his clogs he shuffled along very awkwardly, his body jerking to one side at every step.

The house which Professor Yü made his shelter looked exactly the same as the other University quarters in the alley, old buildings that had survived the Japanese Occupation. It bore all the scars of long neglect. The eaves, door, and windows were mouldering from decay and disrepair. The sitting-room floor was still covered with tatami mats, heavy with years of dampness. They emitted a faint odor of rotting straw that hung in the air at all times of the day. The sitting-room itself was simply furnished: a desk, a tea-table, a pair of tattered armchairs so worn with age that

337

the cotton padding was hanging out of the burst seams. Books were chaotically strewn about the desk, chairs, and tatami mats. These were books in hard covers once, but the binding had come off some, mold had eaten into others, and many were scattered about like so many disembodied corpses with missing heads and limbs. Incongruously entangled in the confusion were a few storybooks of knight errantry bound in brown paper and rented from neighborhood bookshops. Ever since the day Professor Yü chastised his wife in extreme ill-humor, no one had ventured to touch even a single stray page in that pile-up in the sitting-room. Some time before, his wife had taken his books out to air and lost his notes on Byron's poems, which he had left between the pages of an Oxford edition of the poet's works. He had written these notes when he was teaching at Peking University more than twenty years ago and they contained the fruits of long study and reflection.

Professor Yü went into the sitting-room and dropped onto one of the tattered sofas, panting slightly. He massaged the joints in his wounded leg a few times vigorously with his hands because whenever the weather turned damp and cold they would start to ache. In the afternoon, just before his wife went to Professor Hsieh's next door for a game of mahjong, she had specifically admonished him: "Don't forget! Stick on that plaster from the Yü-shan Herb Clinic."

"Please be back early this evening, all right?" he had replied solicitously. "Wu Chu-kuo is coming."

"What's all the fuss about Wu Chu-kuo? Won't you be enough company for him by yourself?" She wrapped up some bank notes in her handkerchief and walked out the front door.

He was holding a copy of the Central Daily in his hands, and had wanted to stop his wife to show her the photo of Wu Chu-kuo with a caption: "Professor Wu Chu-kuo, world-renowned historian residing in the United States, gave a lecture at the Academia Sinica yesterday. More than one hundred scholars and dignitaries attended." Unfortunately he was not quick enough. His wife had raced out the door before he could get in another word. Mrs. Hsieh scheduled mahjong games for Tuesday, Thursday, and Saturday, and his wife never missed a single session. Whenever he would begin to protest, she would seal his mouth with: "Don't spoil the pot, old man. I'm going to win a hundred dollars and stew a chicken for you." He couldn't impose economic sanctions on her because she invariably came back on the credit side and had her own private horde to draw on. Earlier he had suggested that they invite Wu Chu-kuo over for a family dinner, but as soon as he brought up the subject, he was vetoed.

As her ample broad back stomped out the door, a feeling of helpless resignation suddenly overwhelmed him. If Ya-hsing were still here, she would help him welcome his guest properly; she would go to the kitchen herself and prepare a whole table of Wu Chu-kuo's favorite dishes. He remembered the time they entertained Wu Chu-kuo when he was about to leave for the States. They were living in Peiping then. Wu Chu-kuo ate and drank till he was quite lit up and red in the ears. It was then he said to Ya-hsing, "Ya-hsing, I'll have more of your Peking duck when I'm back next year." Who could have known that the next year Peiping would fall? So Wu Chu-kuo's one trip abroad lasted twenty years.

At Sung-shan Airport the other day when Wu Chu-kuo finally arrived in Taipei, he was engulfed in such a flood of people—government officials, newspaper reporters, and curious onlookers—that not a shadow could have slipped through. Yü Chin-lei saw him, but was elbowed out to the fringe of the crowd and didn't even have a chance to greet him from a distance. Wu Chu-kuo was wearing a black woolen overcoat and a pair of silver-rimmed glasses. He had a rich crop of snow-white shiny hair. With pipe in hand, he looked completely poised answering the questions put to him by the reporters. He had mellowed with the passing years; now he carried himself with the eminence and deportment befitting a scholar who inspired immediate respect wherever he went. In the end it was Wu Chu-kuo who spotted him in the crowd. He squeezed his way forward and, gripping Yü Chin-lei's hand, whispered close to his ear, "Let me come to see you in a couple of days. It's impossible to talk here."

"Chin-lei . . ."

Professor Yü got up hastily and limped to the door to welcome the caller. Wu Chu-kuo was already walking up the entrance-way.

"I had been waiting for you at the alley entrance. I was afraid you couldn't find your way." Professor Yü then knelt down and fumbled in a low cupboard near the doorway. It took him a while to produce a pair of straw slippers which he gave to Wu Chu-kuo to change into; one was so worn that the front section had popped open at the toe.

"The alleys in Taipei are ̄ like a labyrinth." Wu Chu-kuo smiled. "Even more confusing than the *hu-tung* [1] of Peiping." His hair was dripping wet and tiny drops of water had formed a film on his silver spectacles. He took off his overcoat, shook it a few times, and handed it to Professor Yü. He was wearing under the overcoat a jacket of padded silk. As he was sitting down, he pulled out his handkerchief and gave his head and face a brisk rub. When he was finished, his silvery-white hair was all fluffed and dishevelled.

"I've been wanting to bring you here myself." Professor Yü took out the thermo-glass which was reserved for his own use, brewed some Dragon Well tea in it, and placed the glass before Wu Chu-kuo; he still remembered that Wu Chu-kuo did not drink black tea. "But knowing how busy you must be these few days, I thought I wouldn't go and jostle with the crowd."

"We Chinese do have a weakness for lavish entertainment, don't we?" Wu Chu-kuo shook his head gently and smiled. "I've been attending banquets every day for the last few days, and each time it was twelve courses, fifteen courses . . ."

"At this rate, if you stay on longer, you'll eat your way back to your old stomach trouble," Professor Yü said, smiling. He sat down opposite Wu Chu-kuo.

"I'll say. It's already been too much for my stomach. Shao Tzu-ch'i gave a dinner tonight and I just couldn't eat anything at all . . . He told me it's been several years since you last saw each other. The two of you . . ." Wu Chu-kuo fixed his gaze on Yü Chin-lei, who, passing a hand over his smooth, bald head, heaved a quiet sigh and smiled, "He is a government official now and a busy man. Even if we were to see each other, we wouldn't find anything to talk about. Besides, I'm not good at idle talk, least of all with him. So it might be just as well that we don't run into each other. You remember, don't you, the year all of us joined the

[1] Traditional term for alleys.

Society for the Common Cause? What was the first oath we all took?"

Wu Chu-kuo smiled, "Not to join the Government for twenty years."

"And to think that it was Shao Tzu-ch'i who led the oath-taking that day! Oh, of course, of course, the twenty years have long expired." Professor Yü and Wu Chu-kuo both laughed at the same time. Wu Chu-kuo held the cup of green tea in both hands, gently blew aside the tea-leaves swimming on the surface, and took a sip. The tea was hot and the vapor fogged up his spectacles. He took them off and, while cleaning them, squinted as if he were trying to concentrate, then sighed deeply. "Yes. Now I have come back and most of our old friends in the Society have passed away . . ."

"Chia I-sheng died last month," Professor Yü replied. "It was tragic the way he died."

"I read about it in the papers abroad. They didn't report it in detail though."

"Very tragic . . ." Professor Yü murmured. "I saw him on campus the day before he died. By then, his neck had gone stiff, and his mouth was twisted to one side. He had fallen six months earlier and ruptured an artery. When I saw how terrible he looked, I did my best to persuade him to go home and rest. All he did was force a smile. It was pitiful. I knew, of course, that he was broke and, on top of it all, his wife was in the hospital. That same night he had to teach evening classes. At the school entrance, he tripped on a shallow gutter, and that was the end." Professor Yü threw out both hands and gave a dry laugh. "So Chia I-sheng breathed his last, just like that."

"Really. So that's how." Wu Chu-kuo mumbled vaguely.

"I heard that Lu Ch'ung had also passed away. Living abroad, you probably know more about this than we do here."

"Yes, and I guessed what was coming long before it happened," Wu Chu-kuo sighed. "During the 'Let A Hundred Flowers Bloom' backlash, the students at Peking University tried to purge him. They accused him of championing Confucianism in his *History of Chinese Philosophy* and forced him to write a confession. How could a man of Lu Ch'ung's temperament take that? So at that point, in front of all the students, he jumped off a building."

"Good! Good for him, I'd say!" Professor Yü suddenly exclaimed and gave his knee two sharp slaps. "What a man. I bow to him. He died a martyr, a 'Confucian man of character!' "

"Still, the irony of life in his case was too cruel perhaps," Wu Chu-kuo shook his head. "For after all, wasn't he one of the big denouncers of Confucius and Company?"

"Precisely," Professor Yü laughed helplessly. "Just take the few of us—Shao Tzu-ch'i, Chia I-sheng, Lu Ch'ung, you, me, and that great traitor who was executed, Ch'en Hsiung—what was the resolution we made together when we were at Peita?" [2]

Wu Chu-kuo took out his pipe, lit it, inhaled deeply, then blew the smoke out slowly, his mind for the moment lost in thought. Then all of a sudden he began shaking his head and laughing to himself. He leaned forward towards Professor Yü and said, "Let me tell you something, Chin-lei. Most of the courses I give at universities abroad cover Chinese history only up to the T'ang or Sung Dynasty. I've never offered a course on the Republican era. Last semester, at the University of California, I gave a course on the T'ang political system. This was the time that student riots were at their peak in America. Our students were the worst—they burned down classrooms, chased out the Chancellor, and beat up the instructors. I must confess, that sort of stupidity really bothered me. One afternoon, I was lecturing on the civil examination system in the early T'ang. Outside the students were scuffling with the police, who were spraying tear gas all over campus. The whole place looked like a madhouse. It was beyond endurance! Just imagine—I was lecturing on seventh-century China. Under those conditions, what interest could that hold for our tousle-haired, barefooted young American kids, only screaming for action! They were sitting in the classroom, but their attention was constantly drawn to the scene outside. I put down my book and announced: "So *this* is what you call a 'student riot,' is it? I have a few things to tell you. More than forty years ago, the students in Peking started a revolt which was a hundred times more explosive than yours." This seemed to jolt them all right. They looked incredu-

[2] "Peita" is the short form of "*Pei*-ching *Ta*-hsüeh," i.e., Peking University.

lous, as if to say, "Chinese students revolting? Don't be ridiculous!" Wu Chu-kuo and Professor Yü burst into laughter at the same time. "And so, I explained. 'On May 4th 1919, a bunch of Peking University students, rising in protest against the Japanese, fought their way into the compound of a treacherous Government official, set fire to his house, and then dragged out the envoy to Japan who was hiding there and gave him the beating of his life.' By this time, the room was dead silent and the students were listening with awed attention. After all, they had been prattling about the war in Vietnam, but they never had enough guts to burn down the Pentagon! Then I went on. 'Later, this group of students, about a thousand of them, were imprisoned in Peita's Law Building.' Seeing that I had their attention, I slowly announced: 'The leader of the group who beat up the envoy is standing here in front of you.' The whole room roared with laughter, some of the students stamping their feet, others clapping. They didn't even hear the sound of the gunfire outside." Professor Yü was shaking with laughter himself, and his bald head was bouncing up and down in response.

"Everybody asked at once how we attacked Chao's Pavilion.[3] So I told them that we climbed into Ts'ao Ju-lin's house on each other's shoulders, forming a sort of human pyramid. The first man who jumped over the wall lost his shoes and then, barefooted, ran like mad all over the garden setting fire to everything in sight. 'Where's that student now?' they asked in one voice, and I said, 'He is teaching in a university in Taiwan, teaching Byron.' They doubled up, laughing hysterically."

Professor Yü couldn't help blushing and his wrinkled face broke into a boyish smile. He sat there grinning with embarrassment and then looked down at his feet. He did not have his slippers on, but was wearing a pair of coarse woolen socks with two large black patches sewn on at the heels. Unconsciously, he brought his two feet together and rubbed them against each other several times.

"I told them: 'When we were prisoners in the school building, a lot of college girls came to give us moral support. One of them, the beauty queen from a woman's normal school, and the barefoot

---

[3] "Chao's pavilion" was the historical name for Ts'ao Ju-lin's mansion.

arsonist, became China's Romeo and Juliet of the moment and got married eventually.' "

"You're pulling my leg, Chu-kuo," Professor Yü ran his hand over his bald head. There was a nostalgic expression in his smile. Then, noticing that Wu Chu-kuo's tea was getting cold, he got up and limped over to pick up the thermoflask. As he was refilling his friend's glass with boiling water, he retorted, "And why didn't you tell your students who it was that proudly bore a flag that day, and had his glasses broken during a fight with the police?"

"Well," Wu Chu-kuo said, somewhat embarrassed, "I did tell them how Chia I-sheng slit his finger and wrote in his own blood 'Tsingtao back to China' on the wall, and how Ch'en Hsiung paraded in the streets, dressed in mourning and carrying a funeral scroll with the inscription 'Ts'ao, Lu, Chang stink.' "

"Chia I-sheng . . . All along, he hoped to achieve something important in life . . ." Professor Yü sat down and drew a long breath.

"Do you know if he finished writing his *History of Chinese Thought?*" Wu Chu-kuo asked with concern.

"Actually, I'm in the process of editing his manuscripts. He only got to the Neo-Confucianism of the Sung and Ming. But . . ." Professor Yü knitted his brow, "Well, he seemed to have been in a great hurry over the last chapters. His thinking was not as perceptive as before. I haven't been able to find a publisher for his book yet. We even had to pool our resources—a few of us, his old friends—to pay for his funeral."

"Oh?" Wu Chu-kuo could not hide his surprise. "Was he really that . . ."

The two men sat facing each other and fell silent. Wu Chu-kuo slipped his hands into his sleeves while Professor Yü tapped his rheumatic leg absent-mindedly.

"Chu-kuo . . ." Yü Chin-lei hesitated, then lifted his head and looked at his visitor. "There's no question about it, you are the most successful of our group."

"Me? Most successful?" Wu Chu-kuo looked up, startled.

"It's true, Chu-kuo!" Professor Yü's voice betrayed a note of agitation. "Look at me. What have I accomplished all these years?

Absolutely nothing! Every time I picked up the papers and read reports of your performance abroad, I couldn't help feeling mortified . . . yet comforted, too, that there's you at least to vindicate all our lost hopes." As he spoke, he stretched his arm and gave Wu Chu-kuo a gentle squeeze on the shoulder.

"Chin-lei . . ." Wu Chu-kuo blurted out as he tried to free himself from his grasp. Professor Yü found his friend's voice filled with agony. "Don't talk like that, please. You leave me nothing to stand on!"

"How? . . ." Yü Chin-lei mumbled confusedly and withdrew his hand.

"Chin-lei, let me tell you something and you'll understand how I felt to be out of the country all these years." Wu Chu-kuo put his pipe down on the tea-table, took off his silver-rimmed spectacles, and with his other hand kneaded the heavy wrinkles between his eyes. "I know what most people are thinking. They think I am having a good time visiting this country and that, giving lectures here, attending conferences there. Well, last year, I was at a convention of the Oriental History Society in San Francisco. In one session there was an American student freshly graduated from Harvard, who read a paper entitled 'A Re-evaluation of the May Fourth Movement.' From the start this young fellow tore the movement to pieces. He was obviously convinced by his own eloquence. But it was his conclusion. His conclusion! These over-zealous young Chinese intellectuals, he said, in an iconoclastic outburst against tradition completely wiped out the Confucian system that had prevailed in China for over two thousand years. They were ignorant of the current condition of their country, they blindly worshiped Western culture, and had an almost superstitious belief in Western democracy and science. This created an unprecedented confusion in the Chinese intellectual climate. That is not all. As the Confucian tradition they attacked cracked up, these young people, who had grown up in a patriarchal system and lacked both independence of inquiry and the will-power to hold their own, found that they were in fact losing their only source of spiritual sustenance and, gripped by a sense of panic, they began to wander about like lost souls haunted by the spectre of a murdered father. They had overthrown Confucius, their spiritual father, and so they had to go through life carrying the burden of their crime. Thus began the long period of their spiritual exile: some threw themselves into totalitarianism; some retreated and took refuge in their tattered tradition; some fled abroad and became wise hermits concerned only with themselves. Thus what started as a revolutionary movement disintegrated and changed its nature. Then he concluded: 'Some Chinese scholars like to compare the May Fourth Movement to a Chinese Renaissance. But I consider it, at best, to be a cultural abortion!'

"By the time he finished reading the paper, there was a great deal of excitement in the room, especially among the several Chinese professors and students. Everyone turned to look at me, obviously expecting some sort of rebuttal. But I didn't say a thing, and after a while, quietly left the room."

"But, Chu-kuo . . ."

"To tell you the truth, Chin-lei, some of the youngster's conclusions wouldn't be difficult to refute. The only thing is . . ." Wu Chu-kuo spoke with a lump in his throat. He hesitated a moment, then gave a nervous laugh. "Just think, Chin-lei. During all these years of living abroad—they add up to several decades— what have I been really? A plain deserter. And on an occasion like that, how could I have mustered enough self-respect to stand and speak up for the May Fourth Movement? That's why, too, in all my expatriate days, I've never talked about the history of the Republican period. That time at the University of California I saw how excited the students were in the middle of their movement, so I mentioned May Fourth only to humor them—it was no more than a joke. The glories of the past are easy to talk about. I don't have to feel ashamed when I tell my students, 'The T'ang Dynasty created what must have been the most powerful, and culturally the most brilliant, empire in the world at that period in history.' And I have been making such pronouncements abroad all these years. Sometimes I couldn't help laughing to myself and feeling like one of Emperor Hsüan Tsung's white-haired court ladies, who just kept telling foreigners the anecdotes of the T'ien-pao reign."

"But Chu-kuo, what about all your writings?" Professor Yü tried to cut him short with a vehement objection.

"Yes, I've written a few books, like *The Power and Office of the*

T'ang Prime Ministers, Frontier Commanders of Late T'ang, and a monograph on *Pear Garden Actors of Emperor Hsüan Tsung.*[4] Altogether, I must have put on paper several hundred thousand words, but they are just empty words, all of them . . ." Wu Chu-kuo was sawing the air with his hands and almost shouting. Then he laughed. "These books are stacked in the library gathering dust. Who will flip through them except perhaps, now and then, a student working on his Ph.D.?"

"Chu-kuo, your tea is getting cold, I'll go get you a fresh cup." As Professor Yü stood up, Wu Chu-kuo suddenly grabbed his wrist and, looking up at him, said, "Chin-lei, I'll tell you this frankly. All that stuff has been written only to fulfill the requirements of the American university system: 'publish or perish.' That's why every couple of years I would squeeze out a book. If I hadn't been required to publish, I would certainly not have written a single word."

"I'll go make you a fresh cup of tea," Professor Yü repeated vaguely. He noticed that a slight twitching had begun to show on Wu Chu-kuo's scholarly looking face. He dragged himself over to a table at one corner of the sitting-room, emptied the cold dregs into the spittoon, and made a fresh cup of Dragon Well tea. Then, holding the thermo-glass in both hands, he limped slowly back to his seat, betraying signs of great exertion. His right leg was feeling more and more stiff from prolonged sitting, and the numbing pain seemed to come in waves, seeping out from the very marrow of the bones. After he had sat down, he began to knead his leg firmly with one hand.

"You seem to have hurt your leg pretty badly," Wu Chu-kuo said. There was a note of concern in his voice as he received the hot tea.

"It's never recovered from that accident. Still, I suppose I'm lucky that I'm not a cripple."

"Have you tried everything you can with the doctors?"

"Don't even mention doctors to me!" Professor Yü shook his hand emphatically. "I stayed five months in Taiwan University Hospital. They operated on me, they gave me electro-therapy,

[4] "Pear Garden" is the location in his palace where Emperor Hsüan Tsung established the well-known operatic company and training institute.

they did this and that to me, and the result was that my leg got steadily worse. Eventually I became paralysed. Then my wife, in spite of my objections, got—I don't know where—an acupuncturist to treat me. And after a few jabs with some needles, believe it or not, I could walk again!" Yü Chin-lei threw his hands up in a gesture of resignation. "We Chinese are a funny lot when it comes to being ill. Sometimes Western treatment just won't work and we simply have to turn to some secret cure of native therapy, like acupuncture. A few random jabs of the needle sometimes unlock the secret of the trouble." They both shook their heads slowly and smiled. Then Wu Chu-kuo stretched out his hand and gave Professor Yü a gentle pat on the troublesome leg, "You don't know, Chin-lei. Whenever I thought of you and Chia I-sheng, I couldn't help feeling ashamed of myself. Look what hard lives you lead here, and yet you still stand firm, educating our own young people." As he spoke, his voice began to quiver. He gave his friend another light pat and continued, "Chin-lei, it's really not been easy for you."

Professor Yü fixed his gaze on Wu Chu-kuo without saying a word. Then he scratched his bald head and broke into a smile, "All my students are girls now. There wasn't a single boy in my courses last semester."

"Well, you're teaching Romantic literature, and girls naturally take to it."

"Yes. There was this girl who asked me, 'Was Byron really that handsome?' And I told her, 'Byron was a cripple. I'm afraid he was worse than me!' There was such a painful expression on her face that I had to comfort her, so I quickly added 'But he did have a ravishingly handsome face.' " Professor Yü and Wu Chu-kuo burst out laughing. "In my final exam last semester, I asked them to define Byron's romantic spirit. One girl wrote down an impressive list of Byron's mistresses, including his sister Augusta!"

"Still, I must say, teaching young girls has its rewards. How is your translation of Byron's *Collected Poems* selling? It must be in great demand here."

"I've never finished translating it."

"Oh . . ."

"Actually, only the last few cantos of *Don Juan* remain to be translated. These seven or eight years I haven't written a single word. And even if I had translated the whole of Byron, I'm afraid there wouldn't be many people who would read it now." Professor Yü heaved and looked directly at Wu Chu-kuo. "Chu-kuo, all these years, I haven't been doing what you imagined at all. 'Standing firm' as you put it, has been the last thing in my mind. To tell you the truth, I have spent my time figuring out ways to go abroad . . ."

"Chin-lei, you . . ."

"Yes. I've not only wanted to go abroad, I have also tried to grab every opportunity to leave the country. Each year, as soon as I learned about any foreign grants to our Arts Faculty, I was always the first to apply. Five years ago, after a great deal of trouble, I finally got a Ford Foundation fellowship for two years of research at Harvard. I was to be given almost ten thousand U.S. dollars a year. All my travel arrangements and formalities were being taken care of. The day I went to the American Consulate to have my visa signed, the Consul even shook my hand and congratulated me. But—can you imagine—as I was stepping out of the Consulate gates, a Taita [5] student, riding past on his motor scooter, drove straight into me. The next thing I knew, I had a broken leg."

"Oh Chin-lei!" Wu Chu-kuo was speechless.

"Anyway, when I was in the hospital, I should have given up the fellowship immediately. Instead, I wrote to Harvard to say that my injuries were only minor, and that I would leave for the States as soon as I was better. But I wound up staying five months, and by the time I came out, Harvard had withdrawn the fellowship. If I had given it up right away, then Chia I-sheng would probably have gotten to go."

"Chia I-sheng?" Wu Chu-kuo exclaimed.

"Yes, he had applied for the fellowship as well. That's why when he died I felt so wretched; I felt I'd done him a bad turn. If he had been able to go to America on that fellowship, he wouldn't have died the way he did. When he passed away, I went all over the place to collect contributions for his funeral expenses. His wife, as I told you, was also very sick in the hospital. I wrote to

[5] Short form of "Kuo-li *T'ai*-wan *Ta*-hsüeh," i.e., National Taiwan University.

Shao Tzu-ch'i, but he didn't come himself. He just dispatched someone with a contribution—and only a thousand Taiwan dollars at that."

"Ah," Wu Chu-kuo sighed.

"The fact is, Chu-kuo," Professor Yü blushed slightly, then looked directly at his friend, "I needed that fellowship very much myself. When Ya-hsing passed away, my two sons were still small. Before she died, she made me promise to bring them up properly and to give them the best education possible. When my older son went abroad to study engineering, he was not on any scholarship. I had to borrow money—and a considerable amount as it turned out—to finance his studies. I have been repaying it for a number of years, but I'm still in the red. That's why at that time I thought that if I got the fellowship and used it sparingly I would be able to pay off all my debts. How would I know that . . ."

Wu Chu-kuo raised his hand and was about to say something, but his lips only moved a little and then he fell silent. After a while, he forced himself to smile, "Ya-hsing—she was really an unforgettable woman."

Outside, the rain came down more heavily, beating on the rooftop with increasing insistence. The cold crept into the room through every available crack along the door and windows. Suddenly the front door opened and banged shut, and a young man entered through the narrow doorway. He was tall and wore a navy blue plastic raincoat. His jet-black hair glistened with raindrops. He was carrying a pile of books under one arm. He nodded with a smile and continued on his way towards his room.

"Chün-yen, come meet Uncle Wu," Professor Yü called to the young man. Wu Chu-kuo glanced briefly at his fine, handsome face.

"Why, Chin-lei, you two . . ." Wu Chu-kuo laughed in spite of himself and gestured toward Chün-yen: "Chün-yen, if I had seen you first when I came here, I would have thought your father had regained his youth! Chin-lei, you know you looked exactly like that when you were at Peita?" The three of them burst out laughing.

"Uncle Wu is teaching at the University of California. Didn't you say you would like to study there? Well, here's your chance. You can ask Uncle Wu all about it."

"Uncle Wu, is it easy to get a fellowship in Physics at the University of California?" Chün-yen asked with interest.

"Well . . ." Wu Chu-kuo hesitated a moment. "I'm not too up on that. Of course, there is more financial aid in the sciences than in the humanities."

"Is it true that the Physics Department often spends more than half a million dollars on one single experiment?" Chün-yen's youthful face gleamed with envy.

"America is a very rich country, after all," Wu Chu-kuo responded. Chün-yen stood there for a while, then excused himself. Watching the retreating figure of his son, Professor Yü whispered, "Every young man nowadays dreams of going abroad to study science or engineering."

"Yes, that's the trend, that's the trend."

"We went all out for 'Mr. Science' in our time, didn't we? Now look what science does—it's almost snatched away our rice-bowl!" The two men laughed. Professor Yü stood up to fetch some fresh tea, but Wu Chu-kuo stopped him hurriedly and stood up himself.

"I am scheduled to give a lecture early tomorrow morning at the National Cheng-chi University.[6] I think I ought to be leaving." He hesitated, then resumed in a low voice, "Day after tomorrow, I'm flying to West Germany to attend a conference on Sinology. Please save yourself the trouble of seeing me off. I'll say good-bye here."

Professor Yü handed Wu Chu-kuo his overcoat and said apologetically, "Really . . . now you've finally come back, and I haven't even asked you over for dinner. My present wife . . ." Professor Yü mumbled embarrassedly, but Wu Chu-kuo interrupted him, "Oh yes, I almost forgot! I haven't met your wife."

"She's next door," Professor Yü squirmed slightly, "playing mahjong."

"Oh, well, then please give her my regards, will you?" Wu Chu-kuo walked towards the door as he spoke. Professor Yü slipped on his wooden clogs, took up his tattered umbrella, and followed behind.

"Oh no, no, don't come out. It's too difficult for you."

6 "National Cheng-chi University" is a college in Taiwan supported by the government; "cheng-chi" means "political."

"You didn't bring your hat. Let me walk you part of the way." Professor Yü put one arm around Wu Chu-kuo's shoulders and held the paper umbrella over his friend's head as they made their way carefully out into the alley. The alley was steeped in darkness, and the rain fell endlessly, a torrential downpour swept furiously about by the wind. Leaning against each other, their feet soaked in pools of water, their backs staggering under the weight of the wind, the two men trudged slowly along, taking one sluggish step at a time. When they were almost at the entrance to the alley, Wu Chu-kuo's voice dropped, "Chin-lei, I'll probably be coming back in a short while—this time for good."

"You're coming back?"

"I'll be retiring in a year."

"Really?"

"I'm all by myself over there. Ying-fen passed away, and it is too difficult to live alone. My stomach is giving me trouble all the time, and then, well, I don't have any children, you see."

"Oh . . ."

"I think the area around Nan-kang is a good quiet neighborhood. Besides, the Academia Sinica is there, too."

"Yes, Nan-kang is not a bad place at all to live in."

The rain streamed through the hole in the umbrella and splashed their faces. They hunched their shoulders against the cold. Just then, a taxi approached and Professor Yü raised his hand to signal it. As the driver pushed open the door, Professor Yü extended his hand to Wu Chu-kuo for a last farewell. Holding the latter's hand in his, suddenly he said with a quivering voice, "Chu-kuo, there's something I haven't been able to bring myself to say."

"Eh?"

"Do you think you could recommend me . . . I mean, I'd still like to go abroad to teach for a year or two, and if there is a university in the States that happens to have an opening . . ."

"Well, I'm afraid they might be reluctant to hire a Chinese to teach English literature."

"Of course, of course," Professor Yü cleared his throat, "I wouldn't go to America to teach Byron—what I mean is, if there is a school which needs someone to teach Chinese or something like that . . ."

"Oh . . ." Wu Chu-kuo hesitated a moment. "Sure, I'll give it a try."

After Wu Chu-kuo was seated in the taxi, he put out his hand and gave him a firm handshake. Professor Yü trudged back home. The bottom of his long gown had become thoroughly soaked by now and clung cold and wet to his legs. His right knee was hurting more than ever. He hobbled into the kitchen, took the plaster from the Yü-shan Herb Clinic that was being warmed on the stove, and pressed the steaming hot dressing firmly over his knee. As he entered the sitting-room he noticed that the window over his writing desk had been blown open and was flapping noisily in the wind. He hurried over and bolted it. Through the cracks, he could see that the light in his son's room was still on. Chün-yen was seated at the window, studying with his head bent down low. His son's handsome profile caught Yü Chin-lei by surprise. For a split second he thought he was looking at himself when he was a young man. It was so long ago that the memory of what he looked like then had gradually slipped away. He remembered that he was twenty, the same age as Chün-yen, when he first met Ya-hsing. They were together in Pei-hai Park. Ya-hsing had just emancipated herself by bobbing her hair, and it was blowing loosely in the wind. She was wearing her dark blue college skirt and standing by the lake. Her skirt fluttered in the breeze. The evening clouds, a brilliant red, gathered in the western skies, transforming the surface of the lake into a sea of fire and throwing flickering crimson shadows on Ya-hsing's face. He had even contributed a poem to *New Tide*. It was written for Ya-hsing:

> As you recline on the emerald waves,
> Red clouds in the evening sky
> Melt into lotus flowers
> That gently lift you up,
> To waft freely with the drifting wind.
> Hsing, Oh Hsing,
> You are the goddess of the waves . . .

Professor Yü shook his very bald head and smiled shamefacedly. Then he noticed that tiny pools of water had collected on the desk by the window, and that the books strewn over it were sprinkled with raindrops. He swept his sleeve over them with one quick wipe and then picked up a book at random. It was *The Knight-Hermit of*

Willow Lake. He sat down on the sofa and leafed through a page or two. But under the dim light his eyes wouldn't stay open and soon he began to nod and his head slipped forward. Half-asleep, he could still hear the sound of mahjong tiles being shuffled and women laughing.

Outside the window icy rain continued to fall, as the night in Taipei deepened into winter.

A NOTE ON THE EDITORS

Joseph S. M. Lau received his B.A. in English from National Taiwan University in 1960 and his Ph.D. in Comparative Literature from Indiana University in 1966. He has written *Ts'ao Yü: The Reluctant Disciple of Chekhov and O'Neill* (Hong Kong University Press, 1970) and translated Bernard Malamud's *The Magic Barrel* and *The Assistant* into Chinese. Dr. Lau had taught English and Comparative Literature at the Chinese University of Hong Kong and the University of Singapore before assuming his present position as Associate Professor of Chinese at the University of Wisconsin at Madison in 1972.

Timothy A. Ross, the assistant editor, obtained his Ph.D. in History from the University of Iowa in 1972. He has translated *The Whirlwind (Hsüan-feng)*, a novel by the Taiwan novelist Chiang Kuei, and has written a monograph on the same author for the Twayne World Authors Series. He is currently Assistant Professor of History at Arkansas State University.

355

A NOTE ON TRANSLATORS

Ch'en Chu-yün (Mrs. Wang Wen-hsing) received her B.A. and M.A. from National Taiwan University, where she is now Lecturer in English.

Cheung Chi-yiu completed his undergraduate work in English at New Asia College, the Chinese University of Hong Kong. He is at the present time a doctoral candidate in Comparative Literature at the University of Southern California.

Dennis T. Hu received his bachelor's degree in Mathematics from Case Institute of Technology and subsequently studied Computer Science at Cornell University, where he earned his M.S. in 1972. He is now a doctoral candidate in Chinese Linguistics and Literature at Wisconsin.

Jon Jackson is Managing Editor of the *Iowa Review*.

Jeanne Kelly's undergraduate interest was in Russian (B.A., Indiana University) but she took up Chinese when she entered the M.A. program at the University of Wisconsin at Madison.

John Kwan-Terry studied English at the University of Hong Kong and Cambridge University, where he took his Ph.D. in 1969. He is now a Senior Lecturer in English at the University of Singapore.

Stephen Lacey received his Ph.D. in English from the State University of New York at Buffalo and is currently Assistant Professor of English, Howard University.

Lorraine S. Y. Lieu studied English, French, and Chinese at the University of Hawaii where she received her B.A. in 1975. She is at present a graduate student in the Department of East Asian Languages and Literature, the University of Wisconsin at Madison.

357

Earl Wieman received his B.A. in General Studies from the University of Maryland and studied Chinese at the University of Hawaii, where he was awarded an M.A. in 1972. He is now Special Correspondent to Hong Kong's *Orientations, Insight,* and *Modern Asian* and is Contributing Editor of *Echo Magazine* in Taipei.

GLOSSARY

Authors and titles of stories are arranged in the order in which they appear in the table of contents:

AUTHORS

Ch'en Jo-hsi　陳若曦
Wang Wen-hsing　王文興
Ch'en Ying-chen　陳映眞
Ch'i-teng Sheng　七等生
Wang Chen-ho　王禎和
Yü Li-hua　於梨華
Chang Hsi-kuo　張系國
Huang Ch'un-ming　黃春明
Lin Huai-min　林懷民
Yang Ch'ing-ch'u　楊青矗
Pai Hsien-yung　白先勇

STORIES

"The Last Performance"　最後夜戲
"Flaw"　欠缺
"My First Case"　第一件差事
"I Love Black Eyes"　我愛黑眼珠
"An Oxcart for Dowry　嫁粧一牛車
"In Liu Village"　柳家莊上
"Earth"　地
"A Flower in the Rainy Night"　看海的日子
"Cicada"　蟬
"Enemies"　冤家
"Winter Nights"　冬夜

MAGAZINES

Chung-wai wen-hsüeh　中外文學　　*Wen-chi*　文季
Hsien-tai wen-hsüeh　現代文學　　*Wen-hsüeh chi-k'an*　文學季刊
Ch'un wen-hsüeh　純文學　　　　*Wen-hsüeh tsa-chih*　文學雜誌